MW00450581

Also by Richard Bogovich

The Who: A Who's Who (McFarland, 2003)

Kid Nichols

A Biography of the Hall of Fame Pitcher

Richard Bogovich

McFarland & Company, Inc., Publishers
Jefferson, North Carolina, and London

LIBRARY OF CONGRESS CATALOGUING-IN-PUBLICATION DATA

Bogovich, Richard.
Kid Nichols : a biography of the hall of fame pitcher / Richard Bogovich.
p. cm.
Includes bibliographical references and index.

ISBN 978-0-7864-6522-4
softcover : acid free paper ∞

1. Nichols, Kid, 1869–1953. 2. Baseball players — United States — Biography. I. Title.
GV865.N485B65 2012
796.357092 — dc23
[B] 2012038037

BRITISH LIBRARY CATALOGUING DATA ARE AVAILABLE

On the cover: Charles Nichols in a photo taken in 1899 by Elmer Chickering of Boston (courtesy of Kid Nichols' great-grandchildren's collection); background image: baseball stadium grandstands, 1910 (Library of Congress)

Manufactured in the United States of America

McFarland & Company, Inc., Publishers
Box 611, Jefferson, North Carolina 28640
www.mcfarlandpub.com

Table of Contents

Preface

Thank goodness Charles "Kid" Nichols was a successful pitcher, and by virtually all accounts a genuinely nice guy. A natural impulse in any biography is to accentuate the positive, and when the subject is a likeable person such as Nick, the temptation can be even stronger. Still, unless a biographer has an ax to grind or chooses to write about an unappealing person, my sense is that the typical reader is actually expecting an emphasis on the good and a minimization of the bad. Whether that's true or not, I have tried to be conscious of the potential for bias, though I didn't lose any sleep over it because of how clearly successful he was. That is, if a pitcher wins two games for every one he loses over his entire career, which is a good approximation of Kid Nichols' major league winning percentage, then the simple fact is that there was generally twice as much good news during his career as bad.

Also, despite a few questions raised early in his major league career about how his ego may have been inflated — and those accusations aren't omitted from this book — starting in the middle of his playing days there was practically a waiting list of baseball figures wanting to express their fondness for him. This praise didn't just come from the most predictable sources, namely teammates, managers, and local newspapers. There were also plenty of opponents, many of them highly regarded themselves, who seemed to have no reluctance about singling him out for admiration. This continued long after he retired.

Kid Nichols probably wasn't an extrovert, but he was clearly thoughtful and well spoken, so when he was given a chance to offer opinions and insights, he would often seize them. Every once in a while a newspaper would print a lengthy statement from him, verbatim. There were also a few times when he took the initiative to write and submit pieces for publication himself. Though he contributed biographical information to the Hall of Fame and provided lengthy answers to questions posed by a would-be biographer at one point, there are no real signs that he attempted anything close to an autobiography. It became my priority to let him speak within this book when appropriate, and sometimes at length. There were, however, various instances when I omitted his commentaries, such as when he offered opinions of other players, especially his own teammates. When he talked about opponents it was usually to name those who hit him particularly well or whose skills seemed particularly impressive. He was a good cheerleader, so some of his comments about teammates need to be taken with a grain of salt, and that was also true about predictions he'd make about his team's chances in the pennant race. On the latter point, though, when you played for a couple of pennant winners, nobody would fault you for envisioning one more.

Also omitted from time to time are his extensive commentaries on pitching, though plenty are included. He'd often be pretty repetitive, as is common when a person's views don't change much over time, but I think he assumed, wisely, that few people reading a specific treatise of his had any prior knowledge of his viewpoints on the subject. Even at his most repetitive he'd often provide some interesting nuances or new depth, so I have sometimes risked a little rehashing in order to set the stage sufficiently for those fresh insights.

In addition to giving Kid Nichols his own voice to the extent feasible, I chose to quote heavily from newspapers of the era. I did this partly because I thought it might help get readers into the mindset of the era a little more, but also because I found the style of writing in those days to have such flair.

This book has been very humbling. I've been a diehard baseball fan since I was old enough to read my first baseball cards, and I also love history, so I didn't consider myself to be ignorant about baseball in the time before Babe Ruth. I was wrong.

Until recently relocating, my wife and I had lived in Madison, Wisconsin, for twenty-five years. As a voracious reader and someone who considered himself both observant and astute, I assumed that after living there for five or ten years I had learned everything important about the city's connection to baseball, both minor and certainly major. My rude awakening came about a decade ago when I was flipping through the book *Out of Left Field* by film critic Jeffrey Lyons and his brother Douglas Lyons. They had compiled a list of Hall of Famers' birthplaces where little had been done to honor their native son. On that list was Kid Nichols, opposite Madison, Wisconsin.

I was bewildered because I didn't know that Madison claimed a Hall of Famer. I also admitted to myself that I really knew nothing about the man, and in fact barely recognized his name, at best, from such lists as career leaders in victories. I didn't look into this much for awhile, but when I eventually did, I assumed that every Hall of Famer must've had at least one entire book profiling him. Wrong again.

Eventually I did discover that David L. Fleitz included a chapter on Kid Nichols in his 2004 book, *Ghosts in the Gallery at Cooperstown: Sixteen Little-*

Known Members of the Hall of Fame (McFarland, 2004), and that provided far more depth than websites I had found. Still, I wanted to know much more about Nick's years in Madison, so because I lived in the same city, I decided to explore local resources. The Wisconsin Historical Society had just made some very helpful city directories available online, and their online catalogue included listings for other promising holdings, but those I'd need to check out in person. When I started finding information about the Nichols family beyond where they lived and what the father did for a living, I was hooked.

Along with humbling me, this book has stunned me in two ways. Despite knowing about the Society for American Baseball Research (SABR) for many years, when I finally got around to joining it, I was blown away with not only the size of its membership but also the depth and vastness of research being conducted energetically by so many of its members. And yet as I looked into minor, obscure aspects of Kid Nichols' career, I was struck repeatedly by how many facets of the game still cry out for illumination.

Before starting this introduction I drew up a very long list of people who helped foster my love of baseball or my interest in writing, as well as the dozens who have offered wonderful encouragement when they first heard about this project. I couldn't believe just how long that list eventually became, and I ultimately concluded that I shouldn't run the risk of readers perceiving that I had gone overboard.

Nevertheless, I absolutely have to thank my family for listening to me enthuse ad nauseum about various finds while researching; my mother for keeping me company on incredibly valuable trips to Kansas City; Steve Newell of Express Photo in Kansas City for his amazing restoration of many photos, some more than a century old that seemed far too faded or damaged; Amber Posner for research assistance; Suzanne Alexander for early editing and encouragement; George Dreckmann and my old C&D soccer team in Madison for encouragement; Freddy Berowski at the National Baseball Hall of Fame for copying materials in the Kid Nichols file; baseball-reference.com for not only compiling data exhaustively but presenting it in several different formats; and the archivists and programmers who've made so many millions of very old newspaper pages available online in searchable format. Lastly, I can't thank Kid Nichols' great-grandchildren enough, particularly Sharon Everett for being receptive to this project; Sister Ann Everett for maintaining her great-grandfather's archives and joining Sharon and me in going through everything; Tom Jones for some initial input plus some very detailed editing of my first draft; and Christy Jones for timely encouragement and additional editing.

1

B.C.: Before Charles

On the day in 1869 that Charles Augustus Nichols was born in Madison, Wisconsin, one local newspaper printed a stirring report from the *Boston Herald* about a dramatic storm they dubbed "The Great Gale of New England."[1] It was in intriguing coincidence. By the end of that century, Kid Nichols would be a crucial player for one of the two franchises in existence today that has operated continuously since the start of the National League.

The future Baseball Hall of Famer was born on September 14, 1869, which is also a significant date in baseball history for another reason. On that day the Cincinnati Red Stockings, which that year had become baseball's first fully professional team on its way to a perfect 57–0 season, departed for a month-long tour of California to become the first team to play on both coasts in the same season, thereby helping to nationalize the game. Twenty-four years later, Nichols and some Boston teammates would make a similar trip after having won their third consecutive pennant and having posted the National League's first-ever 100 victory season.

To understand how an athletic champion arises, or, for that matter, how *any* prominent and successful person is molded, it can help to appreciate his or her family's history. For example, Bill Nowlin, a Society for American Baseball Research officer who has written more than twenty books about the national pastime, devoted two hundred pages in one about Ted Williams solely to that Boston legend's years in his hometown of San Diego and added another hundred covering Ted's family roots.[2] Kid Nichols would demonstrate throughout his adult life that his large extended family was important to him, by acts such as reconnecting in person with nieces and nephews in Wisconsin years after he left the state. Understanding his family's experiences and often-changing situation, including events that ocurred before he was born, are keys to appreciating his journey to baseball stardom.

Kid Nichols was born into a large family that had lived in Wisconsin's capital city since 1856. His mother was the former Christina Skinner, who was born February 10, 1831, in Vermont. His father was Robert James Livingston Nichols, born January 8, 1819, in Rhinebeck, New York.[3] Christina married Robert between 1850 and 1855.

Robert and Christina's family included three half-siblings to Charles from Robert's earlier marriage to the former Sarah Jane Luffman: Mary Elizabeth, James, and John, had been born in Saratoga Springs, New York, 1842 and 1846.[4] Little is known about the first Mrs. Nichols, but buried in Saratoga Springs' Greenridge Cemetery is Frederick Nichols, "son of R. & S. Nichols," who died December 30, 1849, at the age of 4 months, 8 days, next to Sarah Nichols, who passed away less than a month later of consumption (tuberculosis) on January 16, 1850, around the age of 27.

Living with Robert and the three surviving children at the time of the 1850 census was Robert's mother Eve, who was still living with them at the time of an 1855 census there. Also part of the Nichols household in the latter year, along with Christina, were Robert's brother John, then 19 years old, and sister Gertrude C. Nichols, then 27. In both the 1850 and 1855 censuses Robert's occupation was listed as painter, and as a landowner and homeowner in 1855, his property was valued at $1,150.

Robert and Christina's first child, Sarah, was born in Saratoga Springs on April 6, 1856, and soon their nuclear family moved to Madison.[5] Their children William, Fannie, and George were born there in the few years prior to the Civil War, and Jessie was born shortly after it ended.

Wisconsin had graduated from a territory to a state in 1848, with its capital city having only become a village two years earlier, its population well under 1,000 people. In 1856 Madison became a city and had grown to a population close to 7,000. Dominant among its earliest settlers were migrants from northeastern states, like the Nichols family.

During most of the family's many years in Madison, both before and after Charles was born, Robert's line of work was butcher or grocer. By the end of 1856, his name appeared in the city of Madison's personal property tax listings, but with holdings valued only at $200, primarily due to his store. In 1858, the city's tax rolls showed him having personal property of much higher value, $700.

By mid–1857, Robert was listed in a local business directory as having one of eight meat markets in the young city of Madison. Robert had meat markets or grocery stores at a minimum of five locations before Charles was born. Shortly after the Civil War's conclusion in 1865, Robert went into business with an army officer, Joshua W. Tolford. The "Nichols & Tolford" grocery ended after about seven months when the latter bought out Robert, who quickly teamed with a second established butcher, James E. Rhodes, to open the "Nichols & Rhodes" shop. After about five months, Nichols bought out Rhodes.[6]

The location of the Nichols family home also changed a few times between 1856 and the birth of Charles in 1869. They lived as renters in at least two locations before 1860, when they bought a home for the first time. In 1863 they relocated to a home a short distance away at the end of South Hamilton Street, a landmark on the National Register of Historic Places called the Stoner House in honor of the very next owners. Harriet and Joseph Stoner followed the Nichols family in that home for a stint of about two decades. Joseph is known in the fields of photography and history for taking panoramic "bird's eye" photos of cities all across the nation. In 1983 the Stoner House was moved a few lots north, closer to the Capitol, and in this century it is the headquarters of the AIA Wisconsin, a society of The American Institute of Architects. Before the Nichols family sold the house to the Stoners it was valued at $1,800.[7] However, by 1867 the family became renters again elsewhere, and didn't own another home before Charles arrived.[8]

A few other experiences before Charles was born defined his family. One was his brother John's decision in 1861, at the tender age of 14, to join the military at the onset of the Civil War. He may have been the youngest in the state to enlist in 1861. For his first three months he was enlisted in Company K, 1st Wisconsin Volunteer Infantry, for its three months of existence before being reconstituted. After his short time in Company K, John re-enlisted as a drummer in the 11th Regimental Band, until Congress discontinued bands at the regimental level about a year later.[9] After about eighteen months back in Madison, in March of 1864 Johnny was among former members of the 11th Regiment's band recruited to fill the ranks of the 1st Brigade's band, in which he served for the duration.

Pride and worry may have competed for the dominant emotion in the Nichols family during John's enlistments, but in between them a third emotion, grief, overshadowed all others for a reason unrelated to the war. Under the front page headline "Fatal Accident," on September 25, 1863, the *Wisconsin State Journal* reported, "A little daughter of Mr. Robert Nichols, of the 4th Ward aged about four years, was burned to death on yesterday. She obtained some matches, and ignited her dress. Before it could be extinguished, she was so badly burned that she lived but a few hours, dying at 10 P.M. last evening." Lower on the same page was a brief obituary for "Fannie, youngest daughter of Robert and Christina Nichols, aged three years and 11 months. The funeral will take place from their residence on Hamilton street to-morrow afternoon at two o'clock. The friends of the family are invited to attend."[10] About a week later a different local paper provided additional details, including that another girl was with Fannie, but "the flames spread so quickly as to defy the efforts of the girl, who was near, to extinguish them."[11]

This horrific incident was even reported in the *Milwaukee Sentinel*, and in 2002 it was included in a book profiling some of the people buried in Madison's Forest Hill Cemetery.[12] Though this tragedy occurred six years before Charles was born, it wasn't kept from him; in a handwritten document compiling some of his biographical information around 1949, now in possession of the Baseball Hall of Fame, Kid Nichols listed Fannie among his siblings (though he omitted James) and noted her cause of death.

Conversely, a joyous event for the Nichols family occurred in 1864 when Mary Elizabeth was united in matrimony on the second official Thanksgiving Day in United States history to Samuel E. Griffiths, son of a minister. The ceremony was performed at the Nichols residence, as reported in a local newspaper.[13] The couple's first two children were born in 1867 and 1868, before Charles. He would later have many more nephews and nieces.

Young Johnny Nichols proved to be a headstrong boy by enlisting in military bands, but sometime during the decade before Charles was born his oldest full-blooded sibling, Sarah, demonstrated that she was a strong-willed girl by joining a band of a very different kind before she was a teenager. In June of 1859 an organization for youngsters was formed in Madison called the Band of Hope, and it existed for ten years. During that span, close to 1,100 young Madisonians took a triple pledge of abstaining from alcohol, tobacco, and profanity.[14] It is likely that the first of these commitments, firmly sustained by Sarah while her youngest brother was growing up, led to one of the distinguishing characteristics of Kid Nichols as a professional athlete.

Meanwhile, in the spring of 1867 Robert Nichols was elected to a two-year term as a Madison alderman. In fact, he was the top vote-getter among all candidates for the Council. Robert set the stage for this success by having become very active in local Democratic Party politics within five years of moving to Madison. He opted not to seek reelection in the spring of 1869, but he did remain active in the Democratic Party during the 1870s.

There are almost no instances of Kid Nichols engaging in activities of a political nature during his long adulthood, but he and his father did have a common passion: baseball. Still, over the years very few writers connected any of Kid's relatives to the sport, much less his father. One who speculated about some sort of familial connection was Brian A. Podoll in his *The Minor League Milwaukee Brewers, 1859–1952*, when he noted that Madison's Capital City team, beaten by the Cream City team of Milwaukee on August 1, 1868, included a John Nichols at catcher and a James Nichols in left field. "Whether either of both of these men were related to Hall of Fame pitcher Charles 'Kid' Nichols, Madison-born himself, is unclear," Podoll added.[15]

Kid Nichols was only mentioned in passing in Podoll's book, so there is no reason to have expected him to know that the connection had been identified many years earlier. In a *Baseball Digest* article in June 1951, author Sam

Smith had noted that Kid's "two older half-brothers played some [baseball] with a Madison team in 1865."[16] Kid Nichols never went out of his way to mention that any of his older relatives were ballplayers.

It is significant enough that Kid's two half-brothers were among the players on Madison's first organized team, and faced some prominent baseball trailblazers, but handwritten score sheets for the Capital club from 1866 through 1869 reveal that their father apparently also played, at the age of 48. The team's surviving scorebook doesn't include games from 1865, and the few times that James and John appeared in games during 1866 were when two local squads battled one another.[17]

On April 26 and 30, 1867, an "R. Nichols" joined James in games between Madison clubs, playing center field in the first and shortstop in the second. In the first, the Nichols duo was on the side that won easily, 40–9, but James was the losing *pitcher* in the second, 43–38. On May 2 John and James were on opposite sides of a contest between Madison teams. Five days later John served as the sole umpire for a game in which James was on the winning end of a 26 to 18 score. John was listed as affiliated with the Capital Junior Club, which isn't surprising given that he was barely out of his teens. On May 17, James played on the "First Nine" against the local Fielders team, which included his brother and "R. Nichols." A rematch occurred ten days later, and this time the latter player's first name was given, "Rob." City directories in that era listed no other Nichols family in Madison, nor did the 1870 census report any other "R. Nichols" in the area. What's more, he only played when James or both Nichols brothers did, though his main function was apparently to give the starting players a team of foes to hone their skills against.

James, at least, was finally able to face teams from other cities. On June 13, 1867, he was in the Capital City lineup when they began their regular season in Beloit with a loss to their college's Olympian team, 23–12. One Madison player was singled out by a newspaper for high praise: "Nichols, l.f., was pronounced by all who saw him play, to be one of the best, if not the best, left fielder in the State."[18]

Robert played against James's team that month and in July, and those may have represented the elder Nichols' finale. In any case, one of the Nichols men was in the lineup on August 21 when the Capital team beat a squad from St. Louis, 42 to 20. One of them also traveled to Beloit for a game on September 3, 1867, that ushered in Wisconsin's baseball tournament.[19]

Though the club's record book then skips almost two years, newspapers helped fill in the gaps. On June 11, 1868, the Capital City club traveled to play their first match game of the year, beating the Milton College Club, 67 to 28. Though catcher John Nichols batted fifth, center fielder Jim Nichols, batting eighth, was perhaps Madison's top offensive hero. From a batter-by-batter account it sounds as if Jim tripled three times (one "a splendid hit" and another "a sky scraper") in the first four innings, homered twice in the fifth, and tripled again in the sixth.[20] Other games following over the next few weeks included one against the Everett club visiting from Oshkosh[21] and a blowout in which John's 5 runs scored were the fewest for the winners, with the 11 that James scored tying for the team lead.[22]

Within days, however, the Nichols brothers and the rest of the Madison club were crushed by what was arguably the brothers' most noteworthy opposition: the Rockford Forest City club featuring several future NL players, most notably Ross Barnes and Hall of Famer Albert Spalding. The Madison club managed to keep the game close for three innings, and one account drew attention to John Nichols "astonishing some of the Rockford spectators by his diminutive proportions and skill." In the second inning, John managed "a fine hit" off of Spalding, driving in a run. The Rockford players were gracious victors, complimenting the Madison team for "playing a better game than any of the twenty clubs they have played with this year, aside from Chicago, Brooklyn and Philadelphia."[23] A rematch "witnessed by some 500 people" was played in Madison a week later, with Rockford prevailing, 43–12. On defense, John was again behind the plate and James in the outfield. John again had some offensive success, reaching safely in the sixth inning and driving in a run in the seventh while trying unsuccessfully to stretch a single into a double.[24]

At the beginning of August was the aforementioned loss in Milwaukee, 41–15, which Podoll described in his book. A game against another club of historical significance followed when the Madison team hosted the Unions of Morrisania, New York, a team that was led by future Hall of Famer George Wright and included Cuba's Estevan "Steve" Bellán, credited as the first pro ballplayer in the United States born in Latin America. "The Unions were known to be the champion base ball club of the United States, and had won nineteen games in succession on the present tour," wrote the *Wisconsin State Journal*. In Madison's 77–12 loss, "John Nichols won the most laurels, making three runs, his only defect being that he has not muscle enough to send the ball to bases as quick as is desirable sometimes."[25]

On August 10, the Madison club embarked on a weeklong tour of Wisconsin cities, and both Nichols brothers went. Against Oshkosh's Everetts, Appleton's Badgers, Green Bay's Stars, and a Beaver Dam squad they racked up wins ranging from 33–17 to 100–10. Against the Badgers each of the Nichols brothers scored ten runs, and in the 100–10 win over Beaver Dam, John, "as short stop, played first rate," according to the *State Journal*.[26] After the tour a rematch against Milwaukee took place there on August 27, but the Cream City victory was even more lopsided at 67–22. John Nichols played shortstop and scored twice.[27] At the end of September the Madison club finally won a game against Milwaukee at the State Fair, though the victim was the Juneaus, not the Cream City club. The score was 48–16. "The play of the Capitals was among the best they have shown this season," wrote the *Wisconsin State Journal*. "Nichols, as short stop, was lively, and plays his position well."[28]

Charles Nichols in the 1870s; by Madison, Wisconsin, photographer E.R. Curtiss, who photographed all governors and legislators there for decades, starting in 1866.

When the Capital Base Ball Club was revived for 1869, its scorebook included an entry for a game on August 27 in one county to the south of Madison. John and James both played, but the Capital Club lost, 14 to 8. However, on September 3, 1869, just eleven days before Charles was born, John helped the Capital City club win the rematch in Madison, 19 to 17.[29] With several family members having played the game in the decade before the debut of the National League, and with Charles eventually being named to the Hall of Fame, a strong case can be made that Robert Nichols and his sons deserve the title of "Madison's First Family of Baseball."

2

Kid Nichols as a Kid

On September 14, 1869, Charles Augustus Nichols was born in his family's home. In 1939 a fan named Harlan Forker of Danville, Illinois, submitted written interview questions to Kid Nichols for an unpublished writing project. One question was whether he was named after anyone. "Not that I know of," Nichols replied.

Exactly where in Madison that Kid Nichols was born is a little murky. In a 1936 interview he told a local journalist that he was born on North Carroll Street,[1] and a 1970 article in that same paper further specified that his home on that street was "on the site of what is now the Madison Area Technical College."[2] A different location was listed on the birth certificate for Charles Augustus Nichols, which wasn't created until mid–1941 so that he could obtain Social Security. According to that document, the Nichols family was living on Johnson Street. Local tax records for 1869 place the family's home on Madison's Block 98, and East Johnson Street is the longest of that block's four sides. The tax records for 1870 place the family's home on the block that is now occupied by Madison College, and the records from 1871 through 1877 put the Nichols home one block away. Perhaps in 1936 Kid Nichols had only identified the first home that he could *recall.* The different location on his birth certificate filed in 1941 may have come from the witness listed on it, his sister Sarah. Her recollections may not have been sufficiently sharp in 1941, when she was 85, but in 1869 she was 13 and certainly old enough to have formed a clear memory of where her youngest brother was born.

Though the Nichols family was quite large, on many days baby Charles experienced hours of comparative calm because at least three of his siblings were enrolled in public school at the time. In that era, attending school was by no means a given but the Nichols children were faithful attendees. Early in 1870 a daily newspaper in Madison listed a few groups of pupils who were not absent or tardy for a month, and among the ones at Central Intermediate (aka Central Grammar) were "Georgie" and Willie Nichols.[3] A similar list in November for the same school included both as well.[4] According to that year's census, 14-year-old Sarah was also in school that year.

The fact that the Nichols family lived at just one location during most of Charles's first seven years, atypical of their quarter century in Madison, may have been due to the relative stability and success of Robert's work as a butcher. Shortly before Charles was born his father had reunited in business with J.W. Tolford. This time they limited themselves to a meat market rather than a general grocery, and they reversed the order of their surnames. Tolford may have been motivated to take on a partner again due to lingering effects from an event in early 1867 when his solo grocery, which had previously been the "Nichols & Tolford" meat market, sustained costly damage from a fire at the adjacent Draper butcher shop. The Tolford & Nichols meat market that opened in 1869 was located at the corner of Mifflin and Hamilton. Decades later the building that housed it became a city landmark, and it still exists at this writing, occupied by the Blue Marlin Restaurant.

According to local historian Stuart Levitan, "Madison began the decade [of the 1870s] down, still mired in the lingering recession from the late 1860s."[5] Nevertheless, Tolford & Nichols did well enough to employ two clerks, named Frank Jenkins and Anthony Victor, as indicated in a city directory during those years. Additional evidence of the meat market's success can be found in the records of a state government facility. Starting in mid–1869, Tolford & Nichols made considerable sums by supplying the local Soldiers' Orphans' Home. For example, over a 12-month span starting in the fall of 1870 the Home logged purchases from Tolford & Nichols on roughly a monthly basis for close to $190 on average, making them one of the facility's most-compensated vendors.[6] As noted previously, about 15 years earlier the Nichols family's personal property in its entirety was valued at a mere $200. Sarah Nichols, who became a teenager in 1869, was among the local supporters "who used to go week after week to help teach the little ones in the Sunday school there.[7]

A day of much celebration for the Nichols family occurred in the spring of 1872, though Charles was undoubtedly too young to recall it because he was only two years, eight months old. On May 15 both of his half-brothers were married.

John was united in marriage to Mary White "Mattie" Garner by Baptist clergyman E.H. Page, with John's siblings James and Sarah serving as the official witnesses. John's father-in-law was in the lightning rod business, while his mother-in-law would become famous in Madison decades later for living to the ripe old age of 102.[8] When Elizabeth Garner finally died in 1923, she was buried in the same set of Madison plots as John, Mattie, and other Nichols family members. James was united to Ellen M. "Nellie" Wright in a ceremony performed by John Twombly, who was not only a Methodist minister but also happened to be President of the University of Wisconsin! Twombly's involvement may have been due to the fact that Nellie's father, David H. Wright, Sr., was a prominent figure in local academic circles, as reflected in his biographical entry in a local history.[9]

The Nichols family experienced change of a very different sort two months later, when Tolford & Nichols dissolved. This resulted from Tolford's decision to move more than 100 miles northwest of Madison due to his investment in a telegraph line originating in Neillsville, Wisconsin. Robert continued as sole proprietor at the same location, and remained a major supplier to the Soldiers' Orphans' Home. The city directory for 1873 (published in 1872 but after Tolford's departure) listed Robert as employing two clerks, just as Tolford & Nichols had. One was named Fred Omen, whom the directory also listed as a boarder at the Nichols residence. The other was Mathias (aka Mathew) J. Hoven,[10] a future three-term mayor of Madison. In 1897 Hoven would become both the first German and first Catholic mayor of Madison.

The event of 1872 that most directly affected young Charles occurred on October 16, when his sister Dora was born. She was the last child born to Robert and Christina, his eleventh and her seventh. The newlywed Nichols brothers started having children in March of 1873, the first being Addie, born to James and Nellie.

An economic depression struck the nation in 1873, and Madison wasn't exempt from its effects. Fortunately for the Nichols family, sales by Robert to the Soldiers' Orphans' Home remained steady well into 1873. However, by early November of 1874 the Home's occupancy had dwindled to 34 residents, and by Thanksgiving that number had dropped to 21. It closed for good shortly thereafter. By the end of 1875, Robert Nichols was getting out of the butcher business, and Hoven became the new owner at the same location.[11]

In August of 1874, following up on the Band of Hope pledge she had made before Charles was born, Sarah Nichols became an officer in a local chapter of a temperance group, the Independent Order of Good Templars (which still exists today, as IOGT International).[12] Many chapters of this organization at the time were open to both men and women of all ages, as well as to non-whites. Charles and Sarah's brother-in-law, Sam Griffiths, was also very active in the IOGT in Madison. A month later Sarah made her debut as an amateur actress as Mary Morrison in the play *Dora, or The Farmer's Will*, an adaptation of a poem by Alfred Lord Tennyson. The performance was by a local troupe in which Sam was well established, and he joined Sarah in this performance.[13] When Capital Lodge No. 1 celebrated its 22nd birthday a few years later, it was reportedly the oldest IOGT lodge in the world.[14] Sarah would serve additional quarterly terms as an officer of her lodge from time to time until early the next decade.

Sarah also took part in IOGT performances aimed at younger Madisonians, presumably to offer them opportunities to socialize that didn't involve alcohol. In late 1875, at age 19, she portrayed Lillie Ashton in a play called *The Last Loaf*, and another cast member was Robert La Follette as Henry Hanson.[15] La Follette, then 20, later became one of the most famous people in Wisconsin history, serving as a Congressman and Governor and earning 17 percent of the popular vote nationwide in 1924 as the Progressive Party's candidate for United States president. Sarah Nichols and Robert La Follette were simultaneously officers of Capital Lodge No. 1 during at least two terms.[16]

The second half of 1875 also brought baseball back into the lives of the Nichols brothers, and probably into Charles's for the first time. "For the five years after the Civil War, baseball bordered on a mania [in Madison]; then it died down for several years only to become extremely popular again in the middle and later 1870s," wrote local historian David Mollenhoff.[17]

In August of 1875 it was announced that a new Madison ballclub was forming and would face the Sioux of Oregon, a village a few miles to the south. John Nichols was initially listed as the new team's shortstop, but soon became its catcher. Though the Madison team was thumped, 63–24, there was talk of a rematch.[18] Early the next month it was announced that a new Capital City Nine had been formed to play a second game in Oregon, and John was named as their catcher, but due to some misunderstanding the home team failed to show.[19] The new Madison team seems to have fizzled quickly, but the baseball resurgence was not over. In June of 1876 a team representing the city's bankers played a team representing telegraphers. John was scheduled to catch and Jim was to be the shortstop. Only one of them played, at catcher and as the leadoff hitter, in an 18–8 loss.[20] Less than a week later, the Capital City Base Ball Club played the University of Wisconsin's team but lost 36–2. The box score listed one of the Nichols brothers batting third and playing shortstop.[21] On August 1, the Capital City team was scheduled to practice, in anticipation of games with clubs from nearby Edgerton and Stoughton,[22] but again the team faded from view.

In June of 1877 a Madison ballclub did travel to Stoughton for a game, and, with two of Charles's brothers in the lineup, won 23–11. This time, though, Will and George represented the Nichols family. George, in right field, was only sixteen years old, and Will, about nineteen, was the winning pitcher![23] The many subsequent articles about this team usually identified few if any of the players, but a mid–July game was expected to include one of the Nichols boys in right field.[24] Alas, when stockholders announced the official formation of the Madison Base Ball Association in August, neither Will nor George were on the roster.[25]

Will and George were by no means newcomers to the sport. Back in the autumn of 1870, the *State Journal* had reported that "juveniles have taken it up and been playing some lively games lately." Their brief report included a box score for a game between the "Shoo Flys" and the "Polar Stars." Though the Shoo Flys fielded only eight players to the other team's nine, they won 41 to 37. Batting fifth and playing second base for the victors was George, three months shy of his tenth birthday, and batting second was winning pitcher Willie, about 12 years of age, who was the winning pitcher, as he would be again in 1877.[26]

That makes *five* members of the Nichols family who were baseball trailblazers in Madison. What about Charles himself? It's unclear whether he played the game in any organized manner while living in Madison. Years later he was very vague about his introduction to baseball. In 1904, a New York newspaper's article on the expertise that Kid Nichols offered as a player-manager said he drew upon "twenty-eight years at the national pastime," which would place Kid's initial involvement in baseball around 1876, squarely amid his years in Madison.[27] A decade earlier the nationally read weekly *Sporting Life* stated that Kid Nichols "commenced his base ball career as pitcher on a ward school team."[28] However, this may have referred to the 1880s, after the Nichols family moved to Missouri. When Nichols talked directly about his baseball origins, he usually began with his time on organized amateur teams in Kansas City.

Charles's schooling was also sketchy. "I only attended the Ward schools," he wrote of his time in Madison in the aforementioned biographical document that he prepared around 1949. In the spring of 1876 his sister Jessie, who was about three years older, was chosen as one of a few girls from the First Ward school who would put flowers on soldiers' graves during a Decoration Day ceremony,[29] and it's likely that Charles was enrolled in that school at the same time. "The First Ward School building is hardly a credit to the ward; it is kept neatly, but it is by nature a stone barn, illy ventilated and awkwardly constructed," wrote the *State Journal* around that time.[30]

In the spring of 1877 a "Josie" Nichols was among the Fourth Ward schoolgirls selected to place the flowers on Decoration Day, and this was probably referring to Jessie again.[31] In that case, Charles would have been in that school as well, though the family's residence was back in the First Ward a year later. In the 1880 census the family was still listed in the First Ward, though Charles was the only child listed as "at school."

He isn't easy to get a consistent picture of the Madison of Charles's school days. Because of its lakes it was a popular destination for out-of-state tourists as a resort town. The *State Journal* even devoted an entire four-page issue in mid–1877 to the city's attractions,[32] and yet from time to time it would editorialize about rampant unsightliness. "There are scores of localities in town, where swill and all manner of household refuse are thrown out upon the street," it once complained.[33] Madison experienced noticeable population growth between 1870 and 1875, expanding by more than 900 residents from about 9,175 to almost 10,100,[34] but by 1880 it had added only 250 more. In at least one respect Madison kept up with the times, having brought the telephone to town in 1877, a year after it was invented.

The *State Journal* editorial about swill and refuse nonetheless noted that in other respects Madison was "naturally one of the healthiest places on the continent," but of course that didn't mean its children were safe from the many diseases of the era. In the autumn of 1879, for example, there was a scarlet fever scare in Madison's schools.[35] The Nichols family was devastated on January 8, 1878, when diphtheria claimed the life of Charles's young cousin Addie within two months of her fifth birthday.[36] After Fannie had died in 1863, Robert had purchased more than half a dozen other plots in the same area of the cemetery, and Addie was placed in one of them.

The decade ended with a career change for the family patriarch. In April of 1879 Robert Nichols was appointed the city's police officer for the First Ward, at a wage of $1 per day. It's unclear what he had been doing for a living after handing his meat market to Matt Hoven at the end of 1875, though working for someone else as a butcher is a distinct possibility. Regardless, his one year in the new position wasn't entirely a quiet one. In July, Robert arrested a man named William W. Hunt on a charge of beating his wife. Hunt, in turn, charged his wife with bigamy and prostitution. A judge sorted it all out in due time, and fined Mr. Hunt $2 plus costs, which the man paid.[37] By the time the 1880 census was taken in the middle of that year, Robert's term on the police force had expired and the census listed him as having "no business." He did have at least one additional experience with law enforcement late in 1880, this time as one of six jurors who were asked to confirm the cause of death of a local merchant.[38]

Soon thereafter, for reasons unknown today, the Nichols family decided it was time to try life in a new city, and so Robert, Christina, and all of their children relocated to Kansas City, Missouri. Charles's three half-siblings and their spouses all stayed behind. Because of Madison's hot and cold attitude toward baseball, the move was a good one for a budding ballplayer.

3

KC and Pre–MLB

Kansas City, Missouri, experienced steady population growth from the Civil War onward, with about 4,000 residents in 1860, about 32,000 in 1870, roughly 56,000 when the Nichols family arrived around 1881, and about 133,000 a decade later. One big reason for this occurred in 1869, the year of Charles's birth when he Hannibal & St. Joseph Railroad opened a bridge over the Missouri River in Kansas City. The bridge was the first to cross the Missouri and facilitated transportation between Chicago and Texas. The local stockyards also contributed to the city's boom. At five times the size of Madison, the Nichols family must have experienced some culture shock. Milder winters probably helped ease the strain.

Some sources state that Kid Nichols moved to Kansas City when he was 11 years old, which was most of 1881, and others when he was 12.[1] Other sources disagreed when pinpointing the year rather than his age, usually specifying 1881 or 1882.[2] Many of these articles appeared no earlier than World War II, but back in 1898 the *Kansas City Journal* specified 1882.[3]

Robert Nichols was listed in tax records for Madison in 1881 and in the 1882 city directory for Kansas City. The directory identifies the Nichols residence as 505 Locust, a spot which today is just south of the Heart of America Bridge across the Missouri, and two blocks east of the Arabia Steamboat Museum. There was no occupation identified for Robert, but George and Willie also lived there, and both were messengers for the Pacific Express Company.[4]

The family's home changed almost every year for the remainder of the decade. In 1883, it was clear that Sarah was also still living with her parents, though she worked for the Woolf Brothers clothing company. In 1884, Willie and George tried a meat market of their own, at 936 Wyandotte, with their residence on the same street, but the next year they were back at the Pacific Express Company. In 1885, Charles was listed for the first time, as an express driver. In 1886, Robert had a meat market one final time, in partnership with Phillip T. Jones. The Nichols & Jones market was at 2220 E. 18th, and the

Nichols family lived a block away. It apparently lasted about as long as Willie and George's. The next year, that address belonged to the Jones & Carroll market.

Eighteen-eighty-five was likely the year, according to veteran sportswriter Ernest Mehl, that Charles saw his first pro baseball game,[5] featuring Kansas City's Cowboys, previously the Unions. In 1884 the Unions were the local entry in a major league that existed for a single year, the Union Association. In 1885 its team was a founder of the first Western League.

As with the year of the family's move to Kansas City, there have been differing reports about when Charles began to play organized amateur ball there. In 1903 a *Kansas City Star* profile said that Nichols "learned to pitch when only 12 years of age,"[6] but that doesn't mean he was playing in any formal league. One place where Charles was known to have played was on a vacant lot across from Second Presbyterian Church at Thirteenth and Central, a fact which came to light two decades later when a minister's complaint led to the arrest of three kids playing ball there.[7]

"I started my baseball career with a local amateur team at the age of fourteen," Kid Nichols recalled in 1949.[8] Kid Nichols was fourteen in the spring and most of the summer of 1884. However, in the biographical document that he prepared around 1949, and which is stored at the Baseball Hall of Fame, he wrote, "The first team I played on, was the Blue Ave. Club of Kansas City, MO in 1886." As a man of about 80, he certainly deserved tolerance for a lack of precision about events that occurred more than 60 years earlier.

The Blue Avenue club made it into Kansas City newspapers a few times during the summer of 1885, with home and away games against the Independence Garden Citys, and a 9–8 loss to the Distillery Company's team.[9] Ernest Mehl reported that they played at Fifteenth and Brooklyn.[10] A photograph of Nichols in 1949 showed him gripping "an 1885 souvenir bat [which] bears a silver plate with the names and positions of members of an amateur team on which Nichols played in 1885."[11] Today Kid Nichols' great-grandchildren still have that bat, which commemorates a championship. A smaller gold plate simply states that it was won by the Blue Avenue Base Ball Club, and the silver plate lists ten names. Three belong to Charles and his brothers Willie and George. Also listed is their future brother-in-law, Sam Nickells. Among the other names, some of which are now difficult to read, are W. Morris, W. Kennedy, R. Cliver, and G. Axtell.

The Blue Avenue nine also received coverage in the *Kansas City Times* from June to August of 1886. Twice they played the Wyandotte Reds, who were from just over the border in Kansas, and another time mention was made of a win in Bonner Springs, Kansas. One article announced a game against Beaton's nine of Armourdale, Kansas, for a purse of $50, to be umpired by

Gus Axty (aka Axtell) of Independence, Missouri, who was also a Western League arbiter around that time.[12] He could be the "G. Axtell" listed on the 1885 baseball bat's silver plate.

One of the more detailed accounts about Nichols' amateur days was provided by the *Kansas City Times* in 1895. Around the time that Charles organized the Blue Avenue club, a local by the name of Harry Childs reportedly taught him "the secret of curving the ball.[13] (Around 1909 Childs would be the Captain of the Kansas City Athletic Club and a fixture as a pitcher in the local Blue Diamond Baseball League, well known for his bean ball![14]) The *Times* listed the following as Blue Avenue players: W. Kennedy, c.; C.A. (Kid) Nichols, p.; Morris, first; Wilmot, second; Nickells, s.s.; W.H. Nichols, third; Newman, left; G.W. Nichols, center; Cliver, right.[15] At least seven of the names match the silver plate on the team's 1885 baseball bat.

Nichols didn't spend much time on organized amateur teams before setting his sights firmly on playing ball professionally. "In 1886, when I was 16 years old, being confident in my ability as a ball player, I was determined to get on a Base Ball team," Nichols wrote around 1949. "The Kansas City club was in the National League. I applied for a trial with them, and with two other National League clubs, but was turned down. (Guess they must have taken me for a bat boy.)"[16]

"In 1887 I again applied to the K.C. club, who were then in the Western League," Nichols continued. "They also refused me." One local paper's account just a few years after Nichols' 1887 attempt said that during the spring of that year, "every afternoon found him at the old 'hole in the ground' on Independence avenue, anxiously awaiting for Joe Ellick, manager of the Kansas Citys of the Western League to sign him." After being spurned, Nichols "started a billiard hall on East Fifteenth street."[17] In fact, the Nichols Brothers establishment, 2309 or 2311 E. 15th, was a partnership among George, Willie, and Charles, and their father was also involved. At that time the Nichols family was living at 1806 or 1804 E. 12th.

By that spring Nichols had decided that even though he had had success playing with and managing the Blue Avenues, he couldn't advance much further in his career with them. That feeling grew when a local minister insisted that they stop playing games on Sundays.[18] Many accounts of Kid Nichols' amateur career mention only the Blue Avenue club, but in 1887 he played on at least one other noteworthy amateur club, the aforementioned Beaton club in nearby Armourdale, Kansas. In fact, at least one source stated that Nichols played for the Beaton nine in 1886 as well.[19] After his stint with that club in 1887 the *Kansas City Times* asserted that it was the team's manager, Joseph M. "Dick" Juvenal, who "developed Nichols into a great twirler...."[20] The Beaton nine lost very few games during 1887, and the next year Juvenal transformed the club into the Newton, Kansas, franchise in the Western League.[21] Nevertheless, on the rare occasions in the twentieth century when Nichols's association with this Armourdale team was mentioned, Juvenal wasn't credited.[22]

A few years after he played for Juvenal, Kid Nichols had a very good reason to keep from mentioning him: a scandalous murder mystery in which Juvenal was a central figure. His stormy first marriage late in the 1880s ended in divorce after three years — during which time one particularly heated argument culminated in a single gunshot, though which one fired it was never established. In the summer of 1891, a woman to whom Juvenal was briefly engaged *before* his divorce was finalized, Millie Pfaffmann, was charged with blowing up the home he shared with his second wife, whom he had married about two months earlier. This was reported in newspapers in cities as far away as New York and Dallas. A month after the explosion, Juvenal and his second wife were poisoned, and she died. Miss Pfaffmann was charged with the crime and Juvenal then tried to stab one of Miss Pfaffmann's lawyers in court. These developments were also reported across the country. Shortly thereafter he was seen traveling out of town with his first wife, and he also appeared in court with her. In November it was announced that he had moved to Cleveland, Ohio.[23] On Christmas Eve, Millie Pfaffmann was released due to lack of evidence. The case sounds like one well suited for Sherlock Holmes, who made his literary debut in 1887.

Whether or not Kid Nichols deliberately sought to disassociate himself from Juvenal, a game he pitched for the Beaton nine was reportedly his springboard to greater things, and at least four sources are in general agreement about it. In 1903 the *Kansas City Star* said that one game in particular that Nichols won was "a remarkable game, which was the talk of the town." Three later sources identified the victims as a team from nearby Olathe, Kansas, one maintaining that he shut them out 6–0 and the other two even claiming that he blanked Olathe without allowing a hit. The no-hitter claim is dubious because from time to time Kid Nichols said he never pitched a no-hit game at any level. In any case, all three sources agree that this game inspired Ed Menges, then the secretary of Kansas City's entry in the Western League, to rethink his team's earlier rejection of Nichols. One account said that Menges was actually at the Olathe game, but the other two reported that he heard about it second-hand.[24]

Due to the sparseness of reporting on amateur games at the time, it's uncertain when this game took place. On June 6 the *Kansas City Times* reported briefly on a decisive victory the previous day by the Beaton nine over the visiting Olathe Reds, but the score was 13–1. None of the players were named.[25] Nichols' handwritten recollection around 1949 was that the Kansas City club determined on June 1st that "they were short of pitchers [and] then sent for me," in which case his impressive win over Olathe presumably occurred in May. A newspaper account less than a decade after Nichols' pro debut agreed that he was summoned around the first of June.[26]

Before Charles could become a professional ballplayer, he had to obtain his mother's blessing. In 1951 he recalled her saying, "I don't want you to play that roughneck game," to which he replied, "But, Mother, it looks like a fine chance to me. I want to play and maybe some day I can get into the big league and make good money." Christina started to soften, but replied, "Promise me you'll never drink." When her youngest son did, she gave in.

"June 10th I joined the K.C. club in Lincoln, Nebraska," he noted in the aforementioned biographical document that he prepared around 1949. In the 1951 account he elaborated: "I wanted to play ball so badly I didn't even bother to get a contract when the management asked if I'd join the team at Lincoln. The club gave me a hundred dollars and I went to work."[27]

His debut took place on June 14, 1887. "I shall never forget the first time I pitched professional ball," Nichols recalled after the turn of the century. "Nervous? Why, of course I was. But along toward the third inning the nervousness began to wear off."[28]

Nerves apparently got the better of Nichols at least twice while facing Lincoln batters, because one newspaper reported that stray pitches by Nichols "crippled Hoover and struck Dolan in the head, knocking him down."[29] Charlie Hoover, second baseman for the Tree Planters, would go on to play two years as a major leaguer in the American Association, and catcher Tom Dolan had already spent six years in the major leagues, with one more to come the next year. In fact, most of Lincoln's lineup played in the majors at some point. Without question, the most notable Lincoln player was first baseman and future Hall of Famer Jake Beckley, who was also destined to be a teammate of Nichols more than a decade later.

Kansas City was losing 2–0 after the first inning but led 6–2 after the fourth. The next inning their lead shrank to a single run. Neither team scored in the sixth or seventh innings. Nichols ended up winning his first game, 7–6, and produced the decisive run when batting in the eighth. "By some lucky accident I connected with a good one and lined it out for three bags," he said. "I rode back to the hotel that day in the same carriage with the captain and manager, and they could not do enough for me."[30]

"Nichols, the Kansas City amateur, showed up well in the box at Lincoln, yesterday and proved himself a valuable player," raved one of the Kansas City papers on its front page the next day. "He was four times at bat and hit safely three times with a total of five bases. Manager Patterson telegraphed Secretary Menges that Nichols's timely batting and daring base running won the game."[31] Nichols' first manager was John B. Patterson, who had taken over when Ellick resigned in May. Patterson was sports editor for the *Kansas City Journal* but not a ballplayer. Nichols' first catcher was Frank Ringo, who had spent four years in the major leagues before 1887. Tragically, Ringo would commit suicide just before the 1889 season at the age of 28.

In addition to the two hit batsmen, Kid Nichols struck out two but walked none. He tossed one wild pitch. Only four of Lincoln's six runs were earned, due to five Kansas City errors (one by Nichols). Nichols scored three runs.

Legend has it that Charles Nichols received his nickname upon joining the club, when the older players either mistook him for a batboy or at least thought he looked more like one than he did a professional player. His weight at the time was estimated to be no more than 135 pounds. This tale would appear to be accurate, because it only took a week for one local daily to call him "the 'kid'" at least three times in print,[32] and less than a month after his debut, the nationally read periodical *Sporting Life* felt compelled to acknowledge "the masterly pitching of Kid Nichols" for Kansas City.[33]

Kid Nichols followed up his successful entrance with another road victory two days later, beating Omaha 7–5. This time he was quiet at the plate, with no hits in three times up. He committed two errors and struck out none but also walked nobody. Most importantly, he got the job done again for the pitching-starved franchise.

The Cowboys soon followed the debut of a homegrown pitcher with the introduction of new uniforms. "The caps and shirts are white with maroon trousers, stockings and belt," reported one local paper. These garments were unveiled at home on Sunday, June 19, a day on which Kid Nichols was in uniform as a reserve pitcher. He pitched his first pro game in front of his fellow Kansas Citians two days later against the St. Joseph team. Unlike his first two games, this contest wasn't close, a 16–5 win for Nichols. He was eighth in the batting order and responded by collecting three hits in six at bats and scoring twice. He only walked one batter and his teammates' five errors meant that only three of St. Joe's runs were earned.

Because many fans were aware of his two road wins, early in the game there was "very generous applause when the 'kid' stepped into the box," reported one local paper. "The main thing about his pitching is its swiftness. He sends the ball across the plate like chained shot out of a cannon, and even without his curves it would be troublesome to hit him hard. He also has a good drop-curve and an in-shoot, besides, his control over the ball is first-class."[34]

From time to time during Nichols' pro career newspapers made reference to him throwing curveballs, but there has been some debate among baseball historians over the years regarding the extent to which he actually used such pitches. The general agreement these days about Nichols' career overall was summed up well by Bill Felber, who wrote that "Nichols was widely understood as almost exclusively a fastball pitcher who changed speeds and relied on control for effect but rarely if ever delivered breaking balls."[35]

Whatever his pitching repertoire was during his first pro season, it appears that many fans of the Kansas City team were sold on Kid Nichols early on. His win over Leavenworth on June 27 put the Cowboys in a tie for second place in the standings with that team, so grumbling was heard when other members of the staff lost back-to-back home games in early July. "A number of people were heard to say yesterday, that if Nichols had been pitching in either game there would have been a different result," reported the *Kansas City Times* about the Independence Day crowd.[36]

According to the autobiographical document that Nichols wrote around 1949, he didn't have an initial contract with the Kansas City club. After his early winning streak, however, "they gave me a letter of some kind and fifty dollars more."

The *Times* dubbed Nichols "the young wizard" after an impressive outing in late July. Pitching in front of an unusually large home crowd of at least 1,500 fans, the youngster refused to succumb to nine errors made by his teammates. He allowed Denver four hits, no walks, and no earned runs on his way to a 10–4 triumph. Nichols even thrilled the home fans with a two-out triple in the third inning.[37]

For an exhibition game on August 7, a few weeks before Kid Nichols' eighteenth birthday, he was chosen to face his former Beaton team, which later that year was deemed "undoubtedly the strongest amateur club ever organized in the west" by one local daily.[38] Close to 4,000 people turned out to watch. As a sign of how far Nichols had progressed in less than two months, he limited his former team to one hit and faced the minimum 27 batters.[39] Adding insult to injury, the Cowboys won 20–0. At first base for the club from Armourdale was Morris, perhaps the man who had been first baseman for the Blue Avenue club when Nichols led it in previous years.

By the end of that season, the Cowboys finished fourth in the league with an official record of 49 wins, 53 losses. (The Western League chose to omit games played against two of the four teams that folded during the season, Wichita and Emporia).[40] In contrast to this mediocre result, Nichols compiled a win-loss record of 18–12 for the team that had been reluctant to sign him, with an earned run average of 3.37. He also completed all 30 of his starts.

The offseason saw Nichols take part in some unusual forms of entertainment. In between his sister Jessie's wedding to Sam Nickells on October 2 and his sister Sarah's wedding to Thomas Colyer on February 7, Kid Nichols played at least two baseball games on roller skates, and probably played in a football game as well, each involving several of his Cowboy teammates and covered by the *Times*.[41]

With four Western League teams having folded during 1887 and the season having ended a little earlier than scheduled, its franchises faced an uncertain winter. "At the end of the season," Nichols wrote around 1949, "I was told I could go where I pleased for the next season." Just before Christmas, Walt Goldsby, who had played a little major league ball, made Nichols an offer to play with the team he was to manage in the Southern League during 1888, the Birmingham Maroons. By February Nichols refused Goldsby's "good" offer because Robert and Christina Nichols objected to their son going south, so far from home. At the start of that month Nichols denied a report that he had signed with the Beatons of Armourdale[42] as Dick Juvenal was grooming that amateur team to become a new professional franchise in the Western League.

Meanwhile, Kansas City was preparing to have two professional clubs in 1888, with the "Cowboys" name being taken by a new entry in the American Association, and the Blues entering the new Western Association. The latter team was managed by one of Nichols' prominent teammate's from 1887, former NL player Jimmy Manning.

Instead of staying in Kansas City, it turned out that Nichols signed with one of the other three teams that would play in the Southern League in 1888, the Memphis Grays. His parents, who had opposed letting him play 700 miles away in Birmingham, apparently decided that it was acceptable for their son to be about 450 miles away in Memphis. On March 9 he was instructed to report for duty three days later.[43]

On March 30 Kid Nichols pitched his first game for Memphis, an exhibition against the major league St. Louis Browns, who would win their fourth consecutive American Association crown that year. "Manning heard of this," Nichols recalled in 1903, "and for weeks and weeks I was besieged by letters and telegrams from Manning begging me to come back."[44]

Despite this impressive showing, when Memphis made a trip to New Orleans in mid–April, that city's *Daily Picayune* reported that Nichols was "left behind in Memphis while the three highest priced twirlers were taken along," only to be summoned urgently after one of them was injured. Hours after he arrived on the 17th he faced the local team "and proved to be quite formidable. He was hit a little at first but later on he pitched a steady, brilliant game, rising to each emergency. He studied the weak points of his opponents with rare judgment, and promises to give good account of himself before the season is over." Nichols won, 6–5.[45]

Kid Nichols' great-grandchildren still possess a Memphis team photograph from 1888, and among his teammates shown are Dick Phelan, Joe Crotty,

Memphis's 1888 team. Kid Nichols is standing, third from the left.

and Davy Force, all former major leaguers. In fact, Force's 15-year career in the National Association and then the National League dated back to 1871. Memphis's manager was Jimmy Wood, the manager and player in the National Association[46] who is credited with having pioneered the practice of spring training while leading the Chicago White Stockings in 1870. The photograph apparently also includes Phil Reccius, who had spent at least parts of the previous six seasons as a major leaguer in the American Association.

By early June, not only was Kid Nichols pitching well, but league statistics in the New Orleans paper ranked him 19th in the league for batting average, as .274, having appeared in 13 of the team's first 37 games. Their box score for June 4 showed him playing right field and batting seventh for Memphis.[47] Unfortunately, all four of the Southern League franchises were struggling financially in the small circuit, and late in June the Memphis team announced that it would have to suspend operations. The entire league then collapsed and disbanded. Nichols' win-loss record for the Grays was 11–8, and his ERA of 2.28 was a full run lower than the year before. He finished all 18 games that he started.

By July 1 Kid Nichols had been signed by the Kansas City Blues, and on July 3 he left with his new team for a trip to Omaha. On July 6 he won his first game there, 8–5. For the remainder of the season he rarely lost. At least one local paper appeared to realize that the city was in early stages of something special before the month was even out, declaring that "Kid Nichols seems to be a sure winner."[48] On top of that, another Kansas City paper declared that "Kid Nichols is one of the most gentlemanly and accommodating players in the profession."[49] Through mid–August he lost only one game, and that took 13 innings.

As the season wound down in October, despite the very successful stretch that Nichols was finishing, his many local fans were told to prepare for an uncertain future—one for the entire Blues franchise, in fact. "They can not play in Kansas City as a professional base ball team next year; the laws of base ball will not allow it," said the *Kansas City Times*.[50] Within a few days that paper was speculating that Nichols would switch to the Kansas City Cowboys for 1889, though because of an excess of players, "even Kid Nichols may be sold to a high bidder."[51]

The 1888 Western Association season ended with Nichols winning 16 games and losing only 2, finishing all of his games and shutting out his opponents four times. His sparkling 1.14 ERA led the league. Nichols had obviously played a crucial role in the pennant race, though it ended with confusion because Kansas City finished half a game ahead of Des Moines despite the latter team having a slightly better winning percentage. It was determined that the Blues finished on top.

In early November, baseball fans in Kansas City had a bigger worry. "Manager Watkins of the consolidated base ball clubs of Kansas City is in Denver trying to sell that city a franchise in the Western association and team of pennant winners," reported the *Times*. "A first class club could be spared from the list of Kansas City players." First on the list of pitchers was Kid Nichols.[52] Late that month the Omaha club asked that a price be put on him, but within days it was announced that the entire Blues franchise had in fact been sold, though not to Denver. Instead owners from St. Joseph "paid $3,000 cash for the franchise and Cartwright, Ardner, Johnson, Hasamaear, Bradley, Nichols, Kreig and perhaps one or two others."[53]

Kid Nichols had several distractions to keep his mind off of this turmoil. For one, the Nichols Brothers business was trying to determine what type of establishment would bring the most success. At some point from 1887 to 1888 the brothers changed from being operators of a billiard hall to confectioners at the same address, though Robert was listed as being in the cigar business there. A year later, George, Willie, and Charles appear to have followed their father's lead, and Nichols Brothers became a cigar store. George played it safe for a while, at least during 1888, by moonlighting as a messenger for Wells Fargo.

During the first few months of 1889 Kid Nichols kept himself fit with a few activities. During January and February two local papers reported on a series of roller skating races in which he participated, two of which he won. Some 800 people watched one of his victories. In March, the Kid and his brother-in-law Sam Nickells were named as proud buyers of new Traveler safety bicycles. The latter announcement identified Nichols as a member of "the Kansas City base ball team," though it wasn't more specific than that.[54]

As the 1889 baseball season approached, both St. Joseph and Omaha remained interested in Nichols. With his status still up in the air, he didn't pitch for either club on April 5 when they faced each other in an exhibition contest. He was again conspicuously absent on April 14, as Omaha played against the African-American Beacons team,[55] while St. Joseph played an exhibition game against the Kansas City Cowboys.

Omaha began its regular season on April 20 with the issue still unresolved. A few days later it was reported that Nichols would play with them that year, but the decision had been reversed before the season was a week old. "It is now definitely settled that 'Kid' Nichols of last season's Kansas City Blues will not play with the Omaha Western Association club," announced the *Kansas City Star*. "Last week he accepted the club's terms and wired them to send him a contract. The reply he received was that his services were not wanted. Manager Selee of the Omahas arrived in the city this morning and explained to Nichols that the directors had decided that no more pitchers were wanted."[56]

A baseball version of a cat-and-mouse game played out on the *Star*'s front pages during the first two days of May. On the 1st, the paper wrote:

> A dispatch to THE STAR from Omaha states that President McCormick of the Western baseball association club of Omaha was to-day notified not to play Charles Nichols, the pitcher, as he had not been released by St. Joseph. The Nichols referred to is "Kid" Nichols of last season's Blues, and the local base ball authorities declare St. Joseph has not the shadow of a claim upon him. The only club that did have a hold on him was the Kansas City Western association club which now has no existence. Kansas City did not sign him and he has been free since April 1, when, under base ball law, if the officials of a club want a reserved man they must either sign him or make him an offer. The Western association franchise was sold to St. Joseph last fall by Mr. Watkins, who also tried to transfer seven of the players to that city. ... The statement that St. Joseph has not released Nichols is absurd as St. Joseph did not have a club last year and consequently had no reserved men to release. Manager Lord of the St. Joseph club came here last fall and asked Nichols for his terms. The player agreed to sign for $1,100, but Lord refused to give it and thus lost a good man.[57]

The matter was settled after one more day. "Yesterday when Manager Selee of Omaha was notified not to play 'Kid' Nichols, as St. Joseph had not released him, he referred the matter to Mr. Nicholas Young of Washington, president of the National League and chairman of the board of arbitration, to which all disputes are referred. A dispatch received at THE STAR office to-day says that Chairman Young overrules St. Joseph's protest and allows the Omaha ball club to play Nichols."[58]

In 1903, Kid Nichols explained why he resisted playing for the St. Joseph club. "I was sold to St. Joseph," he recalled, but refused to play with that team, owing to the poor salary I was offered."[59] In the biographical document written around 1949 Nichols elaborated, noting that the St. Joe team wanted "to pay less than I had been receiving" in 1888. Thus, he began what was likely the most important partnership of his career, Omaha manager Frank Selee.

One of several 1889 "cabinet cards" of Kid Nichols, used for the Old Judge baseball cards.

Kid Nichols took the ball for Omaha for the first time on May 2, when they hosted Milwaukee. According to one Omaha paper, the team's uniforms for the season were mostly white — caps, stockings, and belts — but the white flannel shirts had navy blue stripes, and players wore navy blue pants.[60] In his debut Nichols struck out seven and won, 4–3. As had been the case when he joined the Blues in the middle of 1888, he got off to a fast start for Omaha. For example, on May 22 Nichols showed St. Joseph what they were missing by beating them 7–2. Omaha committed seven errors behind him but he scattered five hits. "Kid Nichols is pitching a great game for Omaha," observed the *Kansas City Star* the next day. "It may be that Kansas City made a mistake in permitting him to leave home."[61]

At the beginning of August, Nichols received some attention on the east coast. "'Kid' Nichols, the rising young pitcher of the Omaha Club, is being closely watched by many managers," wrote the *Philadelphia Inquirer*. "On Saturday last Nichols pitched two successive games against Minneapolis and won both. In the first game three hits were made off him, and in the second seven."[62]

With rare exceptions, Kid Nichols was brilliant for the next two months.

On August 8 he shut out Milwaukee in Omaha, 11–0, again giving up only three hits (though they clubbed him the very next day, 13–6, thanks in part to Omaha's four errors). On August 23 he hurled another three-hitter, this time against Sioux City. The game was tied at two until Nichols decided it in the ninth by homering. This time it was the *Kansas City Times* that twisted the knife about decisions made before the season. "Nichols is doing grand work for Omaha, and without a doubt he is the peer of any pitcher in the Western association," the paper stated. "Every time he wins a game President Speas and Manager Watkins think of the days when Nick beseeched them to sign for $1,200."[63]

Two days later Nichols beat Sioux City, 2–1, and this time he allowed only *two* hits. While reflecting on these games some days later, the *Sioux County Herald* wrote at length about Nichols. "At home the favorite is often pelted with silver dollars after a brilliant play, and he is said to have won an overcoat worth $100 by his last victory over Sioux City. It is also said of him that, young though he is, he is one of the provident men of the base ball profession." The paper quoted Nichols on this point: "We get paid off every month, and just as regularly as pay day comes, I bundle up a couple of centuries and make for the bank. I send this home to my banker, and he stores it away for me. I have a snug sum saved already, and it's growing every month and every day." The paper implied that Nichols was saving up for a wedding.[64]

On September 4, one of the Kansas City dailies speculated that the local hero might return home. "Charley Nichols, the Kansas City boy who has been pitching the best ball in the Western association this year, was in town a few hours yesterday but left in the evening to join the Omahas at St. Joseph. He wants to play in Kansas City, and he will probably be seen in a Kansas City uniform next year. There is a provision in his contract with the Omaha club that he can not be reserved for next season, and he is therefore free to go where he chooses."[65]

Kid Nichols didn't let such considerations weigh on him. On September 8, he defeated St. Joseph 5–3 at home, allowing his foes only four hits. Two days later, he whipped Sioux City yet again, shutting them out on another three-hitter, 2–0.

Nichols won another 2–0 game on September 15, the day after his twentieth birthday. This time it was a home game against Denver, and it was the pinnacle of his season. Over one hour and fifty minutes, he struck out eleven and walked only two. The Kid allowed just one hit.

In Minneapolis on September 17 he slipped past the opposition with a 4–3 win, but Nichols wasn't done with hurling low-hit games. At home on September 20 he shut out Des Moines on a two-hitter, 5–0. Back in Kansas City, the optimism about Kid Nichols playing there in 1890 was growing.

"Nichols, the Kansas City boy who has been the star pitcher of the Western association this season, will be signed," the *Times* insisted on September 22.[66]

Still, on September 24 the paper reported on other interest in Kid Nichols' services. He was one of ten Western Association players mentioned as having received overtures from the Brotherhood of Professional Base-Ball Players to join what would commonly be called the Players' League, a new major league that debuted in 1890.[67] This was the beginning of a flood of conflicting declarations about Nichols' status over the next two months.

The next day a story in a St. Louis paper claimed that Boston's National League team had bought the entire Omaha club, with Kid Nichols being one of the two "fine" players who were as included.[68] A day after that, a Boston paper confirmed that Omaha manager Frank Selee had announced this wholesale acquisition.[69] One more day later, another Boston daily included a short article out of Chicago that read, "It is reported on the quiet that 'Kid' Nichols, the great young twirler of the Omahas, has agreed to play in Boston next year. Nichols has had much to do with bringing the championship to Omaha this year, and he is the best pitcher in the Western league."[70] However, the season wasn't quite over, and in the midst of all this, Kid Nichols beat St. Paul in an unremarkable game on September 25 by a score of 10–2.

For Kid Nichols, the 1889 season concluded back in the state of his birth, in a series against the Milwaukee Brewers. Word was that he might pitch for Omaha near his birthplace, in the county fair, against a University of Wisconsin team led by Brewers pitcher George Davies, who'd soon pitch three seasons in the majors. For the first game, one of the Boston franchise's owners, William Conant, dropped in to watch the team that he had reportedly purchased. Kid Nichols was on the field that day, but only as an umpire when the appointed one didn't show up. The *Milwaukee Sentinel* reported that "Nichols, or 'Kid' as he is facetiously called by the comedians he is associated with, was fair and honest in his decisions, but, if the truth be told, his judgment was at times a trifle uncertain."[71] The Kid pitched on the 29th, the final day of the season, and was pounded by the Brewers, 15–6. If Conant also watched that game, Nichols had to hope that the owner was aware of how he pitched in all of those other games during September.

For the Omaha franchise, which that year was called both the Omahogs and the Lambs, Kid Nichols finished with a win-loss record of 39–8, and he still hadn't been taken out of a game in which he was the starting pitcher. Eight shutouts contributed to his ERA of 1.75. Perhaps most startling was the fact that he jumped from 173 strikeouts in 1888 to a league-leading 368 for Omaha (albeit increasing his innings pitched from about 310 to 438). His walk totals those years were 34 and 95. Around 1949, Nichols recalled that for the 1889 season the league required *four* strikes to retire a batter. The major league rule had only been permanently set at three strikes for the 1888 season.

Kid Nichols' year with Omaha would be immortalized by two baseball cards issued by Goodwin & Co. to promote its Old Judge cigarettes, cards #318 and #348. There are seven known variations of the latter, and one of the Old Judge cards would be dubiously adapted for use on the Mayo's Cut Plug card of Kid Nichols for 1895.

By mid–October, within two weeks of the season's end, Nichols' future turned very murky. "The Bostons have been caught asleep, and a deal has been completed with Omaha looking toward the release of Nichols to the Reds," according to a report out of Cincinnati.[72] A day later, under the headline "Pitcher Nichols Signed," the *Cincinnati Commercial Tribune* wrote, "It is understood that Nichols will sign on the 20th to play with the Cincinnati team of next season." That paper added that "Boston, Chicago and St. Louis all made offers for him."[73]

As if to prove just how confusing this situation was, the *Sioux County Herald* printed conflicting announcements about Nichols. "The Omaha management has sold Kid Nichols to Ted Sullivan for $3,000," it reported first. "It is not definitely known whether the purchase was made for St. Louis or Cincinnati. Sullivan is still in Omaha endeavoring to close a deal for Nagle and Clarke." Then it paraphrased a report by the *Cleveland Leader* that Boston management had paid $4,500 for Nichols, a sum which the paper said he was well worth.[74]

In its October 23rd edition, *Sporting Life* shed a little more light on the situation. "Boston lost pitcher Nichols because it haggled over the price of his release. The Triumvirate [the Boston team's three owners] stuck to $2800, when Cincinnati came along and gobbled up the man for $3,000," the weekly wrote. They also noted another missed opportunity. "Kansas City counted on getting Kid Nichols, and consequently that city is in mourning over Cincinnati's scoop. Watkins could have signed the young man at the beginning of the season for $1,200, but did not consider him good enough for the Cowboy team."[75]

Absent from these reports was any comment from Kid Nichols himself, with good reason. "My home was in Kansas City, but I was on a visit to friends in Madison, Wis. The first I knew that any other club was after me was when I received a telegram from Ted Sullivan," Nichols recalled a decade later. "I never answered his telegram. Next I received a letter from my brother urging me to sign with the Reds. It was Brotherhood year, and the Cincinnati team was one of the few that was going to have its team of 1889 intact for 1890. My brother thought I would have a better chance with the Reds on this account, and urged me to lose no time in signing."[76] The Kid's half-brothers James and

John were still both living in Madison at the time, so it would have been either George or Willie who was recommending the Reds.

While visiting his birthplace, Kid Nichols was trying to have some fun. On October 19, a ballgame was played in Delafield, Wisconsin, between St. John's Military Academy and a squad representing the University of Wisconsin. In a long and entertaining account in which he figured prominently, a Madison paper reported that for the latter team, "Nichols was to pitch under the name of Johnson, but the first fellow the boys met was a Kansas City lad who knew 'Nick' and let it all out." Since a ringer of their own was not similarly banned, the military team won the game with a late 8-run outburst.[77]

On October 25, Kid Nichols returned to Kansas City to winter there. "I have heard from Sullivan only once and that was a telegram in which he said he would be here to sign me," Nichols said upon his arrival. "I would like to play in Kansas City, but I hardly think I would be able to get my release from the Omahas. Omaha had a good club this year and Frank Selee is the nicest kind of manager to be with. I know little of the report that he will manage the Bostons next year but he has been their western agent and it is not unlikely that he will be Hart's successor." The paper that interviewed him noted that Omaha's sale of Nichols to Sullivan, representing Cincinnati, was less than final because Nichols had "a provision in his contract that he shall receive a half of the money which his release brings. The Omaha club owners are quite reluctant to give up 1,500 plunkers, but the pitcher will hold them to the letter of the contract."[78] It was subsequently reported that on November 1 Nichols received a telegram from Selee "to the effect that his release had been purchased from the Omaha club for $3,000 and that he would receive half of the release money. Nichols said that he would sign with the Bostons, although terms have not been agreed upon."[79] That remained in limbo over the next few weeks.

If Nichols felt a need to let off some steam during this saga, the St. Louis Browns gave him a good opportunity—and the chance to provide evidence that he was worth all the fuss. The Browns visited Kansas City to play an exhibition game on November 4 against a mix of local players, mostly pros, with Nichols as their pitcher. Attendance estimates were from 1,100 to 1,500. The hosts made five errors and thus St. Louis only notched two earned runs off Nichols. The game ended in a 5–5 tie after eight innings due to darkness.

"He easily proved that he is fast enough for any company by striking out 12 of the Browns, though he had only an amateur catcher to support him," wrote one St. Louis paper.[80] "Of course everybody scrutinized Nichols' work closely and if the Boston magnates had been among the spectators they would not have regretted that they paid $3,000 for the young fellow's release," added a Kansas City paper. "His speed was great and such batsmen as O'Neill,

Comiskey and Latham could [do] nothing with his curves." The receipts were divided equally among the players, so for an afternoon's work against a major league team that had recently finished at 90–45, Kid Nichols pocketed $20.[81]

Meanwhile, from late October into November the *Omaha Daily Bee* offered pertinent comments a few times in defense of their local franchise. On October 30 it called Selee a "very smooth man" in a headline for a very long article about the tug-of-war over several Omaha players, including Kid Nichols. The paper seemed hostile to the manager who had just brought them a pennant, even passing along an allegation by Cincinnati "that Selee spirited the Kid away; that he took him to Boston, where he is now," a charge supposedly "verified by the telegrams from Boston, which have repeatedly announced Nichols as a member of next year's team." A few days later it took a jab at their team's star pitcher: "It has leaked out that the nature of the hitch in the Boston-Omaha deal for Kid Nichols is that Nichols insists on one-half of the purchase money. The Omaha management would be foolish to allow the presumptuous youth a single nickel." The paper dropped any hostility two weeks later when it reported that "the coming great twirler" arrived in Omaha from Kansas City and would stay a couple of weeks. "He says he has not signed with Boston yet, as the form of the contract submitted to him did not suit his ideas of what it should be. He accordingly returned it for alteration. When asked where he would rather play, if he could have his choice, he replied unhesitatingly, 'Omaha, but like the rest of the ball players I'm out for the stuff.'"[82] That sounds like his version of "I'm in it for the money," and it may have been that Kid Nichols was just blowing smoke by saying he wanted to play in Omaha, but he would demonstrate in February that he had a genuine fondness for that city.

November 24 was apparently the day that the future was settled for the promising young pitcher. "Charles (Kid) Nichols, the star pitcher of the Omaha 'Western League' team last season, has signed a contract to play with the Boston league team next season," announced papers in Kansas City and Boston.[83] Nine years later Nick provided insight on his dominant thoughts at that time to Harry Weldon of the *Cincinnati Enquirer,* while visiting that city.

"It was not because I didn't want to play in Cincinnati. The fact of the matter was that I could not come here without breaking a promise," Nichols explained, referring to one that he had made to Selee. "He asked me early in the season, along in July, if I would go with him next season. He told me that he expected to make a change. I promised him that if the club he went to would give me as good as I could get any place I would go with him."

"At the same time the Kansas City Club wanted me. Although Kansas City is my home, I made up my mind I would play anywhere else for half the money," Nichols added. "They treated me too meanly to make me want to stay there. Why I was released twice by Kansas City clubs. Released, too, when I was pitching winning ball."[84] His bitterness was directed at Jimmy Manning specifically, though years later it would appear that Kid Nichols was not one to hold grudges.

One event that winter overshadowed all others in the life of Kid Nichols: his wedding on January 29, 1890, to Jane Florence Curtin, who often went by Jennie or Janey. Her parents were Dennis and Jane, both born in Ireland, but Jennie was born in Missouri on August 18, 1873. In 1887 and 1889, city directories listed her as a domestic living at 1225 Broadway, but in 1888 she was listed as a dressmaker living with her parents, on the south side of 27th between Jefferson and Summit.

According to the couple's marriage license, they were married at a Catholic church, Sacred Heart, by John Hogan. Assuming that there weren't two priests named John Hogan in the area in 1890, then Charles and Jennie were married by the first Bishop of the Diocese of Kansas City, who had assumed that position ten years earlier. The most detailed description of the event was probably provided on the front page of *Sporting Life*:

> The bride was attired in a beautiful garnet silk dress trimmed with velvet and wore diamond ornaments. After the ceremony they were tendered a banquet by the brothers of the groom at 2309 East Fifteenth street. The invited guests represented relatives only. A sumptuous repast was served, after which the guests were treated to a musical programme in which "the Kid" was a lively participant, after which the happy couple left for Omaha. They will return within a few weeks, as "the Kid" must report for duty March 1 to receive instructions under Clarkson.[85]

In Omaha the newlyweds stayed at the relatively new Millard Hotel,[86] which was known as the city's leading inn for decades afterwards. Though he was on his honeymoon, Kid Nichols couldn't keep his name out of the local newspapers. On January 31 he accepted a challenge from a local bicyclist named Jack Prince to race a few nights later at the Coliseum. Each man would reportedly put up $20. Nichols, though, wouldn't also be on a bicycle. Instead, his transportation would be roller skates! "The 'Kid' is one of the swiftest skaters in the country and has been looking for some one to beat," said one Omaha paper. "The 'Kid' will be given one-half lap start by the terms of the agreement and the distance will be one mile."[87] A few days later the paper reported the venue "was fairly well filled last night." Sadly, Nichols wasn't able to claim the prize for his new bride.[88]

About a week later the paper said that Mr. and Mrs. Nichols would remain in Omaha until February 16, "when they go to Boston for permanent residence."[89] It is assumed, though, that they first traveled back to Kansas City, for the wedding of Charles's baby sister Dora to Charles B. Northrop

This is believed to be a photograph after Nick and Jennie's wedding in 1890. The Kid (at the rear) is the one holding what appears to be a stalk of celery.

on February 17. In fact, if the happy couple did soon depart for Boston, then they took their sweet time getting there. On March 11 a newspaper in his birthplace of Madison, Wisconsin, announced that he was "spending a few days with relatives here previous to leaving for the east. He is accompanied by his wife and also by his sister, Mrs. Sam. Nichols."[90] The paper must have meant his sister Jessie *Nickells*, wife of Sam. A week later he did draw near to his ultimate destination, stopping briefly in Springfield, Massachusetts, to look up Jim Canavan, his Omaha teammate. On March 18 he was expected to meet up with the National League club in Boston.[91]

On March 19, 1890, Kid Nichols was among eleven members of the Boston Base Ball Club who reported to the Boston YMCA Gymnasium for practice. "Manager Selee was present, and under his eye, the 'boys' exercised under the direction of Instructor Chadwick of the gymnasium," reported the *Boston Daily Journal*. "The 'boys' first took a turn at the bar bells, then ran half a mile and finished up with the medicine ball. Instructor Chadwick then dismissed them and each exercised as he pleased."[92] On April 2, the paper summarized a practice game for some of the Beaneaters against a team from the Boston Athletic Association. Not surprisingly, the pros won, 11 to 3. "Nichols, the new accession as pitcher, showed up well, displaying both speed and curves," the *Journal* noted.[93]

On April 14, Boston continued to prepare for the regular season with a game in Delaware against the Wilmington Blue Hens of the Atlantic Association. Kid Nichols shut them out on three hits, 9–0.[94] On April 18, Nichols pitched again in New Haven, Connecticut, against that city's Atlantic Association team. At least 1,100 people surrounded the Howard Avenue grounds and saw the Kid win, 7–3. He allowed only four hits, and five Boston errors meant that only one of New Haven's runs was earned.[95]

The start of the regular season was just a few days away. For Kid Nichols, it was so far, so good. Soon, so great.

4

Boston Was Boastin'

"A sultry day, with prospects of showers," was how one New York newspaper described the weather in Boston that afternoon. "There were about 700 people present when the game began."[1]

The home team had won two of the first three games to start the season, but with a brand new rookie pitching that day in the fourth game against the Brooklyn Bridegrooms, local fans had to be anxious about whether they'd have to settle for a split. Though the franchise was new to the National League, in 1889 it had won the championship of the American Association, also a major league. The *Boston Daily Journal* noted that the pioneer sportswriter Henry Chadwick was present for the entire series at the South End Grounds, having "witnessed the contests from the scorers' seats." Whether the rookie hurler understood who Chadwick was, and that the man was watching, nobody knows.

Though they were the home team, Boston batted first, as sometimes happened in that era. Nothing much happened during that half of the inning. The date was April 23, 1890, and of course the pitcher who made his major league debut for the Boston Beaneaters in the bottom half of the inning was Kid Nichols.

Catching for him was Charlie Ganzel, who was about halfway through a 14-year major league career. Nichols walked the first Brooklyn batter, and the second hit a single to right field. The third Brooklyn batter, Oyster Burns, watched Nichols and Ganzel get their signals crossed on a pitch and then saw Herman Long fail to field his drive over short, and in short order the first two Bridegrooms had crossed home plate while Burns stood on first base with nobody out. Neither run had been earned, but that was small consolation for the rookie pitcher.

It appeared that Nichols was digging the hole deeper when he uncorked what looked like a wild pitch, but the *Journal* was delighted to report that "Ganzel made a magnificent stop and threw to Long, who had covered second, in time to catch Burns, who was trying to purloin the base." Nichols then bore down and struck out Brooklyn's cleanup hitter. He retired the next hitter easily, and escaped his first inning down only two runs.

Boston was retired one-two-three by Brooklyn pitcher Mickey Hughes, who was beginning his third year in the majors and was three years older than Nichols. In the bottom of the second Brooklyn advanced a runner to third with two outs, but Nichols threw out Hughes at first to end that threat. Pop Smith then led off the top of the third with Boston's first hit, singling to right field.

That brought Kid Nichols to bat for the first time. Nichols also singled to right field. Smith later scored but Boston stranded Nichols at third. At least they had cut Brooklyn's lead in half.

In the bottom of the third Kid Nichols struck out Brooklyn's leadoff hitter, but if he was pumped up after getting a hit in his first major league at bat, it didn't last long. Hub Collins of the Bridegrooms followed by smacking a fly ball that just grazed the fingers of Boston's rookie right fielder, Steve Brodie, for a double. Up next was Oyster Burns. In the words of the *Journal*, "Burns sent a high fly between left and centre, which [center fielder Patsy] Donovan captured after a hard run, and with no time in which to recover sent the ball to 'Pop' Smith at second in season to catch Collins, who had started for third on the hit—a double play which evoked the most intense enthusiasm."

The next three Boston batters weren't sufficiently energized by this great play, because in the top of the fourth they were again retired in order. The first Brooklyn batter in the bottom of that inning reached when one of Nichols' teammates dropped a bloop, but the Kid induced a double play ball and then got out of the inning without difficulty.

Kid Nichols went up to bat for the second time with one out in the fifth inning and singled again, but his teammates couldn't advance him past second before the inning ended. In the bottom of the fifth Nichols experienced his first 1–2–3 inning on three balls hit to Long. After five innings, Nichols was still on the hook to be the losing pitcher, as Brooklyn continued to lead Boston, 2–1.

Finally, in the top of the sixth, the Beaneaters "fell on Hughes savagely and gave as fine an exhibition of scientific hitting as is often seen," according to the *Journal*. The newspaper elaborated:

> Tucker, the first man at the bat, drove a grounder between third and short. This set Long and Donovan right on edge, and some lively coaching was heard. "Let's win the game right here," "line her out, now," "play ball" and kindred cries floated out on the air, to the great delight of the crowd. Tucker stole second. Then Capt. Ganzel placed the ball very scientifically to short right field, Tucker scoring. Lowe got in a rattling drive to left, on which Ganzel reached second. Brodie struck a slow

> liner to Hughes, who got it easily on the fly, and also doubled up Ganzel at second, who had started for third as soon as the ball was hit. Lowe stole second, aided by a wild throw. Smith hit to Collins, who gathered the ball well, but threw low to Foutz, and the ball went through the latter's legs. When he received it, Lowe had scored, and Smith was on third. Nichols drove a single between second and third, and Smith scored. Long got in a rattling three-bagger to left, and Nichols scored. The enthusiasm at this point was unbounded and found vent in yells of all varieties.

The next batter was retired easily to end the inning, but suddenly Boston was ahead, 5–2. In short order, Nichols had logged his first run batted in and first run scored, while notching his third hit in as many at bats. Boston would not add any more runs that day.

In the bottom of the sixth Brooklyn managed to get runners on first and second with two out, but the *Journal* reported that third baseman "Lowe made a very fine running stop of Pinkney's hard bounding hit and caught the runner at first with a lightning throw."

Kid Nichols allowed Brooklyn one runner in each of the seventh and eighth innings, but without consequence. It all came down to the ninth. Though the crowd may have numbered only 700 early on, other accounts of the game put the official number of witnesses by the end of the game at 1,392. A groundout to short and a flyout to right left Brooklyn with one final chance. That batter hit it back to Nichols, who threw to first to end the game and win his first appearance! "Judging from yesterday's showing he will prove a very valuable acquisition to the team's pitching," the *Boston Journal* enthused the next day, at the risk of jumping to conclusions.[2]

Back where the Nichols family made their home, one of the newspapers couldn't resist making a snide remark on the Kid's behalf: "The Kansas City boy, Charley Nichols, pitched his first game for Boston yesterday and won it, Brooklyn managing only five hits. And yet this is the lad ex–Manager Watkins didn't think fast enough for the Kansas City club last year."[3]

Kid Nichols' focus that day was certainly on the game at hand. Nevertheless, the maneuvers and rumors surrounding his acquisition had to have made him aware of the great turmoil surrounding the National League in general and the Boston franchise in particular. The addition of the American Association's 1889 champions was the least of the NL's worries. The new Players' League was a much bigger threat to the NL, and Boston's roster was among the most devastated by defections to that new rival.

Nichols would provide some stability soon enough, but he wouldn't begin his major league career with a winning streak. His second start on April 26 later was also at home but this time it was opposite the highly regarded Amos Rusie of the New York Giants, a future Hall of Famer. Though Rusie was close to two years younger than Nichols he had managed to break into the major leagues in 1889. The Beaneaters only managed four hits off of Rusie and lost, 3–1.

Kid Nichols had benefited from a triple play turned by Long, Tucker and Ganzel, but four of his teammates committed errors and he demonstrated some wildness. In addition, brief accounts that appeared in multiple newspapers said that "Nichols was batted hard," though one of the few independent accounts, in the *Philadelphia Inquirer*, said that like Rusie, "Nichols also pitched well and not an earned run was made off him, but the visitors bunched their hits with Boston's errors."[4]

Nichols' third start was a rematch against Hughes, only this time in Brooklyn on April 29. The score was the same as when the two pitchers first met, except that this time Brooklyn won. The Kid gave up only four hits but experienced some wildness, and a few runs against him were due to teammates' errors. Nichols and Hughes squared off yet again in Brooklyn on May 2, and Boston won the rubber match easily, 11–2.

On May 5 Kid Nichols lost a close game to Philadelphia, 6–5, though he yielded 15 hits. He faced them again on May 8 and had a no-hitter going until one out in the sixth inning but ended up losing by one run again, 5–4.

A truly momentous rematch against Rusie occurred in New York on May 12 as a Players' League game was taking place in an adjacent field. Though fewer than 1,000 fans were watching the NL game, the tension became thick as the Nichols–Rusie matchup approached the ninth inning because both pitchers were almost unhittable, and neither had been scored upon. When the game went into extra innings, many fans watching the Brotherhood game reportedly began trying to watch the drama unfolding in the NL's Polo Grounds. The game remained scoreless after twelve innings, yet it still hadn't reached the two hour mark.

The *New York Herald* provided this account of slugger Mike Tiernan's at bat against Nichols in the thirteenth inning:

> The first ball he tapped foul, and it flew back into the grand stand. A new ball was torn from its case, but before the umpire had tossed it into play the old one was thrown back into the diamond and it rolled to Pitcher Nichols.
>
> "This ball is all right, isn't it?" he asked of the umpire, remembering that in the eighth inning Tiernan had hit a new ball safely.
>
> "No; the new ball was on the field first," said Umpire Powers, "and you'll have to use it."
>
> "Oh, all right," said Nichols, as he exchanged the balls.
>
> "Now, Mike!" cried five hundred folks.
>
> And the first time that sparkling new ball came toward the plate was its last. It was shoulder high, and the end of Mike's bat met it with one of those solid whacks that mean every pound of the batsman's power has been applied to perfect advantage.

> Centre Fielder Brodie and Right Fielder Shellehasse [sic] both started as if to make a catch, but the ball, though only some thirty or forty feet high, had no time to shake hands with them. On it went beyond the fielders, on beyond the bank, on beyond the fence on top of the bank, on beyond the vision of the happy spectators.[5]

As with Kid Nichols' major league debut, the visiting team had batted last, but Boston couldn't muster much of a response in its half of the thirteenth, and thus the game ended 1–0. The *New York Daily Tribune* called it "probably the most remarkable game ever witnessed in this city. Most games may be forgotten the day after they are played, but to-day's battle will take a prominent place in the modern history of base ball."[6] Such assessments aren't uncommon to this day, such as one from baseball historian David Fleitz, who agreed that the game remains "one of the most famous pitching duels in baseball history."[7]

Sometimes a duel that ends so dramatically can have a lasting negative effect on the reputation of the player who is responsible, but such was not the case for Kid Nichols. The *Tribune* observed, "Both Rusie and Nichols gave a brilliant exhibition of strategic pitching, the young twisters having remarkable control of the ball, only seven hits being made, four for New York and three for Boston. The pitching of young Nichols would have won ninety-nine out of a hundred, and was almost as clever as that done by Rusie."[8]

Nichols' support wasn't better for him when he faced Chicago on May 16. Boston newspapers praised his pitching and put the blame squarely on the team's hitting as they lost, 5–0. The turning point in his rookie season, in terms of winning regularly, occurred on May 21 as his first month was drawing to a close.

In a game at home, it was Nichols against fellow rookie Jack Wadsworth of Cleveland. As in the duel against Rusie, neither team scored during the first nine innings. Boston won it for Nichols in the tenth when Long led off with a single, stole second, was sacrificed to third, and came home on another sacrifice.

After this nail-biter, Kid Nichols began a streak during which he won nearly two-thirds of his starts into early autumn. That would include another 1–0 shutout before the end of May against Jesse Duryea of the visiting Reds, though this time Boston's lone run was scored in the first inning. Nichols scattered five hits and walked none.

It was clear after a few weeks that Manager Selee would stick to a rotation of Nichols, Pretzels Getzien, and future Hall of Famer John Clarkson. Getzien (sometimes misspelled Getzein or Getzin) started his major league career in 1884 but was new to Boston. Clarkson had only a little more major league experience than Getzien did, but was in his third year with Boston and well into a Hall of Fame career.

According to recently published research by Frank Vaccaro of the Society for American Baseball Research (SABR), the first significant use of a three-man rotation was in 1887, by Charles Comiskey's pennant-winning St. Louis Browns. After that, "Frank Selee's 1890 Boston Nationals were the most committed team to the three-man agenda, a decision no doubt spurred by Boston's failed use of the one-man rotation in September of 1889."[9] That one man was Clarkson, who finished that season having pitched a staggering 620 innings.

By mid–June the fans in Boston had grown very appreciative of Kid Nichols' strong work, including an 8–5 home win over Philadelphia. On June 16, he returned to the field to pitch the second game of a doubleheader, again at home against Philadelphia. "As Charley Nichols walked to the front of the grand stand and began tossing the ball to Bennett in preliminary practice he was compelled to lift his hat to the spectators who were applauding him vigorously," observed the *Boston Daily Globe*. The Beaneaters faced Phenomenal Smith, who was in his seventh year of major league ball. Boston didn't score until the eighth inning, netting a pair to tie the score, and the game went into extra innings tied 2–2. Nichols found himself in another 13-inning contest. The home team was again batting first, and Brodie opened the Boston half of the thirteenth with a single. He was bunted over to second, and remained there as the next batter fouled out. That brought up Charlie Bennett, and when the Philadelphia second baseman fumbled the ball that Bennett hit to him, Brodie came around to score the tiebreaker.

In the bottom of the thirteenth Boston's rookie pitcher struck out the first batter. "'Nichols! Nichols!' sprang from every portion of the grounds," recorded the *Globe*. Brodie hauled in a fly-out in right field for the second out, and then Nichols faced Philadelphia's cleanup hitter, Sam Thompson. The Kid struck him out to end it.

The *Globe* commented that during this match "there was more excitement than has been seen on the home grounds this season." As for Nichols, "he again demonstrated his ability yesterday in a way that caused wonderment and admiration for his science, pluck and energy."[10]

Boston had started the season slowly, but the start of summer brought a two-month hot streak. About two weeks after the Beaneaters started playing dominant ball, Tim Murnane, the prominent *Globe* sportswriter and a former major league player himself, expressed concern about the effect of success on Boston's rookie pitcher: "Kid Nichols is said by the League scribes to have a dose of the swelled head."[11]

As often happens today when someone achieves celebrity status, minute details begin to be reported by the media, and not just in the city where the person works or lives. For example, two weeks after Murnane's comment, a newspaper back in the city where Nichols pitched in 1889, Omaha, printed an item about him that was only tangentially about baseball: "Kid Nichols has developed into the premier sprinter of the Boston team, and Selee offered to back him for $100 a side against Tiernan of the New Yorks, but Murtie [sic] refused," referring to Giants manager Jim Mutrie.[12]

On August 12, 1890, rookie Nichols was Boston's pitcher in another game that went into extra innings scoreless. It was his second extra-inning game in Boston opposite Philadelphia's Phenomenal Smith. According to the *Boston Evening Journal*'s account, only once "had a Bostonian reached third, and not until the 11th inning did one of the visitors reach second." In the 12th inning, Charlie Bennett won it in grand fashion for Boston with a homer. Kid Nichols ended up with a three-hit, 1–0 shutout.

"Nothing like the work shown by Nichols has been seen on the grounds this year," raved the *Journal*. "Not only did he have perfect command of the ball, but his speed was very great. A remarkable feature of his work was that only four hits were made to the outfield, two flies and two hits. In the fifth inning he succeeded in retiring the side on strikes in one, two, three order."[13]

It was a big win for Boston. Brooklyn was in first place with 60 wins and 31 losses, but Boston was a close second, with a record of 59–34. Adding to the excitement, Philadelphia and Cincinnati were right on Boston's heels. Alas, Boston was only able to sustain its surge for about two more weeks.

On September 13, Kid Nichols figured in rumors about the Brotherhood's upstart league. "Captain Charles Comiskey has been secured by President [J. Earl] Wagner to pilot the Philadelphia Player's [sic] Club to victory next season," reported prominent newspapers. "The deal was to be kept secret until after the season. It was leaked out through Pitcher Nichols, of the Boston League club, with whom Mr. Wagner had a dicker."[14] In other words, Nichols had also been negotiating with Wagner. That same day, the *Philadelphia Inquirer* wrote that Wagner "last night stated that Comiskey, of the Chicago Players' Club, has as good as signed a contract to play first base, captain and manage the Brotherhood club of this city next season."

"Two first-class pitchers are yet needed to complete our team for next year, and unless I mistake very much you will see a couple of the greatest twirlers in the business on our nine," the *Inquirer* quoted Wagner as predicting. "Nichols of the Boston Club, and Rhines, of the Cincinnati Reds, are the men we are after, and we have every reason to feel that they will sign Philadelphia Brotherhood Club contracts."[15] However, the *Philadelphia Record* of the same day reported that, "the attempt to secure Nichols, of the Boston League Club, has been abandoned. Nichols wants too much money."[16]

On September 20 the weekly *Sporting Life*, which was headquartered in Philadelphia, printed an item from the *New York World* that read, "A report from Boston says that 'Kid' Nichols, of the Boston National League Club, has signed with the Philadelphia Players' League team for 1891." The *Sporting Life* then added this rebuttal: "Well, he hasn't, and does not intend to unless he can get a salary far beyond his merits. He is simply — to use his own vernacular — 'pulling the leg' of the Boston triumvirs [the three owners] for a larger salary next season. About $5000 is what he thinks he is worth; and he won't get that or anything like it in the Players' League, where he would be an experiment."[17] In the end it was the Players' League that was the experiment, for it folded after the 1890 season, ending any flirtation that Kid Nichols may have had with the new circuit.

When the 1890 season ended in early October, Boston was in fifth place out of eight teams, though close to Cincinnati and Philadelphia above them, and 12 games behind Brooklyn, the pennant winners. With 76 wins and 57 losses, it was a good year for Boston. The same was true for its rookie hurler. Kid Nichols started 47 games and completed all of them, in addition to pitching in relief once. He compiled 27 wins against 19 losses and seven of his wins were shutouts, which led the league. In 424 innings pitched, he struck out 222 batters and walked only 112, the best ratio in the league. His earned run average was an impressive 2.23.

About two months after the season ended, Kid and Jennie Nichols had a very different reason to be happy: on December 8 their only child, Alice, was born, while the couple was wintering in Boston. Over time Alice would prove to be her father's most fervent fan. Within a few days he visited the *Boston Globe*, which reported that Nichols "wore a wreath of smiles this morning when he entered THE GLOBE office. A 10-pound daughter arrived at his South End home Monday. Mrs. Nichols and baby are doing splendidly."[18]

In mid–January the *Kansas City Times* noted that the Nichols family had returned to that city for a few weeks.[19] The paper later announced that on the 27th Charlie Nichols had spent the day with his Boston battery mate, Charlie Bennett, who had been hunting in Kansas.[20] This was perhaps the first of many indications over the years of the strong friendship that the two developed.

Nichols' return to Kansas City seems to have lasted longer than originally expected. It was announced that in mid–March he would prepare for the upcoming season there with two players on the roster of the Kansas City Blues for 1891, pitcher Frank Pears and outfielder George Hogriever, along with manager Manning.[21] At least one of the dailies in Omaha was also keeping tabs on the former Omaha player, as the *Bee* reported on April 5 that Kid Nichols had just left Kansas City for Boston after making this prediction: "He says the 'bean-eaters' are going to win the pennant and then he and Herman Long will come out west for a world's championship series and show how it was done."[22]

Nichols had at least three good reasons to be optimistic. In the wake of the collapsed Players' League, Boston signed some of its top players, namely infielders Joe Quinn and Billy Nash and pitcher Harry Staley. Staley and Nash would be solid contributors in 1891, and Quinn ended up in the lineup almost every day.

The Boston club had scheduled a trip south for spring training, but in late March a change of plans was announced. "The League team will not go South, as was originally intended, but will take its practice at home, playing games with local clubs until the opening of the regular season," announced one Boston paper. "With good weather the club can get as much practice here as in the South, and the Southern trip would be a losing one financially in any event. Manager Frank Selee is strong in his belief that the team is a winning one, and is hopeful of the best of results."[23] Nichols got in some work when the Boston club hosted Brooklyn for an exhibition game on April 2. Boston also played a few games with Harvard in April, and again two or three of Selee's pitchers saw action.

On April 23, exactly one year after his major league debut, Kid Nichols and the Beaneaters defeated the Giants in New York, 11–6, in their second game of the 1891 season. Nichols followed up by winning Boston's home opener, 5–0, over Philadelphia. Little did he realize that he'd be called back into action the very next day. After eight innings Boston led 11–2, and Selee decided to replace John Clarkson in order to allow rookie pitcher Jim Sullivan to make his first major league appearance. Pitching in front of more than 2,200 spectators, Sullivan "was rather nervous, and allowed four men to score." The rookie did manage to get one man out but walked three and made an error. It was now 11–6, with two runners on base. "Nichols succeeded him at this point and closed the game by striking out Delehanty [sic] and retiring Thompson on a weak hit toward first, Tucker assisting."[24] Sullivan would pitch in only one more major league game that year, doing so for Columbus of the American Association (though he would pitch a few more years for Boston starting in 1895).

Boston had won its first six games, and Nichols had a hand in half of them by making back-to-back appearances. He would replicate that feat in May. On the 5th he won 3–2 in Brooklyn. The next day Getzien was winning there 6–2 after five innings but he struggled mightily in the sixth and suddenly it was 6–5. Nichols came in to extinguish the fire, and Boston ended up winning comfortably, 12–6. Nichols then pitched for the third day in a row, beating New York 13–6 back in Boston.

Kid Nichols found himself pitching another extra-inning game in Pittsburgh on May 25, though this one only lasted ten innings. In that frame, Herman Long tripled and scored, to give Boston a 4–3 victory. Nichols struck out 12 batters.

Though Boston had won its first six games of the season, as of June 9 it had only won 19 of its first 40. The team then went on a nine-game winning streak that propelled it into the pennant race. The third victory, on June 12, was similar to the game on May 25: the opponent was again Pittsburgh, Boston earned another one-run victory in its final at bat, and Nichols again reached double digits in strikeouts.

It must have been an especially satisfying performance for Nichols because, as he had done in his major league debut, he contributed in many ways. "Nichols pitched a beautiful game for the home team; not a run was earned off his delivery," wrote one Boston paper. "He struck out eleven men and played an excellent fielding game also, while at the bat he made two very timely singles and an equally timely sacrifice. In fact, he was very much in the game from start to finish, though having, as usual, his one unlucky inning—this time the eighth, in which Pittsburg tied the score."[25] With that victory, Boston rose to third place in the National League.

Kid Nichols started off July with a bang by allowing Brooklyn batters only three hits in a 6–0 shutout. (Boston papers said he threw a two-hitter but their box scores weren't in agreement about which Brooklyn players achieved them.) Had Nichols picked up something from one of his greatest rivals? "The peculiar delivery of Rusie, the Giants' strong boy, gives promise of becoming universal with speedy pitchers," commented one newspaper. "Nichols used that bewildering rotary motion with the arm before delivering the ball with remarkable success."[26]

Facing Brooklyn again on July 22, a generous act by Billy Nash and Kid Nichols during an 11–5 win earned praise in *Sporting Life* from George H. Dickinson, sports editor of the *New York World*. Dickinson wrote about replacing a player called "Hub" in Boston, which happened to have the same nickname, the Hub:

> It isn't very often that one hears of one ball player doing an act of courtesy to a fellow player on the field. Here is a story, however, that reflects credit on Captain Nash and pitcher Nichols, of the Boston team. When Hub Collins was hurt a few weeks ago the Brooklyn Club management found it necessary to utilize the proffered services of John J. Burdock at second base, he played two games with Ward's men at Boston. No man who ever played ball at the Hub is more popular than Jack. Once he was Boston's idol, and when he made his appearance on this occasion he was given a tremendous ovation. In fact, he was the star of the game. Jack is still better in the field than many second basemen, but he is weak at the bat. This day he was more than anxious to make a hit. "Let him hit it, Nick," said Captain Nash to Nichols. The "Kid" sent in a straight ball and Jack promptly cracked out a single. The applause that followed will probably long remain in the ears of the veteran, who perhaps then made the last hit that will ever be recorded for him in a National League championship game.[27]

"Black Jack" Burdock, who starting playing in the National Association in 1872 at the age of 20, played for Boston from 1878 until 1888, but didn't play in the majors during 1889 or 1890. The trio of games he played in July of 1891 was indeed his swan song. In the games before and after he faced Nichols, he went a combined 0 for 8 at the plate.

On August 6, Kid Nichols had a very unusual experience while facing a team which he had never beaten in his young career, Cap Anson's Chicago Colts. The game was his third significant 13-inning contest in less than two years. The crowd at Boston's South End Grounds was very large, numbering over 5,000. Jack McQuaid was the umpire. After the scored was knotted at 6–6 for a few innings, Nichols quickly found himself in trouble in the thirteenth, with Colts on second and third and only one out.

The well-known baseball analyst Bill James, writing in 1990, summarized what happened next, and what long-term effect resulted:

> Just as Nichols would get set to pitch, Anson would jump to the other side of the plate, switch around as if to bat left-handed, then right-handed, etc. Nichols looked at him as if he was half-crazy, which wasn't necessarily false, and waited for him to stand in and hit. Anson kept jumping from side to side.
>
> At last Billy Nash, the Boston coach, asked the umpire to tell Anson to cut it out, to stand on one side of the plate or the other. The umpire, named McQuaid, said there was no rule that Anson couldn't do that if he wanted. Nichols refused to pitch, Anson continued to jump around, and the umpire, perhaps intimidated by Anson, refused to order him to stop. At last the umpire went Anson to first base, ruling that he was entitled to first base since Nichols refused to pitch to him. Nichols said he couldn't pitch because Anson's body was in the way.
>
> So they made a rule about that, that if a hitter switches positions in the batter's box after the pitcher is set he is called out. The rule is still in the books; you may remember it was the subject of a beer commercial a few years ago.[28]

Because James was focusing on the origin of this rule, what he didn't add was that Nichols' first pitch to the next batter hit the man and forced in the winning run. David Fleitz, an Anson biographer, said that Chicago's leader "figured that the 21-year-old Nichols could be rattled with the game on the line, so he chose this moment to test the young pitcher's nerve."[29]

Other than the previous year's showdown with Tiernan during the pitchers' duel with Rusie, this at bat probably garnered more press coverage at the time than any other during Nichols' first two years with Boston. The day after this game, one Boston paper added important details when it explained that "Anson stepped up to the box and Bennett stood to one side so that Nichols could pitch wide balls. Anson crossed over to the other box and Bennett moved to the opposite of the plate. Anson returned to the first position and so did Bennett. At last it became evident that Nichols would not pitch to him, and he was sent to first, the play being scored a base on balls."[30]

A summary in *Sporting Life* characterized the at bat similarly: "In the ninth inning of the game mentioned the Boston catcher, when Anson came to the bat stood away from the plate and instructed pitcher Nichols to pitch wide so as to give Anson his base on balls. Anson didn't want it that way and changed his batting position as often as Nichols started to pitch. The latter then refused to pitch unless Anson stood still, whereupon the umpire gave Anson his base on balls, taking the ground that he would have gotten it anyhow, according to Nichols' evident intention.[31]

The account printed by the *Chicago Herald* on August 7 (which overlapped considerably with the *Boston Daily Globe*'s version), added the detail that Cliff Carroll, the batter who followed Anson, "never moved, and the ball glanced off his knee to the grass, forcing home the winning run." It also reported on the crowd's reaction: "Few on the grounds understood why Anson was given first in the last inning, and several people blamed the umpire. A young colored man made a move to hit McQuaid as he was walking to the dressing-room, but was taken care of by Lieutenant Daily, who was in the crowd, and taken to the station house."[32]

That same day, a *Boston Daily Globe* sports columnist who signed his name only as "Chatterbox" (though odds are it was Murnane) reported on his interview of Anson:

> I had a talk with Anson this morning.
>
> I found the doughty captain quite incensed at the way a local paper treated him in its report of the game yesterday.
>
> "I did nothing but what was perfectly proper," said he. "Nichols was ordered to send me to my base on balls, and of course I objected. There were two men on the bases and one run needed to win the game. I wanted to hit the ball, but they were not willing to give me a chance.
>
> "Nichols started to pitch a ball wide of the plate, and I shifted over to that side of the plate to get a chance to hit, and then he pitched on the other side.
>
> "Well, of course I shifted over, too, and finally to avoid all this the umpire said I had better take my base, and I did so.
>
> "The next man up was hit by a pitched ball; that forced in a run, and the game was over. That's all there was to it.
>
> "Nichols did not refuse to pitch the ball, but was bound to send me to my base. I thought I stood a better chance to sacrifice that run in than the next, and tried to got a chance to hit, but could not.
>
> "I violated no rule. I have a right to stand on either side of the plate I choose, provided I do not shift around while the ball is in the air. The man who says I was guilty of anything out of the way simply shows his ignorance."[33]

On August 8, Tim Murnane followed up with one of the other actors in this drama:

> Umpire McQuade [sic] was seen after the game and asked why he gave Anson his base on balls in Thursday's game, and he said: "When Anson came to the plate

Nash instructed Bennett to give Anson his base on balls. Anson was anxious to have the ball pitched. I saw that Anson was booked for a base on balls, and when Nichols would not pitch, Anson finally consented to take his base.

"I had the right to forfeit the game if Nichols refused to pitch, but decided that it would be the fairest way to give Anson his base, as it was the play Boston was trying for. The Chicagos won the game fairly."[34]

Also on the 8th, when the *Chicago Herald* reported that Boston had protested the game, it added a characterization of Nichols' role that doesn't square with these other accounts: "Nichols wanted to give him his base and rather than take chances on a wild pitch he refused to pitch the ball at all and finally McQuaid sent the batsman to first though no ball had been pitched. The local management think they see a chance for exceptions and claim that Nichols' action was unauthorized and that McQuaid should have insisted on the ball being pitched."[35]

For some reason, the paper wouldn't let this matter drop. One might expect that Boston's protest would be based on Anson's shiftiness or even Carroll's failure to make any effort to avoid the next pitch. Instead, on August 10 the *Herald* asserted that the basis of Boston's protest was that the umpire "should have forced Nichols to pitch or ordered him out of the game. The proper course, it seems, would have been for the umpire to declare the game forfeited to Chicago."[36]

In any case, on August 11 the *Herald* offered this additional perspective, coupled with a partial retraction:

Had Umpire McQuade [sic] lived up to the strict interpretation of the rules in the thirteen-inning game at Boston last Thursday, he would have given Nichols one minute in which to pitch, and on his failure to do so forfeited the game to Chicago. Instead of taking this arbitrary action he sent Anson to first on balls, which he had a perfect right to do, as he is the sole judge of play. If Nichols did not want to pitch he could have made an illegal delivery, which would have sent Anson to first and not advanced the runners on bases. As to the rumored protest, it will probably never come before the board. Boston will not protest the game. As far as known the case has no precedent.[37]

Around this time Joe Murphy, baseball editor of the *Chicago Tribune*, couldn't resist getting into the act, though his forum was *Sporting Life*, the nationally read weekly:

... Boston protested the game on Anson's going to base on balls or rather on his being sent there by the umpire. The protest is the most absurd I ever heard of. Nichols and Bennett plainly intended to give Anson his base on bails, and McQuade [sic] seeing it sent him to base to avoid delay. What difference there is between sending Anson to base and having Bennett stand half way up the line towards first base while Nichols tossed four balls to him, is one of the things I cannot understand. It looks like a weak subterfuge on the part of the Bean-eaters to try and shift the blame of defeat on McQuade's shoulders, but it won't do with intelligent people.[38]

Nichols, Bennett, Nash and Selee either had little to say about all of this fuss, or reporters had little interest in asking them about it. Regardless, Nick and Bennett would extract some revenge of sorts against Anson in a similar situation in mid–1892. At least Nichols rebounded quickly from this frustrating farce, as he beat Pittsburgh comfortably on August 10 and two days later entered a tied game against the same team in the same team and shut them out over the final three innings to pick up another win. In fact, his most remarkable work of the season was just around the corner.

On August 17, Kid Nichols was again competing with Amos Rusie in the Polo Grounds, this time before a much larger crowd, counted at 3,776. Nichols pitched perfect baseball during the first four innings. By the start of the seventh, the only New York baserunner had reached on an error. Rusie, at the same time, had kept Boston from scoring. In the seventh inning, Long preserved the no-hitter for Nichols with a grab of a line drive that earned him considerable applause. When New York came to bat in the eighth inning they were trailing, 3–0, but that was when the no-hitter ended, on a ball hit by Roger Connor just over Nash's head. The ball struck Nash's hands and bounced into left field for a single. New York had a third baserunner in the ninth on a second Boston error, and Nichols ended up with a one-hitter, having struck out nine and walked none.

About a month later began a saga that could fill an entire book. Chicago led second-place Boston in mid–September by six and a half games with only fifteen games remaining on its schedule. However, on September 16 the Beaneaters began an improbable run of winning 18 of their final 19 decisions—and all of them consecutively. Other than a tie on September 17 against Pittsburgh, the only game they didn't win from September 16 onward was the final match of the season on October 3.

The extraordinary 18-game streak began in an unlikely manner: Kid Nichols beat Chicago 7–2, after having gone 0–9 against the Colts previously. Nichols won seven games during his team's string of 18 straight victories.

In late September Chicago grumbled loudly when the Giants failed to field several of their stars, particularly future Hall of Famers Buck Ewing, Roger Connor, and Amos Rusie, in some or all of the crucial five games that they played in Boston. Nichols won the first and the fourth games handily, 11–3 on the 28th and 16–5 in the first game of a doubleheader on the 30th.

Whatever New York did or didn't do, the fact remains that at the end of the season Chicago went 6–9 (plus a tie), and that one of those six wins came when Pittsburgh forfeited. Cleveland ended up with a losing record but ended up taking two of three from Chicago thanks to Cy Young. In addition, Chicago only managed to win half of its six games during the final weeks from seventh-place Cincinnati. Thus, on September 30 Kid Nichols' victory helped Boston move into first place that day, and on October 1 the Beaneaters clinched the pennant. On October 2 Kid Nichols notched his seventh win during the streak, and the final one for his club in 1891. It was his 30th win, against only 17 losses. In only his second major league season, he was a champion in more ways than one!

Unfortunately, it was probably difficult for Boston to celebrate robustly. When Boston moved into first place on September 28, newspapers in many cities immediately began making accusations. Of course Chicago papers screamed at the top of their lungs, and even some New York newspapers took Chicago's side, including the *World*, the *Evening Telegram*, and the *Press*.

On October 1, the *Chicago Daily Inter Ocean* printed an extensive quotation from the famous baseball pioneer Henry Chadwick, who said in part, "Had the New York club desired that Boston should win the pennant they could not have arranged matters to help the Eastern team better than they have done, except by openly giving away every game."[39] That same day *Chicago Herald* published these comments from Boston scribe Tim Murnane: "The last five games between Boston and New York have been a farce, as the Giants have played indifferent ball and had in their weakest batteries. What is more, the signs of the New York pitchers were given to the Boston men, who have known just the kind of balls to hit at. I do not think the players gave the games to Boston, but I do think they were anxious to see Boston beat Chicago out for the pennant and were pleased when Boston won each game."

After expressing more disdain for the New York players, Murnane turned his attention to Boston, noting that the ballclub "has put up a good, steady game for the last two weeks. The patrons of the game here have found no end of fault with the careless work of the visiting teams during the last three series, and I don't blame them a bit. Although anxious to see the home team win the pennant, I would much rather see the visiting clubs play with a little more life. Manager Selee is of the same opinion. This monkey business will do the game no good."[40]

Absent from most of the other coverage was any discussion of the Boston team's role. One example of a newspaper that did shine a spotlight on the Beaneaters during this turmoil, yet without ignoring Chicago's fury, was in a city that didn't have a horse in the race. "If any team is deserving of a pennant the Hub team is," wrote the *Trenton Evening Times* on October 4. "From the opening game to the present time they have played steadily, strongly, conscientiously, and their work reflects the greatest credit upon the players and management."[41]

This pennant race has remained suspect to this day. Baseball historian David Fleitz explained that "rumors soon abounded that former Players Leaguers in New York (where the Brotherhood was formed six years before) and other cities conspired to throw the flag to Boston to keep it out of the hands of Anson, their sworn enemy. Anson believed as much for the rest of his life, though conclusive evidence of an orchestrated effort is lacking."[42]

This alleged effort was reportedly based as well on the fact that one of the Boston owners, Arthur Soden, owned considerable stock in the New York club. This charge was made vociferously by James Hart, to whom Chicago owner Albert Spalding was in the process of handing over control of the franchise.

"Hart protested with the league," noted Cubs historian Peter Golenbock. "His protest was thrown out, much to his embarrassment, when it was revealed that Al Spalding owned more stock in the Giants than even Arthur Soden did!"[43] Some commentators have mocked an internal investigation that the New York club conducted, which they say had the foregone conclusion of the club exonerating itself, though they may not realize that the Executive Committee of the club included Al Spalding's brother Walter among its three members.[44]

The Boston team and its fans did celebrate the pennant in October, even though it wasn't until November 11 that the pennant was officially awarded, after the National League had considered and rejected four charges filed by Hart.

On October 5, the *Boston Journal* announced that the team's ownership was planning several special events for the 9th, centered on a benefit game for their players, including "a football contest between the Technology and Boston Athletic Association elevens [for which] two 15-minute innings will be played. Souvenir score cards containing photographs of each player will be distributed."[45]

In the meantime, the Boston team played an exhibition game in Norwich, Connecticut, on October 5 against New York, a game in which Clarkson and Nichols shared the pitching duties for the pennant-winners in a 9–3 victory. Boston also took on a team in Pittsfield, Massachusetts the next day and lost! The reason? Kid Nichols and catcher Charlie Ganzel defected to Pittsfield, and were instrumental in the 12–6 conquest of the champions.

Nichols and Ganzel remained traitors during the benefit game on the 9th and were joined by Clarkson and Mike "King" Kelly on the makeshift Old Timers, which included some actual retirees, including Tim Murnane and Ezra Sutton, the latter having played for the franchise from 1877 through 1888. Because Clarkson pitched, Nichols played first base. In the end, the Old Timers lost 13–9. After the game, Kid Nichols, Herman Long and Bobby

Lowe competed in a 100-yard dash, which Long barely won with a time between 10 and 11 seconds. The key was that Nichols had given him a five-yard head start.

In addition to the pennant and his 30-win season, Kid Nichols had plenty of other reasons to celebrate. He completed 45 of his 48 starts and saved three games for other Boston pitchers. He increased his total strikeouts and decreased his total walks over 1890, with 240 and 103, respectively. He cut his number of wild pitches almost in half, from 30 to 16. With five shutouts, his ERA of 2.39 was close to that of his rookie season.

By the end of October Kid Nichols was making his way back to Kansas City. First, though, on the way he visited the city of his birth, as he had done in October of 1889 and again in March of 1890. Of course he had to get into a baseball game, which was reported on back on the East Coast: "Kid Nichols, of the Boston League Club, pitched for the Wisconsin University against the Madison team last Saturday, defeating them 6 to 3," wrote *Sporting Life*. "Only two hits were made off his delivery."[46]

Nichols then spent a fairly quiet winter in Kansas City, rarely drawing any attention from the press. However, at least one paper in his final minor league city was keeping tabs on him, as reflected in an unflattering remark similar to one that appeared in *Sporting Life* halfway through the 1890 season. "They say down in Kansas City that Kid Nichols' head is so large that it makes him humpbacked to carry it around," quipped the *Omaha Daily Bee* in November.[47]

In addition to his wife and young daughter, Nichols still had a shop in Kansas City to keep him busy. As it had in the late 1880s, the Nichols Brothers business changed its nature a few times in the early 1890s. By mid–1891 the Nichols Brothers cigar store reverted to a pool hall, and about a year later it became a confectioners' shop for a second time. The address remained on the 2300 block of East 15th, aka Blue Avenue.

On February 19, 1892, the *Kansas City Star* announced that Kid Nichols had received orders from Frank Selee to report for spring training about a month later in Charlottesville, Virginia. The plan was to use the grounds of the University of Virginia and play three games against the school's team.[48] The *Bee* reported on March 6 that Nichols had just left Kansas City for the east coast, but this was corrected by the *Star* two weeks later.[49]

In late March, during the second of the three games against the University of Virginia, Boston loaned Clarkson and three others to the collegiate club but Kid Nichols still whipped them, 20–3.[50] About two weeks later Boston also flexed its muscles against another university team, in New Jersey against Princeton, but only won 7 to 4. Nichols and Clarkson shared pitching duties.[51]

In mid–December the rival American Association disbanded after ten seasons as a major league, leaving the National League as the only one of its kind. As a result, Boston gained pitcher Jack Stivetts and outfielders Hugh Duffy and Tommy McCarthy from AA franchises that folded. In the middle of the decade the latter duo would be given the nickname the "Heavenly Twins," and in the mid–1940s they would be selected a year apart for the Baseball Hall of Fame. Four AA franchises moved over to the National League and thus increased its size by 50 percent. The new NL cities were Baltimore, St. Louis, Louisville and Washington. There was one more substantial change in the NL: its only split season except for 1891 when a strike interrupted the schedule. The NL would play half of a season and declare one winner, which would play the winner of the second half.

Boston opened the 1892 NL season on April 12, the day after it faced Princeton, by beating Washington 14–4. Its second game wouldn't be until April 16, in Baltimore. Nichols pitched that one in front of more than 2,188 fans and won 11–5. Boston benefited from five Baltimore errors. Kid Nichols drew a walk and had two of his team's six hits, including a triple. His personal celebration was presumably short-lived, however, because his half-brother James died back in Madison two days later.

On April 21, Kid Nichols pitched the home opener, facing Baltimore again. Despite drizzle, Massachusetts Governor William Russell and 3,800 other spectators turned out. Nichols scored an important insurance run in the eighth inning after walking; Baltimore scored twice in the ninth to make it close, but Nichols prevailed, 7–6.

Kid Nichols lost 4–0 in St. Louis on April 29 and the team had an open date two days later, so he took that opportunity to travel over to his home in Kansas City. On the 30th he watched a game between the Cowboys and Milwaukee. One of the Brewers was Fred Lake, who had played five games for Boston in 1891. Lake already had a double, triple and homer when he went to the plate one final time against Jim Hughey. Starting in the fifth inning, after it became clear that Lake was in the midst of a daylong power outburst, the *Kansas City Times* told about the rest of Lake's performance in some detail:

> ... "Kid" Nichols, the Boston pitcher, who played with Lake last year, and who was watching the game from the upper grand stand, remarked that if Hughey would give Lake a curve ball he couldn't hit it. A note was sent to Jimmy Manning asking him if he had any "pull" with Hughey, and if he loved his native land, to try and induce the young man to give Mr. Lake anything on earth but a straight ball. Jeoms walked over to the box like a man with a tip on a 20 to 1 horse, held a caucus with Hughey and went on his way rejoicing. The next time Lake came to the bat he struck out, and "Kid" Nichols remarked: "I told you so."[52]

As if to prove that its 18-game winning streak late that season was less implausible than many newspapers perceived, Boston won 10 of its first 11 games, and 15 of its first 18. They barely slowed down in May when John Clarkson developed a sore arm, though this led to rumors of his release, which were denied by the club. Nevertheless, when Boston ended June with a staggering record of 45–18, Clarkson's was only 8–6. As it turned out, Boston needed to comply with a relatively recent league agreement to reduce rosters to 13 men, so they released Clarkson on June 29, after having already done the same to Harry Stovey on the 20th. Clarkson ended up with Cleveland and pitched well for them during the remainder of 1892. There was absolutely no chance that Kid Nichols would be one of the players released, but when Stovey was let go, it was also announced that Nichols was among the first players asked by two of the owners, Arthur Soden and William Conant, to take a salary reduction.[53] This request was likely what caused Nichols to approach his salary discussions with bitterness on several occasions over the next decade. Across the league, salaries were slashed by 30 to 40 percent.

Nichols' response on the field was to pitch one of his finest games of the season, against a team that was playing almost as well as Boston. Brooklyn was visiting on June 22, and Nichols blanked them, 6–0, allowing them only three hits. The *Boston Daily Advertiser* reported that Nichols would receive "as fine an umbrella as can be made," a promise from a friend that would apply when the Kid hurled his first shutout of the season.[54] At least that gift partially offset the looming reduction in salary.

Nichols followed up on June 27 in New York with a 3–1 victory over the Giants, this time allowing just four hits. "Nichols pitched superbly," declared the *New York Tribune*. "This youngster, who looks so diminutive yet weighs 170 pounds, is to-day about the best pitcher in the country."[55] Two days later, Nichols beat the Phillies on the road, winning 9–1 and again only yielding four hits.

In a game at St. Louis on July 5 that shaped up to be a slugfest early on, Nichols relieved Staley in the third inning and kept the home team at bay so that Boston could win 14–8. Then in Chicago on July 11 he won 3–2, with each team managing only five hits. Half of the account that appeared in one of the Kansas City papers focused not on the pitching performances but rather the attire. It began, "The bean eaters created a great deal of merriment today by appearing in calico and gingham suits of the loudest pattern and color, and all wore false beards of various descriptions."[56]

Tim Murnane confirmed that Kid Nichols was among the players taking part, by sporting fake whiskers. Murnane added that "the make-ups were furnished by a local costumer, with Eddie Foy, the actor, to make up the players." This was the same Eddie Foy whom Bob Hope would portray in a movie about his famous family of entertainers more than sixty years later. Murnane was bemused enough to begin his account of the game with a detailed description of the Bostons' playful stunt, but he saved plenty of space for the actual competition.

"It was one of the prettiest games of the season, and resulted in a victory for Boston, with the most sensational kind of a finish," he wrote. "With two to win and one to tie, Dahlen was on third and Ryan second, with Anson at the bat. Nichols got one strike on the old man and then was ordered to give him first base. Bennett stood out one side and Nichols tossed him the ball. Anson threw his bat and missed, making it two strikes. Then Bennett went back of the plate, as Nichols would then try to strike him out. The Boston infielders were playing in close. Nick shot the ball over the pan and the old man met it square. It was a hot liner, but Joe Quinn made a jumping catch, helped the ball and beat Ryan back to second base, accomplishing a great double play and ending the game right there."[57]

Thanks in no small part to all of this excellent work by Kid Nichols, Boston finished the half-season on July 12 as champions, at 52–22, two and a half games ahead of second place Brooklyn. Nichols reached a personal milestone early in the second half, during a home game on July 29. Batting with the bases empty against Gus Weyhing of Philadelphia in the fourth inning, the Kid knocked a pitch over the fence for a home run, the first of his major league career. Every Boston run proved to be important that day, as they only won 6–4.

The high points for Kid Nichols during August began with the announcement that Boston and St. Louis would do battle in Kansas City. On August 21, the excitement in the newsroom of the *Kansas City Times* caused one of their journalists to lose sight of the vocabulary of the typical baseball fan, and he sent his readers scrambling for the nearest dictionary. He hyperventilated about the return of two local boys made good, the "immortal" Herman Long and the "alutaceous Charlie Nichols, both now of Boston, but to whom Kansas City's proud lips still allude with joy as stellar lights which first shone here."[58] The adjective "alutaceous" means leathery, or leather-colored; as such, it's not exactly a counterpart to "immortal."

In the handwritten document compiling some of his biographical information around 1949, which is stored at the Baseball Hall of Fame, Kid Nichols recalled the basic details of three big days for him with a high degree of accuracy:

> On August 23rd the Boston Club played a double header with St. Louis in Kansas City, Mo. I pitched one of the games. Winning 5 to 3.
>
> On August 24th Boston played ... in St. Louis. I pitched ... and won 3–1.
>
> On August 25th, Boston played in Louisville, Ky. against the Louisville Club. I pitched winning 6 to 1.

Kid Nichols was clearly quite proud of the unusual accomplishment of beating three different teams in different cities on three consecutive days, but on the 23rd the people of Kansas City were simply proud to see him in a major league game there. The *Times* reported that "Nichols was given a roaring reception."[59]

A top candidate for Nichols' favorite memory during September was a big moment on September 19 in Baltimore. When he came up to bat against reliever Tom Vickery in the sixth inning, Boston already had a healthy lead. After two outs the Beaneaters filled the bases, and Nichols responded with a blast to center field that produced the only grand slam of his major league career. Nichols suffered a hand injury on a batted ball that inning and in the seventh ran into some trouble while pitching, so for the remainder of the game he switched with Jack Stivetts, who happened to be playing left field that day. Stivetts was hit harder than Nichols but hung on until darkness mercifully cancelled the ninth inning, and Boston prevailed 14–11, their last four runs coming when Nichols homered. The Kid also tripled that afternoon.

When the second half-season ended in mid–October, Boston's combined record of 102 wins and 48 losses was considerably better than Cleveland's record of 93–56 but the latter won the second half, edging out Boston by three games in the standings. As a result, Cleveland met Boston in a best-of-nine world series, so to speak. It began in Cleveland on the 17th with a scoreless tie. Cleveland's Cy Young battled Stivetts for 11 innings before the game was ended due to darkness.

Boston won the next two games in Cleveland, beginning with Harry Staley outdueling recent Beaneater John Clarkson, 4–3. Stivetts then beat Young, 3–2. The series then shifted to Boston for three games, and the remaining ones would be played in New York if necessary.

On October 21, about 6,500 fans crowded Boston's South End Grounds to watch Kid Nichols face Cleveland. He didn't disappoint, blanking the Spiders, 4–0. The next day Boston overcame an early 6–0 deficit and Stivetts beat Clarkson 12–7. The Beaneaters were one victory away from a sweep.

On October 24, a cold day in Boston, fewer than 2,000 fans showed up. That day's showdown would pit Kid Nichols against Cy Young. Early in the game Nichols twice made a difference on offense. In the third inning he singled to left with one out. Later in the inning he stood at third base with Tommy McCarthy at first and two out. "'Mac' made a bluff to steal second to give Nichols a chance to score; Young threw to [first baseman] Virtue and 'Jake,' seeing a chance to catch Nichols off third, threw to Tebeau, but his arm was poor and Nichols not only scored but McCarthy trotted around to third. 'Mac' came in on Duffy's long drive to left centre for two bases." At the end of three innings, Boston trailed 3–2.

In the fourth, Nichols came up with two men on base and singled to drive in the tying and lead runs. That fourth run proved to be the winning one, as

Nichols blanked Cleveland the rest of the way. With his 8–3 win, Boston won the NL championship for the second consecutive season!

Kid Nichols' statistics glistened once again in 1892. He increased his total wins by five to 35, yet actually decreased his losses by one, to 16. He completed 49 of his 51 starts and hurled five shutouts. His earned run average was 2.84.

Fans of the Beaneaters were invited to show their appreciation at a benefit game for the players on October 27 at the South End Grounds. The team's owners ponied up $1,000 for the occasion. The main feature was a five-inning game between Boston players and a picked nine, including minor league players. Stivetts pitched for the champs but Kid Nichols did so for the picked nine, with Charlie Bennett behind the plate. Behind him in the infield were Jimmy Canavan, Nichols' friend and former Omaha teammate, from Anson's Colts, and former Beaneater and Omahog Joe Kelley, from the Baltimore Orioles. The picked nine won, 7–3. Other scheduled activities included a throwing demonstration and several footraces. "On this occasion Kid Nichols beat Tommy McCarthy in a 100-yard sprint, in 11 seconds, and Herman Long sang an Irish song in Dutch," reported a paper in Omaha.[60] The world record for the 100-yard dash at the time, set in 1890, was 9.8 seconds.

Among the other Boston players competing in this race were Bennett and Staley, who were given 20-yard head starts. Tim Murnane signaled the start of the race, and Arlie Latham of the Reds was the timekeeper. "There was not a very large crowd present at the Boston base ball nine's annual benefit at the South End yesterday afternoon but this did not dampen the spirit of the players," one Boston paper reported. "They gamboled around like school children out for a recess and a majority of them seemed to rejoice that the season was at a close." The paper also reported on how various players planned to spend the offseason, noting that Nichols would winter in Kansas City.[61] Before he left town, Kid Nichols joined Selee, Staley, McCarthy, Bobby Lowe, and Canavan as spectators at a football game in nearby Cambridge between Harvard and Chicago.[62]

Nichols was soon spotted in another NL city, when Chicago's Richelieu Hotel hosted league meetings in mid–November. Nichols stayed at the Indiana House, near the stock yards, which may have reminded him of home.[63] Speaking of home, Nichols was planning a new one in Kansas City. As evidence of the Kid having become something of a national celebrity, the *Philadelphia Inquirer* reported in early February of 1893: "Pitcher Nichols last week purchased two Kansas City lots for $2250. On this tract he will this spring begin construction of a house, to cost about $4000, and which he intends as his future home."[64]

Around this time there was an early indication of Kid Nichols' interest in another sport, one that would be a passion of his for half a century: bowling. He was among more than 40 members of the city's bowling club, and in a tournament on February 10 he duked it out with his own brother George for the trophy but ended up losing to his elder by a whisker, 165 to 162. He walked away with a trophy himself on March 3 after his score of 216 ranked first in a tournament at Scharnagel's alley. The tournaments became a weekly occurrence and by the end of March Kid had won four in a row. His new hobby was reported on back in Boston and even in *Sporting Life*.[65]

It may be that this success in another sporting arena is what made Nichols decide to reject a baseball-related offer that he received during the first half of March. He received a telegram from Charlottesville, Virginia, that offered him the opportunity to coach the University of Pennsylvania baseball team during its preseason, but he quickly declined it.[66] Around that time he was considering another document that had been sent to him: his contract with Boston for the upcoming season. The *Boston Daily Globe* reported on March 19 that several of the champions were refusing the terms proposed by the club's ownership. The paper named Kid Nichols among them, and from his home in Kansas City he declared that he "would prefer his release to signing the contract sent him." According to the *Globe*, however, "A release would be poor satisfaction, as Charley Farrell and others have found out, as other clubs refuse to negotiate with released players."[67]

Kid Nichols ended up signing, at the club's terms, by the end of March.[68] He arrived in Boston on April 1, but so enthused was he about bowling that two days later he wrote a letter to the *Kansas City Star* about his new hobby. It read in part:

> I have been out to a bowling tourney between two of the leading bowling clubs of Boston and find that they bowl a little different from what we do in Kansas City, that is, in regard to the rules. The most important difference is that all dead wood is taken off the alleys and another is that after delivering the ball you are not allowed to touch another ball until the ball you have delivered goes into the pit. If a man crosses over the 60-foot line an inch after delivering the ball it is declared a foul, and all pins knocked down are reset and the bowler loses the ball. I visited General "Hi Hi" Dixwell's private alleys last night and witnessed a hot game between the general's team and an opposition team....
>
> I shall endeavor to get thoroughly posted as to the manner in which they run their tournaments in the East, with the view to arranging for a bowling tournament in Kansas City on my return home at the close of the base ball season the coming fall.[69]

As part of its brief spring training, on April 11 Boston met Harvard's team for a game in Hartford, Connecticut. Nichols and Stivetts shared the pitching duties for the Beaneaters, and Boston won easily, 10–2 (though Boston dailies disagreed on which of the two pitchers surrendered the Harvard runs).

Some major rule changes took effect before the 1893 season that would change the sport substantially. During the 1890s major league baseball changed in many dramatic ways, as described almost a century later by baseball analyst Bill James: "The tactics of the eighties were aggressive; the tactics of the nineties were violent," James wrote in his *Historical Baseball Abstract.* "Players spiked each other. A first baseman would grab the belt of the baserunner to hold him back a half-second after the ball was hit. Occasionally players tripped one another as they rounded the bases. Fights broke out from day to day. Players shoved umpires, spat on them, abused them in every manner short of assault. Fans hurled insults and beer bottles at the players of opposing teams."[70]

"As to offensive styles, many people have written that the baseball of the 1890s was the first 'modern' baseball," James continued, and explained why such commentators often looked at the game from the wrong perspective. "But it is true that the rules attained essentially their modern form after 1893, when the pitching distance was moved back to its present 60 feet, 6 inches."[71]

Many sources state that the distance was increased by more than ten feet, from the previous distance of 50 feet, but that was measuring from the front of the pitching box. The specified box was 5 feet, 6 inches deep and the pitcher was required to keep one foot in contact with the back line while delivering the ball to a batter, so the actual pitching distance in 1892 had been 55 feet, 6 inches. Kid Nichols had understood this when he spoke with *Sporting Life* contributor Elmer E. Bates about the change at the Chicago meetings the previous November. "I don't object to going back five feet, but when you put us down behind the centre fielder, I'm afraid there would be an occasional base on balls," Nichols quipped.[72]

Not only did pitchers have to contend with five more feet, but their box was eliminated in favor of a rubber slab that originally measured one foot by four inches. As is true today, the pitcher was required to place his rear foot against this rubber. Another change to the pitcher-batter dynamic was disallowing bats with a flat side; instead, they were required to be round and made entirely of hard wood. One more change affected batting averages, an exemption from a time at bat for anyone who sacrificed. Lastly, the split season format tried in 1892 had been very unpopular, and wasn't replicated.

The first game of the regular season for the Beaneaters was on April 28. Kid Nichols received the Opening Day assignment at New York's Polo Grounds. When the home players first went onto the field they were of course cheered by the local fans, but the *Boston Daily Journal* said that a large contingent from Boston had traveled down for the game and nearly drowned out New York's supporters with something other than cheering.

After five innings Nichols trailed, 2–1. Boston had already regained the lead when Nichols came to bat in the sixth with Charlie Bennett on second base. The Kid promptly put his terrific speed to great benefit. "He made a three base hit over Lyon's [sic] head and galloped home on Fuller's short nap while handling the fielded ball," reported the *Journal*. "When 'Shorty' received the ball Nichols was just turning third base. 'Shorty' thought he would stop there and took his time picking up the ball. Before Fuller could be brought to a sense of the situation Nichols had gone home." It was scored as an inside-the-park homer.[73] Boston never looked back, and won 9–2.

The Boston club was playing .500 ball into late May, but that changed on the 29th when they won the first of eight in a row. Their sweep of a doubleheader from Chicago the next day, one game of which was won by Kid Nichols, moved them into fourth place in the NL. One of the bigger thrills during the first half of the season for him was probably beating Chicago in a Fourth of July doubleheader in front of more than 9,000 fans in the Windy City.

After a loss on July 24, Boston's record stood at 46–27, good enough for second place just behind Philadelphia. Boston then went on a 24–2 tear to improve its record to 70–29. Both losses were to Philadelphia. Nichols' batch of wins during this 26-game stretch included one on August 5 in Brooklyn when he took over for Stivetts in the first inning, after the starter wrenched his side. Nichols fell behind 4–1 after three innings but Boston had a big rally in the seventh and the Kid added two more with a ninth-inning homer off of Ed Stein, to win 12–5. He then won his regular start two days later as well.

His loss to Philadelphia on the 14th ended a 9-game winning streak, Boston's second of that length within a month. It was also their only loss during a 13-game road trip. He roared right back two days later by shutting out Philadelphia 4–0, after which the Phillies wouldn't be shut out at home for a record 367 games straight.

Shortly thereafter, beginning with the second game of a doubleheader on August 30, Boston enjoyed a third nine-game winning streak. Yet when Chicago ended that streak and first-place Boston immediately lost the next game to second-place Pittsburgh, their lead had slipped to nine games ahead. Pirates fans contracted a case of pennant fever and were salivating for a sweep, but Kid Nichols prevented that with a 7–3 win on September 16. Sometime later he reported that an incredibly ugly incident had happened after the game:

> We were stoned as we left the grounds. Boston and Pittsburgh were fighting for the league lead and hometown fans were infuriated that we won the game. As we left the park they followed us carrying sticks and stones. Tom Tucker, our first baseman, and Hugh Duffy, outfielder, and I were in the last of the coupes in which we were driving away. The crowd let go at us with their missiles as we started down the street. I was hit on the head fully a dozen times and several of the sticks

and stones hit Duffy and Tucker. I got out of the coupe and chased some of the rowdies and asked a policeman to arrest them. He didn't make a move so I climbed back into the carriage. The bombardment was renewed and we were called every vile name you can imagine. It was only by whipping the horses into a fast getaway that we escaped the mob.[74]

More than a week later, one paper noted that "Pitcher Nichols is carrying a few scars as the result of the last game at Pittsburg where the hoodlums threw stones after the Boston's coach on leaving the grounds."[75]

Boston clinched its third consecutive pennant with more than a week left in the season, though Pittsburgh won its final eight games and trimmed the Beaneaters' lead to five games by the end of the season. Boston became only the second franchise to top the National League three seasons in a row—Chicago had done this about a decade earlier. In four years as a major leaguer, Kid Nichols was already three times a champion!

Newspapers all over the country sang his praises as Boston's mainstay and workhorse, if not the best pitcher in the game. His manager echoed this sentiment shortly after the season ended. "Kid Nichols is the steadiest pitcher in the league and the most reliable, as he always keeps himself in good condition," Selee told a newspaperman.[76]

Kid Nichols had 34 wins, and the next best Boston pitcher was Stivetts, who won 20, yet his 14 losses were only two more than Stivetts experienced. Nichols pitched 425 innings while Stivetts worked fewer than 300. Kid Nichols was the winning pitcher in about 40 percent of his team's victories. He completed 43 of his 44 starts and finished 7 games as a reliever. One dramatic improvement over 1892 was slicing his wild pitches from 24 to 5.

The season ended for Boston in St. Louis on September 30, and the club immediately traveled northeast to Milwaukee for an exhibition game on October 1. This was the beginning of a series in midwestern cities between the champions and a team of stars assembled from other NL teams. The game was an inauspicious start to the tour: on a cold and raw day Boston won before a crowd of about 500, 10–1, on a field that had been rendered very sloppy by recent rains.

On October 6, ahead of games scheduled between Boston and the "All-America" team for the next two days in Kansas City, Kid Nichols arrived home. He pitched both games there. On the 7th, before about 1,500 fans, he was leading a slugfest going into the ninth inning, 16–9, but then he weakened and the all-stars rallied to tie the game. The lineup Nichols faced that day included an outfield consisting of future Hall of Famer Joe Kelley of Baltimore, Dummy Hoy of Washington, and Philadelphia's Kid Carsey, the next day's pitcher. The All-America infield, from third to first, was Charley "Duke" Farrell of Washington, "Voiceless Tim" O'Rourke of Louisville, former major leaguer and Kansas City manager Jimmy Manning, and future Hall of Famer Jake Beckley of Pittsburgh. Malachi Kittridge of Chicago caught teammate Ad Gumbert, who won had 22 games in 1893.

Actually, the scoreboard showed the all-stars leading by one, but after much debate, a ruling was made that the score was in fact 16–16. In either case, Kid Nichols was looking like a goat in front of family and friends as Boston began the bottom of the ninth. The *Kansas City Times* reported on that half inning in detail:

> Nichols was first at bat. He tried to knock the cover off the ball, but failed to connect and, remembering that Gumbert had caused him to fan the atmosphere on two previous occasions, he gave up the attempt and tried for a bunt. The first two attempts resulted in fouls, but the third one dropped in the diamond and Gumbert grabbed it. He threw it at Jake Beckley's outstretched mitt, but missed by several feet, and the ball rolled safely off toward the club house, while Nichols flew around to second base. Long tried to send him home by driving the horse hide into right field. Beckley unlimbered himself like a seven-jointed telescope, however, and nailed the sphere in time to catch the flying Dutchman before he reached the initial bag. Nichols reached third on the sacrifice. The excitement had shattered Ad Gumbert's nerves, and a moment later he pitched such a wild outshoot to Lowe that Kittridge failed to reach it and Nichols cantered home with the winning run. The game was of the kind that the base ball fiend loves to see, with plenty of free hitting and lively base running and a close finish.[77]

Kid Nichols pitched the entire rematch the next day as well. The umpire was also the same, Billy O'Brien (specified as "Big Fat Billy O'Brien" in at least one newspaper's line score, befitting an era in which baseball nicknames often weren't kind).[78] This time the local turnout swelled to between four and five thousand fans. There were a few lineup changes for the All-Americas, most notably that their pitcher would be Kid Carsey, who was a 20-game winner for Philadelphia in 1893. O'Rourke moved from shortstop to right field, and stepping in at short was future Hall of Famer George Davis of the Giants. Boston led 4–3 after five innings, and Nichols then cruised to a 12–4 victory. It was probably this postseason contact with Kid Nichols that prompted Kittridge to say, "He is about the most perfect husband and father I ever met, and there isn't a player in the League that doesn't admire and respect him."[79]

At the end of the eighth inning (not the first, as originally intended, and as stated in other sources), a formal trophy presentation was made to Boston captain Billy Nash. He was given the Dauvray Cup, which was donated to the major leagues in 1887 by actress Helen Dauvray, the wife of Giants shortstop John Ward. It was supposed to be given permanently to the first franchise that won three consecutive championship series between NL and American Association pennant-winners. The Giants won this series in 1888 and 1889 but then conflict between the leagues caused their post-season playoff to be cancelled. After the AA folded, a decision was made to award the cup permanently to the next NL team to win three consecutive pennants. The last known sighting of the Dauvray Cup was the next month, when Boston pitcher Henry Gastright exhibited it in Newport, Kentucky. This trophy has remained lost to this day.

The Boston and All-America teams played again on October 11 in Omaha, where cold and dusty conditions limited the crowd to fewer than 500. They played seven innings, and Kid Nichols won again, 2–0. The All-America lineup was the same as in the second Kansas City match.

The tour continued with stops in Sioux City and Cedar Rapids, Iowa, over the next three days, but Kid Nichols finally received a break. When Boston beat the all-stars again in the latter city, 6–3, on the 14th, not only did Staley pitch for Boston, but Stivetts was in the lineup at first base in case a reliever was needed. Due to bad weather in at least three cities the tour may not have been a big moneymaker for the two squads, but a Cedar Rapids paper reported that it wasn't a dud, either: "The Bostons and All-America ball teams are ahead about $3,000 on their tour of the west."[80]

Nichols then headed back to Massachusetts to umpire a benefit game played on October 21. The game was played in support of striking employees at the T.G. Plant shoe company. Two years earlier owner Thomas G. Plant had reduced wages, but the Knights of Labor union decided not to fight the action. In August he made another cut, and workers had gone on strike in September. Listed in the lineup for one of the two teams was Jimmy Bannon, the St. Louis Browns rookie who Boston had already lined up for its 1894 roster, and his brother Tom, who would go on to start a brief major league career in 1895 with the Giants.[81] If Nick's receptiveness to the upstart Players' League during September of 1890 was in fact intended to send a message to the Beaneaters' owners, this announcement may have been made at least partly with them in mind as well.

In any case, in late October Kid Nichols and his wife checked into San Francisco's New Western Hotel with teammate Herman Long, Tommy McCarthy and his wife, and a few other major leaguers.[82] On the 29th, a team billed as the Boston team played the first of many games on the West Coast, although only five players in the lineup were Beaneaters. In addition to Nichols, Long, and McCarthy, the lineup also included regulars Duffy and Nash. Also mixed in were four All-America stars, each from a different club: Hoy, Beckley, Davis, and Kittridge. Kid Carsey accompanied them as a second pitcher, and filling in for Frank Selee was Billy Barnie, manager of Louisville's NL club.

The Friscos lineup that this "Boston" team first faced was led by pitcher

Phil Knell, who was twice a 20-game winner in a short stint in the majors and who would pitch the next two years in the NL. Among others in the lineup with major league experience were Pete Sweeney, who split time in the NL and AA from 1888 to 1890, Hi Ebright, who played 16 games in the NL during 1889, and Pop Swett, who played 37 games for Boston's Brotherhood franchise in 1890. Twenty-five cents was the admission charge, and seven to eight thousand fans turned out.

Despite the seeming mismatch, Boston had to produce a run in the eighth inning to tie the game at 5–5, and it went into extra innings. With two out in the tenth, two future Hall of Famers who weren't Beaneaters gave Boston the victory, when Jake Beckley doubled and George Davis followed with a run-scoring hit. Three days later the Bostons faced another nine from the four-team California League, the Oakland Colonels. Carsey pitched instead of Nichols, and Boston came from behind in the ninth thanks to a fatal wild pitch for a 3–2 win. It was back to Nichols the next day, November 2, for a 10–2 win over Oakland again, only this time the game was played in San Jose. The next day Carsey defeated Oakland in Stockton, and the day after that Nichols blanked them 8–0 in Sacramento, on five hits. It was then Carsey's turn to blank Oakland, back in their home park, on November 5, to extend Boston's unbeaten streak in California to six. The *Sacramento Daily Record-Union* called the Boston squad "the finest aggregation of ball-players that ever played the national game on the Pacific Coast."[83]

Oakland's roster at the time had two players on it with vastly more major league experience than anyone on San Francisco's, led by Jerry Denny, who had 12 years in the majors, including 44 games for Barnie in 1893, and George Van Haltren, who was seven years into a 17-year major league career. Van Haltren, who spent 1893 with the Pirates, often appears in discussions of the greatest players not currently in the Hall of Fame. (The name "Tip" O'Neill was shared by three baseball figures in the 19th century, and the one on Oakland then was apparently Norris, a lifetime minor leaguer and former teammate of Carsey who was well known on the West Coast.)

Boston let the two California teams have a few days off, and when Kid Nichols faced the San Francisco team on November 12, he found that they had added his Boston teammate, Bobby Lowe, at third base, and promptly inserted him into the cleanup spot in their batting order. His familiarity with Nichols didn't seem to make much of a difference, as the Friscos only managed six hits in a 7–2 loss.

Around Thanksgiving, Kid Nichols was considering his second offer of the year to do some collegiate coaching. This time it was Princeton that was making an effort to reel in Nichols for the coming spring. That school was still hoping for this in early December, when they were joined in the hunt for

Nichols' services by Brown University, which was hoping to land one of three future Hall of Famers, Nichols, John Clarkson, or John Ward.[84] While those colleges were waiting, Boston continued to play the two San Francisco and Oakland clubs into the new year, and by Christmas the Californians started having semi-regular success against the Beaneaters.

As a Christmas gift to his daughter Alice, or as a third birthday present for her earlier that month, Kid Nichols could have bought her a new item with her father depicted on it: (Chief) Zimmer's Base Ball Game issued by McLoughlin Brothers, a tabletop item highly sought after by collectors today. Only ten are known to still exist.

Early in 1894 Kid Nichols and his Boston teammates received terrible news. On January 10, their longtime catcher Charlie Bennett lost both of his legs in an accident. During a train trip he got off to speak to a friend in Wellsville, Kansas, and slipped under the wheels while trying to reboard. Bennett and former teammate John Clarkson had been preparing for a hunting trip together, so Clarkson immediately helped Charlie's wife tend to him. Kid Nichols and Bennett were close, and this tragedy affected him more than most others on the Boston club.

Word of this horrific event likely reached Nichols before he was to take part in an unusual baseball game in Oakland on January 13. As a major change of pace, the Bostons and the Colonels played an indoor baseball game, at the Second Regiment Artillery (or "Battery B") Armory, in San Francisco, at the intersection of Page and Gough. They used a ball seventeen inches in diameter on a diamond that measured 27 feet on a side. Kid Nichols pitched, and among the Boston nine, three men were listed at positions created especially for this venue: McCarthy at "left short," Davis at "second base and center field," and Carsey at "right short." Beckley was at first and Hoy in right but Long played catcher, and Kittridge covered left field. Missing from the Oakland lineup were Van Haltren, Denny, and O'Neill, but in the outfield for them was Clark Griffith, another future Hall of Famer. Boston won, 13 to 9. The victors probably didn't care much that earlier in the day Carsey lost a "real" baseball game to the same team (which did include Denny and Van Haltren in its lineup, but not Griffith).[85]

A report out of California five days later predicted that the Bostons' visit to California would end early. "They came to the coast with the intention of giving exhibition games to March 1, but circumstances have rendered to make their stay not only unprofitable but disagreeable," noted *Sporting Life*. "Their games, as has been frequently stated in this correspondence, have within the past seven weeks failed to draw enough money to net them living expenses, on account of weather conditions, and the expressions of discontent are becoming more frequent every day."[86] Sure enough, the Bostons played their last game in the Bay Area on February 4, and added one a week later against a picked nine in Los Angeles. By then, Kid Nichols was long gone. On January 15 or 16, he, Jennie, and young Alice had left town.[87]

"Pitcher Nichols packed up his belongings last Monday and started Eastward with his wife and child," reported *Sporting Life*. "The sad accident that befell Catcher Bennett, of the Boston Club, was in a great measure largely responsible for Nichols' sudden severance of connection with the winter team. When the press dispatches brought the news of the awful accident, Nichols wired for particulars, and received a reply from Mrs. Bennett confirming the newspaper story. There has been a strong bond of friendship between Mr. and Mrs. Nichols and Mr. and Mrs. Bennett, and the pitcher concluded to cut short his stay on the coast in order to hasten to the bedside of his stricken comrade."[88]

Nichols' visit to tiny Williamsburg, Kansas, led the *Topeka Journal* to observe: "With 'Kid' Nichols, John Clarkson and Charley Bennett all at Williamsburg that place is getting almost as distinguished as Washington."[89] Nichols concluded a visit with Bennett and by February 3 was back in Kansas City, where he recommended two West Coast players to KC Manager Jimmy Manning.[90]

In addition to all of the admiration that Kid Nichols was receiving for his pitching, with increasing frequency he was praised for his character. "He is quiet, unassuming, gentlemanly and certainly deserves the position he has won," wrote *Sporting Life* during the spring of 1894, apparently not buying the accusation floated from time to time that Kid Nichols was becoming an egomaniac.[91] However, in its previous issue it quoted Giants pitcher Dad Clarke as saying that "Kid Nichols wouldn't spend a dollar to see Heaven."[92] Clarke had been a teammate of his at Omaha in 1889.

If Nichols was indeed becoming more frugal, he could have pointed to several considerations. For one, by mid–1893 the Nichols Brothers business had ceased to exist. Willie had become a depot agent for the American Express Company, while George was an express messenger, and their father was working again as a butcher. Though Kid's brother-in-law Sam Nickells had worked some years as a pharmaceutical agent for Parke, Davis & Co. and then the K.C. Drug Specialty Co., from 1889 to 1893 he and Jessie were sharing quarters with her parents and brothers. While Robert and Christina Nichols were still alive, the extended Nichols family never seemed to be living high on the hog, as the saying goes.

Charlie Bennett's plight may also have provided a cautionary tale to Nichols. "The famous catcher was not left as well off as most people supposed," commented the *Boston Daily Advertiser* just before the 1894 season began. As a result, "Nichols has become a business man if not a capitalist within the last few days. He is starting a tobacco store in Detroit with Bennett."[93]

While in Kansas City during February and March, Nichols did not give his arm a complete rest, choosing instead to mix other physical activity in with light baseball workouts. "The 'Kid' has devoted much of his time this winter to bowling and in a pennant race now on between six local clubs leads his team, which stands first in the race," *Sporting Life* said. "He claims that next to pitching itself nothing equals bowling in keeping the pitching arm in condition. For the past week Nichols has reported daily at the grounds with members of the local team and loosened up his assortment of curves." He left for Boston on April 1 for a few weeks of preparation with the club's full roster.[94] Sadly, just before his departure, Hugh Duffy's wife passed away from tuberculosis. She had been ill for months, and Duffy had hoped that the team's trip to California would restore her health.

5

Regrouping and Rebuilding

Kid Nichols signed a contract for the 1894 season on April 13, and pitched some against local teams around that time, such as the Brockton club on the 16th and the Holy Cross collegiate team the next day. Opening Day for Boston was at home on the 19th against Brooklyn, and the Beaneaters won easily, 13–2. Stivetts pitched for Boston instead of Nichols, but Tim Murnane mentioned "Mrs. Charles Nichols and sister from Kansas City" in his list of "the prominent lovers of the game" among the 7,000 fans who welcomed the three-time champions.[1]

Kid Nichols pitched Boston's second game, on April 21 in Brooklyn, before more than 19,000 people. He scattered five hits and blanked the Brooklyn batters, 3–0. Three days later he took part in an odd game in Baltimore that saw Stivetts nurse a 3–1 lead until the home team came to bat in the top of the ninth inning. Stivetts loaded the bases with nobody out and then was ejected on a count of three balls, one strike after complaining about umpire Tim Hurst's strike zone. Nichols entered the game, walked in a run, and then surrendered a two-run single, giving Baltimore the lead. The Orioles piled on more runs but it was getting late, so Boston decided to avoid ending the inning, hoping that the game would be called due to darkness and thus the score would revert to that of the previous inning. They didn't prolong the inning long enough to fulfill their aim, but by the time it ended the Orioles had scored 14 times.

Years later, Boston catcher Jack Ryan had cause to reminisce about this game:

> Big Jack Stivetts was pitching for Boston. Baltimore was starting to hit him hard, and Ryan was directed to warm up Kid Nichols. In those days the bull pen was not in a corner of the field, in full view of the spectators. In Baltimore the warming-up pen was between the grandstand and bleachers and behind big gates that opened on the field. No sooner had Nichols and Ryan left the field and shed their sweaters to warm up than each was surrounded by ten or twelve men.
>
> "What do youse tink yer goin' to do?" asked a burly oyster shucker of Ryan.
>
> "Going to warm up."

"Yous thinks yer goin' to warm up," said the ruffian. "I sez yer not goin' to warm up until I sez yer kin. Ryan and Nichols pleaded, but it was no use. Manager Selee sent another player to tell them to hustle in, but the gangsters grabbed him, too. Finally, the score-board showed Baltimore had scored 14 runs off Stivetts.

"Now yer kin warm up, if yer wants to, replied the leader of the gang.[2]

Ryan misremembered Nick's role in the bloodshed, but otherwise this sounds like an accurate characterization of the reputation that the Baltimore fans and players were developing. In any event, Nichols shook this off and made his scheduled start there the next day. Though he gave up two hits each in the second and third innings and walked three in the sixth, he escaped all three jams unscored upon and came away with a 6–3 victory. He closed out the month by beating Philadelphia 6–5 in ten innings on the 30th.

Nichols' early-season success peaked on May 7 in New York before 3,000 spectators. He opposed Amos Rusie again. Second baseman John Montgomery Ward made two errors in the first that gave Boston an unearned run. That was it for the scoring, and Nichols handcuffed the Giants, with no walks and only three hits off his deliveries.

Little more than a week later, the Boston franchise was shaken to its foundations. On May 15 (not 16, as is often stated), the Beaneaters were hosting Baltimore at the South End Grounds in front of 3,000 to 3,500 fans. The home team finished its turn in the third inning and ex–Beaneater Steve Brodie stepped toward the plate to face Boston pitcher Tom Lovett, who was new to the team that season. There was suddenly a flurry of activity in the stands near the right field corner, followed by a line of smoke. It turned out that a pile of rubbish had caught fire. Boston right fielder Jimmy Bannon tried to extinguish it without success, hindered by a lack of water nearby. The fire spread rapidly, and within three hours had decimated more than 170 buildings in the neighborhood, including a large school. The "Great Roxbury Fire" left nearly 1,000 families homeless.

For upcoming home games the Bostons shifted to the Congress Street Grounds, which had been the home of the pennant-winning Boston Reds of the Players' League in 1890 and of the American Association in 1891. Soon a new (third) South End Grounds was under construction.

Nichols blanked New York again on May 21, 3–0. This would have been no mean feat under normal circumstances, given that the Giants had future Hall of Famers batting second, third, and fifth in the form of "Monte" Ward, George Van Haltren, and George Davis. At this particular time a shutout was even more impressive because the left field fence of the Congress Street Grounds wasn't very far from home plate.

As a starting pitcher, Kid Nichols would benefit from this short distance in a historic game on May 30. In the first game of a doubleheader Boston had prevailed against Cincinnati in a 13–10 slugfest, but the second game was one for the record books. Taking maximum advantage of the Congress Street ballpark's inviting left field fence, Bobby Lowe homered twice in the third inning, and two more times later on, to become the first man in major league history to club four home runs in a single game. All four sailed along the left field line. Boston won 21–11, and it wasn't even that close until Nichols eased up in the ninth inning and the Reds then scored five times. For anyone not convinced of just how vulnerable pitchers were in that yard, two days later Stivetts also allowed more than 20 runs in a lopsided loss to Cleveland.

At the beginning of June, Charlie Bennett provided Boston fans with some insight into his life since his tragic accident in January. In a lengthy interview that appeared in the *Boston Daily Globe*, Bennett also shed light on his friendship with Charles "Kid" Nichols. Bennett noted that Nichols had visited him more than once that past winter, but that wasn't a surprise. "We lived together last summer in Boston, and my wife and Mrs. Nichols think as much of each other as Charley and I do," Bennett revealed.[3]

In June, Kid Nichols was one of a few pitchers in the league who received strong praise from baseball pioneer Henry Chadwick in a long column reporting on the NL's most successful pitchers to date. Chadwick noted that Nichols was responsible for half of Boston's first 20 wins. What's more, while the Kid's win-loss record was 10–1, three other Boston starters were a combined 10–11. Stivetts was the weakest link at 2–7, and Staley was limping along at 2–2. That left the 30-year-old newcomer, Tom Lovett, at 6–2, but he wouldn't sustain that brief success, and his big league career came to an end within months.[4]

The Boston pitching staff stepped it up shortly thereafter. Starting on June 7 the team won 9 of the next 10 games, and beginning on June 23 they enjoyed a stretch of 10 wins out of the next 12. From June 7 to July 7 the Bostons improved their record from 22–14 to 43–20, and rose from fourth place to first.

One of their few times that Boston lost during that span came in the second game of a doubleheader at home on June 18, and it was only the second loss of the season for Nichols. In the first game Boston had scored 16 runs in the first inning of a 24–7 humiliation of Baltimore, with Hugh Duffy reaching base a record three times when his club batted around twice. After that performance, it must have frustrated Kid Nichols to see three costly errors contribute to a 9–7 loss in the nightcap.

On July 20, the new South End Grounds was opened after ten weeks of construction. Even though Boston had spent almost a full month on the road waiting for their new grounds, they had just barely slipped into second place when they returned home. They returned to first place on July 21 when Kid

Nichols easily netted their second victory in their rebuilt home, and late in the month their lead grew to five games.

That lead had been cut in half by August 24, when Boston played a doubleheader against Cleveland. In the first game, Nichols relieved Staley after a few innings when the starter was unable to escape any inning with a blank state. After six innings Boston trailed 10–8. With a man on in the seventh Nichols hit a ball down the left field line and over the fence for what many in attendance thought was a homer by a good five feet, but umpire Jack McQuaid, the same official who had sided with Cap Anson over Nichols in that infamous game three summers earlier, ruled it foul. The blow would have tied the game, but after that ruling neither team scored again. Boston did win the second game, but a sweep was what they really needed.

On August 27 an event occurred that was long in the planning: "Boston's Tribute to the King of Catchers, Charles W. Bennett." That was the title on the souvenir program for this fundraising benefit for the Beaneaters' crippled comrade. In a letter dated July 5, 1960, to Sid Keener at the National Baseball Hall of Fame, Kid Nichols' daughter Alice told about visiting Bennett's nephew George Porter in Detroit, who was a longtime friend of her family and his uncle's heir. George gave her the program from the 1894 benefit. Her letter is still on file at the Hall, and her grandchildren still have this rare memento.

"Manager Selee and Charley Nichols have worked faithfully since last spring to get attractions and collect money for this deserving affair," said the *Boston Daily Globe.* There was plenty of publicity leading up to the event, even in other cities, such as when the *Cleveland Plain Dealer* mentioned that "officials of the Brooklyn club have subscribed $50 to the benefit of Bennett."[5] The *Globe* also reported that Kid Nichols was living on Tremont Street that summer, where he would host Charlie Bennett and his wife while they were in town. The night before the benefit, Charles and Jennie Nichols entertained not only Bennett and his wife Alice but also Boston's other catcher during their three pennant years, Charlie Ganzel, along with his wife.[6]

There were nearly 9,000 people at the new ballpark, many of whom arrived early. The main feature was a ballgame between the Beaneaters and top collegiate players in the area. All stood as the entire Boston team escorted Bennett, moving laboriously on crutches, onto the field and toward their bench. The *Boston Daily Advertiser* reported that at first there were a few moments of silence, but then "some one shouted 'three cheers for Charley Bennett' and they were given again and again while Charley, with bared and drooped head slowly made his way past the grand stand to the Bostons bench, which in former years he had occupied so often. As he passed the grand stand, he was visibly affected by the tremendous outpouring of sympathetic voices, his eyes were filled with tears, the corners of his mouth twitched and his lips trembled with emotion. In the grand stand, with Mrs. Charlie Nichols, sat Mrs. Bennett, who also was unable to check the rush of feeling which overcame her at the more than rapturous reception given to her husband."[7]

For the ballgame, Boston had all of its regulars in the lineup, except that Hugh Duffy gave his spot in left field to none other than Gentleman Jim Corbett, the famous heavyweight boxing champion. Kid Nichols pitched the first half of the game. Other activities were scheduled for after the game, including a 100-yard dash between Nichols and Jimmy Bannon. Bannon won by two yards. There were other races, including a sprint around the bases, and an amateur high jumper later impressed the crowd by clearing the back of a carriage horse that was brought onto the field. Bobby Lowe and Billy Nash gave a demonstration on accurate throwing from second base to home, and Lowe beat Nichols and Tom Tucker in distance throwing with a heave of 113 yards. The event raised close to $6,000 for Bennett.

Boston won nine of eleven just before the benefit for Charlie Bennett but lost four of five immediately afterward. The first of these losses went to Kid Nichols when the club resumed its National League schedule the day after the Bennett game, at home against St. Louis. Past the game's midpoint it looked like Boston would win, but in the end the Browns won, 9–5. Few would have blamed Kid Nichols if he was totally drained after the emotional intensity of the previous day. The Beaneaters had slipped into second place by the end of the month but treaded water in early September with four consecutive wins, beginning with a doubleheader sweep of Chicago, in Boston. Nichols won the second game that day. Two days later he earned the fourth of those wins as well, edging Louisville, 7–6. After that, the Bostons slowly slid out of the pennant race throughout September, and on the 6th they entered third place.

Kid Nichols kept plugging away, including on September 8 in Chicago when he held the Colts to five hits and won, 3–1. He also maintained his cool in Cleveland on September 13 until his teammates rallied to pound Cy Young, 11–4. On the 17th Nichols lost in St. Louis by a run, 6–5, but three days later he scattered six hits in a 4–3 win at Louisville. As a team they were playing .500 ball that month, and when their season ended on September 29, they finished in third place, eight games behind Baltimore, the pennant winners, and five behind New York. Though the final weeks were disappointing, finishing third in a 12-team league with a record of 83–49 certainly wasn't embarrassing. Nevertheless, by letting New York overtake them in addition to Baltimore, the Bostons were deprived of a new postseason opportunity: the chance to play in the new Temple Cup series between the top two finishers. New York ended up sweeping the series in four games.

Despite Boston's season ending with a whimper, it was yet another banner year for Kid Nichols. He won more than 30 games for the fourth straight season, and finished at 32–13. As he had every year previously, he toiled for more than 400 innings and completed 40 games. Other stats were somewhat poorer than in years past, as he had his second consecutive year of striking out fewer men than he walked, and his ERA was a run higher than in 1893. Still, as was the case during the pennant-winning season the year before, Kid Nichols accounted for about 40 percent of his team's victories.

Nobody could blame the offense for Boston not winning a fourth consecutive pennant. The 1894 team *still* holds the major league record for most runs scored in a season, with 1,220, and they achieved that in 30 fewer games than teams play in a season today. Kid Nichols contributed his fair share. He scored 39 runs and drove in 34. Among his 50 hits were 11 doubles and 2 triples, and his batting average was an impressive .294. Contrary to some sources, Nichols did not accomplish this as a switch hitter. "I always pitched and batted right handed," he said in the biographical document written around 1949.

Jack Stivetts rebounded from his 2–7 record early in the season to finish at 26–14, but the rest of the pitching staff was mediocre. Harry Staley had averaged 20 wins and 9 losses during the three championship years, but fell to 12–10 in 1894. In 1895 he would pitch poorly for St. Louis in his final major league season.

Though Charlie Bennett would have been a 39-year-old catcher in 1894, he had caught the most games for Boston the previous year, close to half of them, and twenty more than Charlie Ganzel. "Baseball scribes have attributed Charlie Bennett's train accident in large part to the reason that the Boston Beaneaters' 1894 club failed to win the pennant," wrote Donald Hubbard, biographer of Hugh Duffy and Tommy McCarthy. "In a purely baseball sense, he had not hit effectively for almost a decade and had largely stopped drawing walks after 1890. His most significant contribution came in managing the pitching staff and in not acting as a clubhouse lawyer in a tempestuous clubhouse, and Kid Nichols, for one, greatly missed him."[8]

Within three weeks of the season ending the Boston team disbanded for the winter, but first they had an unusual opportunity for some camaraderie. The evening prior to an exhibition game in Wilkes-Barre, Pennsylvania, in early October, the Boston club was invited by the local team's manager to enjoy a theatrical performance at the local Music Hall. On the 4th the famous heavyweight boxing champion John L. Sullivan, the "Boston Strong Boy," starred in "A True American," a three-act romantic drama written for him.[9] With Kid Nichols pitching the next afternoon, Boston prevailed 1–0 on a homer by Jimmy Bannon.[10]

The championship Kansas City bowling team of 1895. Kid Nichols is the taller of the two men standing.

Back home in Kansas City the next month, Kid Nichols joined a six-club bowling league and began adding to his reputation. Around Thanksgiving he came close to rolling the high score for his five-man Kansas Citys in a match against another local team, the Standards.[11] However, he wasn't allowed to keep baseball from his thoughts for very long that winter. Early in 1895 the *Philadelphia Inquirer* reported that for the second consecutive year Nichols had received an offer to coach Princeton's collegiate team during its spring training, starting in February. The paper added that he would probably go to Detroit in February to open the cigar business that he and Charley Bennett had been contemplating.[12]

Nichols would receive attention in that paper before the month was out, when he led the Kansas Citys to a new high mark in an amateur bowling tournament, beating the nationwide record previously held by New England League bowlers. This was news elsewhere on the East Coast, and even in the Utah Territory (which was still eleven years away from being admitted to the Union as a State).[13] Of course this was big news in Kansas City, but Kid Nichols may not have welcomed the attention he received there a few days later, when the *Kansas City Times* reported that he lived at 29th and Vine Streets.[14] His name wasn't in the three city directories from 1894 to 1896, though his brothers and father were listed a block over, at 29th and Flora, first on the northwest corner and later on the northeast corner, which was the side closest to Vine.

Kid Nichols enjoyed making predictions, though his record was mixed. As the 1895 season approached, he offered one about New York's new manager. "George Davis, a fine player, will never be the general that Johnnie Ward was, and it's an even money bet that Ward will be back in command of the New York team before the season is half over," Nichols foretold.[15] Ward had just managed the Giants to second place and victory in the first Temple Cup series, but his teammate Davis was taking over for 1895. Nichols' prophecy about these two Hall of Famers didn't hit the bull's-eye, but he came pretty close: Davis only managed the first 33 games, and his team went 16–17.

If Kid Nichols had followed the instructions that he received from Frank Selee around the 1st of March, he would have departed on the 15th or 16th for spring training in Columbia, South Carolina. There turned out to be one holdup: his contract. Back when the 1894 season was concluding, consecutive issues of *Sporting Life* had hinted that there might be trouble on this front. First, it mentioned Kid Nichols in a story about plans underway to form a second major league, a new American Association. Among the ringleaders were Pittsburgh manager Al Buckenberger, Nichols' California manager Billy Barnie, and longtime Chicago second baseman Fred Pfeffer, who had spent the past few seasons with Louisville. There was word that founders of the New York franchise were looking to hire the manager of the NL's Giants in 1892. "Pat Powers has practically been engaged as manager of the team, and is working hard in getting things in shape. According to Manager Powers, the team that will represent this city in the association will be wonderfully strong. It will consist of Tucker, Lowe, Long, Nash, Duffy, McCarthy, Bannon, Nichols, Stivetts and Ganzel, of the champion Bostons, all of whom, it is said, have already agreed to jump the League."[16] In later coverage of such announcements, speculation, and rumors, a few of these Bostons were mentioned a few more times as looking to join the rival league, though not Nichols.

Still, in the next issue J.C. Morse of the *Boston Herald* confirmed that Nichols was unhappy. "Nichols receives the limit, but can get $1000 more from another club that could be mentioned, and as other players are known to get more than the limit Nichols wants a raise of over $500 next season. When he did extra work for the club last season he did not get a cent therefore, and he has not forgotten that fact," Morse noted.[17] Other journalists didn't really pick up on this at the time, and Kid Nichols didn't grumble to the papers about the matter throughout the winter.

After it became public knowledge that Kid Nichols wasn't going to be making a beeline for South Carolina, lengthy commentary from him that appeared in the *Kansas City Times* didn't make him sound like someone who had a simplistic disdain for franchise owners. "It surprises me that so much sympathy is shown to Fred Pfeffer," Nichols said. "Fred, to start with, was one of the original Brotherhood men and the League took him back after the Brotherhood fight, without a word of censure and paid him a big salary. Then he breaks out with his wild-eyed association scheme."

Pfeffer's cohorts had backed out of the plan by the end of 1894, as the NL threatened permanent banishment, but Pfeffer remained defiant. Louisville fans countered with more than 10,000 signatures on petitions to reinstate him, including one from Cap Anson, and the NL ultimately let Pfeffer off the hook with a $500 fine, which his supporters quickly paid for him.

"His very action in espousing this lost cause shows what he would have done to the League people if he got the chance," Nichols concluded. "Yet he was taken back after one offense and because he was fired for the second he is regarded as a much-abused man. Isn't the League entitled to some protection?"

It should be noted, by the way, that Nichols' primary purpose in speaking with the *Times* seems to have been to voice concern about the rule changes of recent years. For instance, he observed, "It's impossible to stand on the rubber and get a good foot-hold and the only thing to do is to place your feet on the ground, and we would be suckers to place it behind the plate. We will get nearer to the home plate by lodging the purchase foot in front of the rubber."[18]

The position that Kid Nichols staked out regarding his contract was sophisticated, but the next day the *Times* made it clear that it wasn't buying it. "Kid's argument that a club forfeits the right of reservation after March 1 furnishes flimsy ground for him to stand on," the paper insisted on March 18. "He says he is now in a position to negotiate with other clubs. Technically speaking, he may be right, but is there a club in the league that would accept him. Not much. It's one of the Free Masonry tenets; one, and perhaps the only unwritten law in base ball. Nichols will play where the Boston club chooses to place him."[19]

The following day the *Kansas City Daily Journal* countered by siding with Nichols. "Nichols is not unreasonable in his ideas of salary and would be perfectly willing to play for what is facetiously termed 'the limit' if it were not for the fact that there are several other members of the Boston team who are getting more money, and who are not nearly so necessary to the success of the team as he is," the *Journal* wrote. "Without Nichols in the box the Boston team would have no chance of standing in the first four in the league race, and it is, in a great measure, his pitching which keeps the team up to its high position every year. This being the case, he does not see why he should be asked to play for $2,400 when Duffy and Nash are to get $3,000 each."[20] It must be noted that the sports editor of the *Journal* was Tom Bell, one of Nichols' bowling teammates.

That same day the *Times* began its story on the disagreement by quoting a telegram that Kid Nichols received from Boston co-owner Arthur Soden the day before: "Pay you the limit and no more. No extra work required." Though that daily had criticized Nichols' position the day before, this time it then turned the floor over to him:

> That is what I call a cold deal. I received this telegram from Soden late on Monday. Do I intend to reply to it? Not much. I have already written and wired Selee that I would sign the same agreement that held good last year.
>
> That is, I will pitch two games a week and receive extra salary for extra games. I made this agreement with Mr. Soden personally last year. Now he says no extra work will be required this season. He has got to give me more substantial evidence than a bare telegram before I will believe it. For example, I signed at a certain salary and the limited game stipulation and the extra salary; for extra games wasn't agreed on between Soden and myself.
>
> Why, they could put me in the box three or four times a week and I would be wearing my arm out for nothing. I have worked hard for the Boston team, and was always reasonable with management.
>
> Many a time I have pitched three and four games a week. In the fall of '92 I pitched three games within three days. Under the present pitching rules it is impossible for any pitcher to twirl three games a week, even half through the season, and that's why I ask for extra money for extra games. The Boston club has acted peculiarly toward me this spring. In previous seasons, I negotiated with one of the club directors, generally Mr. Soden. This year they have left Manager Frank Selee to do business with me, and the only object I can see in it possibly is to grind me down as much as they can."

The *Times* summarized Nichols' next steps: "He will throw himself upon the mercy of [NL] President Nick Young, who, being the tail end of the league dog, can not offer the 'Kid' much consolation. Nichols proposes to have it out with Selee and the Boston triumvirs if it takes all summer." In the next column on that same page, the paper took a different tone from the day before, heaping praise upon Nichols at length. Its new attitude was summed up when the paper declared that Nichols "is entitled to $2,900 which he received last year."[21]

On March 22, his brothers Willie and George helped keep him from dwelling too much on this contractual dispute by joining him at the Kansas City Bowling Club's weekly competition. The Kid finished first.[22]

In *Sporting Life*'s edition of March 23 the Nichols dispute was covered on no fewer than three pages. This publication seemed to consider Nichols to have a strong leg to stand on legally or procedurally under the rules of reservation within the National Agreement, and it printed Nichols' statement about that on the previous day:

> I do not propose to leave Kansas City until I have signed a contract or received an assurance from President Soden that the club will pay me as much money as I received last year. When the Boston Club lost money it immediately cut down the salaries of the players, and the cut was accepted by me without a kick. Now when the club is making good money again I think they ought to be willing to give the players a fair increase of salary. If I understand the League rules the Boston Club no longer has an exclusive claim to me, having failed to tender me a contract or make me an offer before March 1, as required. If I don't get a favorable response from the Boston Club at once I am going to wire Nick Young, and if he says I am free to go elsewhere I will sign with some strong team which will give me a fair salary.[23]

The *Kansas City Times* then reported that on March 23, Nichols left for Columbia via a Memphis route. Again the paper gave Nichols a forum:

> On second thoughts, I thought I might as well join the team and let that difference with the club remain unsettled until I reach Boston and consult the president, Mr. Soden. I can settle with him on the spot quicker than by writing letters. Manager Seelee [sic] writes me that the boys are anxious to have me hurry and join the team, as they are after the pennant this year and do not propose to allow it to slip from their grasp as they did last season. Seelee says we are strong enough in pitchers this year to get there again. To the surprise and delight of Manager Selee and the whole team Pitcher Heine Stivetts reported in splendid condition. I was never better in my life. In fact, I don't really need any preliminary work.[24]

The media quickly let this all blow over without providing much more detail, but there may have been more going on at the beginning of spring than met the eye, for not many days later the *Times* mentioned a report from the South, "where the Bostons are practicing, that 'Kid' Nichols was giving away money."[25] Yet it wasn't until April 20 that a Boston paper reported that Kid Nichols had in fact signed a contract with the Beaneaters for 1895.[26]

Three years later, Washington owner J. Earl Wagner told a tale that he said took place in the spring of 1894 but his details indicate that he must've been thinking of 1895. Wagner said that "the Senators were practicing in the South and we ran across the Boston team at Columbus [sic], Charley Nichols was one of the absentees from the team, and was in Kansas City holding out for a raise in salary. Selee offered to trade Nichols for Jimmy McGuire, with Fred Tenny [sic] thrown in to make up full measure. But we decided to keep McGuire as a trade would have given Boston a certainty for an uncertainty. Nichols had seen so much service that we suspected his wing would go back on him within a season or so. But he deceived us all."[27]

Probably as a result of Kid Nichols' last-minute signature on a contract, he pitched in an exhibition game in Providence, Rhode Island, on April 18 and the Opening Day assignment at home against Washington the next day was given to Jack Stivetts, who won, 11–6. The two teams traveled to the nation's capital for a rematch the day after that, and this time it was Kid Nichols who won for Boston, 12–4.

In New York on April 25, the home team scored three runs off of Kid Nichols in the third, two on a costly error by Bobby Lowe, before Nichols shut them down the rest of the way. Unfortunately, Boston's success against Jouett Meekin was limited to a 2-run fifth inning, so Nichols ended up on the losing end despite yielding only one earned run. Boston didn't play from the 27th through May 1, but Nichols rebounded on the 2nd with a 9–7 win against Washington and an 8–6 win off of John Clarkson's brother Dad in St. Louis on the 6th. Nichols finally notched a low-scoring, close victory in the first game of a doubleheader in Cleveland on May 15, during which he struck out seven Spiders on his way to a 3–2 win.

On May 18, Kid Nichols topped his previous game, this time in Louisville opposite Mike McDermott. Through eight innings McDermott limited Boston to three hits and no runs, but Nichols was simultaneously shutting out the Colonels. The Beaneaters doubled their hit total in the ninth and left town with a 1–0 win.

After the Kid's shutout in Kentucky the Bostons lost five in a row and slid from third place to the middle of the league standings, but by June 15 it had zoomed to first place, thanks to a stretch during which it won 12 out of 13 games. Boston then stayed atop the standings almost every day through July 1. A particularly significant win during that span was on June 22, when 8,500 fans crowded Boston's year-old South End Grounds. Kid Nichols would counter the red-hot Dad Clarke of the Giants. Boston led 3–0 after four innings but after seven they only led 4–3. Nichols kept New York from scoring in the final three frames, and an insurance run gave him a 5–3 win.

A month later, Kid Nichols was commenting to the *Kansas City Times* about pitching, and that prompted him to tell of the personal challenge he received that day from Clarke, his former Omaha teammate in 1889. "Curves and slow delivery have plenty of admirers," Nichols noted. "They may be good for a change, but give me the speed for a steady diet. In our last game with New York old Dad Clark [sic] began to tell me before the game that he would strike me out every time I came to the bat. But I fooled Dad. I struck left-handed and made two hits, and Dad didn't strike me out. But I made him fan every time he came to the bat. Dad is a hot-headed fellow and easily rattled, and after the game he was so hot that he wouldn't speak to me."[28] The box score a month earlier confirmed his memory regarding his own batting, and he did strike out Clarke twice, but he retired him in some other manner a third time, and yielded a hit to Dad. Still, Nichols could have rubbed it in even more than he did, because he didn't mention also drawing a walk from Clarke and then scoring the decisive run.

Though Boston was in first place on July 1, by the 17th it dropped back to sixth place. The next day Kid Nichols suffered a tough loss in Chicago to starter Clark Griffith, who had crossed paths with Nichols in California. Chicago scored two in the second inning and Boston scored one, and then neither pitcher allowed another run. Both Nichols and Griffith limited their foes to five hits.

To this point in the season, Nichols had pitched in 21 games with an earned run average of 2.86, and opposing batters had a combined batting average of .263 against him.[29]

With the team so far west, Kid Nichols was allowed a brief absence to visit his family in Kansas City, so long as he also did some scouting there. The *Kansas City Times* reported on Kid Nichols' assigned task, the outcome of which would have significant effects on the Boston club over the next five years. "Charley Nichols encased his stocky figure in one of Jimmy Manning's uniforms Saturday morning and 'warmed up' with the Blues," the paper wrote. "He pitched to Martin Bergen, and Martin, though he never before caught the Kid, took excellent care of everything that came up to him. Nichols acknowledged to the writer that one of the incidental objects of his trip to Kansas City was to look over Jimmy's material, though to judge from the Kid's attention to Bergen's play it would seem that Bergen got the monopoly of the look over."[30]

That audition took place on the 20th, and Nichols left Kansas City the next day. He rejoined his team in time to beat St. Louis on the 22nd, 13–2. That was the middle game of a five-win streak that elevated them momentarily to third place again.

Little more than a month after visiting his relatives in Kansas City, Kid Nichols enjoyed a brief respite on the east coast. The Beaneaters were scheduled to play an exhibition game in Newport, Rhode Island, on August 23, with Nichols playing right field. The team arrived the night before, and thus was able to avail itself of the well-regarded resort on the morning of the game. Jennie Nichols and Mrs. Nash accompanied their husbands.[31]

When Kid Nichols next pitched on August 26, he netted a very satisfying win in front of 7,000 Boston fans against Emerson Pink Hawley, the Pittsburgh pitcher who was on his way to a 30-win season. The score was 2–2 after six innings, and the winning run came home from third base in the ninth after a Pirate fielder couldn't come up with Nichols' scorching grounder cleanly. That win helped Boston toward its last hurrah. The Beaneaters reached third place on August 29 but only for that day, and never climbed higher than fourth place after that. During September Nichols probably derived the most satisfaction at home on the 20th when he held off Rusie and the Giants, 5–3. On the 27th he was part of an unusual outcome against Washington, when he singled and scored as part of a 12-run first inning, only to be replaced by Bill Yerrick to start the bottom of the frame, who then sailed to an easy "complete game" victory. When Boston's season concluded on September 30, they finished at 71–60, in sixth place out of twelve teams.

Jack Stivetts, who had to battle malaria for a while, finished an even 17–17, newcomer Cozy Dolan was 11–7, and Jim Sullivan, who had pitched a disastrous third of an inning for Boston in 1891 in an inauspicious major league debut, returned to the big leagues and went 11–9. Four other pitchers combined for 6 wins and 11 losses.

As for Kid Nichols, in many regards the season was better than his previous one; he completed all of his starts for the first time since his rookie year, he notched three saves compared to none in 1894, he reduced his home runs yielded from 23 to 15, hit batsmen from 9 to 5, and wild pitches from 14 to 11, while greatly improving both his strikeout and walk counts. Most impressively, he shaved more than a run off of his ERA with a mark of 3.41, his best since 1892. Despite all of these improvements, his win-loss record slid from 32–16 in 1894 to 26–16 in 1895. Such is baseball.

In late August, J.C. Morse of the *Boston Herald* analyzed Nichols' work in the pages of *Sporting Life*: "Nichols has been doing by far the best work of any of the pitchers, and with good fielding should not have lost a game in weeks. Two games he has pitched in Philadelphia should have been victories and easily."[32] In any case, Kid Nichols' 1895 season was immortalized by a Mayo's Cut Plug baseball card, which poorly adapted one of his cards issued in 1889 while he was with Omaha!

On October 1, the day after Boston's final game, the *Journal* announced Kid Nichols' plans for the immediate future: "Pitcher Charley Nichols will bid adieu to Boston today at 3 P.M., when he takes the train to Cleveland. He will arrive in Cleveland in time to see the Temple Cup game on Wednesday. He will stay at Detroit for a couple of weeks and will winter in Kansas City. Charley Bennett will also winter in Kansas City. Bennett must get a new pair of artificial limbs."[33]

Cleveland started at home in that year's Temple Cup series as a result of finishing second to the repeat pennant winners, Baltimore. The series opened on October 2 with a game in which both teams scored in the final two innings. Cleveland came out on top, 5–4, with Cy Young the winning pitcher. "The Baltimores were nervous and so were the Clevelands, but it is doubtful if either team was more nervous than Charley Nichols of the Bostons, who sat in the grand stand and rooted for both teams without partiality," reported the *Boston Daily Globe*.[34] But it was a correspondent for the *Journal* to whom

Nichols turned after the game and said, "Wasn't that a beauty? It was one of the most glorious games ever contested."[35]

During Kid Nichols' subsequent trip to check in on Charlie Bennett in Detroit, it was announced that he would play on a team made up of other local major leaguers, minor leaguers, and top amateurs. The series would pit them against the Page Fence Giants, of Adrian, Michigan, one of the most noteworthy African-American teams of that decade. That team was led by Captain Grant "Home Run" Johnson, and also on their roster was future Hall of Famer Sol White. The most notable among Nichols' projected teammates were Sam Thompson, a star outfielder for Detroit and Philadelphia in the NL; Detroit native Ed Stein of the Brooklyns, whom Nichols had homered off of in 1893; Jim "Deacon" McGuire, the catcher then with Washington (who was in the middle of an incredibly long major league career); and another Detroit native, Count Campau, who had led the American Association in home runs when Nichols was an NL rookie. The teams were supposed to meet on October 8 but that game was cancelled due to bad weather. When they did play the next day, none of the aforementioned NL players appeared, nor did Nichols, and it was no surprise that the Giants won easily, 16–2, against a lineup with little major league experience.[36]

Less than a month after Boston's 1895 season ended, the team signed Marty Bergen, the catcher whom Kid Nichols had scouted in Kansas City during July. Bergen was two years younger than Nichols. Boston made a bigger acquisition on November 14, when it traded longtime third baseman Billy Nash to Philadelphia for Sliding Billy Hamilton, an outfielder destined for the Hall of Fame, who would take over for another future Hall of Famer, Tommy McCarthy. Filling Nash's spot at third base would be future Hall of Famer Jimmy Collins. The decision about Nash was a wise one, as it turned out, because none of his three seasons in Philadelphia were anywhere near as good as his top years in Boston. The 1898 campaign would be his final season in the majors. These moves were all part of a two-year shakeup of the Boston club.

In December and January Kid Nichols' name turned up in coverage of Kansas City's bowling teams. It was also mentioned at the turn of the year that he'd spend that winter collecting rents for a Kansas City real estate man with extensive holdings, but the news of far more significance was that he had agreed to be on a team that Jimmy Manning and Frank Selee were trying to organize for a tour of Australia during the fall of 1896. That plan had been described in some detail in two *Sporting Life* articles on November 23, but Nichols hadn't been named as a candidate then. Manning had taken part in Al Spalding's baseball tour of Australia in 1888.[37] Alas, the plan pursued by Manning and Selee fell through.

Kid Nichols had a very quiet offseason otherwise, but as is also true today, the dead of winter didn't mean that sportswriters of the 1890s stopped talking about baseball. During February of 1896 the *Boston Herald* decided that it had to take issue with some of the offseason commentary about baseball's top pitchers. "Cy Young, Theodore Breitenstein and Emerson Hawley have been loudly heralded by some of the press of the country as the only pitchers that are in the $10,000 class, but there are people who believe that right here in Boston there is a pitcher who should not be overlooked when big money — or offers — are being passed around. His name is Nichols and it would take more than $10,000 to get him away from Boston."[38]

Before the middle of March Kid Nichols signed a contract for the 1896 season with the Bostons. Though Nichols didn't report for spring training as early as many of his teammates, there wasn't a reenactment of the prior year's preseason conflict. For spring training that year, the team decided to return to the city that served as its base in 1892, Charlottesville, Virginia. Nichols reported on April 3, and if anyone was unsure of the nature of his relationship with the rest of the players, that was settled quickly.

"Nichols received a great welcome from the members of the Boston team as he stepped from the train this noon," reported one Boston newspaper. "The team was at the depot to take a train for Roanoke when the western train pulled in. The first man off was Nichols, bag in hand. 'There's Nick,' sang out Herman Long, and the boys made a line for the old standby. Nichols' good right arm was tested pretty well as he went down the line bowing and shaking hands."[39]

Though Kid Nichols was a late arrival for spring training, for a change he was the Opening Day starter, in Philadelphia on April 16 against his longtime captain, Billy Nash. There were five other NL games that day, with their attendance ranging from 8,000 to about 14,500. Philadelphia stunned the baseball world by drawing 23,000. Boston led 4–0 after two innings, but Philadelphia halved that lead in the third. Boston got those two runs back in the fourth, and after that, Nichols cruised to a 7–3 win, having scattered seven hits. "They couldn't hit Nichols, and that explains it all," concluded the *Philadelphia Inquirer*.[40]

Kid Nichols also received the honor of starting the home opener against Baltimore on April 20, and this time a crowd of 17,000 to 18,000 packed the South End Grounds. It was the biggest opening day crowd in the city's history and was only eclipsed in Boston history by the 20,000 drawn to a Decoration Day game in 1884, coincidentally also against Philadelphia. Nichols would strike out only one Oriole that day, but according to the *Boston Morning Journal*'s box score it was future Hall of Famer Wee Willie Keeler, who would only strike out eight more times that entire season! Keeler was also the only batter the Beaneater pitcher beaned that day.[41] The Beaneaters scored in the first five innings, including an 8-run third and a 7-run fifth, on their way a 21–6 victory. Nichols scattered seven singles while Boston piled up 28. Two belonged to Nichols, in four at bats. With the score so lopsided he was relieved after pitching six innings, and the game was called after the eighth so Baltimore could catch a train.

These two wins were Boston's only victories in its first six games, but then it won six in a row. This streak began when Nichols faced the Orioles in their own park on the 23rd. Nick shut out the defending champions 7–0 on six hits.

Reminiscent of his lopsided win in Boston's home opener, on May 7 Kid Nichols enjoyed a 17–1 win in Louisville, during which he scattered six hits. Boston's other pitchers continued to pick up the pace, and about a week later the team entered into a tie for first place, where they would stay for a few days. Kid Nichols helped the cause in St. Louis on May 18, in a tense game opposite Bill Hart.

The Browns tallied a run off Nichols in the first inning, and that was the only scoring in the game until Boston batted in the eighth. Hart had only allowed two hits at that point, but then issued his only walk of the game. A few hits later, and Boston had a 3–1 lead. Through eight innings Nichols had allowed one walk and five hits. With one out in the ninth he issued his second walk, and a two-out hit brought the potential winning run up to the plate in the form of Browns catcher Ed McFarland. He hit a line drive into the stands near the left field line for what would have been a three-run homer but the blow was ruled a foul ball by Tom Lynch (who late that season would become the first major league umpire to call 1,000 games). After the resulting outcry died down, McFarland flied out to end it.

To regular observers, something must have seemed amiss in Kid Nichols' behavior in the center of the diamond. "Nichols's extraordinary efforts in the box excited suspicion among those who know him, and after the game it was learned that there was a good reason for his apparent desire to do his best," reported the *Boston Journal*. "The 'kid's' home is in Kansas City, and whenever the Bostons play here his estimable wife and beautiful little girl come here to see him play. They occupied prominent seats in the grand stand today, and proved to be great mascots for the 'kid.'"[42]

Nichols notched a nice win at home on June 11 against Cincinnati, allowing only five hits in a 9–1 game, but a few days later the Boston team got stuck in a rut, and sat in fourth place for more than a month. Even winning five in a row starting on June 23 didn't improve the team's standing.

The game that Kid Nichols pitched in Washington on July 2 was declared by *Sporting Life* to have been "the greatest pitchers' battle of the season" to that point. Leading the other side in this battle was James McCutchen James, commonly known as Doc McJames, whose six-year career would peak with 27 wins for Baltimore in 1898. McJames kept Boston hitless until giving up two in the fourth inning, which the Beaneaters combined with Washington errors for four runs. McJames would then keep Boston hitless and scoreless the rest of the way. Kid Nichols extended his hitless stretch longer. With two out in the seventh the Senators got a runner to third when Jack Stivetts, playing third base, fielded a bunt and threw in the general direction of first base, the ball going to the right field fence instead. Stivetts then made another throwing error on a ball hit to him by McJames and the shutout ended. The no-hitter ended after one out in the eighth with a double, and a two-out single brought in the other Washington run.[43] After an uneventful ninth inning, Kid Nichols had a two-hit victory, 4–2. He then pitched two days later in the second game of an Independence Day doubleheader in Brooklyn. Nichols gave up two runs in the first inning but Boston scored six times before the fourth inning, and by scattering five hits across his nine innings of pitching he won, 7–2.

In Pittsburgh on July 15 Kid Nichols and Pink Hawley pitched a dramatic game. The game was tied 1–1 after the second inning and then no runs were scored in the next six. Boston scored once in the ninth and Nichols was able to exit with another close, low-scoring victory to his credit.

Kid Nichols started August by beating Philadelphia 3–1, and then on the 6th he had a duel with McJames that was even more nerve-wracking than their matchup a month earlier. This time, Nichols gave up four hits and McJames gave up eight, but neither man allowed a run to score for eight innings. Nichols gave Washington another zero on the scoreboard in the ninth. In the bottom of that frame, Hugh Duffy was on second with two outs. Marty Bergen drove the ball between third and short for a single, and Duffy tried to score. The throw arrived just when he did but was a foot wide, and the Bostons handed Nichols a 1–0 win.

These two victories were part of a five-game winning streak for Boston at home, but in spite of this burst the team spent almost all of August mired in sixth place.

In Boston on August 13 Kid Nichols experienced one of his shortest appearances as a starting pitcher, when New York led 9–1 after the fourth inning and drove him from the game. Nichols was ultimately tagged with a 10–7 loss. New York was again the opposition the next day, and Kid Nichols wandered the South End Grounds "looking for revenge," according to the *Boston Daily Globe*. "So manager Selee sent him in against the same crowd that knocked him off the perch the day before."

Nichols was also motivated by the fact that Dad Clarke was starting for the visitors. The *Globe* shed light on their rivalry: "Years ago Dad and Nick were members of [Selee's Omaha] team and dividing honors. Manager Selee signed Nichols for Boston, and Clarke has always marked Boston for his prey since that time in 1890."[44] Boston scored two in the second inning and two more in the seventh, while New York's five hits did no damage. Kid Nichols had rebounded with a 4–0 shutout and tagged his rival with another loss.

Boston tied its best streak of the season with six in a row in early September, including two doubleheader sweeps, but that was its last gasp. Still, the club's 1896 finish was a bit of an improvement over the previous year. Boxton finished at 74–57, good for fourth place in the twelve-team NL, two rungs higher than in 1895.

Kid Nichols improved his record from 26–16 the previous year to 30 wins and 14 losses in 1896, and lowered his earned run average from 3.41 to 2.83. He again accounted for 40 percent of his team's victories. In addition, his fielding statistics were impressive enough for the *Washington Times* to circulate an announcement about them. "Unless some official scorer has made an entry that every other scorer in the land has overlooked, Charley Nichols ... will gain the remarkable distinction of playing through the season without an error — the only man of the hundreds who took part in the fight of '96 who can exhibit a fielding average of 1.000. Nichols officiated in forty-nine games, and he had considerable work to do. He is credited with twenty-seven put-outs and eighty-seven assists. That is up to the usual run, for there is not a twirler in the league who has averaged three chances to a game."[45] Back in May, *Sporting Life* had already insisted that Kid Nichols was "doubtless the finest fielding pitcher, though [Win] Mercer, of the Senators, is a close second."[46] For the record, Nichols made no errors while pitching in 1896 but he did make one error that season as an outfielder.

Sprinkled throughout the press coverage of the 1896 season were insightful tidbits about Kid Nichols. For instance, in May the *Cedar Rapids Evening Gazette* asserted that Nichols had "an ambition to become a manager and a magnate, and rumor has it that he will purchase an interest in the Kansas City club." However, the Iowa paper updated this in early July, writing that "Charley Nichols, of the Boston team, has reversed his decision, and will not go into business in Kansas City at the end of the playing season."[47] This reported interest would eventually prove to be true.

Sporting Life was routinely a source of short observations and news items. In the realm of opinion was an item naming Kid Nichols as "the best dressed man on the Boston team." More of an insider's revelation was a reference to Boston having been approached at some point about the availability of their "brilliant and brainy pitcher," but the outcome being that "the Boston management refused to surrender [Nichols] in exchange for Rusie," his counterpart on the Giants.[48] In fact, a year earlier Arthur Soden had directly rebutted a rumor that Nick would be acquired by New York: "If New York offered me Rusie and Clarke both in exchange for Nichols, they should not have him, for he is worth more than the two of them," the Boston co-owner insisted.[49]

An undated Kansas City photograph.

Around the end of the season, the *New York Sun* circulated a report that extended this kind of "inside scoop" journalism to Kid Nichols' family, or so it thought. "Frank Nichols, brother of Kid Nichols of the Boston baseball team, is desirous of attaining a reputation in another field," began the version printed in the *Milwaukee Journal* on September 28. "He aspires to the welterweight boxing championship. Although a young fellow, he has already defeated Jim Lynch at 122 pounds and Dan Murphy of Boston. He has arranged to box twenty rounds with Frank Rogers of Boston at 140 pounds. If he wins, he will try for Joe Walcott, Tommy Ryan or Billy Smith."[50] A one-sentence summary appeared elsewhere.[51]

Corrections appeared in some papers a week or so later. "That story which was told in the East relative to Frank Nichols, a pugilistically inclined brother of the Boston twirler, was a bald-headed fake. Nichols has no brother Frank," acknowledged the *Washington Times*, for instance.[52] The timing didn't prevent *Sporting Life* from publishing the fabrication in its issue dated October 10, which it retracted in its next weekly issue.[53] The perpetrator of this hoax wasn't identified.

About ten days after the season ended, the *Boston Daily Globe* revealed that Kid Nichols' short-term plans were to spend a few days in Chicago and then head home to Kansas City.[54] He'd end up having a fairly quiet winter at home, similar to the previous offseason. In fact, as it anticipated his arrival, the *Kansas City Daily Journal* said there was some question about whether Nichols would even bowl that winter.[55] Sure enough, when his brother George's name appeared in November and December among local bowlers, including teammates Charley and Johnny Kling, Nick's name was nowhere to be found. Johnny, by the way, would not only go on to be a notable Chicago Cub catcher in the 1900s but also a baseball associate of Kid Nichols. Later in the winter it was revealed that Kid Nichols did have a role in the local bowling scene, as the official record keeper for the entire season.[56]

Nichols may have been devoting most of his energy that winter to launching a new business. When *Sporting Life* announced it in early February, the nature of this news may have sent Boston fans into a panic:

> Kid Nichols, the crack pitcher of the Boston team, whose winter home is in Kansas City, may not be seen with the "Beaneaters" next season. He has purchased a laundry in this city with his brothers Will and George, and has been doing a good business. They have worked up a big patronage, and the Kid, it is said, has told close friends that he likes his new trade much better than playing ball, and that he has declared his intention of giving up the game if his new business continues with the present success. He is doing no gymnasium or other work to keep himself in condition. His friends here hope he will not give up the game and they point to his playing record with much pride.[57]

The Nichols Brothers laundry was located at 2200 E 15th (now Truman Road), at Brooklyn Avenue. In that low-tech era, its telephone number was 1270. At that time the three brothers and their parents were all living very close by, at 1429 Brooklyn.

On March 11 his many admirers in Kansas City, at least, were given some comfort by the *Journal*, when it reported that Nichols was "anxious to remain in Kansas City and do his preliminary work here as long as possible, so that he can give his attention to his business. He wrote to Selee yesterday asking for permission to stay here until a few days before the first game to be played in Boston on April 19, promising to report then in the pink of condition. Nichols has accepted terms, his contract calling for the limit, as usual."[58] Nick didn't get his wish, or perhaps he didn't desire it very strongly, because on March 20 he left to join the Bostons for spring training in Savannah, Georgia. By the end of that month Nichols saw action in a game between Boston and a local club, except that he was one of three pitchers loaned to the other team. As a result, Boston lost 4–3.[59]

In the 1897 season, several more changes to the Boston lineup surfaced. For one, Fred Tenney, in his fourth year out of Brown University, took over at first base for Tom Tucker, Kid Nichols' teammate during all of his previous seasons in Boston. Meanwhile, rookie Chick Stahl replaced outfielder Jimmy Bannon. On the pitching staff, Fred Klobedanz and Ted Lewis emerged, and the rotation grew to four. Each of them had pitched fewer than a dozen games in their only previous major league season, with Boston the year before.

The Beaneaters were scheduled to start the regular season by hosting

An undated photograph, on the back of which the group was identified as the Boston team, in Florida. Though the team's spring training took place as far south as Georgia, there is no known instance of the team traveling south of that state's border.

Philadelphia on April 19 and then play eight games on the road. Kid Nichols drew the Opening Day assignment on a sunny but very windy day in Boston. Through eight innings his team failed to score, but he did all right and was only down by three. With two on and two out in the ninth, he surrendered a homer to future Hall of Famer Nap Lajoie and suddenly Philadelphia had doubled its lead. That ended up making a huge difference, because it meant that Boston's five-run rally in the bottom of the ninth, which started when Nichols drew a walk, wasn't quite enough.

Nick's second start was on April 23 in Baltimore, which had won the last three NL pennants. After seven innings Boston led 5–4, despite complaining that the home team was exploiting umpire Tom Lynch's inability to monitor behavior on the base paths while the ball was in play across the field. Nichols got into trouble in the eighth and Baltimore tied the game on a bad throw during a double steal. After an error by Jimmy Collins and two more hits, the Orioles led 7–5, which proved to be the final score.

It would get worse before it got better. In Philadelphia on April 27, Kid Nichols lost for the third time in a row. He was relieved after the eighth inning down 10–4, and another big ninth-inning rally by his teammates only served to give the false impression that the game had been close as the 10–8 score that was entered into the record books.

The Boston team as a whole took its cue from its ace, and ended April dead last in the NL standings, among 12 teams. Meanwhile, Baltimore fans were envisioning a fourth consecutive NL title, and on May 4 that team took over first place, where it would perch for more than a month.

Kid Nichols received a ten-day break in early May, and it helped, at least at first. He made his fourth start of the season at home on the 6th against Washington. He excelled for eight innings, giving up only one run on three hits. Meanwhile, the Boston offense gave him five runs. However, the Senators loaded the bases with two outs thanks to two singles and an error by Herman Long, and suddenly the tying run was at the plate. That batter was third baseman Charlie Reilly. Reilly only averaged about two home runs a season but some of the Bostons may have remembered his first-of-its-kind major league debut in 1889, when his four hits that day included two homers. In any event, the Boston fans were undoubtedly well aware of their star pitcher's three previous losses, and there was suddenly palpable tension.

Pitch one, a swinging strike. Pitch two, another swinging strike. Pitch three was the same, and the game was over.

Nichols' troubles weren't, at least not immediately. At the start of a seventeen-game road trip on May 10, against Pittsburgh, Nick was victimized by errors made by three future Hall of Famers, Collins, Billy Hamilton, and Hugh Duffy in the fourth inning. The three unearned runs that inning made the difference, as Nichols was on the losing end of a 4–2 final score.

Shortly afterwards, Kid Nichols spoke about the challenges of being a fielder in a baseball game. He wasn't speaking specifically about Collins, Hamilton, and Duffy, but he did suggest that fans shouldn't be so quick to judge fielders harshly. "One of the hardest plays for me to make and one that I think bothers every pitcher is crossing to first to receive an assist from the first baseman," he said. "Casual observers do not realize how hard this play is. Other things are to be considered. The pitcher has to watch for the base, and he has also to watch to time his step on the bag with the throw from the first baseman. It is very difficult to look for the base and the ball at the same time, not to say anything about the batter, with whom you are sure to make a head finish at the bag. This is the hardest part of the game for me. I don't know how it strikes other pitchers. I'm telling of my own experience."[60]

The game in Cleveland on May 13 represented a turning point for both Nichols and the team as a whole. Starting for the Spiders was Cy Young, but Nichols outdueled him. Rookie sensation Louis Sockalexis lived up to his reputation by hitting a double and a triple off of Nichols, but the Kid only allowed two other hits and won 4–1. Boston finally reached .500 at 8–8, and they had jumped from twelfth place to sixth in two weeks. On May 21 Nichols would again limit an opponent to four hits, this time in an 11–1 win at St. Louis.

Nichols started the final game of the long road trip, in Cincinnati on May 29. He allowed the second-place Reds a run in each of the first two innings, one on an RBI that came after Fred Tenney dropped a foul popup, but he shut down the Reds from then on. His teammates were only able to score in the eighth inning, and then only once, so Nichols ended up on the short end of a 2–1 game.

After a day off, on May 31 Boston enjoyed a home stand of sixteen games. The first time that Kid Nichols pitched during this streak was on June 3, with Cleveland in town. Nichols hadn't traveled with his team, reported the *Journal*, because he had been "detained in Cincinnati on account of the sickness of his daughter."[61]

For the second time in less than a month, Cy Young was the opposing pitcher. The Spiders managed but one run, unearned due to two errors, and none of their five hits came in the same inning. Kid Nichols won comfortably, 6–1. "Nichols Is King," bellowed the headline the next day in the *Boston Daily Advertiser*.

On June 7 Nichols shut out Pittsburgh, 4–0, and the Kid helped his own cause with three hits in four at bats. As a result of this win, Boston moved into second place ahead of Cincinnati, and only two games behind Baltimore.

On June 12 Nichols faced that Reds team which Boston had recently overtaken. The Beaneaters scored three in the first inning, and Kid Nichols held Cincinnati scoreless for the first five innings. The Reds threatened after Jake Beckley's double put two runners in scoring position. Nichols retired the next batter, and the play after that brought back memories of his start in Baltimore during April, when Boston insisted that umpire Lynch was missing cheating by the Orioles when he had his back turned. This time, while umpire Tim Hurst was watching the second out made at first base, not only was the runner on third scoring behind him, but Beckley was somehow right on his teammate's heels! Hurst instantly decided that Beckley had come nowhere near touching third base on his way home, he ruled Jake out for taking a blatant shortcut. The ensuing argument caused both benches to empty onto the field, but Hurst stood his ground. After things quieted down, Kid Nichols cruised to a 5–1 victory, thanks in part to issuing no walks.

A chart in the *St. Louis Republic* showed that in his first ten games, Kid Nichols had given up 97 hits in 404 at bats for an opposition batting average of .240, to go with only 19 earned runs allowed.[62] He continued his full recovery on June 19 against Chicago, the final game of the sixteen-game home stand.

Nichols won that one as well, 7–3. He was on a personal hot streak but his team's was more impressive, because they had won *all* of their games during that span, and won a seventeenth consecutive contest in Brooklyn.

After starting the season with a very uncharacteristic win-loss record of 1–4, Kid Nichols had subsequently won nine of ten to stand tall at 10–5 at the conclusion of Boston's stunning 17-game win streak. The fandom in Boston was elated, and back home in Kansas City, the *Journal* gloated that "'Kid' Nichols gave only eleven bases on balls in the five games he pitched of the sixteen straight victories at home."[63]

The seventeenth straight win put them in first place, ahead of Baltimore, which had recently won nine in a row itself. Their loss in Brooklyn on the following day dropped them back to second, and winning the rubber game of the match on the 23rd put them back on top by half a game. With first place on the line, Boston hosted Baltimore for a crucial three-game series starting on the 24th, a Thursday. Nichols started that first game.

With first place on the line there was a huge turnout, and that inspired the *Advertiser* to provide this account of the game on its front page the next day:

> The game was played before more than 15,000 people, one of the largest crowds that has ever been on the grounds, and by far the greatest throng that has ever seen a week-day game in this city. At 2:45 P.M., three quarters of an hour before the game was to be called, there were more than 5000 people on the grounds, and from that on, they came in hordes.
>
> They overran the stands and bleachers long before 3 P.M., and encroached upon the field. Ropes had been stretched in the outfield, but not enough space was behind them to wedge in the people. They mocked at ropes and the insufficient police force present. They crowded up toward the diamond from the outfield, and from the foul lines on either side. They sat on the ground in front of the bleachers, and in the corners of the grounds until a solid wall of faces rose from near the diamond, unbroken to the fence-tops.

The paper acknowledged that these circumstances had an effect on the game, though not as great an impact as Oriole fans likely believed.

> It was necessary to make a ground rule that hits into the crowd should yield one base to the batsman, and base-runners being allowed to take two bases. This rule worked somewhat to Boston's advantage on the whole, but did not change the result. It was feared that the game would prove a farce because of the interference of the crowd but it is safe to say that every spectator got his money's worth of good clean, snappy ball. ... Each pitcher was well supported by his infield, the outfield having little chance because of the crowd that limited its field.[64]

Boston jumped out to a 4–0 lead after two innings but Baltimore cut that lead in half in the third. Boston didn't look back after that, and totaled 20 hits on their way to a 12–5 victory. Whatever harassment Baltimore fielders may have experienced from the local fans during the game, they undermined their own cause by hitting into three double plays. The Beaneaters won the next day as well, and then for the series finale the first game's starters, Nichols and Joe Corbett, each took the ball again with only a day of rest in between. Corbett was the younger of the boxing champion who had moonlighted in left field for the Bostons during the benefit for Charlie Bennett in 1894.

Because the finale was on a Saturday, the turnout swelled to 17,000 fans. Each starting pitcher impressed, especially given that they shared the same intense spotlight a mere 48 hours earlier. The goose eggs started piling up on the scoreboard, and Nichols finished by allowing only five hits. Corbett was just as good, so it came down to the ninth inning. In the top half, with two outs Nichols faced outfielder Jacob Charles Stelzle, more commonly known as Jake Stenzel. As the *Journal* reported, Stenzel proceeded to drive "the ball over the low fence at the 25-cent gate. A majority of the spectators expected the umpire to give the batsman a single only, but he very properly let Stenzel make the circuit. While the crows was mulling over the situation in a semi-dazed way, [Tom] O'Brien went out on a grounder to Nichols."[65]

In the bottom of the ninth, a one-out single by Jack Stivetts was all that Boston could muster. Even though Kid Nichols thus ended up on the wrong end of a 1–0 shutout, the Orioles left town trailing by a game and a half.

To start July, Nichols found himself in New York matched up with Amos Rusie. Boston scored first, with a pair of runs in the fourth, and the Giants picked up a run in the next inning after horrible throws by Collins and Duffy. With two teammates on base and two out in the sixth, Collins more than made up for his gaffe with a blast that turned into an inside-the-park homer, and suddenly Kid Nichols enjoyed a 5–1 lead. Though the first six innings Nick allowed only two hits, but the Giants produced two runs in the seventh.

It remained 5–3 going into New York's half of the ninth. "For a week past the Bostons have played a successive series of games in which each has been won or lost in the ninth inning, with the spectators wrought up to the highest pitch of excitement," noted the *Boston Journal*, "but none of them equaled the terrific battle between the Bostons and 'Giants' which was fought out on the Polo Grounds this afternoon."

Rusie himself started off the inning with a hit. He soon scored to make it a one-run game, and the Giants had runners on first and second with only one out. The next Giant to face Nichols was George Davis. "A vicious swing and the ball went toward second like lightning," the *Journal* observed. "The noise of that crazed crowd went up to heaven."

"Vain was the hit. Vain was the joyous intoxication of the crowd. Herman Long, crippled and sore, leaped into the breach. In a twinkling he had made a grand stop, had touched second, and with Joyce almost on top of him, with hands upraised to block the throw, he lined the ball to Tenney just ahead of the runner and completing a double play which was a marvel of speed, all was over."[66] Kid Nichols escaped with a 5–4 win.

Kid Nichols suffered one of his few losses that summer in Chicago on July 8, in a genuine duel against Clark Griffith. The score sat at 1–1 after nine innings and Griffith ended up driving in the winning run himself with one out in the tenth. Fans could have reasonably expected another such duel in Cleveland on July 12 when it was Nichols against Cy Young, but Nichols won their head-to-head contest easily. The final this time was 8–2, and Nichols produced the big blow in a four-run fourth inning with a homer to the center field fence. Young was replaced midway through the next inning.

Nichols ended July the same way that he started it, with a game on the line in the ninth inning. The difference this time that instead of toiling to protect a lead, the question came down to whether it would be Boston or host Washington that would break the deadlock. Neither Nichols nor his counterpart, Doc McJames, was sharp in the first five innings, after which the score was 6–6. Both pitchers turned over new leaves in the next few innings, and the score stayed that way going into the ninth. Only Boston scored that inning, and Nichols had another one-run win, 7–6. It was his 20th victory of the season, and there were two months remaining.

Boston had held onto the NL's top rung throughout July, though for more than three weeks after Independence Day it was Cincinnati that occupied second place, not Baltimore. Boston's lead was always less than six games. Boston retained first place throughout August as well, but when Baltimore regained second place on the 12th, that team wouldn't drop lower in the standings the rest of the way.

Baseball fans were beginning to sense that the race was going to come down to a lengthy fight between the decade's pair of three-time champs, so it's no surprise that many observers in Boston, perceived the looming struggle as one that pitted good against evil. As noted in Bill Felber's detailed account of the 1897 pennant race, foremost among these commentators may have been the well-regarded John Morrill of the *Boston Globe*. "In the eyes of Morrill and many in the sporting world, Oriole baseball corrupted the game, legitimized underhanded tactics, and compromised virtue in the Machiavellian pursuit of victory," Felber noted. Felber provided examples of leading baseball writers in other NL cities who shared Morrill's concern, such as Joe Vila in New York, Ren Mulford in Cincinnati, and Hughie Fullerton in Chicago.[67]

As pennant fever increased in Massachusetts and Maryland, Kid Nichols pitched a real gem on August 23 when Louisville visited for a doubleheader. The home team used two hits to produce a run in the first, but Nichols gave them almost nothing else the rest of the way. Meanwhile, Boston scored in the third, fourth, and fifth innings, and the first game ended as a three-hitter for Nichols, 4–1.

Shortly thereafter the Beaneaters lost three in row at home, the third on the 27th when Cleveland beat Nichols 7–1, and Boston ended August tied with Baltimore for first. Through September 10 the two clubs remained in a virtual tie.

Kid Nichols pitched in five games during the first ten days of that month, which Boston spent at home. On the 1st, he came on in relief to help preserve a 7–4 win against Chicago. Two days later he pitched a complete game against the Colts, went three for three as a batter, and won 9–1. On the 6th, he had an easy time with Cincinnati in front of 12,000 fans, and won 10–2. On the 9th he gave Stivetts a break for the final two innings of 13–6 win over St. Louis, and the next day he had a six-inning relief stint against the same team, after Boston fell behind 9–2. Nichols entered the game with runners on, induced a double-play ball, and shut down the Browns on three hits from then on. Meanwhile Jimmy Collins led an impressive Boston comeback, finally tripling home two runs in the ninth to tie it. Collins then scored the winning run on a groundout by Nichols, and Boston won, 10–9.

Nevertheless, Baltimore was keeping pace with Boston, and by September 14 the Beaneaters had actually slipped into second place. There were little more than two weeks left in this intense pennant race. That day Kid Nichols defeated visiting Philadelphia, 6–4, and on the 17th he moved to within three games of 30 wins with a 17–0 romp versus New York, also in Boston. The Giants had only five hits, and never got a runner to third base. Nichols also contributed to the offensive onslaught with three hits in five at bats.

Boston's last home game of the season was scheduled for the 22nd, but one day earlier it hosted Brooklyn for a doubleheader. The first inning of the first game was one for the record books, as it was the worst frame of Kid Nichols' major league career. His catcher, Charlie Ganzel, dropped not one but two foul popups during the first at bat, and Nichols ultimately walked the batter. After a single, Nichols succeeded in retiring the third batter, but the cleanup hitter drove in both runners with a hit. A couple of lousy plays added to Brooklyn's lead, but Nichols also gave up a bunch of additional hits, and when the dust settled, the Bridegrooms had a staggering twelve runs. When the game reached its merciful end, the score was 22–5. "And with the loss of the game the possibility of the pennant coming to Boston becomes very doubtful," moaned the *Boston Journal*, despite the fact that the Beaneaters had gone on to trounce Brooklyn in the second game of the doubleheader.[68]

Undeterred by that paper's pessimism, the Beaneaters also won the finale from Brooklyn and moved back into first place by a razor-thin lead of half a game. The *Journal* was undoubtedly looking ahead to the fact that Boston's next three games, half of their remaining ones were going to be played in Baltimore.

Thus, three days after his humiliation in the thick of the pennant race, Kid Nichols faced a far more imposing starting assignment in game one of this decisive series. It was the third significant game of the season in which the other starter was Corbett. September 24 was a Friday, and 12,000 to 13,000 turned out. Newspapers counted 135 to 140 in the organized delegation from Boston.

Baltimore drew first blood, and did so immediately. John "Mugsy" McGraw led off by walking on five pitches, and after Willie Keeler failed to advance him, decided to steal second base. Hughie Jennings followed with a hit and McGraw raced home with the first run. Joe Kelley followed by driving a ball over Hugh Duffy's head in left field, and Jennings raced around to make it 2–0. Baltimore left Kelley in scoring position when Kid Nichols bore down to induce a pop up from Jake Stenzel and then fanned Jack Doyle.

The Baltimore fans had high hopes in the third when McGraw led off with a single. Keeler surprised nobody by laying down a bunt toward third, which he would have beaten out if Jimmy Collins hadn't made a barehanded grab of it and a lightning throw to first. Though it was a close call, there was little argument when Keeler was ruled out. The next two batters could do nothing to advance McGraw from second, and the brief opportunity ended with the score staying 2–0. Stenzel reached third to open the fourth when Billy Hamilton misjudged a ball that landed in front of him and then rolled through his legs. On the next batted ball Stenzel proved too eager to add to the Orioles' lead, and Collins easily threw him out at home.

Corbett was stingy early on, but Boston finally broke through with a run in the fourth, and took a 3–2 lead in the fifth. Keeler led off the sixth inning with a single, but he was soon cut down by Marty Bergen when trying to steal second.

Kid Nichols singled off of Corbett in the seventh inning, and that apparently rattled the Oriole ace. Billy Hamilton followed with a weak tap right back to the pitcher, but Corbett hurried his throw and it sailed away, the result being that Nichols stood on third and Hamilton second, with no outs. Tenney was up next, but before he could do anything, Corbett hurled a wild pitch and Nichols scored to make it 4–2. Tenney decided to take advantage of Corbett's nerves and dropped a bunt that became a base hit and brought in Hamilton from third. The Bostons added one more in the eighth to make it 6–2.

Just as Nichols had started an inning by singling in his previous at bat, Corbett's replacement, Arlie Pond, opened Baltimore's half of the eighth inning with a base hit. McGraw walked. Keeler then fouled off nine of Nick's pitches, according to *St. Louis Republic* correspondent Charles Dryden, but Nichols didn't succumb and Keeler finally flied out. Jennings followed by hitting the ball toward short and Pond ran into the ball, so he was declared out. It could have been a mistake, but he may have done it to prevent a likely double play. Either way, Kelley drew the second free pass of the inning to load the bases. That brought up Stenzel, who had homered memorably off of Nichols, and lethally, three months earlier. Stenzel lined one sharply toward left field, but, as Dryden described it, from his position at shortstop "the rubber-legged Long bounded high in the air and pulled the wanderer down."

Darkness started to become a concern as Baltimore faced its last chance. Doyle opened their ninth frame with a single up the middle. Heinie Reitz followed with a bloop single. As the pressure mounted on the field of play, the spectators surrounding it did what they could to pile on. "The din the crowd turned loose in an effort to stampede Nichols was something terrific," reported Dryden, "but the veteran kept his head where it belonged, and the bedlam passed by unheeded."[69] Wilbert Robinson then drove in Doyle with a single to left. It was now 6–3, and the tying run was at bat with nobody out. Joe Quinn was called on to pinch-hit for Pond and Nichols retired him, but the runners moved up. McGraw then followed with a hit that drove in Reitz to make it 6–4. Keeler didn't repeat his time-consuming at bat of the previous inning, instead swinging at a pitch from Nichols that was low and away. The runners were moving on what first seemed like a surefire hit, but Long grabbed Keeler's liner and easily doubled the runner off second to end the contest. It was Kid Nichols' 30th win of the season.

Baltimore bounced back the next day with a 6–3 win at the expense of Beaneater starting pitcher Fred Klobedanz, and Boston's lead was again reduced to half a game. Sunday was an open date, so when the deciding game of the series was played on Monday, September 27, it was Nichols versus Corbett yet again. The crowd was about twice the size as Friday's, in the range of 25,000 to 29,000.

Boston batted first, and leadoff man Billy Hamilton started the action with a single. He eventually scored on a groundout by cleanup hitter Chick Stahl. Corbett was forced to make a very early exit because of this play, since Stahl whacked the ball right back at the pitcher's bare hand and the Oriole ace was unable to continue with severely jammed fingers. Another successful starter, Jerry Nops, took over the pitching chores. Boston ended up with just the one run; Baltimore countered with two in its half of the first. In the top of the second Boston quickly tied the score and had runners on second and third. Nichols smashed a pitch to right field and drove in both runners. His 4–2 lead didn't last long at all.

Kid Nichols was hit hard by Baltimore in the bottom of the second, and an error contributed to the damage. He ultimately gave up three runs and now it was Baltimore 5, Boston 4. He erased a potential run, however, when Kelley tried to squeeze with McGraw on third only to have Nichols pounce on the bunt and throw the runner out at home.

Oriole manager Ned Hanlon quickly decided he had seen enough of Nops, and at the next opportunity sent Saturday's winning pitcher, Bill Hoffer, up as a pinch hitter. Hoffer also took over the pitching for Baltimore. Boston then tied it in their half of the third. The Beaneaters scored three more in the fourth, and Kid Nichols had a little breathing room with a lead of 8–5. Nichols had actually kept the home team from scoring in the third and fourth innings, and added zeroes in the fifth and sixth as well. Hoffer blanked Boston in the fifth and sixth as well. For all practical purposes, the seventh inning decided it. Boston exploded for nine runs, and though Nichols allowed three in the bottom half, Baltimore was now losing 17–8. Doc Amole became the fourth Oriole pitcher in the eighth inning. It was very rare in 1897 for any major league team to use that many hurlers in a game.

There'd be a little more scoring, and Kid Nichols ultimately won his second game of the series in Baltimore by a score of 19–10. Though this game clearly wasn't anything like the many low-hit gems Nichols pitched throughout the season, half of Baltimore's runs came after the game was out of reach, and box scores indicated that only four or five of the ten runs were earned. That same day, Western Union delivered a message from Boston to Mr. C.A. Nichols at the Eutaw House in Baltimore which read, "Hurrah for Boston accept my congratulations on your work," and which was signed by Alice and Jennie. Kid Nichols' great-grandchildren still have this telegram.

The Bostons left for Brooklyn with a game-and-a-half lead and three contests still to play. Baltimore had four remaining games at home against Washington. The Beaneaters hadn't clinched the pennant, but the reaction across the baseball world the next day was no less intense. For example, beneath its main headline the *Cleveland Plain Dealer* added, "Little Hope Left for Baltimore."[70] The *Washington Times* ran a story about the large and fervent crowd that surrounded its own bulletin board awaiting the posting of updates via telegraph.[71] The *New York Times* was quick to note that "this all-important series" made both teams "extremely nervous" at the beginning of the third game, as reflected by sloppy play by both defenses, but the paper didn't dwell on that. "Nothing can detract from the glory of the victory," it concluded.[72]

The *St. Louis Republic* quickly declared Boston the pennant winners, and editorialized at length. "The victory of the Bean Eaters was a popular one, not only in this city, but in every town in the country outside of Baltimore," the paper wrote. "When it is understood that among ball players it is considered the hardest feat in the world for teams to win from Baltimore on those grounds and with that crowd, the full significance and great merit of Boston's victory will become apparent." The *Republic* also commented about Kid Nichols specifically a few times. "Nichols' record in the series is a superb one. To win two games out of three from Baltimore on the latter's grounds before an intensely partisan crowd and from a team that has grown gray winning pennants hands down is surely one of the grandest achievements of modern baseball." The paper concluded that he was "entirely unconscious of his eminence as a pitcher, and correspondingly unassuming."[73]

One of the most forceful descriptions of Nichols' achievement appeared in a paper that no longer had a National League team of its own to cover, the *Providence Evening Telegraph*, which declared that in the series, "the imperturbable Nichols took upon his shoulders the herculean task of winning two games, and his indomitable pluck carried him through. If ever a ball player deserved to be raised upon a pedestal of honor that man is 'Charley' Nichols."[74]

Some merchants also demonstrated that they were inspired by this showdown, including one who immediately took out an ad in Washington that read:

Beaneaters Too Much for Orioles.

The Baltimore rooters had to take a back seat again yesterday, and great was the wrath thereat. Great was the wailing and gnashing of teeth, and many the potations that it took to soothe their feelings. Let us hope that they called for Tharp's Pure "Berkeley" Whisky, for it is a good and true comforter and leaves no bad after effects. $1 a quart at Jas. Tharp's, 812 F st.[75]

An ad on the front page of the *Boston Journal* on the day after the game also jumped on the Nichols bandwagon. It read:

PITCHER NICHOLS
OF THE BOSTONS

He's a dandy it would seem. So are nickels all and brasses, when they're polished with Putz Cream. Send four cents in stamps for trial sample of Putz Cream Metal Polish. Meyers' Putz Pomade Co., 285 Devonshire St., Boston, Mass.[76]

Boston and Baltimore both won on Wednesday, September 29, and it was looking even less likely that the Orioles would pull out a fourth straight championship. Baltimore fans were convinced more than ever of a league-wide conspiracy against them, but Kid Nichols could have pointed to the 12-run first inning he suffered against Brooklyn a week earlier as solid evidence to the contrary. Regardless, Baltimore needed to keep winning, but after the Beaneaters won again on the 30th, the Orioles failed to do likewise, and the outcome of the pennant race was written in stone. Boston wrapped up its season on October 2 and finished with a record of 93–39 versus 90–40 for Baltimore. The 1897 Beaneaters achieved the best record of the decade to that point.

"A great movie could be made about the 1897 pennant race," wrote Bill James in his *Historical Baseball Abstract* in 1988. "It's good versus evil, clean baseball versus Mugsy and assorted thugs — and good triumphs. It's so easy to root for Kid Nichols and Jimmy Collins and Herman Long and Hugh Duffy against McGraw and Jennings and Reitz."[77]

Kid Nichols finished twenty games over .500 with 31 wins versus 11 losses. Though Kid Nichols had won 30 games in 1896 and had an earned run average under 3.00, in 1897 he managed to improve in multiple categories, including wins, losses, saves, home runs given up, hit batsmen, walks, strikeouts, wild pitches, and even ERA. In recent years baseball statisticians have grafted new measures of effectiveness onto the careers of 19th century players, and a popular one is WHIP, the sum of Walks and Hits divided by Innings Pitched. In six of his first nine seasons Kid Nichols led NL pitchers in either WHIP or Strikeout-to-Walk Ratio (K/BB), and 1897 was the one year in which he ranked first in both categories.

When Gus Weyhing pitched his last game in 1896 he was the active major league hurler with the most career wins at the time, with 226. Prior to Kid Nichols' 28th birthday in 1897 he leapfrogged Gus, off of whom he had hit his first major league homer, and ended the season as the active pitcher with the most lifetime major league wins, at 245. It was a distinction he would retain during his remaining years with the Bostons.

Both on and off the field, Nichols might have been described as clean cut. Usually he was known for being clean shaven as well. Nichols rarely sported a mustache in his long life but he wore one in team and individual photographs from the 1897 season. In a radio interview during the summer of 1939 he explained that this was a fad among some of teammates, and that "we had an agreement that we wouldn't shave them until we won the pennant."[78]

Though the regular season was over, Boston and Baltimore were still obligated to play in the Temple Cup series, which proved to be "a bust from the word *go*," wrote baseball historian Jim Baker. "Boston and Baltimore fought a terrific battle in September of 1897, but if they immediately turn around and play again, what are they playing for? The Temple Cup undercut the pennant race and was anticlimactic in itself."[79]

The first game of this postseason series took place in Boston on October 4, two days after the season ended. Kid Nichols started for the pennant-winning team and Nops for the runner-up. Every Beaneater was cheered loudly by the crowd of 9,000 to 10,000 when he came to be the bat, the biggest ovations going to Hugh Duffy and Nichols. The *Journal* complained that "the fielding of the Bostons was the slowest exhibition they have shown this year. Duffy was about the only man who was awake and many 'Orioles' are credited with hits which the Boston fielders would have gathered in had they played with their usual dash."[80] Nevertheless, after six innings the champs led the Orioles 11–10. Kid Nichols managed not to issue any walks but his arm was spent, so he turned the game over to Ted Lewis. Baltimore scored two off of Lewis in his first inning but Boston responded with two, and the game ended as a 13–12 win for the Beaneaters.

The Beaneaters lost the next two days, but before the teams left town to continue the series, a formal victory party was held in their honor at Faneuil Hall. At the head of the main table was Congressman John Fitzgerald, grandfather of future President John Fitzgerald Kennedy. According to the *Advertiser*, Mayor Josiah Quincy III "presented each member of the team with a diamond-set watch charm suitably engraved." The newspaper was equally impressed with some of the non-politicians in attendance. "Another pleasant feature was the presence of the Baltimore players, and the heartiness with which the members of the two teams fraternized showed how little the hard feelings of the diamond endure when the game is over."[81]

Before reaching Maryland, the two teams played exhibition games in Worcester and Springfield, Massachusetts, and Baltimore won those. It won the next two games at home as well, and claimed the Temple Cup. There may have been fewer than 1,000 spectators for the final game. A month later the NL announced that the Temple Cup series would cease to exist.

Kid Nichols didn't play again after leaving the first game's slugfest with a thin lead. At the conclusion of the series, the *Globe* said that Nick, Jennie and Alice were heading to Detroit for an annual visit to Charlie Bennett.[82] They arrived in Kansas City on October 21. He spoke at length that day with a *Star* reporter about the Temple Cup and the decisive series in Baltimore toward the end of September.

"The opening game did not hurt me apparently but towards the close of the third game I felt myself growing weak, and after it was all over my pitching arm was so sore I could scarcely raise it," Nichols revealed. "It needed rest, and after a fruitless attempt to pitch in one of the Temple cup series, I decided that it would not be wise to strain my arm further."[83]

Nichols was rested enough to pitch on the 24th when the Orioles and a traveling team of "All-Americas" stopped in Kansas City. Among Nichols' teammates were fellow Beaneaters Collins and Stahl, plus former Boston captain Billy Nash. Others included Pat Tebeau from the Cleveland club at first base and Tim Donahue from Chicago as the catcher. About 7,000 fans gave Nichols "a grand ovation" when he appeared. Baltimore led 4–1 after four innings but Nichols improved over the next four innings, and going into the ninth the All-Americas trailed by only one run, 5–4. Baltimore made it 6–4 after an error by Nash and that was the final score.[84] Only half of Baltimore's runs were earned, so Nichols may have judged correctly about the extent of his recuperation.

His brothers Will and George bowled on a team with the Kling brothers that autumn, but their kid brother's name didn't turn up in newspaper listings. A brief newspaper item in early December offered a likely explanation: "'Kid' Nichols, of Boston, complains of a strained arm, and will treat it sympathetically this winter." With 7,000 fellow Kansas City residents having watched the game against Baltimore, it's quite possible that Kid Nichols felt compelled to go the distance, and overdid it in the process.

In early December, *Sporting Life* reported that Nichols was "negotiating with the management of Princeton College Athletic Association to train the Princeton Base Ball team next year."[85] The school had approached him twice before, in 1893 and 1895. The third time didn't pan out, either. Starting in November, Kid Nichols had a far more important matter to concentrate on, and from December to February the last thing on his mind would be baseball.

Just before Christmas, the three Nichols brothers were sued for $10,000 in circuit court over an incident at their laundry. "Among the employees of the laundry was Edna E. Weaver, who was engaged on November 4 last in attending to a tablecloth as it traveled through a patent steam propelled ironing machine, commonly known as a mangler," reported the *Kansas City Journal.* "In this instance the machine was well named, for it not only mangled the tablecloth, but it fastened onto the young woman's right hand and drew her arm into its rapidly revolving rollers, with the result, she declares, that she will be a cripple for life."[86] The sum that the plaintiff sought was equal to more than four years of Kid Nichols' major league salary. The ultimate outcome of this legal action was not announced.

Kid Nichols' spirits may have been uplifted momentarily when Frank Selee stopped in Kansas City on December 29 on his way east from the Pacific coast. Selee utilized the *Star* to take issue with recent comments about Nichols by Tom Brown, the 16-year major league outfielder then with Washington. "Brown is reported as saying that Nichols's success is rather due to his condition than to headwork," the *Star* summarized. "Frank says that Brown must be talking through his hat if he thinks the 'Kid' is not on to the angles of the game, as Nichols is probably the closest student of National league batsmen's strength and weakness of any pitcher in the business, and that with each recurring season his value as a pitcher increases. While it is true that few pitchers keep in the same condition as Nichols, there are fewer that excel him as a pitcher."[87]

January would be a very sorrowful month for the entire Nichols family, because Christina Nichols died of cancer on January 29. The Rev. J.M. Boon of the Brooklyn Avenue M.E. Church officiated during the funeral, and she was buried at Elmwood Cemetery. How much or how long their mother suffered wasn't revealed.

Weeks later, the *Boston Globe* noted that Kid Nichols still "feels keenly the death of his mother at Kansas City," but that his team anticipated their "old reliable" joining them for spring training on March 21 in Greensboro, North Carolina.[88] After a difficult winter, few could blame Kid Nichols for wanting to escape before then. His sister and brother-in-law, Jessie and Sam Nickells, provided a pleasant opportunity for him to do so.

Sam's work had prompted them to move to New Orleans, so they invited him down for Mardi Gras, which that year was held on February 23. Jessie, Sam and their three children were living at Berlin (now General Pershing Street) and Saratoga, in the Milan neighborhood. The *Daily Picayune* publicized his arrival, and noted that he'd only remain a few days. A day later, the paper announced that on the 27th he had been lined up to pitch for the city's pennant-winning amateur team, the Levys, against another local club. It rained on the day of the game, but local sports fans were told that Nichols would square off in a game between the same teams on March 6. He didn't show up, and the paper was unsure of whether he had cancelled or whether the local team had overstated his interest.[89]

Around this time, one of Tom Brown's Washington teammates had kinder things to say about Nichols. "The eight-year record of Charley Nichols as a League pitcher proves to me that he is the king of all twirlers and for all time since base ball became a professional sport," declared pitcher Win Mercer, who had won more than twenty games in each of the two previous seasons. "Of course, Amos Rusie is a master of the downshoot and of thunderbolt, wind-splitting speed, but Amos has had at least one off season, and I regard him as a trifle shy of the class that Nichols occupies all by himself."[90] If Kid Nichols read this comment, it probably cheered him more than his own manager's praise at the end of December.

When spring training was starting, Tim Murnane of the *Globe* checked into the whereabouts of Boston's ace, and learned that "Nichols has refused to sign a Boston contract at the salary offered him by Soden, Conant and Billings. As the schedule calls for 22 more games than last season Nichols figures it out that he will have more work than usual the coming year. Nichols' demand is for a salary of $3000, $500 more than he received last season. The Kansas City man says that he cannot last forever, and must get the money out of the game in the next two or three years. Nichols has written one of the Boston players from Kansas City saying that he has no intention of joining the Boston club until the club has come to his terms. The players to a man sympathize with the pitcher who has done so much for Boston."[91]

The *Kansas City Journal* also believed that Kid Nichols was back in town at this time, but in fact he, Jennie and Alice were still in New Orleans. A humanitarian relief ship was expected to leave New Orleans for Cuba by the end of March, and the *Kansas City Star* announced that the ship would "have several Kansas Cityans on the dock to bid her Godspeed," with Kid Nichols among them. With the Spanish-American War looming, the *Star* publicized a local charitable drive for Cuba's "Reconcentrados," enemies of Spain who had been forced into history's first concentration camps. Kansas City residents responded in droves, with Nick's old Kansas Citys bowling team helped the cause by staging a benefit tournament. Sizable donations were also collected in cities like Omaha and sent to the New Orleans docks.[92]

On the 30th, the *St. Louis Republic* reported that Kid Nichols was still holding out, and took that opportunity to quote an anonymous source at length about the situation:

> "The Boston Club management is the stingiest outfit in the League," said a ball player. "The idea of refusing Charlie Nichols' request for a $600 raise is about the cheapest move that ever happened. Nichols has won two pennants for the Boston Club, and enabled Soden and his associates to make more money than any set of club owners in the League. Their profits last year were in the neighborhood of $125,000. In the face of this fact, however, they refuse to allow Nichols one cent of an increase and insist that he sign for the limit—$2,400. Rusie, Meekin, Mercer and other crack twirlers are known to be getting more than the limit. The Washington Club makes no secret of the fact that Mercer is getting $3,000. That is what makes Nichols sore. He knows that if Mercer is worth that money he is entitled to it. I hope he holds out for it. Without him the Boston team will not finish one, two, six."[93]

The next day, Tim Murnane gave a little hope to readers from Greensboro: "Manager Selee wrote Nichols last week saying that he would like to have him with the boys even though he had not come to terms yet. Today Selee received a long friendly letter from Nichols, in which he said the weather had been perfect at New Orleans for the last month." On April 9 Nichols reported to the team, which was then in Virginia, along with Jennie and Alice. "He says he is in perfect condition, as he has practiced every day since Feb. 22 at New Orleans, and gained 12 pounds while doing the work," Murnane wrote. "He weighed today 179 and says he could pitch a full league game tomorrow. Nichols has not put his name to a Boston contract, but will go along with the club and fix his business with Pres Soden later on."[94]

6

Twirling Twilight?

Kid Nichols had to scramble to get in a little game action prior to the 1898 regular season, which he did with three innings on April 13 in an exhibition game at Allentown, Pennsylvania, and some work the next day in Reading. The regular-season schedule had been extended by about three weeks to 154 games, a length that was to become commonplace around 1904 and remained the standard until the current 162-game season was adopted in the early 1960s. Thus, the 1898 season wouldn't wrap up until mid–October. Fred Klobedanz was Boston's Opening Day pitcher in New York on the 15th, but drizzle and mud caused the game to be called in the third inning.

That gave Kid Nichols an opportunity to earn the team's first decision of the season on April 16, in front of 15,000 New York fans. He responded by shutting out the Giants during the first six innings. The Beaneaters had only scored once themselves during those frames, and New York took a 2–1 lead in the seventh. A controversial decision on a tag of Billy Hamilton at third base in Boston's half of the eighth inning kept a threat alive, opening the door for three runs. The fans screamed, flung cushions onto the field, and eventually rioted, though the turmoil didn't reach a crescendo until Kid Nichols left with a 4–2 win. Nichols had scattered five hits. When head umpire Pop Snyder left the field, it had to be via police escort.

Nichols faced the same team on the 19th, this time in front of polite Boston fans, and surrendered two runs on four hits in the first inning. He gave the Giants no more hits after that, and eventually won 14–2, with Ted Lewis taking over for the last six outs. The *Boston Journal* decided to call their ace "King" Nichols, and noted that he took a later train than his teammates because he was conferring with Arthur Soden. "It is evident that he and Soden came to an agreement on the salary question," the *Journal* concluded.[1] A rumor circulated shortly thereafter that the franchise's owners gave in to Kid Nichols' demands and signed him at a $3,000 salary.[2]

On April 22, 1898, Cincinnati's Ted Breitenstein and Baltimore's James Jay Hughes both hurled no-hitters, the latter having victimized the Beaneaters.

More than a century would pass before this would occur again, when Dave Stewart and Fernando Valenzuela both tossed such gems on June 29, 1990. Kid Nichols pitched in Baltimore the next day, and led 2–1 in the ninth inning when he got into trouble.

With runners on base, Mugsy McGraw was an on-field coach for Baltimore, in foul territory, "and then began an infraction of the coaching rules which calls for the severest criticism," wrote the *Journal.* "McGraw began to run up and down the lines. He was checked by the umpires for a moment, but ... several times went even to the diamond to rattle Nichols. Umpire Connolly called to Nichols to stop pitching, but 'Nick' pegged away without stopping for a moment and Connolly's voice was lost in the pandemonium. The umpire claims, with some reason, that he was forced back to his position so long as the ball was in play. A moment later 'Joe' Kelley lined out a beautifully placed hit to right, and Quinn and O'Brien came home with the winning runs. The Bostons were beaten fairly and squarely, but had not the game been marred by the scene of that last inning the defeat could be accepted with much greater equanimity. Capt. Duffy would have done well to have come in and demanded the enforcement of the rules."[3]

Kid Nichols started May on a strong note, shutting out the Senators in Washington on the 2nd, 7–0. He allowed seven hits and a walk, and none of those runners reached third base. On May 9, Boston played the first of four against Baltimore at home, and the series began with Nichols matched against Hughes. The Oriole hurler came close to another no-hitter, but the Beaneaters did manage two hits. Nichols didn't pitch well, and trailed 6–0 after seven innings. Baltimore then scored seven in the eighth to put the game firmly out of reach, and it ended 13–0. At that point, Boston's record stood at 9–9 and they were in sixth place. The defending champions then rebounded by winning the next two against Baltimore. On May 12, Nichols had a rematch against Hughes.

Boston led 4–2 after four innings but Baltimore scored two more to tie it in the fifth. The Beaneaters broke the tie in the next inning, and exploded for seven runs in the eighth on their way to a 15–6 win. Boston next swept three from St. Louis, and their six straight wins elevated them to third place. They then played three games in Cincinnati against the first-place Reds. In the first game, Jake Beckley had a hand in all of Cincinnati's runs when he tripled three times off of Nichols, scoring each time. It still ended up being a close game, but Nichols was on the short end of a 5–4 outcome. His teammates rebounded to win the next two from the Reds.

Boston had an off day on May 22 and then played the next three days in St. Louis. Nichols didn't pitch again until the 25th, so before then he traveled over to Kansas City to see his brother Will, who was very sick.[4] Nick won his game in St. Louis, 8–4, and he got to watch the Browns turn a triple play.

Boston overtook Cleveland to claim second place on June 1 and after the middle of the month the Beaneaters would stay there, behind Cincinnati, almost without exception for the next two months.

On June 25 Kid Nichols pitched one of his best but also one of his most nerve-wracking games. Boston hosted Pittsburgh, whose pitcher that day was Billy Rhines. Rhines had won 28 games in 1890 as a rookie for Cincinnati, one more than fellow rookie Kid Nichols, and he had won 21 for the Reds in 1897. Nichols and Rhines became locked in a scoreless due for seven innings. Boston finally scored a run in the eighth on a walk and an error, and added one more in the ninth to make Nichols a 2–0 winner. Nichols gave up six hits and walked one.

Kid Nichols and Boston traveled to Cleveland for a game on June 29 against the "Indians," as the Spiders were sometimes called around this time. The Beaneaters outhit the home team 10 to 6 but Nichols ended up on the wrong end of a 3–0 shutout.

His disappointment changed to sorrow on July 1 when he learned that back in Kansas City his brother Will had died at home. He had suffered from Bright's disease, a condition of the kidneys, for more than a year, but had only given up his duties as general manager of the Nichols Brothers' laundry three months earlier. Will was 40 years old and left a widow and two young children.[5]

Kid Nichols soldiered on, and figured in both of Boston's victories on Independence Day in New York. In the first game against the Giants, Beaneater pitcher Vic Willis was breezing along with a 6–1 lead going into the New York half of the eighth inning, when he suddenly got into trouble. He gave up a double to the opposing pitcher, Si Seymour, and then a single that drove in a run. Willis followed those two hits with a walk and hit batsman to load the bases, all with no outs. Captain Duffy summoned Nichols into the game even though the Kid had had no time to warm up. He allowed the three runners already on base to score but wiggled out of the inning with Boston still on top, 6–5. That's how it ended, and Nichols garnered a save. Nick then started the second game, opposite Amos Rusie, and hit a triple on his way to beating the Giants 10–3, in a contest shortened to six innings by rain.

The first-place Reds hosted Boston on August 6 and won, 2–1, then hosted Baltimore the next day and beat them as well, 4–1. Boston then played three more in Cincinnati starting on the 9th. That day Kid Nichols was the starting pitcher for the Beaneaters. He gave up five hits all day and walked none. The Reds didn't advance any runner to second base, and Boston had a relatively easy 8–0 win. With Nichols' shutout, the Beaneaters caught fire, going on to win the final two games in Cincinnati and more.

Boston continued winning until they took first place from the Reds on the 16th, and when they hosted the Reds on the 20th, they had won ten in a row. A crowd of 10,000 turned out to watch the top two pennant contenders do battle. Willis started for the Beaneaters and had a slim 2–0 lead after three innings. He held the Reds scoreless for the first seven innings but Boston wasn't able to increase its lead.

In the eighth inning, Willis loaded the bases with only one out, but escaped with only one Red runner crossing the plate. The score was still 2–1 when Willis walked the first Cincinnati batter of the ninth inning. The next Red bunted, and Willis decided to try for the runner heading toward second base. The pitcher threw poorly, but Herman Long made an impressive catch, getting spiked in the process. With one out, Willis issued a second walk, and Captain Duffy had seen enough. He summoned Kid Nichols, who induced a force play at second. That left the tying runner on third and the lead run on first with two outs. Up came the man batting just before cleanup hitter Jake Beckley, shortstop Tommy Corcoran, who was in the middle of an eighteen-year major league career. Corcoran sent a ball softly to Nichols' left, and Beaneater second baseman Bobby Lowe charged toward it. So, too, did Marty Bergen, who was playing first base for Boston that day. It was Lowe who fielded the ball, but there was no way that Bergen could double back to his post, so it fell to Kid Nichols to race toward the vacated bag and take the throw from Lowe in time to beat Corcoran in a bang-bang play. It was a solid save for Nichols.

Nick had been one of the biggest contributors to the 11-game winning streak, while also enjoying a personal winning streak. "Billy Hamilton and Charlie Nichols, both of whom have warm spots in every one of the local fans' hearts, are just about the whole thing with the Bostons these days. 'Nick' has won eight straight games now," reported the *Kansas City Journal* on August 19.[6] It was a nice way to honor the memory of his brother Will, who had been part of the family's championship amateur team back in 1885.

But Kid Nichols wasn't done contributing that month. By August 29 Boston had slipped back into a tie for first with the Reds, and Baltimore was only a game behind the two of them. Nichols responded on the road by limiting Pittsburgh to four hits on his way to an 8–0 shutout, his second whitewashing of the month.

Nevertheless, Boston spent the first six days of September back in second place, with the Reds again atop the standings. Boston regained first place on September 7 and led the Reds by one game when Kid Nichols faced the Giants and Amos Rusie in Boston on the 9th. Rusie gave up three runs in the first but that would be the extent of Boston's offensive production. Luckily for them, none of New York's seven hits contributed to any scoring off Nichols, and the Kid prevailed with a 3–0 shutout, his third over the span of a single month. Boston continued to lead in the standings as September ended, but it still had games to play during the first half of October.

Boston hosted Baltimore for two important games, on October 3 and 4. Baltimore had jumped over Cincinnati into second place by then, and at the start of October the Orioles trailed the Beaneaters by three-and-a-half games. Boston won the first match, 13–10. Kid Nichols faced Doc McJames in the second game.

Neither pitcher allowed a run in the first five innings. In the sixth, each team scored once, and neither team could break the tie in the seventh. That set up to the decisive eighth inning. According to the *Boston Daily Advertiser*, "Jennings allowed himself to be hit by a slow pitch to start the eighth. A wild pitch gave him second, and Kelly's [sic] safe bunt put him on third. He scored on McGann's long fly." Kid Nichols hadn't been pummeled, but he now trailed 2–1.

Boston had Fred Tenney on second and Herman Long on first in the bottom of the eighth, but with two outs. It looked like Jimmy Collins had ended the threat when he grounded toward first base and McJames ran over to take the throw, but the pitcher "ingloriously muffed" it, and Tenney raced around from second to score "by a daring slide." Though the game was only tied, the error "broke McJames' heart, and a wild pitch let Long in with the winning run. Collins scored a moment later on Stahl's hit, and at the end of the inning [umpire John] Gaffney called the game on account of darkness." Kid Nichols had come away with a 4–2 win, after limiting Baltimore to six hits. "Boston made the league championship practically sure," the *Advertiser* deduced, and they were proven correct.[7] The second victory over Baltimore gave Boston a five-and-a-half game lead, and the Beaneaters only played seven more games. What's more, Nichols' win happened to fall right in the middle of nine consecutive triumphs for his team, and they clinched the pennant before that streak ended.

Kid Nichols had a different kind of contribution to make to his team the day before their final game, in Baltimore. On the evening of October 14 he joined Long, Klobedanz, Duffy and Collins at Wilbert Robinson and Mugsy McGraw's bowling alleys, to challenge Jennings, Keeler, Kelley, McGraw, and Clarke. Nichols bowled the highest game and had the best three-game total, which enabled the Beaneater quintet to best the Orioles. The next day Nichols entered the baseball game during the seventh inning in relief of Klobedanz and locked down a 10–8 win over Baltimore. In light of the chilly weather that day, *Journal* reporter Walter Barnes remarked that nearby him "some one suggested that, as the Bostons had beaten the Baltimores at base ball and bowling they ought to try them at foot ball."[8] The Bostons finished with a record of 102–47, six games ahead of the second-place Orioles. It was their second consecutive pennant, and fifth in eight years.

For the *New Bill James Historical Baseball Abstract*, the author developed a formula for determining the effect that a player had on individual pennant races throughout his career. He wasn't surprised to find that Babe Ruth ranked first, and Mickey Mantle a close second. "There were six pennant races that clearly would have ended differently if Babe Ruth had been merely a good player, and Mickey Mantle also had a decisive impact on six," James wrote. "However, while you might have guessed the numbers one and two men on the list, the number three man was a pitcher who had a decisive impact on the pennant races of 1891, 1892, 1893, 1897, and 1898, Kid Nichols. Nichols won [at least] 30 games in all of those seasons — for teams that won pennants by relatively thin margins."[9]

For the third year in a row, Kid Nichols led National League pitchers in wins. His win-loss record of 31–12 only differed from his 1897 record by that twelfth loss, but in many respects his performance in 1898 was better. His 42 starts represented an increase of two, and he completed 40, an increase of three. His five shutouts were three more than the previous year. Also, he lowered his earned run average for the fourth consecutive year. At 2.13 it was the best of his career to that point, and more than 1.5 runs below the NL average. Most impressively, Kid Nichols had won 30 or more games for the seventh time in eight seasons. His total of seven 30-win seasons is still the major league record, one that is widely considered to be unbreakable.

As the Western League season was winding down, the occasion of the Kansas City Blues winning the pennant moved the *Kansas City Journal* to mention one of that team's biggest fans, Kid Nichols' father Robert. "This man probably has not missed half a dozen games this season, and always occupied the same seat in the front row," the paper noted. Poignantly, the man who had lost his wife and a son that year was described as "an old man with the weight of years upon his shoulders."[10] When the National League season ended a few weeks later, Robert Nichols received more unwelcome news when his pitching Kid decided to winter in Boston.[11]

As was common for the team, immediately after the season the Bostons played a few exhibition games, including one in Bridgeport, Connecticut, on October 17 during which Kid Nichols was one of three Beaneater pitchers in a losing cause. One event in Boston intended to honor the team was held at Music Hall, while another was staged at the Tremont Theater on November 7. "A handsome blue silk pennant was presented to the players of the Boston Base Ball Club by Mr. De Wolf Hopper at the Tremont Theater last night at the conclusion of the second act of 'The Charlatan,'" the *Journal* reported. Many of the Beaneaters had already left town for the offseason, but Selee, Duffy, Nichols and Klobedanz represented the squad in seats to the left of the stage. The three owners of the franchise were in the theater manager's box. "Selee accepted the pennant on behalf of the players, and complimented Mr. Hopper as a lover of honest and clean base ball," the *Journal* continued. "The pennant was lowered from the flies of the stage, and it stretched almost from wing to wing. Inscribed upon it in white letters were the words 'Champions, 1898.'" Hopper, who was most known for his recitations of "Casey at the Bat," ended the program by performing the famous poem.[12]

One night later, the Boston players turned the tables, to the surprise of baseball reporter Jacob Morse. "It is something unique indeed for a base ball club to give a dinner to the friends who have extended courtesies to them," he noted in *Sporting Life*. Foremost among the Beaneaters' guests were the men who had organized the recent event at Music Hall, and the baseball writers for the daily newspapers. At the center of the table was John Morrill of the *Globe*, and the team's three owners sat to one side. Selee was joined as host by Duffy, Klobedanz, Lewis, Long, and Nichols.[13]

On that same page, *Sporting Life* reprinted a *Washington Post* article in which Kid Nichols described his approach to conditioning. "Flannels, witch hazel, liniment, massage and all those quackeries never occurred to me," Nichols said. "If a pitcher is regular in his habits and his muscle and fibre and blood are healthy, there is no necessity of rubbing, bandaging and doctoring. This is my twelfth year as a pitcher, and I attribute the endurance of my arm to good health, regular exercise and total abstinence from intoxicating liquors." He had kept the promise that he made to his mother when entering pro ball, and validated his sister Sarah years of involvement in the temperance movement back in Madison. "Bowling during the winter is about the only exercise I stick to, though I play occasional games of hand ball," his commentary concluded.[14]

A week later, *Sporting Life* positive gushed about him: "Charles Nichols, of the Boston Club, must be accorded the title of the king pitcher of his day, and his record is unique. He has pitched nine consecutive years in the National League for Boston, and in only one year has he failed to secure a better percentage of victories than his club."[15] Such high praise for Nichols became increasingly common after the 1898 season. In fact, there were signs of a flood weeks before Boston clinched the pennant. For example, early in September *Sporting Life* had already declared that "Nichols, the superb, the star pitcher of the League, and the leading twirler of his decade, will rank in history with Keefe and Radbourne." Also, in mid–September, the *Kansas City Journal* was delighted to reprint a tribute to Nichols by the *Ohio State Journal*, which began,

"Kid Nichols is a monument. He's other things, too. But he's a living, breathing, effective argument to all ball players of what they might be if they took proper care of themselves." Around that time Cap Anson and "Father" Chadwick named three pitchers each to their idealized pennant winner for 1899, and Nichols was the only man on both lists.[16] This kind of commentary continued unabated until the eve of the next season, when the *Philadelphia Inquirer* called Kid Nichols "the greatest pitcher of them all."[17]

By early November, Kid Nichols had taken a job with the Continental Clothing House in Boston, focusing on the sale of the "Champion" overcoat. In November it was also announced that he had withdrawn from the Nichols Brothers laundry back in Kansas City.[18] Shortly before Christmas, Nick told the *Globe* that his time as a salesman was going well. "The Champion overcoat was a boom for me, as the customers called for *it* and my friends and the baseball public called for *me*," he said (emphasis added). The primary reason that a *Globe* reporter sought him out, however, was for his reactions to recent talk about the National League dropping four weaker franchises and returning to an eight-team organization. Nichols had plenty to say about that:

> It is the weak clubs that beat us. Against a strong club you go in with the idea that you have got to fight for the game, and you do, and win it. But against a weak club you do not begin to fight until it is too late.
>
> Then the game would benefit. Instead of a lot of weak clubs coming here, we should have the Baltimores, Clevelands, New Yorks and Cincinnatis here three trips instead of two. Then the game might get back to its old standard before the brotherhood.
>
> It would help the Bostons as against the Baltimores. Baltimore won her pennants by beating the weak clubs. With a league of eight strong clubs we would show them a thing or two about which is the stronger club.
>
> I hope they will bring this deal off. I should think they might. The 10-year agreement has only three years more to run, and then the small clubs will be thrown down hard.
>
> If I had one of them I would rather take what I could get and get out now into a smaller league than go on three years longer losing money, and then have nothing.
>
> With Boston, New York, Philadelphia and Washington the east would be well fixed. Washington is a good ball town and I believe it is more likely to stay in the big league than Brooklyn.
>
> Then in the west Chicago, Pittsburg, Cincinnati and St. Louis, with the Clevelands in the latter city, would make a strong western circuit.[19]

Kid Nichols would eventually get his wish, though circumstances in the near future would show him to be wrong about Brooklyn.

In early 1899, about a year after Kid Nichols' mother died, his family had a major health scare. "Charley Nichols had a very unpleasant experience last week in nursing his little daughter, Alice, who was prostrated with a severe attack of pneumonia," Jacob Morse related. "Happily the little one weathered the storm finely and is now all right."[20]

In January, shortly before Alice's health crisis, Kid Nichols had been mulling over an offer to coach the Trinity College (now Duke University) team in Durham, N.C., where the Beaneaters would do their spring training. The college bug seemed to be in his system more that winter than before, as indicated when he started practicing with Harvard players in January, as a result of his teammate Ted Lewis serving as the school's pitching coach.[21]

Then in early February Nichols accepted an offer from Amherst College in Massachusetts, less than 100 miles west of Boston. By the middle of the month he reported for duty, having made an initial three-week commitment. In the *Boston Globe*, Tim Murnane commented that Nick would show "the students a few points about the national game, batting and pitching in particular. This will be Nichols' first attempt at coaching a college team, and the chances are that he will take unusual interest in his work, as he always does. Nick can teach the college boys as well as any one in the art of pitching a ball, also fielding the position. The Amherst boys will find Nichols modest and earnest; the greatest all-round pitcher the game ever produced, and more intelligent than the average college graduate. There is nothing showy about Charley Nichols, but he fills the bill from subcellar to dome."[22]

The first three weeks of coaching must have gone well, because by the end of the month Nichols said he'd like to continue until at least April 1. However, Frank Selee was anxious to get every man on the team to North Carolina on March 21, since Boston was scheduled to begin the regular season on April 15. Within two weeks, Fred Tenney, who was coaching at Dartmouth, expressed a preference similar to Nichols, though Captain Duffy was apparently ready to end his coaching at Boston College whenever told to do so. When the club departed for Durham on the assigned day, it was announced that Nichols would stay at Amherst, Tenney at Dartmouth, and Lewis at Harvard. Also, new catcher Boileryard Clarke, previously an Oriole, would continue to coach at Princeton. On April 4 Kid Nichols headed to rendezvous with the Bostons in Norfolk, Virginia, and around that time signed a contract for the 1899 season. The *Baltimore Sun* said Nichols would "receive $3,000, the same salary as last year."[23]

On April 6 Kid Nichols pitched part of an exhibition game against the Washington Senators in Norfolk. Six days later Nichols also saw some action in a game against the University of Virginia in Charlottesville, and one day after that in a game at Lancaster, Pennsylvania, and then the Bostons spent the night in Philadelphia before Opening Day in Brooklyn on April 15. Nichols drew the assignment as starting pitcher, while for the Superbas it was Brickyard Kennedy. The turnout was in the range of 20,000 to 22,000 fans.

If Nichols hadn't been paying attention during his first inning of work, he might have assumed that his opposition was actually Baltimore. Ned Hanlon had left the Orioles to manage Brooklyn, and in short order Joe Kelley, and Willie Keeler and Hughie Jennings followed. Those three were at the top of Brooklyn's batting order that day. In their first plate appearances, they proved to be no threat.

Brooklyn produced two hits off of Nichols in the second inning, but he escaped the threat when the lead runner was thrown out at third on an attempted steal. The home team didn't get its next hit until the sixth, when Keeler tripled to the center field fence with two outs. Nichols then induced Jennings to ground out, stranding his teammate. The Superbas' fourth hit came in the eighth inning, and after a bunt they had a man on second with one out. Nichols then obtained popouts from Kennedy and Kelley to end that frame. The game remained scoreless after each team batted in the ninth. The same applied to the tenth inning. The Bostons finally scored the game's first run in the eleventh after an error by Jennings was followed by a triple off the bat of Chick Stahl. It then came down to the bottom of the eleventh.

"Nichols tightened his belt and put on some extra steam," reported the *New York Sun*. "Cassidy, who went to bat instead of Kennedy, hit to Lowe and was out. Collins gathered in Kelley's bounder, and Lowe did the same for Keeler. That settled it, and the crowd rushed onto the field to congratulate the victors and sympathize with the losers."[24] At that moment, Kid Nichols probably knew that he wasn't in Baltimore. In any case, he had started the season with a 4-hit, 1–0 shutout, having allowed no hits after the eighth inning. "I never saw Charley Nichols looking better, and the fact that he was applauded almost as heartily as any Brooklyn player when he came to the plate to bat shows how he is held in the good will of the public," commented John B. Foster, sports editor of the *New York Telegram*.[25]

"It was by all odds the greatest game of ball I ever saw at this season of the year," Hanlon told the *Baltimore Sun*. "I just looked at that man, Nichols, in amazement. After a few years in the league most pitchers do not get in their best form until the season is a few weeks old. Yet there was Nichols after eleven years of brilliant and hard pitching with more speed than ever I saw him have in the very first game of the season."[26]

After starting the season with three games in Brooklyn, the two teams met again in Boston on the 19th, the Beaneaters' only home game of the month. Despite the cold that day, the game drew 15,000 enthusiasts. The Opening Day pitchers faced one another again, and the result was another shutout. This time it only lasted nine innings because Boston scored early and totaled seven runs in all. Kid Nichols allowed five hits in his nine innings of work. Alas, his magic didn't continue in his next two starts, both in Philadelphia that same month. First was a 10–8 loss during which his team's six errors meant that only two of the winners' runs were earned. In the second confrontation, the Phillies turned eight hits into six runs while Boston was shut out. Thus, Kid Nichols entered May with a record of 2–2.

A photograph apparently taken in 1899 by Elmer Chickering of Boston, a noted photographer for such public figures as John Philip Sousa.

The Boston team as a whole didn't fare too well in April, and after being shut out again on May 1 in Baltimore, their win-loss record stood at 7–7 and they sat in seventh place in the 12-team league. Kid Nichols pitched there the next day. After giving up two runs in the first he led 5–2 by the end of the seventh, and ultimately won, 9–2. Boston would sustain a winning record over the remainder of the long season.

May 9 was an open date for the Beaneaters, so they enjoyed a little internal rivalry. The collegiate team that Ted Lewis had coached early in the year, Harvard, was hosting Amherst, the squad that Nichols had tutored. Each Beaneater pitcher advised his respective team but it was no contest, a 14–0 win for Harvard on a one-hitter. Other Beaneaters watched the game from the stands.

Kid Nichols had an unusual relief experience in St. Louis on May 22, in a game in which Charlie Hickman was Boston's starting pitcher. A seven-run inning for Boston gave Hickman a lead of 8–1 going into the bottom of the third inning, but he became very wild and walked two batters. Frank Selee decided to take no chances and put in Nichols, who allowed one runner to score but shut down the Perfectos for a 10–2 win. By the end of May the Bostons had climbed all the way to second place, behind Brooklyn.

On June 7, the Nichols family back in Kansas City had more worries. The *Kansas City Journal* reported that the "Nichols Bros.' laundry at Fifteenth and Brooklyn caught fire this morning at 2:40. The fire started in the cellar. The building above the laundry is divided into flats. The people were all awakened and gotten out of the building."[27] By this point, it isn't clear whether the business was still functioning at all. After so many setbacks it must have seemed as though the place was cursed.

A few thousand Chicagoans witnessed an amazing duel between Nichols and Clark Griffith on June 20. Boston scored a run in the top of the fourth, and Chicago tied it in the bottom half. In the process, one of the Orphans, Danny Green, drilled a base hit that struck Nichols and knocked him over. Nick continued pitching. Each pitcher then piled up scoreless inning after scoreless inning. Boston didn't produce a run in the top of the ninth, but the crowd came to life when Green led off the bottom of that frame with a walk. He was then bunted into scoring position, but Nichols retired the next two batters. The Orphans threatened again in the eleventh but a nice play by Lowe got Nichols out of that jam. In the top of the thirteenth inning the Beaneaters exploded for four runs and not long after the game ended, yielding a 5–1 triumph for Nichols. Over the thirteen innings he had allowed only seven hits.

It turned out that Nichols had injured his side during that game, probably on the line drive that ricocheted off of him, and it was still bothering him a week later. About a week later it was announced that he'd probably need at least a few days of rest. He showed during the second game of an Independence Day doubleheader in Baltimore that he wasn't his usual self. He gave up three runs in the first, and though he only allowed eight hits on the way to a respectable final score of 5–4, during that loss he issued seven bases on balls. That was almost one-tenth of his total walks for the season.

It wasn't too long before Nichols looked as though he was back to 100 percent. On July 14, he pitched at home against Pittsburgh, facing future Hall of Famer Jack Chesbro in only the second game of his career. Chesbro was masterful, at least when he was throwing to the plate. He allowed Boston only three hits, and none of those figured in any scoring against him. Chesbro's main problem was his own wild throw, which led to two runs. Another problem for Chesbro was that he was the only Pirate to get a hit. Nichols had a no-hitter until Chesbro singled with one out in the sixth. Nichols ended with a 2–0 one-hitter, with two walks.

Nevertheless, Washington manager Arthur Irwin suggested that something may have been bothering Kid Nichols long before his injury in Chicago toward the end of June. According to Irwin:

> It looks to me as though Kid Nichols is favoring his arm. You know that for years Nichols depended chiefly on his swift raise shoot. It was a peculiar ball, and looked easy to hit, but the batsmen were up against the trio of shells when they went after it. Nick seems to have lost control of that ball, or perhaps he has been pitching it so many years that it is beginning to tell on his arm, and that's why he is probably using a drop ball thrown at a medium rate of speed. It's odd to me that batsmen

> should find his drop easier to locate than his raise ball, but they are discovering it so often that Nick must return to his swift raise if he wants to get back to his old pitching form. He has changed his delivery altogether, with a view, no doubt, to relieving certain muscles in his arm on which a strain has been imposed by throwing the drop.[28]

One possibility, not raised by Irwin, was that Nichols had an inadequate spring training with the team because of staying at Amherst so long, but his astonishing shutouts to open the regular season argued against that theory.

Nichols had another very good outing in Boston on the 19th, against St. Louis. Not only did he demonstrate strong pitching, but he signaled that his batting was no longer affected by his injury in Chicago by homering over the left field fence in the fourth inning. The only run that Nichols allowed was in the sixth when Bergen dropped a good throw to the plate that would have otherwise resulted in an easy out. It ended up being an easy 8–1 victory.

Sitting directly behind home plate that day or the next, and possibly both, was a teenaged pitcher named Christy Mathewson. Weeks before his twentieth birthday he made his professional debut in Manchester, New Hampshire, on July 21, 1899, but stopped in Boston on his way there from his home in Pennsylvania. "I saw my first big league game in Boston back in 1899, when I paid 75 cents to see Kid Nichols pitch against Cy Young at the Old Walpole Street Grounds," Mathewson recalled more than two decades later upon being named president of Boston's NL franchise.[29] In fact, on the 19th, Nichols beat two other St. Louis pitchers, not Young. Young then edged Boston's Vic Willis on the 20th, 3–2. So perhaps Matty witnessed both games.

Nichols was in a reflective mood toward the end of July, and offered one of his longer endorsements of a wholesome lifestyle. "I never drink beer, whisky or chew tobacco," Nichols affirmed. "I scarcely know what intoxicating liquor tastes like. I have been pitching professional ball about eleven years. I can pitch a game every third day. And in a pinch can pitch every other day. Yes, I attribute my powers of endurance to my habits. However, I do not think it hurts a pitcher to take a glass of beer once, in a while."[30]

The Beaneaters were in St. Louis on August 1, and Kid Nichols became locked in a seesaw battle. Against Perfectos pitcher Willie Sudhoff, Nichols and the rest of the Bostons led 2–0 after six innings. St. Louis tied it in the seventh, Boston went ahead 3–2 in the eighth, and St. Louis tied it in the ninth. Both starters continued into the extra innings, though Sudhoff eventually gave way to Jack Powell. Each team scored one run in the tenth to make it 4–4, and up to that point it may have still been appropriate to consider it a pitchers' duel. It became something more than that in the twelfth, when each team scored three runs. Then neither scored in the thirteenth, nor did Boston in its half of the fourteenth. Powell led off the bottom half of that frame by blasting one over Billy Hamilton's head in deep center field. Not being a fast runner, Powell presumably would have stopped at third with a leadoff triple if Hamilton hadn't proceeded to boot the ball. It was scored as a same-ending homer, giving Nichols a fourteen-inning complete game loss, 8–7. His apparent recovery from the injury in June notwithstanding, at that point Nichols' win-loss record was an uncharacteristic 11–11. He wasn't a detriment, but he also wasn't an obvious asset.

The team as a whole did manage to do well anyway. Boston rarely slipped to third place at any point from June through August. On August 5 in Washington, Nichols impressed by issuing no walks to go along with five hits on his way to a 9–3 victory. He gave up three runs in just the first inning of a game at home against Cleveland on the 9th, but he shut them down after that and won, 6–3. That was Boston's seventh win in a row, and Nichols had helped them to move just one game behind first-place Brooklyn.

Boston then lost a doubleheader at home to Cincinnati at the worst possible time, but in their next game, during which the Beaneaters hit into a triple play, Nichols beat the Reds, 6–3, and kept them close to Brooklyn. A week later, on the 21st, Boston trailed the Superbas by three games when Nichols started at home against that team. He was roughed up for five runs in one inning and lost a tough one, 7–5.

In Cleveland on the 29th, Kid Nichols hurled a three-hitter and won comfortably, 9–1. On the whole, however, Boston struggled in early September, and on the 4th they dropped to third place in the NL standings behind Philadelphia. Kid Nichols pitched against first-place Brooklyn on the 8th and gave up five runs, not an impressive figure but also not insurmountable. Yet Boston only managed six hits off of Jay Hughes and never got a man to third base, so Nichols ended up on the wrong end of a 5–0 shutout. Boston would spend the rest of that month in third place.

Late in the month the *Boston Daily Advertiser* assessed some of the problems that individual Beaneaters were experiencing. For one, Kid Nichols and midseason acquisition Jouett Meekin were having "hard luck in the way of support" despite pitching good ball. The paper also noted that Marty Bergen had left the team without permission, and not for the first time. "These frequent absences without leave have not made the rest of the team feel any better, and it is better to get rid of a man whose actions demoralize. It is not dissipation that leads Martin to quit the team every now and then. There is no straighter player on the team from the standpoint of habits. He has too much of a nomadic disposition."[31] Bergen also had gone missing in October of 1897, but the regular season had already ended so that disappearance wasn't disruptive. The *Advertiser* didn't connect Bergen's absences to Nichols' strug-

Another photograph from 1899 by Chickering, this one signed by Nick for his grandson Harlan Everett, Jr.

gles, but the pitcher had always had a strong bond with his catchers dating back to Charlie Bennett.

Though the Beaneaters had spent most of September in third place they didn't throw in the towel, and instead they began their longest winning streak of the season on the 25th. A few games into the streak, on the 29th, Kid Nichols helped them sweep a doubleheader from the visiting Senators. After Washington tied the game 2–2 in the fourth inning, Nichols held the Senators scoreless until Boston could come up with two runs in the eighth. "Nichols pitched a splendid game throughout and broke his spell of hard luck," proclaimed Walter Barnes in the *Journal*, attributing the pitcher's mediocre results of late to mere misfortune, just as the *Advertiser* had.[32] Nichols contributed another win toward the end of the streak, this time at home on October 4 against New York. The Giants totaled ten hits but their runs mainly came in due to errors, and Boston won, 6–4. "Nichols pitched a splendid game and used more curves than is his habit," Barnes noted.[33] Whatever the reason, even in victory Kid Nichols didn't quite seem to be his usual self.

During the ten-game winning streak the Bostons jumped over second-pace Philadelphia, yet Brooklyn led Boston by eleven games at the start of the streak so it didn't even cut Brooklyn's lead in half. The Superbas clinched the pennant prior to Kid Nichols' start at home against Philadelphia, on October 13. Going into the contest, second place was on the line, because Boston only led the Phillies by a single game and had only one more game remaining. The starting pitcher for the Phillies was Wiley Piatt, whose 23 wins led his team that season.

Kid Nichols allowed a two-out single to Ed Delahanty in the first inning, but kept his opponents scoreless through the first five innings. The Phillies' best scoring chance during the first half of the game came in the fourth, when Monte Cross walked, Delahanty bunted him to second, and Marty Bergen's passed ball moved Cross to third base with one out. That brought up cleanup hitter Pearce Chiles, whom Nichols struck out. Next up was the dangerous Nap Lajoie. Nichols' first pitch was a strike. So was his second one. His third pitch was strike three, and Cross was stranded.

Piatt also wasn't scored upon during the first five innings, but with one out in the sixth, Bergen doubled, Boston's only extra-base hit among the five it would get that day. Nichols' out advanced him to third, and Billy Hamilton singled him home. That was the only run for either team over the first eight innings, and the only baserunners allowed by Nichols came when Delahanty singled in the first and Cross walked in the fourth.

Nichols tried to nail down a 1–0 shutout, but with one out in the ninth Elmer Flick singled. Cross hit into a force play, and now there were two out. That brought up Delahanty, who singled sharply and advanced Cross to third. Chiles was quickly down two strikes, though Delahanty stole second base in the process. A third time Chiles swung and missed a pitch from Nichols, but Bergen dropped the third strike. The Boston catcher recovered in time to fire accurately to first base and retire Chiles that way. Nichols was then able to celebrate a three-hit, 1–0 shutout. With that, Boston clinched second place.

"'Nick' received constant ovations, and if ever a pitcher merited them he did," noted Barnes in the *Journal*. "It was a pitcher's contest of the best type, and the honors were with Nichols, though his own game fielding contributed to this end. ... Twice he blocked terrific liners sufficiently to enable the infielders to put out the batsmen at first, but he had his old-time speed and control, and his pitching, when the 'Phillies' had their only two chances to score, was 'the limit.'"[34]

Boston finished with a record of 95–57, eight games behind first-place Brooklyn. When Brooklyn had clinched the pennant, Kid Nichols may have taken some solace in having shut them out in back-to-back games to start the season. Regarding his own performance, he may have taken some comfort from shutouts to start and finish his season, with a one-hitter squarely in the middle.

Compared to all of his previous win-loss records for Boston, Kid Nichols' 1899 season stood out like a sore thumb, at 21–19. Only in his rookie season had he lost that many games, and previously he had always won more than 25. Yet his 1899 earned run average of 2.99 was better than in three of his previous years, including the pennant-winning season of 1893 when he won 34 games. In addition, in 1899 he completed all of his starts, something he had only done previously in his rookie year and in 1895, while his four shutouts represented his second-best mark since 1892. Though his ERA was higher than in 1898, he gave some indications of better control by allowing far fewer wild pitches and hit batsmen, even adjusted for fewer innings pitched. Perhaps the Boston dailies were correct in late September to write off his win-loss record as simple misfortune.

Kid Nichols maintained a low profile during the early weeks of the off-season, with one exception coming at the end of October when he played in a game between two teams near Massachusetts' border with New Hampshire. He batted leadoff and pitched for Newburyport versus Amesbury. Helping the latter club was catcher Jack Ryan, who had spent three years with the Beaneaters in the middle of the decade. Nichols and Newburyport won, 10–3.

Around the middle of November, Kid Nichols received a telegram that his father had become very ill back in Kansas City. Charles and Jennie immediately headed west. Robert had been living with his youngest daughter, Dora, and the rest of the Northrop family at 3607 Thompson Avenue. Charles arrived on the morning of November 20, in time to be "at the bedside of his father at the time of his death," reported the *Kansas City Journal.* "He never missed a base ball game, and, rain or shine, he was to be found in the same seat at Exposition park," noted the *Kansas City World* on its front page on the day of his death. Back in Madison, Wisconsin, the *Wisconsin State Journal* printed a long obituary that same day on its front page. "The rise of his son in the base ball profession was a source of great pride to Mr. Nichols," added the *Kansas City Star*. He had died of old age at the age of eighty.[35]

Sporting Life announced this somber news to its readership on December 2, and noted that Kid Nichols would probably spend at least at week in Kansas City despite Alice being enrolled in school back in Boston. He ended up staying for at least two weeks. While in Kansas City, Nichols was asked how his pitching arm was. "Just as good as ever," Nick replied. "I had my share of hard luck, and I lost six games at a critical time, but I was not discouraged. I knew that I would come around all right."[36]

His father's death couldn't have come as much of a surprise to Kid Nichols, but the tremendous tragedy that rocked the Bostons and the entire baseball world early in 1900 was an earth-shattering shock, even given the warning signs. On January 19 in North Brookfield, Massachusetts, some 60 miles west of Boston, Martin Bergen murdered his wife and two children and then committed suicide in the same gruesome manner. "It is thought the action was due to insanity," claimed one account, which continues:

> The members of the Boston team tell many stories about his actions while on baseball trips, which illustrate Bergen's peculiar mental make-up. Charlie Nichols said recently that Bergen was the most difficult man to get along with that he had ever met. The great pitcher said that there were times when Bergen thought that everyone was conspiring against him, and would treat all the men with entire indifference, in spite of all that could be done to show him their good will.
>
> "On one occasion," said "Nick," "when we were in St. Louis, and Bergen had one of his freaks, 'Chick' Stahl came into the hotel and said, 'Good morning, Marty,' whereupon Bergen struck him in the face, knocking him down."[37]

Bergen, whom Kid Nichols had made a special trip to scout in the middle of the 1895 season at Kansas City, had played four years with Boston. He made his biggest contribution by far during the pennant-winning season of 1898, when he played 120 games and hit .280. In 1899 his playing time had dropped to 72 games and his average had fallen to .258. It all ended at the age of 28. Marty Bergen had caught 105 of Kid Nichols' starts, and only Charlie Bennett caught more, 124. Bergen's life ended up resembling Bennett's in a broad sense, swinging from triumph with the Beaneaters to terrible tragedy. The biggest differences were that Bergen's tragedy wasn't a freak accident, and that Bennett survived his.

It wasn't very many decades ago that fans would hear players mention a teammate with whom they usually roomed on road trips, so one might wonder whether Nichols ever roomed with Bergen. Nichols shed light on this topic many years later when he wrote, "I always roomed alone, never doubled up." That was in 1939 to Harlan Forker of Danville, Illinois, for an unpublished biographical project of Forker's. Kid Nichols' great-grandchildren have the typed interview responses that he prepared for Forker, probably with help from Nick's daughter Alice.

By coincidence, news about Nichols was announced on the same day that the Bergen story broke. Yale University had obtained a commitment from Nick to coach their team before the regular season. His focus would naturally be the pitchers, though he would also advise on batting and the game generally. He became the school's first professional coach since 1894, when Beaneater pitcher John Clarkson had handled those duties. Yale turned to a pro again after a poor record during the previous few seasons. By mid–March Nichols was joined by teammate Charlie Hickman, who would provide pointers about batting. Shortly thereafter, Nichols was afforded an opportunity to try another new sport, polo, and before the month was out, as Nichols was preparing to end his service at Yale, a New York paper drew attention to the fact that one player whom Nichols had worked with was "Cuhna [sic], the 300-pound Hawaiian who played on last year's freshman nine" and who also served as center on the varsity football team.[38] Albert Richard "Sonny" Cunha would go on to be a very well-known Hawaiian musician, politician and entrepreneur.

On March 30, Kid Nichols joined Frank Selee, Billy Hamilton and Fred Tenney as the first small batch of Beaneaters to depart for spring training, with stops in New York and Washington before reaching Greensboro, North Carolina. On the way down Nichols had an opportunity to see Yale open its season against New York University. As a result, during practice on April 2, Nichols "sported a Yale sweater on the field today, a gorgeous affair presented to him by Cuhna [sic], the giant Hawaiian," reported Walter Barnes of the *Boston Journal*, who was traveling with the Bostons.[39]

As Kid Nichols had favored a year earlier, the NL dumped four franchises and became an eight-team circuit. It also shortened its schedule. Boston hosted Philadelphia on Opening Day, April 19, then the two teams played in the City of Brotherly Love on the 20th. That first game dealt a frustrating relief loss to Nichols. Vic Willis had drawn the Opening Day assignment but left after four innings, behind 12–3. Jim Sullivan took over and held on until an improbable nine-run rally in the ninth that sent the game into extra innings. With the teams deadlocked at 17–17, Nichols entered the same in the tenth. He walked Delahanty and Lajoie, but when Nichols induced what appeared to be a double play ball from the next batter, Bobby Lowe misplayed it. Lowe was able to cut down Delahanty when he tried to score on the misplay, but the next batter doubled in both runners. Nichols was pinned with the loss in a 19–17 contest.

It was far more aggravating for Nichols the very next day in Philadelphia when he was the starting pitcher. He hurled into the eleventh inning of a 4–4 game, but ended with a 5–4 complete game loss when Lowe made two errors in the decisive frame. He then lost another one-run game in New York on the 24th, 4–3, despite the Beaneaters outhitting the Giants and drawing the game's only two walks.

In Brooklyn on the 28th Nichols had trouble in the first inning. Stahl and Hamilton did some poor fielding, but Barnes of the *Journal* observed that Nichols only "had good speed but no curves." The Superbas scored five, and Nick was relieved after that inning. After the game, Frank Selee announced "that the veteran pitcher would probably not pitch again for a week or ten days, as he has strained a ligament in the elbow."[40] Subsequent reports projected that he'd be sidelined for at least a month.

While he recuperated, Kid Nichols found various ways to occupy his time besides following the fates of his fellow Beaneaters. For example, he sat on the bench during a ballgame between Yale and Brown. He also submitted a photograph that he had taken of two youngsters dressed as Beaneaters to the *Globe* for publication, which the paper turned into a sketch (or "cut" as the paper termed it), printed with this caption: "Today's cut, 'Hink and Dink,' the youngest battery in the world, is copied from a snapshot taken of Francis Walsh, a young Kansas City lad who has been visiting Boston lately, and Freddy Wiltzinger, a youngster from Dorchester. Both are friends of Charley Nichols of the Boston baseball club, two of whose uniforms were remade to fit the young players."[41] And while the Beaneaters played in Chicago and St. Louis starting in mid–May, Nichols umpired a ballgame at the South End between teams of local actors and reporters. He also watched a game between Harvard and Princeton. It certainly didn't seem as though he just moped at home, which around this time was apparently 4 Massachusetts Avenue, according to that year's federal census.

With few exceptions, Boston was dead last in the eight-team NL from their second game through May 26. Kid Nichols was of course very disappointed not be well enough to join them for the 11-game road trip that began in Pittsburgh on May 12, but he also missed watching them lose the first seven games of the trip. He described his frustration to the *Boston Evening Record* in the midst of that losing streak, during which Herman Long was also disabled by a foot injury. "I hate to be inactive, anyway, but I could stand it a good deal better if the boys were winning," Nichols said. "When they are losing and I am not with them, it makes me feel like a fish out of water, and I want to be where I can help them."[42]

On May 20, the *Journal* provided a status report on Nichols's healing. "'Nick' thinks that his present trouble is due to rheumatism, as last Tuesday, when it was so warm, he worked hard at the South End Grounds, and his arm felt splendidly afterward," the paper reported. "On the colder days of the week, while he could do work without apparently doing any harm to his arm at the time, it pained him afterward."[43]

On May 26, their final game of the road trip, the Beaneaters began an eight-game winning streak, their longest of the year. Kid Nichols was presumably a fixture at the South End when the Bostons began a long home stand on May 30, and would have had the pleasure of watching constant winning. He even took Jennie at least once, on June 1.[44] Finally, on June 7, with Chicago in town, Nick was ready to return. He allowed two homers, a triple, and a double, but only two other hits and two walks, as a nine-run fifth gave Nichols a 13–4 victory in his return to action.

Then with Pittsburgh in town on June 13, he really wowed the locals. The Beaneaters could only manage a single run in the third inning off of Deacon Phillippe, who was on his way to a 20-win season, but Nichols made it hold up. He allowed just three hits and shut out the Pirates 1–0. The win moved Boston into third place, where they would usually remain throughout the rest of June. As was to be anticipated, his comeback wasn't without its bumps, as reflected in his start at home against Brooklyn on June 18.

Nichols was trailing 3–0 in the eighth inning when the Bostons rallied against Superbas starter Joe McGinnity to tie it. The game went eleven innings, and Nichols ended up losing another extra-inning complete game, this time 6–3. A day later, Brooklyn earned a four-game series sweep in Boston. On June 23, Nichols took a step backward at home against Philadelphia. He only allowed one run in the first five innings but ran into big trouble in the sixth. He was then removed, only the second time he hadn't completed a start that season — and something that wouldn't happen again that year. Boston eventually lost, 10–4. He ended the month with an exasperating one-run loss. He breezed through eight innings at Cincinnati with a three-hit shutout, though the Bostons had only scored two runs themselves off of Ted Breitenstein. Suddenly the Reds extracted two walks and slapped three more hits, and won the game, 3–2. In a doubleheader against Pittsburgh on Independence Day he lost another low-scoring game, this time 3–1.

Nichols had still found time to take in at least one more Yale game during June, before the school's season ended. As the school had hoped to do by bringing in a professional to coach, the team did reverse course and meet with success that season, winning 16 of 27 games. That 16–11 record is credited to Kid Nichols as manager in some record books.

When Nichols next started, in Boston on July 7, he faced red-hot Chicago, which had just beaten the Beaneaters twice as part of a nine-game winning streak. Unlike his previous few starts, Nichols received excellent offensive support and won 11–4. The victory was the 300th of his career, though with recordkeeping still erratic nobody was aware of the achievement at the time. Kid Nichols was the youngest pitcher ever to reach that major milestone; he wouldn't turn 31 until mid–September.

In St. Louis on July 11, the starting pitchers were Kid Nichols and Cy Young. For six innings in the drizzle, it was a scoreless duel. Boston plated a run when Fred Tenney homered in the seventh, and the Beaneaters picked up two more runs in the ninth. The stingy Nichols earned a two-hit, 3–0 shutout. Nichols seemed to be regaining his form, but by mid–July Boston had fallen back to seventh place. After a week near the bottom of the standings the team improved enough to return to fifth place and stay there.

During his career Kid Nichols occasionally had experience in major league games at a position other than pitcher, but in Cincinnati on August 6 he took on the new role of umpire. During the second game of a doubleheader, umpire Ed Swartwood started feeling increasingly ill, and at least he yielded to a pair of pitchers from the opposing teams, Nichols and Breitenstein, "who umpired without calling forth a murmur," according to the *Boston Globe*.[45] Boston was down 3–1 going into the final inning but rallied for three to win it.

At Chicago a week later, two pitchers were similarly pressed into service to help umpire Tim Hurst during the first game of a doubleheader. Joining Nichols this time was Chicago's Burt Cunningham, in a game which Boston lost 7–1. In the second game Hurst umpired solo for the entirety, and Nichols was tagged with a 6–4 loss, his fourth straight. Boston didn't play on three consecutive days shortly thereafter, so Nick wasn't afforded an opportunity to end that skid until August 23, which he did with a 6–3 win at home against first-place Brooklyn despite issuing seven walks. Boston then beat Brooklyn again the next day and gained a little pride in doing so by reaching the .500 mark, at 49–49, while at the same time moving out of the "second division" and into fourth place. He ended the month by beating the Giants in Boston, 5–3.

During September Nichols continued his uneven season. At home on September 17 he held Chicago scoreless for seven innings and in the end scattered five hits to win, 8–1. On the 21st he lost to the visiting Phillies, 10–6, when that team produced ten hits good for 25 total bases. Then against the Giants on the 25th, Nichols hurled a five-hit shutout, 8–0.

At least Nichols was able to usher in the final two weeks of the season with a well-pitched game, against the pennant winners in Brooklyn on October 1. In game one of a doubleheader, he was opposite Joe McGinnity, the future Hall of Famer whom he had battled for eleven innings on June 18. The two pitchers traded leads but after six the score was 3–2 in Boston's favor. In the bottom of the ninth, Joe Kelley tripled in a run off Nichols and represented the winning run with nobody out. The next batter was Lave Cross, who flied out to Boston left fielder Shad Barry but not deep enough for Kelley to test Barry's arm. Bill Dahlen was next up and he, too, flied to Barry in left. Kelley decided that he had to try and win it but Barry gunned him down with an accurate throw.

Thus, Nichols and McGinnity again went into extra innings. Neither team scored in the tenth, but the Beaneaters scored in the eleventh. In the bottom of the inning Wee Willie Keeler singled off of Nichols, but the Kid retired Jimmy Sheckard and Joe Kelley to end a 4–3, eleven-inning marathon. Before the second game the Bostons' record stood at 65–63, but the team would only win one more game that month to finish at 66–72, the first losing record of Kid Nichols' major league career. Boston ended up in fourth place out of eight teams.

After a decade of nothing but winning records, Kid Nichols ended 1900 at 13–16. During his first nine years he had started at least 40 games each season, but his total in 1899 had slipped to 37. In 1900, however, his injury limited him to only 27 starts. His earned run average of 3.07 was nonetheless better than that of three previous seasons. He also threw four shutouts, matching his 1899 total. Perhaps the most notable difference was that his strikeout total dropped considerably, from 108 to 53.

Kid Nichols had a very quiet offseason until mid–February, when he started coaching players at Brown University in Rhode Island, his third different collegiate coaching assignment in as many years. Not quite a month into his coaching stint at Brown, Nichols made news on several other fronts. The *Boston Globe* reported that on March 11 he signed a contract for the 1901 season, and that he was even "given a liberal increase in salary by Pres Soden." The paper didn't define what Soden considered to be "liberal." It was reported elsewhere that Nichols had received several offers from franchises in the upstart American League but had turned them all down. At this time the *St. Louis Republic* chose to declare that "Nichols is without doubt the greatest pitcher that ever stepped into a box." If this endorsement ever got back to him, he would have appreciated this willingness to overlook the mediocrity of his two prior seasons and instead survey his entire career.[46]

Around this time, Kid Nichols offered his comments about some rule changes, insights that may be of interest to today's fans who fret that games take too long:

> This rule about pitchers not being allowed to limber after a batter has taken his place is all wrong. Just as soon as the side in the field is retired the next man up at the bat will make a sprint for the batter's box and the pitcher won't have a chance to warm up at all. If he throws to an outfielder it will be called a ball, and even if all nine fielders are not in their places he will be prevented from exercising, as there is a rule saying that there shall be no practice on the field between innings. No matter how lively a pitcher's arm may be he doesn't rest. Under this new rule he will be obliged to deliver one or two slow ones to the batter before he cares to put them in fast, and thus he may throw away two chances to have strikes called.

> I find no fault with the rule saying that a ball must be delivered within twenty seconds. I am satisfied, too, with having foul balls called strikes under some circumstances. It makes it easier for the pitchers. It will be hard on the catchers to make them stand at the plate all the time. More catchers will be needed, and they will have to play at intervals instead of one man working several days in succession.[47]

Nichols followed up on some of these points a short while later, and addressed the length of games specifically. "Persons do not object to seeing games two hours long, provided there is closeness and excitement," he said. "If a game is dull, they do not care for it whether it lasts two hours or only one hour and a half. Our game with New York the other day lasted one hour and twenty-eight minutes. That was too short."[48]

As he was in a coaching mood, advice from Kid Nichols appeared in the *Boston Post* on March 24 under his own byline. It read in part:

> I believe in massaging, and advocated it so much to the Boston Club that last year, they applied it to us. If the arm is massaged immediately after pitching a game it's the best thing in the world for it. After pitching a game a man ought not to touch a ball on the following day, but take the next practice two days later.
>
> Si Seymour, who was with New York last year, has wonderful curves and plenty of speed, but as he lacked control he failed to win his games. However, a man can't depend entirely on a straight ball, so that he must be able to control the curve balls as well.
>
> If you start off pitching a straight ball, you should change and put the curve over. You want to make the first ball pitched a strike, and then you have the batter at a disadvantage.
>
> The ambition of young pitchers is to strike a man out. They think that the more they retire in this manner the better ball they are pitching. They say, "If I put the ball over he'll hit it," and then they throw high and wild. The point is to deliver a ball over the plate and make the batter hit, but use every means of offering him a tough proposition by using a high neck, close or low ball according to the circumstances.
>
> Many a pitcher uses an elaborate swing [i.e., windup], and I have been asked repeatedly to adopt one, but have persistently refused. I don't approve of it because it interferes with the control of the ball, and the one using it has to master two deliveries, since a swing is out of the question when one of the bases is occupied.[49]

Nichols' straight forward delivery led baseball historian Bill Felber to write, "It is impossible, of course, to precisely quantify why Nichols proved so durable a pitcher. But let us not lightly dismiss his own view that his simple overhand motion had much to do with it. The motion Nichols describes is today considered the least stressful pitching motion on elbow and shoulder ligaments, tendons and muscles."

"Unless we make Nichols out to be a freak of nature, or unless we categorize opposing hitters as incompetents, the most logical solution is that his motion minimized the actual physical strains imposed on the act of throwing a baseball in ways that are largely forgotten today," Felber concluded.[50] In his book on the 1897 pennant race, Felber offered Roy Oswalt as a modern version of Nichols.[51]

While Nichols was composing his treatise for the next generation of pitchers, there was word that he had a living legacy. Denver's Western League team had signed a pitcher called "Kid Nichols II," who was described as being a cousin of the real deal.[52] This was little-known Al Nichols, whose professional career was very short and minimally documented. There was a pitcher named Nichols in Kansas City amateur circles from 1896 to 1900, and his name was reportedly Al, but on those few occasions when Kid Nichols' extended family was mentioned in newspapers, the focus was on nieces and nephews, not aunts, uncles, or cousins. The Kansas City amateur named Nichols was sometimes a teammate of Johnny Kling and his brothers, who were known to be friends of the Nichols brothers, so the amateur Nichols of the 1890s certainly could have been from the same family tree. On the other hand, Denver's Nichols may simply have been trying to ride on the coattails of Kid Nichols I.

There was also an out-and-out imposter who appeared in Pittsburgh on the eve of the season. "A gang of Chicago burglars, headed by a man supposed to be 'Kid' Nichols, shot and killed two men here, and in turn one of the gang was wounded, while the others, two men and two women, were captured," reported newspapers across the country. "The man supposed to be 'Kid' Nichols gave the name of Robert Wilcox. His wife, Jennie, confessed they had all recently come from Chicago." No information was provided about how long this thug may have been trying to pass himself off as the noted ballplayer, nor whether he had much success persuading anyone of his claim.[53]

The real Kid Nichols had witnesses to verify an alibi if anyone tried to tease him about this. He had left Brown on March 30, and at the Beaneaters' spring training in Norfolk, Virginia, he managed one team during an intrasquad game on April 4. He and Frank Selee spent Easter Sunday, the 7th, in nearby Old Point Comfort, where the Kid had a chance to catch up with some of his Yale friends from the previous preseason. On the 9th he was one of three Beaneater pitchers to combine for a shutout against the Norfolk team, and during the Bostons' slow return home he pitched three shutout innings against a team in Worcester, Massachusetts, on the 15th.

In Boston on Opening Day, April 19, Kid Nichols drew the starting assignment against New York, with low mercury readings on the thermometers. "Nichols was in great form, considering the weather," reported Walter Barnes for the *Boston Journal.* "He had good speed and worked in benders

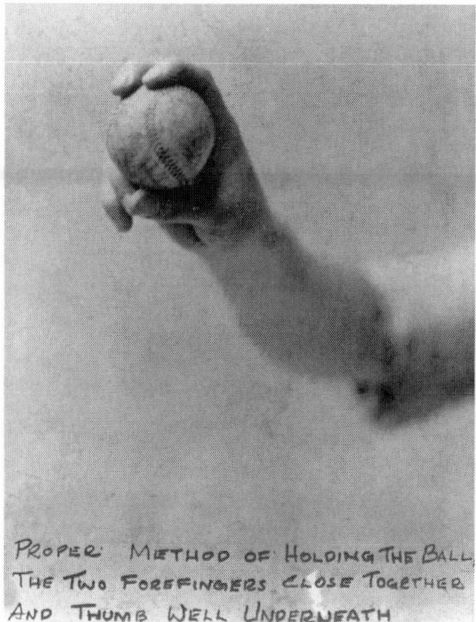

A set of seven undated photographs, a few of which have been widely circulated. The handwritten captions were likely added by Kid Nichols himself.

and his newly-acquired slow ball with great effectiveness. Five scattered hits was the best the 'Giants' could do against him, and if it had not been 'Nick's' own error, not a man would have reached third base."[54] In the end, he had a 7–0 shutout.

Unfortunately, Nichols then suffered a seven-game losing streak that lasted through May and into June. One painful loss came at home on May 3 against young Christy Mathewson and New York. Nichols struck out seven Giants and gave eight of them hits, while Mathewson struck out only three Beaneaters but held them to four hits. Misjudgments by Boston left fielder Shad Barry were responsible for both of New

York's runs, though they were scored as earned, and Nichols lost, 2–1. That was the same result when the two pitchers met in New York on June 1. This time, Nichols limited his foes to four hits while Mathewson allowed five. The first of New York's tallies came when Fred Tenney committed an error at first base on a potential inning-ending double play, so that run was unearned. This isn't to say that all of Nick's losses during the streak were by a whisker; for a counterexample, he was clobbered by Pittsburgh 11–1 on May 25.

In the middle of this streak, Kid Nichols was featured prominently in large ads, taking up nearly one-quarter of a page, in at least one of Boston's dailies. These ads for the Standard Clothing Company, at 395 Washington St. ("Opposite Franklin St."), featured sketches of and endorsements by three NL players and two AL players. The AL testimonials were from Buck Freeman and Chick Stahl. Featured first among the three Beaneaters, along with Captain Herman Long and Fred Tenney, was Kid Nichols ("Charlie" in the ad), labeled "The King of Pitchers." Two days after his Opening Day shutout in New York, he was apparently still in that city, and decided that he couldn't wait to contact the store until he was back in Boston. He wrote, "Will be in after another of your Oswego Serge Suits when I get home. They beat any suit I ever had for the money. Yours truly, Chas. Nichols." In the ad's largest lettering, it was explained that such a suit was priced at $15.00.[55]

As his losing streak grew longer, on June 12 in Cincinnati Nick caught a break. Starting for the Reds was Noodles Hahn (and his catcher was Bill Bergen, Marty's brother). The Reds had a 6–4 lead when the Beaneaters' rookie outfielder, Fred Crolius, came to bat with a man on base. That's when some poor planning by the men in charge of Cincinnati's ballpark figured most prominently in the game. As the *Journal* described the scene, in left field was a "junk shop" where a new grandstand was under construction. "Crolius caught a low ball with a long swing and sent a screeching grounder past third into left," the *Journal* reported. "It bounded against the lumber pile and under some timber, and before it could be found, Grosart [sic], who was on the bags, and Crolius had scored, and the score was a tie."[56] Nick and Hahn then pitched scoreless baseball until the game was called as a 6–6 tie after the 12th.

Togie Pittinger was the starting pitcher for Boston when they hosted Philadelphia on June 17, but when the score reached 4–4 after two innings, Nichols went in for a long relief outing. Boston was down 7–5 after the fifth but then Nichols settled down for four scoreless innings. Boston tied it in the bottom of the ninth, and the game went into the tenth. Philadelphia scored a run in its half, but in the bottom of the tenth the Beaneaters rallied to win it with three singles and then, with two outs, a game-ending double by Nick himself. With his losing streak over, Nichols would win two for every game he lost.

On June 22 he won his start at home versus Pittsburgh the hard way. In the second inning he singled in Boston's first run. In the fourth inning he singled in their next run. In the sixth inning he then doubled in two more, and ultimately accounted for all four of his team's runs in a 4–2 triumph. That victory completed an eight-game winning streak for the Bostons, which, due to doubleheaders, Nick had also started with his win five days earlier. At the end of this brief but successful stretch, the Beaneaters had progressed from a losing record to 23 wins and 20 losses, good enough for fourth place.

It was presumably his offensive spurt that earned Kid Nichols a start in left field when his team hosted St. Louis on the 27th. He responded in the field with four putouts and no errors. At the plate, Nichols contributed a run-scoring double during an early rally. As Boston's starting pitcher, Pittinger led 5–4 going into the top of the ninth but then surrendered the tying and lead runs. In the bottom of the ninth, the first two Bostons made easy outs. That brought up their eighth-place hitter, Kid Nichols. "Then, to the unbounded joy of all, Charley Nichols whacked a home run over the left field fence," exclaimed the *Journal*. This came off of Jack Harper, who was the third of four Cardinal pitchers that day.

Bill Dinneen entered the game to take over for Pittinger, instead of Nichols himself, and that decision paid off handsomely. Otto Krueger had already tripled home a run in the tenth on a ball that got by Nichols, and next up was the Cardinals catcher. "'Artie' Nichols flew out to his namesake 'Charley' in left field and Kruger [sic] started for the plate, but as soon as the ball was caught 'Charley' showed his outfielding worth by making a dead straight throw into Kittredge's mitt and Oom Paul was out by a yard before he reached the goal," said the *Journal*.[57] Boston managed to tie the game again in the bottom of the tenth and to win it with one out in the twelfth, 8–7.

For a game in Cincinnati against Noodles Hahn, Kid Nichols was the second man in Boston's batting order, at first base. He had one of the Beaneaters' five hits that day and the only one for extra bases, a home run in a 4–1 loss. Two days later in a midseason status report for the *Journal*, Walter Barnes wrote:

> Tenney left Boston on the sick list, but that wonderful fellow, "Charley" Nichols, who has suddenly bloomed into an all-round player, has jumped into the breach and performed so creditably, especially at the bat, that he is the talk of the base ball world today. Talk about his being "all in!" Why his nick-name, "Kid," fits him more than ever. May the good work go on! The "fans" the country over rejoice in "Nick's" success.[58]

In a game at St. Louis on July 19 he provided more evidence of just how versatile he had become late in his Boston career when he was pressed into service for some umpiring, for the third time in his career. Boston lost 8–1;

in fact, they lost two of the three games in which Nick umpired. This time he made amends as the Beaneaters starting pitcher the next day, and won, 10–2.

Nichols closed out July on the 29th in New York against his newest nemesis, Christy Mathewson. This one wasn't quite as low-scoring as Matty's prior pair of 2–1 victories at Nick's expense. Boston led 2–0 after it batted in the fourth but the Giants tied the score in the bottom half of that frame. New York took a 3–2 lead in the seventh but Boston promptly tied it. Each team then scored a run in the ninth to make it 4–4. In the top of the tenth, the first two Beaneaters flied out to left but then the next two singled off of Matty. Herman Long then doubled in one of the runners, and Boston ended the inning with a 5–4 lead. After Nichols got the second out George Van Haltren, who was on first, stole second to put the tying run in scoring position. Van Haltren took a long lead off of second and tried to steal third, and the throw to Bobby Lowe there was in time, but it was unclear whether he held onto the ball long enough. The game was officially over, but the field didn't clear until after a heated argument in which several New York players took part.

In August, Kid Nichols and Christy Mathewson would have three more showdowns as starting pitchers, but first they faced each other in a game at the start of the month when Nichols entered a 5–5 game in relief of Dinneen, who had gone six innings opposite Matty. Nick ended up losing, 9–8. Before Nichols and Mathewson squared off again, Nick was bested by young Colt Duggleby of the Phillies in Boston on the 8th. In the immediate wake of defeats by such youngsters, the *Philadelphia Inquirer* referred to Boston's veteran pitcher in a headline as "Pop" Nichols.[59]

New York hosted the next meeting between Nichols and Mathewson on the 13th. It was as much of a gem as Matty's two early-season wins. Neither pitcher was scored upon for the first nine innings. In the tenth, however, Nichols contributed a timely single to what became a three-run rally, and won 3–0. Matty had given up seven hits and Nick five.

After a doubleheader intervened, just two days later Matty and Nick were the starting pitchers again, in the nightcap of another doubleheader. Boston scored a run off Matty in the ninth to tie it at 5–5 and this time the game was called a tie after eleven innings due to darkness. When the two teams began a series in Boston on the 19th, the result was a relatively easy win for Nichols, 11–6, as New York did most of its scoring after the game was out of reach.

Highlights were plentiful for Kid Nichols during September. At home against St Louis on the 5th, his teammates rallied for four runs in the bottom of the ninth to transform a defeat into a 6–5 win. On the 9th the Reds visited, and Nick's own two–RBI triple was a key blow in a 5–3 victory for him. While pitching a good game after the Giants had come to town on the 14th, he hit a two-run homer off Bill Phyle on his way to a 9–2 win, during which he held New York to six hits. Nick had hit one homer a month from June through September. The one off of Phyle was the sixteenth and final home run of Nick's major league career.

The Beaneaters split a doubleheader in New York on September 16, but the whereabouts of two players not in their lineup was revealed the next day by a *Boston Globe* reporter, probably Tim Murnane. "Herman Long and Charley Nichols enjoyed the game yesterday at the American grounds," the paper noted in passing. The AL didn't have a franchise in New York in 1901, so this must've meant that Nick and Herman were back in Boston. The Boston Americans split a doubleheader with Washington that day, so the comment that they enjoyed "the" game was probably the paper's way of saying they enjoyed the action in general. In the first game, Cy Young entered as a reliever in the seventh inning and pitched shutout ball until his team broke the tie with two outs in the bottom of the tenth.

Nichols and Long left to join their NL teammates in Chicago that night, and on the 20th the Kid's counterpart was Jock Menefee, in the first game of a doubleheader. Chicago scored once in the fourth inning and the game remained 1–0 until the eighth. Nick singled to left to start that frame for the Bostons, one of his two hits during the game. Another hit moved him to second, and two errors brought him home to tie the game. Neither team scored in the ninth, but the Beaneaters had two men cross the plate in the tenth. Other than a scratch single, the Orphans didn't do much off of Nick in the bottom of the tenth, and he had a 3–1 win, with only five hits allowed.

On September 24 in St. Louis, Nick found himself matched against Michael Joyce O'Neill, who went by Michael Joyce during 1901. After six innings, the game was knotted at 3–3. Zeroes then accumulated on the scoreboard through the tenth inning. Bobby Lowe singled home a run in the tenth, and Nichols soon claimed victory in an 11-inning three-hitter, 4–3. But Nichols would top that performance as the season drew to a close.

In the meantime, Nichols played CF and batted eighth in a 2–1 loss to St. Louis on September 25. That same day, word circulated that Frank Selee was going to be replaced by Al Buckenberger for the 1902 season, a rumor that turned out to be accurate. Herman Long and Bobby Lowe had been Nichols' teammates during his entire major league career up to that point, and the other fixture had been his manager.

The month's pinnacle for Kid Nichols came on September 27, in the second game of a doubleheader at Cincinnati, which the *Boston Globe* described as the "play-off" of the 12-inning tie back in June. Nichols pitched scoreless ball against two Reds pitchers, and Boston's lone run, in the eighth, came on a dropped fly ball. The game was called due to darkness after the eighth inning. Nick had only allowed one walk and two hits. Perhaps this was Kid Nichols' way of paying tribute to the only manager he had known since Omaha in 1889. The *Globe* discussed the fate of the longtime Boston pitcher in its account of the game. "There is a very heavy-scented rumor going the rounds that Charley Nichols is thinking seriously of accepting a good offer from the new St. Louis club of the American league," the paper revealed. "Nick will no doubt give his old club a chance to bid for his services."[60]

Kid Nichols lost 8–4 in Pittsburgh on October 2, though he tripled in one run and then scored himself. Three days later, Boston finished its 1901 season in fifth place out of eight teams, with a record of 69–69. Pittsburgh won the pennant.

Kid Nichols finished with a win-loss record of 19–16. He started 34 games, seven more than during the previous season, but the second-lowest total of his years with Boston. His earned run average of 3.22 was better than three prior seasons, including his 3.52 mark of the 1893 pennant-winning year, but it had increased for four seasons in a row since his low of 2.13 in 1898. Other positives were hurling four shutouts for the third straight season, lowering his homers yielded by three despite pitching 90 more innings than the year before, and, most encouragingly, seeing his strikeouts skyrocket. He fanned 143 batters in 1901 compared to 53 the previous year, marking his highest total since 148 in 1895, a year in which he made nine more starts. At the end of the season his batting average stood at .282, and he had accumulated eight doubles, seven triples and four homers.

A few days after the regular season ended, the Beaneaters played an exhibition game against the Torrington team at Winsted, Connecticut, and was defeated 5–1 thanks to Nichols and Kittridge playing with Torrington. The next day, October 10, Nichols was preparing to play shortstop in a game in Webster, Massachusetts, but he was struck by a batted ball and had his nose broken.[61] "I was practicing in the outfield," he recalled in the handwritten autobiographical document from around 1949. "A batted ball hit a stone and bounced up and hit me on the nose, breaking it."

Nichols apparently recuperated for a couple of weeks back in Boston, but by the end of October he, Jennie and Alice were in Kansas City to visit relatives. Though he had lost his parents and a brother in recent years, his brother George and sisters Sarah and Dora still lived there. In addition, his half-brother John moved to Kansas City from Madison around this time. Kid Nichols was expected to stay in Kansas City for a month or so.[62] He was still there a month later when the *St. Louis Republic* reported that he had received an offer to coach at Brown University again in the spring of 1902. Nick, however, expressed a preference for coaching at Harvard so he could be in Boston. Yet whether he would play for Boston was also up in the air because he was still unsigned for 1902. By now the Nichols family was expected to stay in Kansas City until shortly after the holidays.[63]

On December 4, a surprising rebellion took place in the Western League that shook up baseball from Kansas City to Denver. Led by the St. Joseph franchise, league president Thomas J. Hickey was deposed and George Tebeau was stripped of his Denver and Kansas City franchises. The Kansas City franchise was to be awarded to Kid Nichols and Jimmy Manning.

Nichols confirmed his interest immediately, and elaborated the next day:

> I am not under contract with the Boston team, and there is no way to hold on to me if I choose to leave. I prefer getting the matter pleasantly straightened out and will work along that line. I expect to have no trouble in getting Boston's consent.
>
> I am pleased with the plans for the Western league, and my local friends have been offering congratulations all day. It does me good to know I have so many friends who want to see me back with the Kansas City team, and I expect to do everything in the world to please them if I take the team.[64]

On December 12, Kid Nichols arrived in New York to meet with the owners of the Beaneaters about obtaining his release. He issued a statement then as well:

> I have a splendid opportunity in Kansas City, and I believe that I would be very foolish not to accept it, yet I do not want to leave Boston except in a manner perfectly satisfactory to the owners of the team, who have always treated me with consideration. I have laid the facts before them and tomorrow they will decide whether I can sever my relation with the club. I am sure the matter will be adjusted satisfactorily.[65]

The headline in the *Kansas City Star* the next day said it all: "Nichols Got His Release." Arthur Soden granted it on the condition that if his venture in Kansas City proved unsuccessful, his first call would be to the Beaneaters. After Nick emerged from their final meeting, he spoke to the press again:

> I can now take up the duties of half-owner and manager of the Kansas City Western league team with the satisfaction that I have acted fairly towards everybody concerned. I did not wish to leave the Boston team on any but friendly terms and that was why I came on here and made a personal plea for my release. Now that I have secured it, I shall go about forming my team for next year. I shall remain in the East a few days to await the developments of the National league meeting and pick up a few players for the 1902 Blues that I have in mind.[66]

And with that, one of the most amazing twelve-year stretches for a pitcher with a single major league team in all of baseball history was over.

7

Curveballs and Comebacks

Kid Nichols' twelve years with Boston's National League franchise offered him much stability at the beginning of his marriage and during his young adulthood, even though there was occasional uncertainty about his contract, and his family relocated within Kansas City frequently. Over the next fifteen years he would experience very frequent change, partly because he couldn't quite find a suitable niche after leaving Boston, but also because he became restless if his talents weren't being put to full use. To his credit, Kid Nichols would prove to be enthusiastic, energetic, and rather fearless in new undertakings, as his new job in Kansas City demonstrated.

On December 17, 1901, Kid Nichols arrived back in Kansas City from his eventful trip to New York. Upon his return, he shed more light on his hectic month, including his new connection to Jim Whitfield, the veteran sports editor of the *Kansas City Star*, who had been named president of the Western League as part of the recent coup that toppled Thomas Hickey and George Tebeau:

> My conference with Messrs. Soden, Conant and Billings of the Boston club was entirely satisfactory, and their united action in consenting to my going into business in Kansas City for myself, under certain conditions, only bears out the confidence I had in their spirit of fairness. When I showed them that the chance offered me to become interested in the Kansas City club was not a wildcat scheme, but backed up by substantial financial support and the good will and assurances of patronage from the best people in this city, they not only agreed to let me go but wished me the greatest success in my new venture. I shall never forget their expression of interest in my future, especially as the severance of my relations with the Boston club leaves their pitching staff lamentably weak. However, Manager Al Buckenberger, who has succeeded Frank Selee in control of the Bostons, is of the opinion that he will be able to fill the breach and congratulated me on the prospects as a manager of the Kansas City Blues. He knows that Kansas City is a first class ball town and is confident that the Kansas City Blues, with Jimmie Manning and myself at the helm, will be a factor in the new Western league pennant race of 1902.
>
> As soon as I can complete my arrangements with Mr. Manning and line up the situation here I shall return East to wind up my affairs at Boston and go on a still

> hunt for Eastern talent that I expect to land within the next few weeks. I did some missionary work in that line while on the way to and from New York, and players and magnates alike congratulated me on my success on getting away from Boston in a manly manner, and promised to extend all the aid possible in assisting Manning and myself to get together a winning club. I shall endeavor to close up some little unfinished business I have in Boston and ship my household effects from that city here with all possible dispatch, in order that I can be at the Western league meeting which is to be held here the second Tuesday in January to complete the circuit, and arrange for the coming base ball season.
>
> The National League magnates, and particularly the Spalding wing of that body, which at present is evidently in the ascendancy, are heartily in accord with the National Association of Minor Leagues, and as President Ban Johnson of the American league had already declared that his organization would work in harmony with the Western, I should not be surprised if a general confederacy of all the base ball organizations, with the exception of the proposed Hickey association, would be effected before the season of 1902 is very far advanced.
>
> President Whitfield of the Western league was congratulated on all sides by magnates of all factions, and his Eastern newspaper friends and ball players generally on his return to active work in the base ball field, President Spalding, Al. Reach, A.F. Abell, Harry Von der Horst, James Hart, A.H. Soden and Frank De Haas Robison individually wished the Western league and himself a prosperous season in 1902.
>
> The National association leaders, Pat Powers, Tim Murnane, Jake Morse and others, also regard Whitfield as a most valuable ally in the West, and showed their appreciation of his base ball experience and ability by electing him as the successor of Hickey on the board of arbitration and on the committee on rules and contracts. ... Manning and I will begin at once looking upon a site, and by the time the weather moderates sufficiently to set the fans thinking about base ball they will find a handsome little plant somewhere in the vicinity of convenient car lines, ready for the season of 1902. We already have our eyes on one or two available sites, but will not be in any too big a hurry to decide as there is plenty of time.[1]

Nick was referring to the fact that George Tebeau, in response to the attempt by Western League rivals to strip him of the Kansas City club, had secured Kansas City's Exhibition Park for 1902. That was the first move in Tebeau's campaign of war on the Western League.

Tebeau planned to field a Kansas City entry in a brand new American Association, and running it for him would be Dale Gear, who had brief major league experience with Cleveland in the NL in 1896 and 1897 plus Washington in the AL in 1901. Early indications were that Gear did not share Tebeau's animosity for his rivals. "Nichols and Gear evidently do not believe in flying at each other's throats, even if both are candidates for the baseball patronage of Kansas City," observed the *St. Louis Republic* on December 19. "Both have always proved themselves gentlemen. Gear is a college-bred man and a capable lawyer and is one of the brainiest men among the ranks of the players. Nichols's long career on the diamond is an exceptionally clean one."

In his new role, Kid Nichols continued to set a wholesome example. The *Republic* observed: "At the recent meeting of the Western League at St. Joseph, Nichols sat at the banquet table with a number of the leading lights in Western baseball. When the wine was brought around, he turned his glass upside down and quietly asked for lithia water. The incident aroused comment, and in a neat little speech the famous Boston twirler quietly asserted that his ability to avoid dissipation [i.e., drunkenness] was in the main responsible for his being able to pitch winning ball year after year."[2]

At the end of the year Nick, Jennie and Alice headed back east. After stopping in Detroit to spend part of a day with Charlie Bennett, they reached Boston on New Year's Eve, where Nick looked for promising ballplayers to sign and tied up loose ends. Less than three weeks into 1902, his connection to another catcher made the news back in Kansas City. The *Star* reported that Johnny Kling had a strong interest in playing for Nichols, if only Kling could shake his contract with Chicago in the NL.[3] Kling, a former bowling teammate of Nick's brother George, had caught for Chicago in 1900 and 1901. As it turned out, Kling remained in Chicago in 1902 and ended up playing for someone who Kid Nichols knew exceptionally well, new Chicago manager Frank Selee.

Toward the end of January, somebody decided to see if they could ignite a fight between Gear and Nichols, despite the *St. Louis Republic*'s assessment of the two toward the end of the previous year. "Catcher Kittridge and Pitcher Nichols are outspoken in their denunciation of Dale Gear," read the brief account in the *St. Paul Globe*. It then attributed one negative remark about Gear to Kittridge, whose reason for weighing in was unclear. Nor was it clear why Nichols was being held responsible for comments made by his former catcher. A week later the *Globe* reported that Kittridge had again criticized Gear, and took a jab at the catcher in the process. The paper noted that Kittridge had been with Nichols when Nick signed a player to his Kansas City roster, which may have been an attempt by the *Globe* at guilt by association, because it again didn't document any actual hostility on Nichols' part.[4] In addition, Kittridge would have been an odd choice for a surrogate or mouthpiece, if such a scheme had even crossed Nick's mind.

In early February, as the Nichols family was preparing to head back to Kansas City, it was revealed that Detroit's AL club had offered him $5,000 per year for two years, but that he had declined because of the commitment he had made to Kansas City's Western League club. Upon his return to Kansas City, it was reported that only during his most recent trip had he officially obtained his conditional release from the Bostons. What's more, he was said to be owed a $600 bonus that the Boston owners were refusing to pay.

The Nichols family made stops in Syracuse, Buffalo and Chicago on their return home, before finally reaching home on February 15. Upon his arrival, the *Kansas City Star* said that his offer from Detroit had been $13,000 over two years. Instead of talking about that, or what he claimed the Beaneaters still owed him, Nichols' conversation with the paper focused on three players he had signed, along with his views about baseball's labor rules, particularly the reserve clause.[5]

Tebeau and Hickey's war heated up as springtime approached. In mid–March, the *Minneapolis Journal* printed a piece that clearly favored the American Association over the Western League, by suggesting that sportswriters in the East were out of touch and had underestimated the AA. At the end, however, it noted that Jim Whitfield had sued the *Kansas City Journal* for libel, seeking $25,000 in compensation for being called a "grafter." On this point, the Minneapolis paper offered a measured response. "While Whitfield has tied himself up with the wrong crowd, the sporting writers should remember that he has borne an honorable name in journalistic and sporting circles for a generation," it wrote. "There is enough material for attack on the Western league without resorting to personal abuse of President Whitfield."[6]

The *St. Louis Republic* also weighed in on the situation on the other side of Missouri. "Kansas City is rent in twain by the rival teams, and even the newspapers are exhibiting signs of partisanship," the paper observed. "By reading one publication, the general public arrives at the conclusion that the Western League is absorbing all the limelight, while a glance at another dispels this idea, and, after a perusal of the article, the reader comes to the conclusion that the American Association club already has the pennant won, and that the club headed by Jimmy Manning and Charley Nichols isn't really in existence."[7]

Early on April 7, James Whitfield took a gun and shot himself to death in his bedroom, while his wife and only child were elsewhere in their home. That day Nichols and his new club were in St. Louis, playing its first game of the spring against that city's NL club. The major leaguers clubbed the Kansas City team, 17–1. Two days later, Kid Nichols was an honorary pallbearer at Whitfield's funeral.

On April 12, Nichols' team made its home debut, at the new Sportsman's Park, on Indiana Avenue at 17th. It would later be called Recreation Park. They hosted the champions of the American League's first season, the Chicago White Sox. His team did a much better job than in St. Louis, and only lost 8–3. Nichols had pitched some in the prior game but wasn't in the lineup against Chicago. The two teams played again the next day and the score was almost the same; the main difference was that Nichols did share in the pitching.

Their regular season opened in Colorado Springs on April 23, with a 5–2 loss, but Nichols' team bounced right back the next day in a big way and won, 22–10. Kansas City rallied late to win the third game of the series,

7–6, and in the ninth inning Kid Nichols made his playing debut as a pinch hitter. The two clubs met for a fourth time on the 26th and this time Nichols was the starting pitcher. He won, 6–4.

The regular season home opener for Kid Nichols' Kansas City Blue Stockings was on May 2 against the Denver Grizzlies. Attendance was estimated at 2,000. Nichols team won 9–6, and if Nick was tempted to insert himself in the lineup at any point, he resisted the urge. The Blue Stockings were pounded in their second game, and that set the stage for Nichols to debut on the new Kansas City diamond on the 4th. In addition to the third game in Colorado Springs, Nick had won his other start, an eleven-inning game in Denver. The turnout was at least as big as two days earlier and Nick won again, this time 6–5.

With his team's record at 7–4, Manager Nichols' club was just behind first-place Omaha among the eight teams of the Western League. Omaha was led by a future Hall of Famer at pitcher, 25-year-old Mordecai Brown. Besides the two Colorado teams, the other four franchises were in Peoria, Des Moines, St. Joseph, and Milwaukee. Nick's old teammate Hugh Duffy starred for the latter club.

The home opener for Gear's American Association club was on May 10, so it was no surprise that his club drew 2,500 fans to Exhibition Park that day, while only 250 attended that day's game at Sportsman's Park. In his recent book on the war between the AA and the Western League, Dennis Pajot described the battle at the ticket windows between the two Kansas City clubs after Gear's club debuted:

> The next day, a Sunday, Gear's Association team drew 4,000, while Manning's Western team attracted 1,800. The weekday crowds showed similar or even bigger gaps in attendance, with the American Association team drawing 600, 1,000, 820 and 850 compared to the Western's 250, 200, 150 and 200. The following weekend Gear's team drew 750 on Saturday and 5,000 on Sunday, compared to 750 and 550, respectively, for Nichols' team. Things were not much different when the American Association club returned on Memorial Day to again go head to head with the Western League club. Facing the Milwaukee Brewers in a double-header, the Blues drew between 5,000 and 6,000 spectators, while the Western League club drew 3,400 against St. Joseph.[8]

In sum, early on Gear's AA club was outdrawing the Western League club nearly 3 to 1. The disparity would soon lessen considerably, to roughly 1.5 to 1, and in the end Gear's club would draw almost 88,000 in paid attendance, compared to 53,000 for the Manning-Nichols club. One factor was that all eight of the AA cities had been or would be major league cities, although briefly in some cases, whereas five of the Western League cities have never been home to a major league franchise. As *Sporting Life* observed that season, "As long as the Western League retains Des Moines, Peoria, St. Joseph and Colorado Springs in its circuit, it will be useless for the press agents of the league to talk of equality with the American Association."[9]

Despite the shaky fan support, the Blue Stockings continued to do well into June, but Manager Nichols decided to give pitcher Nichols more than two weeks off that month. When he put himself in the lineup on June 24 at home against Colorado Springs, he didn't regret it. He beat the Millionaires, 7–2, on a three-hitter. At that point, the Blue Stockings were in first place in the league, with a record of 36–20, ahead of Denver. Meanwhile Gear's team was 27–28 and in fifth place among the eight teams of the AA.

Nichols' managerial success, especially compared to Gear's, must have helped ease any agony that Nick felt about the interleague war its effect on attendance. No doubt it boosted his spirits even more when praise from an unlikely source appeared in the nationally read weekly, *Sporting Life*, in July. "I have always thought Nichols a greater pitcher than Clarkson. Nichols won at least four championships for the Boston nine by his good work on the plate," said one of the Beaneaters' owners, Bill Conant, at an NL meeting. "Nichols could be depended upon to pull a game out of the fire when it appeared to be lost," Conant continued. "We were sorry to see Nichols go, but glad if he could better himself."[10]

On July 19, Nichols would experience the first of two odd outcomes in consecutive months, both of them so unusual that a manager could go decades without ever experiencing either. His starting pitcher, young Norwood Gibson, had a no-hitter going through seven innings in Omaha, but only led 1–0. The Blue Stockings gave him a second run in the top of the eighth but then imploded on defense in the bottom half, and combined with some walks, Omaha took a 3–2 lead. Kansas City couldn't score in the ninth, and Gibson ended up with a no-hitter but also a loss.

In St. Joseph on August 25, Jake Weimer was Nichols' starting pitcher. After one-third of an inning he had walked two batters and squawked at the umpire so rigorously that he was ejected without finishing the frame. In came Gibson, who pitched over nine innings of no-hit ball. The Blue Stockings won a ten-inning no-hitter, 3–0.

By the end of August the *Kansas City Star* had taken to referring to the Blue Stockings as "the Nichols family," such as when it reported on a double-header sweep of Hugh Duffy's Milwaukee Creams, game one of which was a 6–2 win for pitcher Nichols. As a result, the Western League standings at the start of September had Milwaukee in first place with a record of 69–46 and a winning percentage of .595, Omaha and the dominant Mordecai Brown in second with 67–47 and .588, and Kansas City in third at 68–49 and .581.[11]

Of the three, Kansas City surged the most, though Denver came on strongly as well and made it a four-team bottleneck as the season finales approached on September 22. The Blue Stockings entered the final day needing to win to clinch the pennant. Kansas City played in the Mile High City, and Kid Nichols was scheduled to start as pitcher, but didn't. The *Star* explained why: "Nichols had intended to pitch the game, but during practice he was hit on the head by a bat which slipped out of Dud Risley's hands, and he was painfully injured. He did not deem it wise to go into the game, and sent Jake Weimer to the slab when play was called." It may be no coincidence that Risley wasn't to be found on the Kansas City roster the next season.[12]

In Nick's handwritten autobiographical document from around 1949, he described the aftermath of this accident (the only one of his career that he could recall, other than his broken nose in October of 1901):

> It cut a gash one and one half inches long. I was taken to a doctor's office to have it sewed up. I returned to the park with my head so swathed in bandages I was unable to wear my cap. In the 7th inning I had to go into the game (the umpire had ordered the pitcher out of the game on account of arguing). Our other pitcher was unable to pitch on account of the climate so there was nothing else to do but go in and finish the game.

Weimer left after six innings, having pitched well but trailing 2–1. The Blue Stockings scored two to take the lead in the seventh, and Nichols shut down Denver on two hits and a walk, striking out four in his three innings of work. Kansas City picked up two insurance runs in the ninth, and Nichols had saved the pennant in a 5–2 win.

Kansas City finished first in the Western League with a record of 82–54, for a winning percentage of .603. By its finale Omaha had played four more games but split them, and thus finished a very close second with a percentage of .600 after shutting out Milwaukee in their last game. Milwaukee ended up right behind Omaha at 80–55 and .593, half a game better than Denver. Over in the AA, Gear's Kansas City club finished at 69–67.

Kid Nichols finished 1902 with a win-loss record of 26–7 and an earned run average of 1.82. His top rival for the league's pitching honors was Mordecai Brown, who had one more win than Nick but also had 15 losses, to go with an ERA of 2.22. Brown moved up to the St. Louis Cardinals in 1903 and then became a perennial 20-game winner for the Cubs, including two world championships.

Thus, Nick could withdraw to his residence near Harmony Park, at 3007 E. 11th, a very happy man. For the next few years that would be the home he shared with Jennie and Alice, with his brother George joining them for part of that time. Meanwhile, that year or the next their half-brother John moved back to Wisconsin, this time settling in Oshkosh. In 1904 George, who never married, would start living with their youngest sister, Dora Northrop, and her family. He would bounce between living with Nick and Dora for the remainder of his life.

Kid Nichols and Dale Gear were on civil enough terms to conduct a postseason series between their two clubs. Nichols pitched the first game for the Blue Stockings and was tagged with the loss in a very lopsided shutout, but Nick's team was almost as dominant in winning the second game. Gear's team then won game three, only to have Nichols even it up by pitching his team to a narrow 6–5 victory in the fourth game. Nick tried to come back in the very next game but got pounded again, and a second consecutive win by Gear's team gave the AA franchise the series, four wins to two. At the same time, Omaha won a series from the AA champs, Indianapolis, so neither league had bragging rights in October.

In fact, the rival Kansas City clubs quickly took their show on the road, to Winfield, Kansas, for a series. Nichols was the losing pitcher in his team's third straight defeat, 1–0. Gear's pitcher in that game was borrowed from the Washington Senators, Wyatt "Watty" Lee. After that the two teams, though continuing to be led by Nichols and Gear, began mixing in other players. They next played in El Paso, Texas, and in the middle of October they played a five-game series in New Mexico (which was still a territory at the time and a full decade away from statehood) as part of the annual fair in Albuquerque. The Nichols team represented Albuquerque and the Gear team El Paso. In the second game, Lee won 5–3 to come out on top in another pitching battle with Nichols, who was caught by Johnny Kling. On October 18, Nick was the winning pitcher for Albuquerque, over Lee, by a score of 7–4. Nevertheless, Gear's lineup had won three of the five contests, against a Nichols-led club that also included Cleveland outfielder Jack McCarthy. The box score showed that Nichols' third baseman was named Tinker and his first baseman was named Chance, presumably two of Kling's well-known Chicago teammates.[13] The two teams then returned to El Paso to play. Afterward Nichols, McCarthy, and their wives vacationed at the Alamo for a few days before spending time relaxing in Colorado Springs. There Kid Nichols had a brief reunion with his old Beaneater teammate, Bobby Lowe.[14] Their paths would cross again soon enough, on the baseball diamond.

For 1903, the Nichols "family" on the ball diamond would be without two of its key pitchers. Norwood Gibson had been signed by Boston's American League team, and as a rookie he earned a record of 13–9 to help his team get to first modern World Series, though he wasn't one of the three pitchers used against the Pirates to win the championship. Gibson went 17–14 for Boston in 1904 but his major league career turned out to be short. Jake Weimer would win 20 games for the Cubs, an accomplishment he would repeat in 1904. He would then go 18–12 for Chicago in 1905, and win 20 for the Reds in 1906. A third young player whom Nichols lost to the major leagues was Rabbit Robinson. As with Gibson, he'd have a short major league career, though Rabbit played in more than 100 games for Washington in 1903 and Detroit in 1904, at several positions.

Playing in 1902 and part of the 1903 season for Kid Nichols was Roy Hartzell, who would go on to an 11-year career with the St. Louis Browns and the Yankees, usually in those ballclubs' lineups though at multiple positions. All told, Nick would field a much younger team in 1903. Most notable among the newcomers was Otto Hess, whose record of 20–17 for Cleveland in 1906 would be his best by far in ten major league seasons. Another acquisition for the franchise, in February of 1903, was Percy Chamberlain as the team's secretary. He had been sports editor of the *St. Joseph Gazette*, and Nick would count Percy among his very good friends in the long term.

It should come as no great surprise that two of the three best players whom Kid Nichols tutored on their way to the major leagues were pitchers. He never tired of passing along the lessons he had learned in the center of the diamond. When Tim Murnane published a collection of baseball advice for the Spalding Athletic Library in 1903, he included comments from Nichols alongside those of still-dominant stars like Cy Young. "It takes great speed to get a jump on a ball," Nichols said. "It must be thrown perfectly straight with an overhand swing, allowing the ball to slip out from under the fingers as if they were greased. I have found the real jump ball the most effective against both right and left handed batsmen."[15]

On April 3, 1903, Nick and his team departed for an exhibition trip through the Missouri Valley, beginning with three games in Springfield, Missouri, after which they opened a new ballpark in Pittsburg, Kansas. Another stop was Fort Scott, Kansas. In mid–April, the Blue Stockings played two exhibition games with the AL's St. Louis Browns. Nick's team played well but lost both games.

The Sox opened the season at home on April 28 with a 14–5 loss. About a month later, both Kansas City teams were in fourth place in their respective leagues, both having won about half of their games. Then some major flooding struck that part of the country, during which the Nichols family lost some of the Kid's early memorabilia.

Kid Nichols must have enjoyed both sides of a game against Omaha on July 13. In addition to being the winning pitcher in a 7–2 contest, he hit two doubles and a triple. He made sure nobody would forget that he was an excellent pitcher in a home game on the 30th against Denver, which was now led by his old Boston Beaneater teammate Bobby Lowe. The Blue Sox scored their only run in the second inning and were limited to three hits on the day by Carl Lempke, who would spend about half the decade in several minor leagues without making it to the majors. Still, Kid Nichols made that lone tally hold up by hurling a one-hit shutout, which earned him some national attention.[16] The game took one hour. At that point the win-loss record of the Blue Sox was 40–37, good enough for third place but quite a distance behind Colorado Springs atop the Western League.

It wasn't unheard of for Manager Nichols to have an argument with an umpire, but while pitching in the second game of a doubleheader against Denver on August 16 he had one of his most noteworthy tantrums. The incident occurred in the second game, when he was pitching in the eighth inning, trailing 3–2. "It was all because the manager-pitcher would not pitch with a ball that he thought was not exactly right," explained the *Kansas City Star*. "He jumped on the sphere and told the umpire to throw out a new one, but that official could not see things that way and gave Denver the game." The forfeit, with the ninth inning still to play, gave the Grizzlies a sweep of the twin bill. Even though the Sox still had a winning record at 51–44 after the two losses, the *Star* probably hit the nail on the head when it commented:

> For a time it appeared that the Blue Sox had better than a good chance to win the pennant again this year, but the recent reversal of form caused the outlook to be intensely gloomy. Three successive defeats at Colorado Springs and two to Denver, a rather disastrous record that for a team which had all kinds of speed when it rounded into the home stretch of the pennant race.
>
> The exhibition in the second game at Denver yesterday must have been a most interesting and dramatic one and just a little childish. Because the ball did not suit them the Blue Sox played foot ball with it and Nichols finally ripped it to pieces. Then the umpire gave the game to Denver. Nichols is usually very cool on the ball field and is manifestly opposed to "scenes." The ball in question, therefore, must have been very much to the bad. However, the actions of Nichols and the Blue Sox certainly did not do them credit.[17]

Nick regained his composure soon enough, as demonstrated when his timely hits and endurance contributed to a 12-inning win in Des Moines against the Undertakers on the 23rd, and beat first-place Milwaukee 4–2 on the 28th.

On September 17, the Western League abruptly cancelled its few remaining games and ended its 1903 season a week early. It came as no shock that the reasons were financial. James Whitfield's eventual replacement as league president, Michael Sexton, explained that "to have continued would have meant heavy losses for all teams and it is for this reason that the order is issued." He emphasized that not all of the franchises were in dire financial straits, but in doing so he probably painted a rosier picture than the facts warranted. "The season has been unusually prosperous in most instances and, with two exceptions, all have made money," he declared. "Unfortunately, Denver and Omaha have had losing teams, but the patrons have been loyal and the patronage has been exceptional." Did that mean those were the two cities that hadn't made money? He wasn't clear on that point, but what did stand out was how he studiously avoided talking about the cities where the WL was competing head to head with the AA, namely Kansas City and Milwaukee.[18]

Two days after Sexton made his unexpected decision the Blue Stockings played in St. Joseph in a game billed as an "exhibition." On that day Sexton offered these additional comments: "We have made money this year, and are well enough fixed financially to hold out against any unjust changes which they [AA leaders] desire. They must surrender Kansas City if they desire Milwaukee, or vice versa, and unless one of those advances is made there will be no change," Sexton insisted.[19]

The *Colorado Springs Gazette*, for one, didn't take Sexton's assessment at face value, and insisted that same day that the WL's Milwaukee and Peoria franchises were already dead.[20] Would Kansas City be the only front left in the war?

When the season was terminated the Kansas City Blue Stockings had a win-loss record of 66–58, in third place. Milwaukee was the sudden pennant winner. Kid Nichols didn't pitch quite as well as he had in 1902, but remained a considerable asset with a record of 21–12 and an ERA of 2.51.

Gear's team finished with almost the same mediocre record as the year before, this time at 69–66, but as in 1902, they dominated Nichols' team in a postseason series that began during the last week of September. Nichols pitched exceptionally well in the opener and won 8–2, but he ran out of steam in two subsequent starts and was thumped in both. After that first game, Gear's team won five of the remaining six contests.

In mid–October Nick had a chance to let off some steam by returning to New Mexico's annual territorial fair. Three teams played a series in round-robin format, representing El Paso (Texas), Albuquerque and Santa Fe. Each team was allowed to import up to three professionals, and joining Nick on the Santa Fe roster were Carl Lempke, the pitcher he had beaten with a one-hitter in late July, and his Denver teammate Charles Baerwald, a catcher (not to be confused with outfielder Rudolph Baerwald, who played seventeen games in late 1907 for the New York Highlanders under the name Rudy Bell). On October 10, the daily *Santa Fe New Mexican* printed a front-page photograph of their team, with only the three professionals identified.

The host city recruited pitchers Henry Schmidt and Oscar Jones, who had combined to win 41 games for the Brooklyn Superbas in 1903. El Paso brought in a battery comprised of pros named Markley and Adams, the former presumably George Markley, a longtime catcher in the Texas League who had played for Atlanta in the Southern Association in 1903. The pitcher was possibly Reuben Alexander "Rick" Adams, a Texas native who played for New Orleans in the Southern Association during 1903 but spent time in the Texas League before and after that (and in 1905 pitched eleven games for the Washington Senators). But the biggest celebrity brought in for this tournament was the umpire, Cap Anson.

Each team ended up winning two and losing two. On the 14th the Santa Fe battery of Nichols and Baerwald prevailed over El Paso's battery of Adams and Markley, 3–1. Both pitchers struck out fourteen, but Nick limited the opposition to five hits. On the 15th Nick earned Santa Fe's other win as well. A Santa Fe player named Manuel Alarid helped right away with a first-inning homer, and Nichols struck out eleven Albuquerque men on his way to an 8–4 victory over imported pitcher Oscar Jones. In both games Nick batted fifth. Santa Fe could have won the tournament on the final day by defeating El Paso, but Lempke lost the game in the late innings. Nick played right field and homered in a losing cause.[21] The tournament organizers tried to add another round to determine which team would win the purse, but nothing came of it.

More than thirty years later, a longtime New Mexico ballplayer named Henry Alarid reminisced with veteran *New Mexican* sportswriter Dan Ortiz about the tournaments in Albuquerque, focusing on a showdown between the teams representing that city and Santa Fe. Alarid was supposed to play on the latter team in the 1903 tournament but had been very ill, and thus only traveled with the team as a spectator.[22]

If Henry was a close relative of Manuel Alarid, Ortiz didn't say so. Henry didn't specify the year, but he remembered the Santa Fe team importing Kid Nichols, whom he described as the manager of Kansas City at the time, and a catcher from Colorado named "George Bearwald," which was a reasonably close recollection so many years later. The third pro for Santa Fe whom Alarid recalled was a pitcher-turned-first baseman named Frantz, which must be Walter Frantz of Dale Gear's 1903 Kansas City team. Perhaps Alarid remembered Frantz from a different year of the fair. In any case, Alarid offered this version of events:

> Albuquerque had a New York Giants battery, Christy Mathewson, the Big Six himself, his catcher "Chief" Meyers, and another big leaguer whom Alarid doesn't recall. As the tourney was in October the tourney entrants had lots of major leaguers from which to select.
>
> Albuquerque and Santa Fe had the strongest clubs that year and towards the end of the tourney with both teams undefeated they met in the "crucial" game. Kid Nichols was in the box for Santa Fe, and his old National League rival, Christy Mathewson, was the Duke City nominee to beat Santa Fe. The biggest crowd ever seen at the fair grounds jammed the place to see the two National Leaguers stage a beautiful pitchers' battle.

> Both pitchers were at their best pitching shutout ball, and near the end of the game, Mr. Alarid doesn't remember what inning it was but believes it was about the seventh, Mathewson uncorked one of his fast shooters to Manuel Alarid, young Santa Fe outfielder. Alarid, a good left-handed hitter met the ball squarely on the nose, parking it out on the race track beyond center, to beat the Big Six 1–0. There was no more scoring in that game on either side.
>
> Manuel, who fans used to know as "the Santa Fe boy who hit a homer off Christy Mathewson" died here last year. He used to tell of the achievement. Kid Nichols wanted to sign him for his Kansas City Blues [sic], but Manuel turned the offer down, saying he was afraid he would get homesick.[23]

Over many years had the true story of Manuel Alarid homering in support of Kid Nichols evolved into a fish tale with Oscar Jones, a 19-game-winner in 1903, replaced by a Hall of Famer, and other details change to increase the drama? Or had Henry Alarid spliced together halves of true stories? Among the lesser inconsistencies is that Chief Meyers didn't break into professional ball until 1906, and he didn't become Mathewson's catcher in the majors until 1909.

Author L.M. Sutter did mention Nichols and Baerwald when she wrote about the 1903 tournament in her recent history of baseball in New Mexico. Sutter also referred to Mathewson, but not in that context.[24] Matty did play once for a team in Los Lunas, New Mexico, and in November of 1909 he pitched in El Paso, including a duel against Rube Waddell, but several biographies of Mathewson published over the past two decades shed little light on those episodes. At lease Henry Alarid's claim that Kid Nichols offered to sign Manuel Alarid in October of 1903 is entirely plausible.

Soon after this, *Sporting Life* published a one-sentence jab stating that "Charlie Nichols seems to have made a failure at Kansas City under the best possible conditions."[25] It was left unclear whether this referred to not repeating as the pennant winner, not competing well against Gear's club, or having chosen the wrong venture after his years in Boston. Regardless, this provocative comment was forgotten when rumors began to circulate that Kid Nichols was in line to become the new manager of the St. Louis Cardinals. If Nichols had indeed done a horrible job, a major league job would be a bizarre demotion.

Nichols had been a rumored candidate to take over the St. Louis club a year earlier (as were a few others, including Jimmy Manning), but that speculation had died down quickly. In the autumn of 1903, however, the rumors persisted and *Sporting Life* kept them alive with some astute commentary. "So long as the Western League remains in Kansas City Nichols will not leave that point, as his people live there and he has a family growing up around him which he is anxious to provide a permanent home for," its correspondent wrote. "If the Western is forced out of that city, however, Nichols will have to find a position elsewhere, and he himself says that in that case he would rather come to St. Louis than any other place."[26]

Though the future of the Western League in Kansas City looked very shaky and the prospect of a return to the NL had to be tantalizing, Kid Nichols continued to go about his normal affairs. Nick and Jennie put their best foot forward together in late November, as the *Kansas City Star* revealed that "Mr. and Mrs. Charles A. Nichols entertained at their home, 3007 East Eleventh street, Friday night for their daughter, Alice, who is at home from the Sacred Heart academy in St. Joseph, spending Thanksgiving vacation." The guests named included Mr. and Mrs. Percy Chamberlain, Nick's brother George, and eighteen others, about half of whom were probably friends of 13-year-old Alice.[27] It was among the few times in his life that Kid Nichols made a newspaper's society page.

Nick also found time that winter for bowling. Shortly after Alice's party, the formation of the Kansas City Bowling Association was proclaimed, with Charles A. Nichols as president. The recognition of the American Bowling Congress was soon obtained.[28]

As 1903 wound down there was yet more talk of Kid Nichols going to St. Louis as a player-manager. The issue was resolved in early January when he accepted an offer to manage the Cardinals. Nick offered the following insight:

> I assure you that it is very hard for me to leave Kansas City, and that I hesitated a long while before I accepted Mr. Robison's offer. He gave me until the last of the year to decide and I did not accept until the last moment. I hoped that the American association would take some action towards settling the situation here, but it did not. What the Western league will do in regard to a team is doubtful, and so I could not afford to turn down the St. Louis proposition. However, I want it understood that wherever I am I will have the interests of Kansas City at heart, and I think it safe to predict that some time in the future I will again be connected with base ball interests here. Though manager of the St. Louis team I will retain my title as president of the Kansas City Western league team, and while I will in no way allow my interests here to conflict with those in St. Louis, I will do everything in my power towards settling the situation here and reviving the interest that is obviously rapidly killed by base ball politics.[29]

The Western League would continue to exist for decades, but for the 1904 season it dropped its franchises in both cities where it had competed with the AA, Kansas City and Milwaukee. It also dropped Peoria, meaning that it retreated from its two easternmost cities and thus proved that the *Colorado Springs Gazette* had been correct. Sioux City moved over from the Iowa-South Dakota League and the WL thus was reduced from six teams to eight. It wouldn't have eight teams again until 1909. Even though the league no longer had a Kansas City franchise, Nick as a nondrinker must have approved of the

Peoria Distillers being one of the teams dropped, and of the fact that the Des Moines team changed its name to the Prohibitionists. Perhaps those central Iowa fans had been the league's rowdiest.

In St. Louis, Kid Nichols took over a team that had finished dead last under Patsy Donovan in 1903, with a win-loss record of 43–94. They were seven games behind seventh-place Philadelphia. With a losing record in sixth place, by the way, was Boston in its second year since the arrival of Al Buckenberger and the departure of Nichols. In 1902 the Beaneaters had done much better, with a third-place finish and a winning record. That year Buckenberger had two 27-game winners in Vic Willis and Togie Pittinger but couldn't find a winning third starter. In 1903 both aces had losing records and could only manage 12 and 18 wins, respectively, while the unsuccessful search for an effective third starter continued.

The Cardinals' only .300 hitter in 1903 had been Donovan himself, an outfielder, but he was 38 years old. The only other starting players with respectable batting averages were outfielder Homer Smoot at .296, third baseman Jimmy Burke at .285, and second baseman John Farrell at .272. Shortstop Dave Brain easily led the team with fifteen triples, but those came at the expense of two-baggers, of which he only had eight while compiling a .231 average. Whereas Kid Nichols had won at least 20 games in his first ten years in the majors, and usually at least 30, none of the four most-used starters for the 1903 Cardinals won even ten games. Charles "Chappie" McFarland was 9–19, rookie Mordecai Brown was 9–13, Clarence Currie was 4–12, and Mike O'Neill was 4–13. Nick didn't have Brown on his roster because on December 12 he had been traded with Jack O'Neill, who had done most of the Cardinals' catching in 1903, to the Cubs for pitcher Jack Taylor and little-used catcher Larry McLean.

In addition to some ugly hitting and pitching statistics, the 1903 Cardinals also possessed a reputation as an unruly bunch, perhaps the poorest behaved in the NL. Kid Nichols was the kind of person to jump into new endeavors with both feet, especially under these circumstances, but he didn't do so at the expense of previous obligations. Therefore, in his capacity as president of the newly formed Kansas City Bowling Association, on February 7 he left for a national meeting scheduled in Cleveland. He also spent some time visiting Charlie Bennett in Detroit.

On February 11 a major acquisition by the Cardinals was announced: the purchase of first baseman Jake Beckley, a future Hall of Famer, from the Cincinnati Reds. Though Beckley was in his mid-thirties, he was showing no signs of slowing down, having hit over .300 in each of the five previous years and having belted 10 triples in 1903.

Nichols made a brief stop in St. Louis on the 22nd on his way back to

Kid Nichols with the Cardinals, just before the 1904 season.

Kansas City, and reported for full-time duty on March 3. Four days later, Nick's new team had its first spring training practice at the South End Park in Houston, Texas. Manager Nichols worked his squad hard, but before their first week was over they were guests of actor Harry Corson Clarke at the Empire Theater, to witness a production of *What Happened to Jones*.[30] Clarke had had one of the most memorable one-game major league careers ever, for the Washington Nationals in 1889. He was an emergency outfielder recruited from the stands for the second game of a doubleheader at the Polo Grounds, and responded by throwing out two New York baserunners who tried to take advantage of the novice.

Nichols also gave his team half a day off on St. Patrick's Day, and fraternized with them in memorable fashion that evening. New catcher Michael William Grady, sometimes called "Michael Angelo," had been dominating his teammates at billiards during training camp, but Nichols only watched, albeit intently. By that night, Grady, who was only three months younger than his manager, was strutting around the pool hall declaring himself team champion.

"'Nick' quietly invited Mike to take a cue and play twenty-five points straight pool. Grady winked at his defeated comrades and said another Mr. E.Z. Mark. 'Nick' said nothing, but smiled and broke the balls," reported the *Kansas City Star*. Grady made a poor decision on his first shot, and then "'Nick' clicked off twelve balls without hardly an effort. Grady, after viewing the great work of his 'boss,' stood still a few moments and said: 'Oh! That was luck; he is playing above his speed.'" Jimmy Burke then left to summon absent teammates, who then watched Grady pocket only fourteen balls before their manager reached twenty-five. The table was then reset.

"The 'boss,' in order to give the defeated champion a chance, agreed to continue to fifty points," the *Star* continued. "Mike said O.K. and broke the balls. 'Nick' after making a difficult long shot, smashed into them and dropped his ball. He cleared the table. Grady, much crestfallen, refused to play any more...."[31] A few weeks later, just before Opening Day, Grady and Beckley would each manage half of the team in an intrasquad exhibition at League Park, with Nichols on the latter team. In response to some good-natured trash talk by Grady, Nichols responded with the prediction that he and Beckley's team would make "a couple of hundred hits to-day."[32]

Kid Nichols arranged for his team to play exhibition games in Beaumont and Galveston against those cities' South Texas League teams just before finishing up their time in Houston on March 27. Nick also scheduled a game in Little Rock, Arkansas, as they made their way to St. Louis, and several contests in his old stomping grounds of Memphis. In April, the Cardinals played a seven-game series against their American League counterparts, the Browns. At least one paper back in Boston took note when the Cardinals lost the third game of the series but rebounded the next day with Nick pitching them to a 6–2 win.[33] The Cardinals went on to win the decisive match on the 11th.

Kid Nichols (left) as player-manager of the Cardinals, likely in 1904, with co-owner Frank Robison.

Opening Day for Kid Nichols and his Cardinals was at home on April 15. Nick gave the assignment as starting pitcher to Jack Taylor, who faced Deacon Phillippe of the Pirates, the defending NL champions. It was a close game throughout, and though it was generally well-played, two errors by the Cards cost them three runs in a 5–4 loss. The next day, Kid Nichols chose to pitch. Pitching for Pittsburgh was Roscoe Miller, whose best season in the majors by far was in 1901 when he went 23–13 as a rookie for Detroit.

Kid Nichols retired the first man he faced easily but

Kid Nichols with the Cardinals in 1904.

walked the second. After a fly-out, Nick then walked Honus Wagner. The next man singled the lead runner home, but Nick then ended the inning by inducing a foul pop to his catcher, Bill Byers. Nichols' first major league inning since 1901 hadn't gone smoothly, but under the circumstances it wasn't too bad. The Cards promptly tied it in their half of the first inning, and Nick responded by retiring the next three Pirates in order. In the bottom half Nichols batted for the first time but struck out.

The visitors took the lead off of Nichols in the third but the St. Louis offense responded with two and took the lead back. In the fourth, the Pirates tied it at 3–3 on an error by Beckley. In the bottom of the fourth Nick singled, though he didn't end up scoring. After that he allowed the Pirates no runs from the fifth through the eighth, while his team scored pairs in the fifth and seventh innings. In the ninth, Nick loaded the bases for Pittsburgh with only one out. He then gave up a two-run single and allowed the next man to reach, but then secured a strikeout and induced a pinch hitter for Miller to ground out to short and end the threat. He won his playing return to the NL, 7–5.

After winning the third game from Pittsburgh, next up was the first of several significant reunions for Nichols with former allies. St. Louis's next visitors were the Chicago Cubs, led by Nick's only manager in Boston, Frank Selee. The two teams played two in St. Louis followed immediately by three in Chicago. Frank had set the stage for a pleasant meeting more than a month before the season, when he expressed his sincere hope to a Boston paper that Nichols would be a success as a big league manager.[34]

As circumstances would have it, six of the eight NL managers in 1904 had been involved in that famous 1897 pennant race between Boston and Baltimore. Kid Nichols had mentioned that he was aware of this before the season began.[35] In addition to Selee, Ned Hanlon was the manager of Brooklyn, ex–Beaneater Hugh Duffy led the Phillies, and ex–Orioles John McGraw and Joe Kelley skippered the Giants and Reds, respectively. The two exceptions were Fred Clarke with Pittsburgh and Al Buckenberger in Boston.

Selee won two of the first three games and then chose Nick's Blue Stockings protégé Jake Weimer to face Nichols on April 23. Chicago scored a run immediately, but Nick gave them no more. Weimer, though, held the Cards scoreless through six innings. In the seventh inning, St. Louis tied it thanks to a well-executed hit and run. They repeated that strategy successfully in the eighth as well, and Nichols ended up with a 2–1 triumph. Each pitcher allowed only four hits. The Cardinals won another close game the next day, 4–3, and ended up taking three out of the five played consecutively with Chicago. Selee's very talented team would dominate for the rest of the year, taking twelve of the remaining sixteen meetings.

Kid Nichols had a thoroughly enjoyable start to May with the Reds in town before a crowd of 14,000 fans. He was the starting pitcher and contributed two hits plus a run scored in a game that was tied after eight innings, then won by the home team in the bottom of the ninth after two were out, when Byers singled home the winning run.

Less than a week later Nick would be furious when a game at home on May 7 against the Giants ended in controversy. Jack Taylor was trying to nail down a 1–0 shutout in the top of the ninth. With pinch runner John McGraw on first base, pinch hitter Roger Bresnahan hit a pitch deep into left field, an obvious extra-base hit that would score McGraw at a minimum. Bizarrely, first base coach Billy Gilbert actually bolted into fair territory behind McGraw. According to the account in the *New York Times*, "McGraw ran across the plate with nearly every member of the visiting team aiding him. Gilbert, more enthusiastic than the rest, followed his manager around the bases from first. As McGraw was nearing third, one of the team dashed to the plate while the rest stood howling on third base." Contrary to retellings of this incident in recent years, Cardinal captain Jake Beckley was not the left fielder who retrieved the ball. Instead, Beckley hastened to third base to protest, and took the ball from Jimmy Burke there. Then, as the *Times* reported, "another New York player dashed for the plate from the coaching line. Beckley, thinking Bresnahan had made the dash tossed the ball toward home plate, with no one covering the position, and Bresnahan scored."[36] It didn't help the situation that this occurred in an era when players didn't wear numbers on their uniforms.

The Cardinals escaped the inning without further damage, but couldn't come up with a run to tie the game in the bottom of the ninth. Nichols and the Cardinals' front office filed a protest, under Rule 56, Section 17, which the *St. Louis Republic* printed in a prominent box the next day. It read, "If one or more members of the team at bat stand or collect at or around a base for which a base runner is trying, thereby confusing the fielding side, and adding to the difficulty of making such a play, the base runner shall be declared out for the interference of his team-mate or team-mates."[37] The Giants insisted to NL president Harry Pulliam that their bench only emptied after Beckley threw the ball homeward, and at the end of the month he rejected the protest in writing, with a surprisingly venomous tone aimed at Beckley.[38] Pulliam was usually considered gentle.

Then again, this was the same man who couldn't or wouldn't force John McGraw to play the 1904 World Series, which ended up being cancelled. For that and several other reasons the New York franchise grew to hate Pulliam intensely, and after his first reelection was unanimous, subsequent votes saw the Giants dissent. Thus it was unlikely that Pulliam was biased in favor of the Giants; instead, he may have decided that he didn't want to incur the wrath of the Giants on every matter. This would happen in the aftermath of his necessary involvement in the famous Merkle incident as the Giants and Cubs competed for the pennant in 1908, and Pulliam's physicians said that the stress from that controversy contributed to the depression that ultimately caused Pulliam to commit suicide in mid–1909.

In any event, this tough loss for Taylor was the Cardinals' fifth in a row, and left them with a mediocre win-loss record of 7–10. Undoubtedly Nick wasn't satisfied with that, but he could take comfort from having shown that he wasn't too old to play in the majors. "There is no doubt that Charlie Nichols, manager and pitcher of the St. Louis National League team, possesses the most wonderful arm in professional baseball to-day," the *Republic* declared after the protested game. "In the game he has pitched so far this spring he has shown all his old-time strength and cunning, and there is no reason to believe that he will not perform as well on the rubber this year as ever he did." They then quoted the veteran:

> I know of no reason why my arm should be better than that of any other pitcher, except that I take better care of it than do some of the boys who have the reputation of having so-called iron arms. While I have suffered with a sore pitching arm at times, it has never been sufficiently out of condition to lead me to believe that the end of my pitching days was at hand.
>
> Even to-day I have no idea how soon I will be compelled to give up pitching, for my arm feels as good and strong as it did ten years ago. I have never taken anything but the simplest exercise in the spring, never having the aid of a masseur to

> keep my arm from getting sore. When there was any soreness I would resort to the old-fashioned method of giving the arm lots of work under favorable weather conditions to bring it back to its form again. Of course, pitching is a great strain on the arm. At the same time, if the muscles are kept in a good, healthy condition, and one is in other ways physically sound, there is no reason why the general run of pitchers should not last longer than they do. I have hopes that I shall be able to continue in the business for years to come, and I see no reason why I should not.[39]

Shortly after the fiasco with the Giants, Nichols' Cardinals got hot. At home from May 10 through the 22nd, the team won nine of ten games to move into fourth place with a record of 16–12, three-and-a-half games behind first-place Cincinnati.

On June 1, Kid Nichols returned to Boston for the first time as manager of the Cardinals. "I bear no grudge for any one, but ... I would give all my old sweaters, including the one they gave me for coaching the Yale varsity team, to make a clean sweep of the games here with my St Louis team," Nick said.[40]

"The feature of the day was the cordial greeting given to Charlie Nichols," reported the *St. Louis Republic* about that day's pregame activities. "He was kept busy shaking hands and doffing his cap in answer to salutes from the crowd." In brief remarks before the teams started playing, Nick said: "I am delighted to come back to Boston, where live so many of my best friends and most agreeable acquaintances, and I am doubly pleased to be able to return at the head of a first-class ball team."[41] After one inning of play, even the skies wept tears of sentimentality, and the game was cancelled. The teams were also rained out the next day. On the 3rd they finally got in a game, and then some; Boston beat Jack Taylor, 1–0, in 13 innings.

Nick scheduled himself to be the starting pitcher on the 4th. "Charley Nichols was given a warm hand when he walked to the field" by the 6,000 fans present, noted the *Boston Globe*. Starting for the Beaneaters was his old colleague, Vic Willis. Each pitcher kept his opponents from scoring until the home team came up with single runs off of Nichols in the fourth and fifth innings. St. Louis tied the score and the duel between Willis and Nichols continued into extra innings. In the top of the twelfth, Beckley reached on a single and broke the tie when an errant throw sailed over the head of first baseman Fred Tenney, the only man in Boston's lineup other than Willis who had been a longtime teammate of Nick. Kid Nichols retired his former team in the bottom half and earned a 3–2 win. He also delivered at the bat, collecting two hits in four trips. "As the old war horse walked from the field he was kept busy hand shaking with old friends and admirers," the *Globe*'s account concluded. That paper was also inspired to include a cartoon with a caption that read, "Nichols Wins from His Old Team."[42] The Cardinals then left town, with a record of 18–18.

Nick also received a warm ovation when he pitched in Brooklyn on June 10. The home team scored a run in the first inning on two walks and an error, but then Nick settled down. St. Louis's offense came up with two runs in the fifth and two more in the seventh to give its skipper a 4–1 lead. Nichols, meanwhile, carried a no-hitter into the Brooklyn half of the eighth inning. Two hits, an error and a walk not only ended the no-hitter but also jeopardized the victory, but Nick escaped that frame with a 4–3 lead, which was how the game ended. Nichols finished with a three-hitter. Soon thereafter, the *Kansas City Star* was delighted to reprint commentary from the *New York Sun* about Nick being among the "ornaments" of the baseball world, one of the best-liked men in his chosen field, and a pitcher feared across the NL for his arm of steel.[43]

Kid Nichols lived up to that praise on June 20 in a home game against Pittsburgh, the defending champions. He hurled a four-hit shutout, 3–0. And against third-place Cincinnati on the 28th he pitched a 1–1 game into the tenth inning, then watched his offense score four and deliver a 5–2 win. Nick continued his winning ways in early July when Selee and the Cubs came to town. The teams remained deadlocked from the fourth inning until the Cardinals finally tallied a run in the bottom of the ninth. Nichols limited Chicago to five hits in the 3–2 victory. He beat New York in St. Louis by the same score on July 10, in a matchup against "Iron Man" McGinnity, the future Hall of Famer.

In the wake of that victory against the first-place Giants, Kid Nichols' pitching record stood at eleven wins and only three losses. "Not one of those three defeats was what could be called a bad defeat," insisted the *Star*.[44] Jack Taylor was also faring well up to that point, with a record of 10–5. The team struggled in its other starts, as had been the case the year before Nick arrived, so the Cardinals remained in fifth place and continued to hover around the .500 mark.

On July 14 Kid Nichols pitched yet another gem, this time with Brooklyn visiting. The starting pitcher for the Superbas was Oscar Jones, whom Nick had faced in New Mexico. After three innings, the score was knotted at 1–1. The next run was scored with two outs in the bottom of the ninth by the Cards. Nichols scattered four hits in the 2–1 victory.

With Philadelphia in town a week later, St. Louis lost a game due to poor fielding. By the seventh inning, team captain Jake Beckley had grown exasperated by all of the lousy throws made his way. During that frame Nichols made a great stop on a ball hit back to him, but Beckley had to scoop the hurler's low throw out of the dirt. After doing so, he went over to the rubber and chewed out Nick as he might a rookie. "Nichols, appreciating the humor of the situation and the excellence of Beckley's play, walked away with a good-natured smile overspreading his countenance," reported the *St. Louis Republic.*[45]

For the first game of a doubleheader in Pittsburgh on July 30, Jack Taylor reportedly wanted Kid Nichols to replace him as the scheduled starter. If he communicated that to Nick, the manager rejected Jack's request. Taylor and Beckley had indulged in some drinking and gambling the night before the game, and Taylor felt in no shape to pitch. He ended up losing 5–2, allowing only seven hits but issuing five walks and tossing two wild pitches while only striking out one. Months later Taylor would be investigated for his conduct during this period, but in the short term the incident may have damaged his relationship with his manager.

In early August the Cardinals again visited Boston and Kid Nichols gave that city another reason to regret not having him on their pitching staff. The St. Louis offense produced one run in the first off of Togie Pittinger, and that was it for the day. It turned out they didn't need any additional runs, because Nick shut out his former club, 1–0.

In Brooklyn on August 11, Kid Nichols and Oscar Jones were the starters in what proved to be an amazing game. Each team scored one run in the fourth inning. Neither team scored until they both picked up one run again, in the *fifteenth* inning. St. Louis finally scored two in the seventeenth and Brooklyn could only come back with one. Nichols had fanned 14 men while giving up nine hits.

"After the game Captain Nichols had quite a reception in the clubhouse, and several of the Brooklyn players shook hands with the St. Louis manager, and congratulated him on the well-deserved victory of his team," reported the *St. Louis Republic.* "The Brooklyn fans, too, gave to Nichols a 'send off' as he walked off the field — something unheard of in that borough of Superba fanaticism."[46] The *New York World* noted that in the crowd was famous comedian Eddie Foy, who had helped the Bostons have a little fun with costumes in that mid–1892 game in Chicago. Foy was so inspired by Nick's performance that he wrote a verse in tribute; according to the paper, the poem "was pretty bad, but Mr. Foy meant well." The *World* also asked Nick how he kept himself in shape for such a long time, and he was happy to answer. "I work slowly," Nichols said after the marathon that had lasted two hours, 35 minutes. "I keep my nerves quiet. If I find that my arm is tiring I always change to some other kind of delivery so as to rest the overstrained muscles. Of course there are times when I cannot do this, when I have to give a certain batter a certain kind of ball. But generally I can change."[47]

On August 16, Kid Nichols earned a 6–1 win in the first game of a doubleheader at Philadelphia. The Cardinals then won their next seven games, their longest streak of the season. In the middle of that streak he beat the Phillies again, 4–2, while limiting them to four hits.

Shortly after Jack Taylor had to pitch that game in Pittsburgh while in a stupor, the *St. Louis Republic* had commented that Nick was "personally popular with all his players, and is proving a very able and successful leader."[48] Toward the end of August, however, Frank de Haas Robison, who owned the Cardinals with his brother Stanley, felt compelled to dismiss rumors that Nichols' days as manager were numbered and that he might return to Kansas City as part owner and manager of the surviving American Association club there. Robison also downplayed rumors of a feud between Nichols and Taylor. Hoping to put the matter to rest, with more than a month left in the 1904 season he announced that Nick would continue as manager into 1905.

Taylor grumbled to the press that Nichols had given himself the easier assignments as starting pitcher and Taylor the more difficult ones.[49] A few days later, on September 5, Taylor announced he was leaving the team, which meanwhile was in the midst of its longest losing streak of the season, seven games. Taylor's boycott didn't last long; he returned on the 7th in the first game of a doubleheader against the visiting Cubs, 4–3. In the nightcap, Nichols responded to Taylor's return by allowing Selee's men a single in the third and a homer in the eighth. Nick won a two-hitter, 4–1, to snap the losing streak.

On September 11, Kid Nichols decided that his other pitchers were far too overworked, so he pitched both games of a doubleheader in Cincinnati himself. He split them. In the first game he held the Reds to three hits and won 4–2. The Reds beat him 8–5 in the second game, though his best stretch of pitching in that game spanned the seventh through ninth innings. His team's offense just couldn't rally late. If his arm was weakened at all by that feat, it had bounced back by the end of the month. In Brooklyn on the 29th he limited the Superbas to five hits and shut them out 3–0. Curiously, it was reported that the next day he went over to the Polo Grounds to watch Chicago and New York battle, while Brooklyn was defeating his Cardinals.[50] Maybe he was on a scouting mission.

On October 3 in New York, Kid Nichols pitched against his nemesis of 1901, Christy Mathewson. Matty needed to set an all-time record for his franchise in order to beat Nick. As it was, Nichols led 1–0 after seven innings. In the end, Nichols only allowed five hits. Alas, the Giants bunched three of them in the eighth inning, two for extra bases, and an error also contributed to a three-run outburst. The Cards left ten men on base against Matty, but he struck out sixteen St. Louis batters. That is still the single-game record for the franchise, though it was tied by San Francisco Giants pitcher Jason Schmidt 102 years later.

That loss was one of only two defeats in a nine-game span as the calendar turned from September to October, and Nichols' team ascended above the .500 mark with a record of 75–73. The final win was the second game of doubleheader on the day after Matty's milestone, and McGraw's men showed their frustration. The trouble began in New York's half of the first inning, after an apparent homer by Giants leadoff man Johnny Dunn. Beckley appealed to umpire Jim Johnstone that Dunn had neglected to touch first base, and the ump responded by declaring Dunn out. Johnstone was then subjected to verbal abuse from the fans for the remainder of the game.

With the game tied at 1–1 in the fourth inning, the situation deteriorated after a Cardinal runner stole second base. The New York shortstop who took the throw, Bill Dahlen, was so adamant that he had applied the tag in time that the umpire ejected him. Second baseman Billy Gilbert took up his teammate's cause, and was also tossed from the game. Johnstone then walked away only to have a fan rush out and smack him. The umpire refused to file a complaint to the police who were present, but they threw the spectator out. The remaining Giants refused to resume play, and after the time limit specified in the rules, Johnstone awarded a forfeit to the Cardinals. NL president Harry Pulliam happened to be present, and endorsed his umpire's decision.

After starting October well, the Cards lost the last six games of the season and finished in fifth place in the eight-team league, with a win-loss record of 75–79. Though it would have been very nice to have finished with a winning record, they had improved considerably under Kid Nichols from their last-place finish the year before, when their record in a shorter season was 43–94.

Despite the losing record, the Cardinals actually scored a few more runs than they allowed, 602 to 595. Nick's team wasn't particularly successful at home, with a record of 39–36, but they weren't horrible on the road, where they went 36–43. Their best month was 19–11 in July, but they were a little below .500 most other months. The Cardinals were 22–23 in one-run games.

Kid Nichols probably derived a little personal satisfaction from seeing his team finish ahead of Ned Hanlon's Brooklyn club, Nick's old Boston team, and Hugh Duffy's Phillies. Head to head against Hanlon, Nick was 15–7. His record against Boston was 13–9.

Nichols' team made a modest offensive improvement. Under Donovan in 1903 the Cardinals offense hit .251 and scored 3.6 runs per game. Those figures improved to .253 and 3.9 under Nichols, which meant two extra runs per week. Most impressively, the team's earned run average plunged by more than one run per game under Nick, from 3.67 to 2.64. Donovan had tried 17 different pitchers; Nick only used eight.

The players who made a difference on offense for St. Louis included a Nichols recruit, catcher Mike Grady. Though he was 34, Grady played in 101 games and hit .313; he wasn't much of a gamble, having played for four different major league teams from 1894 to 1901, but he spent 1902 and 1903 with Dale Gear's rival AA team in Kansas City.

Rookie outfielder William "Spike" Shannon hit .280, which would be his highest in a five-year NL career, though he would lead the league in runs scored for the Giants in 1907. Shannon had played with St. Paul in the AA during 1902 and 1903. He had been acquired by St. Louis before Nichols signed on.

Jake Beckley, the 36-year-old first baseman and new captain, hit .325. Elsewhere on the infield, 27-year-old Danny Shay had become the primary shortstop instead of Dave Brain. Shay's .256 average wasn't great but it was much better than Brain's had been the year before. Shay's only prior major league experience was 19 games with Cleveland in 1901.

Brain, at age 25, was shifted to a utility role but still played often, and improved from .231 to .266; what's more, he had 24 doubles to go with 12 triples and a team-leading seven homers. The year before, it seemed like all of his hits were either singles or three-baggers. The other two starting infielders were third baseman Jimmy Burke, whose batting average dropped from .285 in 1903 to .227 in 1904, and second baseman John Farrell, whose average fell from .272 to .255. Outfielder Homer Smoot, at age 26, was the only other regular from 1903 who was decidedly an asset to Nichols. Smoot had another good year, hitting .281.

The best line of the year came from none of the above players, and it does not appear to have surfaced in print until the next season. It came from John Bannerman "Larry" McLean, the Canadian-born catcher who grew up in the Boston area. McLean, who stood 6'5" and weighed almost 230 pounds, was the player paired with Jack Taylor in the Mordecai Brown trade that occurred shortly before Nichols was hired. Both of the acquisitions had troublesome reputations, but Nick didn't feel compelled to play Larry.

Here is the anecdote, which originated in the *Seattle Exchange* and was gleefully reprinted in the *Boston Journal*:

> A story told on the Portland bench yesterday coming from J. Bridegroom McLean is worth repeating. The Tall Sycamore who takes care of the receiving end of the Webfooters' battery tells it on himself. He was playing in St. Louis last year and not being in the best of condition and not being on the best of terms with Manager Kid Nichols, warmed the bench many afternoons. Now, McLean comes from good old Methodistic stock and the mother's letters from home were ever freighted with the best of advice. She laid particular stress upon desecrating the Sabbath by playing ball and wrote as only a mother can, counseling against any Sunday playing. Mac read the letter more than once and then telegraphed this answer: "Don't worry, mother; am not even playing week days."[51]

In 1915, McLean would be demoted to the minors by John McGraw after an incident at the Buckingham Hotel in St. Louis. Larry would die in 1921 back in Boston, after he was shot by a bartender during a brawl in a tavern. If Kid Nichols heard about that, he would've had a cautionary tale to use when counseling young ballplayers during the final decades of his life.

In 1904, Nick's win-loss record as a pitcher was 21–13. By winning eight more games than he lost, he achieved his highest difference since 1898, his final pennant season with Boston. He threw as many shutouts as he did wild pitches, three. His three homers yielded was easily the lowest total of his career to that point. He had more than twice as many strikeouts as walks, 134 to 50. It was only the second 2-to-1 ratio of his career and the first since 1891. Most impressively, his Earned Run Average of 2.02 was the best of his entire major league career.

Jack Taylor was the only other obvious bright spot on the Cardinal pitching staff, and even then his 20 wins were offset by 19 losses. More important was his ERA, an excellent 2.22. Chappie McFarland and Mike O'Neill weren't as bad as they had been in 1903, at 14–18 and 10–14 in 1904, and their ERAs weren't bad: McFarland's was 3.21, and O'Neill posted a sparkling 2.09 ERA.

In addition to the quartet of Taylor, Nichols, McFarland and O'Neill, Nichols had tried Joe Corbett, his Baltimore nemesis in 1897, for 14 starts. The result was a record of 5–8 and an ERA of 4.39. Corbett had gone 24–8 for Baltimore during the famous 1897 season had been out of the majors since then. Joe requested his release from the Cardinals at the end of July, and never pitched in the majors again. He was six years younger than Nick.

At the close of the regular season, the Cardinals played a postseason series with their AL rivals, the Browns. The Browns won three out of the first four meetings but the Cards won the next two, and the AL club lost interest in continuing, so the series was split. Afterwards Kid Nichols headed home to Kansas City. At some point during the offseason he probably had the chance to peruse *Spalding's Official Baseball Guide* for the next season. On a page containing photographs of the 1904 Cardinals, the first one was incorrectly identified as Manager Nichols.[52] Somebody made a note to that effect, in Nick's personal copy, which his great-grandchildren still possess. The note was probably jotted by Alice or by the Kid himself.

The NL season was less than a month over when his name turned up in the rumor circuit again. At the beginning of November, Louie Metz of the Metz Brothers' Brewery in Omaha went public with details of a discussion he had with William Rourke, a co-owner of that city's Western League franchise since 1900. According to Metz, "Manager Rourke has offered us the Omaha team. Our plan is to have Kid Nichols become manager and part owner. As the Western league is on an unsatisfactory basis the chances are that Omaha will be in the American association next year. This is the end we are working for at present." Rourke was in the east at the time but he returned within days and the sale was reportedly imminent.[53]

This plan seems to have evaporated pretty quickly and Nick had a quiet three months. In mid–December he did make a trip to St. Louis, during which he scheduled preseason games with the Browns. For Christmas that year he received a photograph of the St. Joseph team from his friend Percy Chamberlain, which Nick's great-grandchildren still have.

At some point during this offseason Nick's Kansas City bowling team finished in first place. He made much bigger news in mid–February, when he traveled east to participate in the NL's investigation of Jack Taylor's conduct prior to the Cardinals' doubleheader on July 30. The *Philadelphia Inquirer* offered a detailed report, which read in part:

> The charges against him were preferred by Secretary Locke of the Pittsburg Club and the first count was that he conspired with divers gamblers and others to lose the game in question. The second count was that he had been guilty of conduct in violation of the constitution of the National League and prejudicial to the best interests of the National game. His inquisitors were Garry Herrmann, who, although having declared his belief that the player was guilty of the charges, yet accepted the proxy of Barney Dreyfuss, who claimed to be ill, and sat in judgment on the player whom he had already unofficially declared to be dishonest. Arthur Soden and President Pulliam, ex-officio members of the board, were the others present. James A. Hart, who has also made accusations against the pitcher, declined to appear, and John T. Brush, the other member of the board, was conveniently absent. However, as three constitutes a quorum, the action of the league is quite legal, although it may be susceptive to a charge of peculiarity. The Pittsburg Club was fortified by the presence of three lawyers, who unloaded a bushel of affidavits on the case, and gave the proceedings a very legal aspect.
>
> Charley Nichols, manager of the St. Louis team, was called before the board, and is supposed to have testified in favor of Taylor, but the manager refused to say anything whatever on the case or what was his attitude. Frank De Hass Robinson [sic], president of the club, also appeared as a witness and did what he could to straighten out the tangle for the pitcher. The hearing was behind closed doors and not a whisper came forth until the solemn triumvirate emerged shortly before 7 o'clock.[54]

The League officials had met for more than four hours. The following day's paper reported the outcome, which was that Taylor was deemed guilty of drunkenness only, and fined $300. The *Inquirer* explained that the NL panel decided the matter that way "largely because if he were adjudged to have been guilty of dishonesty he would have to be expelled from the league and would thus lose his means of making a livelihood."[55] Taylor thus was exonerated for the second season in a row of such charges; the first had come after he was accused of throwing games during a postseason series between the Chicago teams in 1903. In 2003, baseball historian Arthur D. Hittner, observed, "The inability of league officials to deal decisively with the menace of gambling would have profound consequences in the years to come."[56]

Later that month, Kid Nichols was given the chance to comment on a more pleasant subject than the Taylor matter. The *Kansas City Star* published his thoughts about pitching, which read in part:

> ... I think the principal thing is that I have never been afraid to let the batter hit the ball. I always remembered the fact that a good batter cannot put more than one in three safe, a poor batter one in four, or even less. I never, or seldom, anyway, throw my arm off trying to strike a man out. It's might hard to fan a good hitter, and it doesn't pay to try it on a poor one. I let them hit it, but try to keep them from hitting it safe, never forgetting that I have eight men behind me just as eager as I am to retire the opposing batter. Years ago I practiced and developed a high, jump ball, one that passes over the plate at a man's shoulder and changes its course ever so slightly as it passes him. It's a hard ball to hit safe. To make a hard hit the batter must meet the ball squarely on the center, and my aim has always been to keep him from doing that. If he hits under it the result is a fly that can almost surely be gobbled up by one of the fielders. If he hits it on top a grounder goes to one of the infielders. While this jump ball has been my most effective argument, I never worked it to death.
>
> Another thing that I never believed in is throwing wide balls on purpose. A good many pitchers think it is policy to waste one or two occasionally. Not for me. I never could see the advantage of it. What's the use of deliberately throwing a ball that only wastes your strength and puts you in the hole?
>
> Of course, I give bases on balls and pitch many wide ones, but it is never intentional. Study the batter; keep him guessing, make him hit, but keep him from hitting it safe if you can; don't be afraid to trust your fielders, and always keep in good condition. Those are my rules, and I am pitching yet in the big league, though I started nineteen years ago.[57]

In early March, Nichols' charges convened in St. Louis and left for spring training, in Marlin Springs, Texas, about twenty miles from Waco. Around St. Patrick's Day they began a slow, winding trip to St. Louis. They played games in such cities as Oklahoma City and Waco, and starting on the 25th they played three against the Kansas City Blues. Managing the Blues for 1905 was former NL manager Arthur Irwin; Dale Gear had been replaced partway through the 1904 season. Nick pitched part of the first game, and in the end his Cards swept the series.

During the first half of April Nichols' men played their preseason series with the Browns, which proved to be very popular. For example, when the Browns won the second game on Sunday, April 2, it was before 25,000 fans at League Park. The Cardinals ended up losing the series in a ten-inning seventh game.

The Cardinals hosted Chicago on Opening Day, April 14. St. Louis lost,

6–1, but won 2–1 the next day and split two more with the Cubs. After seven games Nick's club had a win-loss record of 3–4 but then lost five in a row through May 1. They won the next two days to conclude a short home stand with a record of 5–9. On the evening of May 3 Kid Nichols was relieved of his managerial duties, though he would stay on the team as a pitcher. The players were reportedly surprised. Nick was mystified but also seemed to accept the decision. "I have tried to make a winner out of the team and suppose I have failed, according to the present aspect of the percentage table," Nichols said. "There is material in the team, however, and the season is still young."

"I will have a chance now to get in condition and will take my regular turn in the box, I suppose," continued Nick. "I am with the team and will do the best I am capable of for its success. I know of no reason for the shift beyond the desire of the management to lift the crew out of the rut which it seems to have gotten into."[58]

Jimmy Burke was named player-manager by the Robison brothers, though in recent months control of the team had shifted from Frank, who was in declining health, to Stanley, with whom Nichols had a mediocre relationship. The team reacted to Nick's demotion by losing its next four games in Chicago, and three out of four in New York.

On June 21 the Cardinals began their longest losing streak of the season, fourteen, which lasted through July 6. At the end of the streak, Kid Nichols was unconditionally released. Nick had made seven starts for the Cards in 1905, compiling a 1–5 record and an earned run average of 5.40.

After Nichols was replaced as manager, the 1905 Cards never won more than four consecutive games. Jimmy Burke didn't finish the season as manager, and his replacement was none other than Stanley Robison. Their winning percentages were almost identical, and the Cardinals ended up in sixth place, at 58–96, a much poorer record than during Kid Nichols' full season as manager, when the team had almost broken even. St. Louis would perform even worse in 1906, sliding to seventh place with a record of 52–98.

Under Nick in 1904 the St. Louis offense hit .253, but in 1905, when Burke and Robison managed 91 percent of the club's games, the Cardinals hit .248. The decline of the team's earned run average was much more significant, increasing by almost a full run per game, from 2.64 to 3.59. Part of this was due to Jack Taylor's ERA jumping from 2.22 to 3.44.

"I expected my release some time before I received it, which was on July 5," said Nick shortly after his fate was confirmed. "I am glad that it is an unconditional document. To-day I received an offer from the Philadelphia Club, which I will consider particularly."

"I haven't any concern for my baseball future," he added. "I am as good now as I have been for years, and on my last three games I feel that I showed form which could hardly have been dissatisfying to any club. When I was deposed as manager of the club I should have perhaps asked for my release. I remained and there is not the slightest friction between Manager Burke and myself or Mr. Robison. I have supported the club loyally and they certainly supported me as well."

According to the *St. Louis Republic*, "Mr. Robison refused to talk of the release of Nichols and Manager Burke likewise asked to be excused." The next day, the paper suggested that Nichols might join Nap Lajoie in Cleveland or become a part owner of the Kansas City Blues. Possibly to Nick's surprise, Jack Taylor gave him a blanket endorsement as an available pitcher.[59]

Years later, Kid Nichols revealed that his release came about when he was ordered by Stanley Robison to work the gate in a game against the Reds on July 5. Ticket-counting wasn't an uncommon assignment for less experienced players, but Nichols felt it was beneath his dignity. Nick told Robison that instead he'd take the day off and go to a racetrack.

On July 14, it was announced that Hugh Duffy's Phillies, also sometimes called the Quakers, had signed Nichols, their leader's longtime teammate in Boston. He would reportedly receive $3,000 for the remainder of the season, and his family planned to join him in the City of Brotherly Love. Word was that the second-place Pirates and first-place Giants had both expressed some interest in signing Nick. In fact, the *Boston Globe* said that the Giants inquired one day too late, and that if Nick hadn't already signed with Duffy, New York would have been his preference.[60]

By the time Kid Nichols made his debut with Philadelphia, the team had fallen into fourth place in the NL behind Chicago. His first appearance was in a home game on July 21, the second game of a doubleheader against the Pirates.

"When Nichols was trotted out for the second game he received a great ovation" from the 6,635 spectators, reported the *Philadelphia Inquirer*, adding that "Nichols was repeatedly applauded for his work at the end of nearly every inning."[61] The only time he gave up as many as three hits in an inning was the sixth, when the Pirates scored their only run. He followed that with hitless frames in the seventh and eighth, and won 5–1. That gave the Phils a win-loss record of 49–35, ten games behind the Giants.

On July 26 with Frank Selee's Cubs in town, Nichols added to his career list of extra-inning triumphs. Through the first seven innings, Nick allowed his old manager's team only two hits, and no runs. The Cubs then scored once in the eighth and again in the ninth to tie the game. The Quakers won it for Nick in the bottom of the eleventh, 3–2. Nick even singled and scored during the game. Nick faced Selee's squad again on the 31st in Chicago, but this time the Cubs prevailed, 3–2. By then, however, the Phillies had regained third place.

In the second game of a doubleheader in St. Louis on Sunday, August 6, Kid Nichols faced his old team. Undoubtedly to his satisfaction, the Phillies had already won three of the first four games in the series. The starting pitcher for the Cardinals was rookie Jake Thielman, who would end the season tied with Jack Taylor for the team's leader in victories with fifteen. "The sympathy of the fans was clearly with Nich, and on every side could be heard, 'I hope Nich will win,'" reported the *Inquirer*. The Cardinals scored a run in the first off of their former skipper, but their offense was pretty quiet after that.

Batting seventh for St. Louis in that game was the man who took the reins from Nick, Jimmy Burke. By this time, Robison had demoted him and taken the job himself. "When Burke went up to bat the first time, in the second inning, two ex-managers of the Cardinals confronted one another," noted the *Inquirer*. "Nichols smiled sweetly, as much as to say, 'I won't do a thing to you,' while Jimmie looked as serious as a prisoner on the dock. The Kid was cruel, however, as he never allowed Jimmie a hit out of three times up."

The Cards did threaten in their half of the fourth inning. Jake Beckley led off with a triple, the only extra-base hit off of Nick that day. After one out, George McBride grounded toward Nichols. As the *Inquirer* described it, "Nich got the ball, ran Beckley down, who was trying to return to third, and whirling around got George at second. It was quick, heady work and deserved the round of applause the play evoked."[62]

Though Nick was piling up scoreless innings following the first, after five he was still trailing, 1–0. The Phillies then came up with two in the sixth frame, and that was it for the scoring. Nichols, won 2–1, while scattering four hits. He also had the satisfaction of singling against his old team.

The next day, the Phils began a seven-game losing streak, and they started another one on August 23, dropping them back into fourth place. Nick won a rain-shortened game on the 15th by a score of 3–1, but during the losing streaks he had three losses in which he received almost no offensive support. In those three games he gave up a combined thirteen runs, not great but not horrible, while his offense only scored a total of two. He did finish the month on a positive note, in New York.

The other starting pitcher was Joe McGinnity, and this time the Phils gave Nichols plenty of offensive support early, driving the "Iron Man" from the game in the early innings. Nick pitched shutout ball through seven innings but weakened considerably in the eighth, and Duffy decided to bring in former Beaneater Togie Pittinger to save the game. Nichols earned an 8–5 win.

"This was Nichols' first appearance here in a Quaker uniform, and he was given a rousing reception as he walked into the box," wrote the *Inquirer*. "Even when the heavy hitting drove him to the bench in the eighth, the cranks rose and cheered him for his good work in the early innings."[63]

Even though Philadelphia had two very rough patches during August, the team ended the month with a win-loss record of 63–55. In September, Nick took advantage of his elder statesman status to offer one of the final extended treatises on pitching of his major league career. This time, he wove several of familiar themes together:

> A pitcher's powers come to him naturally. A man may be able to hurl a ball with the speed of a catapult, but he does not necessarily become a star. Speed is needed, but one must have something besides that. First of all, he must be absolutely rattle proof. In a tight pitcher's battle one lapse will prove his undoing. He must always be on the alert, ready to dash in and field the bunt or scurry to first and cover that bag on a hit to the first baseman. Above all things, he must study the batsman and find out the balls they can hit and the balls that puzzle them. A young twirler cannot learn that in one season or two seasons. It requires experience to master these fine points.
>
> There are nine men in a game of ball, and each acts as a unit to attain success, but the fact is certain that the pitcher is handling the ball most of the time and he can make or break victory. At the same time the greatest pitcher in the world cannot win unless he has support, and here again is where he must show sand. In a hard game an unfortunate blunder on the part of one of his fielders will demoralize many near stars. It is the man who goes ahead and retires the side with runners on the bases that is successful. A pitcher's most valuable asset is his arm, and his arm should respond to a clear head. Liquor tends to destroy the usefulness of both, and no player can survive long in fast company who has improper habits. Pitchers in recent years have had the upper hand of the batsmen, as modern averages attest, but I don't believe that it is because the batting has gone back. Years ago a club was fortunate to have one star twirler. Nowadays clubs are supplied with three and sometimes five first class men. That is what has kept the batting down.[64]

From the last day in August through late September, Kid Nichols enjoyed excellent success. He won five of his six starts, including a four-hitter at home against Boston on the 9th, 4–2. On the 15th, he won in Boston by the same score, the final time in his long career that he would win a game in the city where he had starred for so long. His last two wins during that span were a 2–0 shutout in Pittsburgh against the NL's second-place team, on the 23rd, and a 5–1 victory in Cincinnati on the 28th.

If fate required Kid Nichols to lose a start in October, it seems fitting that it would be against Frank Selee's Cubs, on the 2nd. For Philadelphia, Kid Nichols finished with an earned run average of 2.27 and a win-loss record of 10–6. Combined with his record in St. Louis, he was a combined 11–11. The Phillies finished at 83–69, in fourth place among the NL's eight teams. After the sour start to the season, it had to feel good for Kid Nichols to end the season with a winning team that stayed out of the second division.

Nick's plans after the season were unclear, other than that he wouldn't be on his Kansas City bowling team when its winter season began. There'd be enough other current and former major leaguers to fill his shows on different teams in the league, namely Johnny Kling, Joe Tinker and Dale Gear. Kid Nichols was expected to be staying elsewhere during the bowling season.[65] In February, the *Philadelphia Inquirer* reported that Kid Nichols was in New Orleans, as was Phillies infielder Frank Sparks.[66] Presumably Nick and Jennie, and perhaps Alice, were staying with his sister Jessie, brother-in-law Sam Nickells, and their brood, as had been the case before the 1898 baseball season.

That month Nick offered his views on the spitball, which had become very popular in the American League. "The spit ball will never be used long by any pitcher who wants to save his pitching arm," Nick predicted. "The throwing of the spit ball calls into play an entirely different set of muscles from those used in hurling the other curves or straight balls. The result is that the pitcher who uses the spit ball builds up muscles that can be used only for this ball. In building up this set of muscles the other muscles naturally suffer, and when the pitcher tries his other curves he finds he has lost much of his former effectiveness. I would not advise any budding pitcher to try to cultivate the spit ball, for it means an early death to his diamond career."[67] More than a decade would pass before the spitball was banned, and even then certain practitioners excepted.

During spring training, talk about Kid Nichols and the Kansas City Blues surfaced again, this time in *Sporting Life*, which wrote that "Johnny Kling, catcher for the Chicago Nationals and Kid Nichols, of the Philadelphia Nationals, have offered George Tebeau $22,000 for the Kansas City team's franchise in the American Association."[68]

Nichols spent the spring in New Orleans working out with members of Connie Mack's Philadelphia Athletics. Opening Day for the Phillies was April 12 but Kid Nichols didn't pitch until the 21st. He was the starter in Boston in a slugfest that the Phillies won 18–8, but he left the game very early after giving up most of his former team's runs.

On the 25th in New York, he was the fourth Phillies pitcher in a shutout by the Giants, 7–0. Three days later he also pitched in New York, as the starter. He shut the Giants out for the first four frames but then allowed runs in each of the next four innings and lost, 7–2. Something was clearly wrong, and Nick didn't pitch again until May 18, in Chicago. He pitched briefly as the third of four Phillies pitchers in a blowout loss, 14–5. The gap between major league action hadn't helped; in just one-third of an inning Nick allowed two walks and two hits, plus he threw a wild pitch. He didn't even have the consolation of losing to Frank Selee, because Selee had stepped down as manager of the Cubs due to declining health.

Not long afterward, Nick threw in the towel. In his handwritten autobiographical document from around 1949, he explained, "I developed pleurisy and was unable to get into condition." Pleurisy is an inflammation of the lining of the lungs and chest, which often causes sharp pain when a person coughs, and even simply takes a breath. As a result, Nick wrote, "I asked for my release and I obtained it." There'd be talk off and on about Kid Nichols joining some other franchise, but his major league career was over.

For Philadelphia in 1906, he had only made two starts and two relief appearances. He earned no wins and suffered one loss. In 11 innings he gave up seventeen hits, made two wild pitches, hit two batters, walked thirteen and only struck out one. Though four runs against him were unearned, his earned run average was 9.82.

Those ugly numbers, however, couldn't make the slightest dent in an astounding career record. Kid Nichols won 361 games, lost only 208, and saved 17. He completed 95 percent of his career starts. To this day, only six pitchers in baseball history have amassed more victories than Kid Nichols.

8

Choices and Changeups

From early June into July of 1906, Kid Nichols either received offers from or expressed hope about latching on with several teams. His old Boston teammate Billy Hamilton said that Nick would be welcome on his Harrisburg club in the Tri-State League, and by early summer the Kid was working out at the Polo Grounds and looking to sign with the Giants or Highlanders. Highlander manager Clark Griffith, at least, was interested.

Over the remainder of the year, Nick's name would come up regularly in various contexts. First he was to appear in an exhibition game with the likes of Cap Anson and Nap Lajoie in Columbus, Nebraska, then he was likely to become manager of Denver's Western League team. In October it was the team in Buffalo and in November it was Jersey City. One of the more persistent reports, spanning December to at least March, had Nick and Jake Beckley seeking to run a new Western League franchise in St. Joseph, Missouri, if that league expanded from six teams to eight. However, expansion turned out to be two years away.

In the midst of this, two dailies in Washington, DC, provided an interesting lesson in journalism by publishing contrasting announcements about Nick a few days apart. First up is the *Post*, and second the *Times*:

> Charlie Nichols thinks he made a mistake in giving up bowling. He will go in for the sport this winter, in the hope of getting back into big-league pitching shape for next season.
>
> Charley Nichols thinks he made a mistake when he took up bowling. He was always a successful pitcher until then. He will get a trial with the Boston Nationals next year.[1]

Setting aside spelling, the first seven words were the same, but the opening sentences concluded very differently. Which accurately represented Nick's thinking at the time? Given that he had opened his own bowling alley at the time, it's unlikely he would try to harm that activity's reputation as 1906 was drawing to a close. Also, he hadn't bowled during the offseason leading up to 1906, and it's quite conceivable that he regretted it. *Sporting Life* resolved any doubt when it reported that "Kid Nichols has resumed work on the alleys to restore his arm."[2]

If Kid Nichols was feeling like an old man at the beginning of 1907, he didn't act like it. In January he brought the game of broom ball to Kansas City from New York, but with a twist: the contests were conducted on roller skates, and Nick served as referee. It was basically like hockey, five on a side, with a basketball. One match that month was witnessed by more than 3,000 people at the city's Convention Hall.[3]

As the major league teams were conducting spring training in preparation for the 1907 season, Kid Nichols reflected on his career and the changes he had witnessed:

> ... I am still a "kid," and good for a few more years on the diamond. There are men in the game older than I, but I've been pitching longer than any of them. Even the ancient Cy Young has to give me precedence, and some of the fans believe it was Cy who pitched when the dove struck out from the ark. Joke, eh?
>
> There have been many improvements in the game since I first faced the fans, and I suppose there'll be more in years to come, although I can't see where unless radical changes are made in the sport. I would hesitate to suggest any myself.
>
> Baseball nowadays, and especially as played from the pitcher's box, is a science. The old-time corner lot rules that went when I broke into the game have gone into oblivion, and along with them the players who couldn't keep up with the procession. Unless a player is a student nowadays, he soon loses out. The game is still baseball, but it's not the game we played twenty years ago. It's faster, it's more exacting and it is more exciting.
>
> One of the best changes ever made was the foul strike rule. It has lessened the pitcher's work and quickened the game. Before that rule a batter could foul until he wore the pitcher out or got a base on balls. In a tight corner such tactics sometimes won the game by finally bringing to the bat hard hitters who would not ordinarily get a chance at the ball.
>
> Another change that has come about, and it was brought about by the brotherhood fight, is that the young man gets his chance in the game. Before the days of the brotherhood the magnates kept their old men year in and year out, fearing to change. Nowadays the managers are always on the lookout for young blood, meanwhile not forgetting to hold on to the old men that are still making good. But the old player must make good or out he goes. The men get better treatment, too, than they did in the old days. They are quartered at the first-class hotels, they travel first-class, and they have better accommodations all around.
>
> Salaries? Well, I don't know about salaries being any better, although you hear a lot about big ones. You hear about $8000 and $10,000 ones, but none of 'em ever came "Kid" Nichols' way. I've always drawn good salaries, but I don't believe the average now is any higher than years ago. There may be some "phenoms" who are getting them, but nobody ever showed this Missourian the color of any of the real big ones you hear about.
>
> I don't even know yet — that is, I haven't decided — whether I'll play this summer. Retire? No, no, no; but I've got this bowling alley here, and I may have to stay here

> to run it this summer. If I make it go then next year I'll get into the game again. I'm too young to retire yet, unless I can make more money at something else.
>
> The future of the game? That's hard to tell, but it will always be the national game. It's distinctively American. The kids play "one o' cat" at school and graduate into the amateur leagues. When they get into business they're fans and they stay fans till they die. Until the kids quit playing, baseball will be the national game."[4]

On March 24 the *Washington Post* reported that Kid Nichols "had several offers from Eastern clubs, among them one from the Philadelphia Nationals."[5] How serious or appealing those may have been is anyone's guess. During the 1907 season he did end up staying away from the majors, and the minor leagues as well, but naturally he couldn't erase baseball from his life entirely. By May, he was incorporating baseball into his business.

"The once-famous pitcher 'Kid' Nichols is erecting on the third floor of his bowling academy in Kansas City, a device for reproducing every play in the baseball games the Blues play away from home," *Sporting Life* explained. "He will have a diamond painted on a large board and electric lights at each position. The lights will be so arranged as to show how each fielder handles a hit ball, whether cleanly or whether he bobbles it. Lights will show the progress of men on bases. A song will indicate each run while a buzzer will signify a hit. The batting order will be posted and a light will show what man is at bat. Cards will show the balls and strikes as registered, against players."[6]

Such scoreboards had been around in one form or another for at least a decade, but leave it to Nick to improve upon it. The *Kansas City Star* reported that on one occasion in May, Kid Nichols drew more than 900 people to "watch" a Blues game in Milwaukee.[7] On August 6, Nick actually filed a federal patent application for his unique design.

From June into early October, Kid Nichols' name would pop up in the Kansas City papers with some regularity, and occasionally elsewhere. For example, on June 19, the *Star* shared Nick's good news that "Miss Alice Nichols returned last night from Sacred Heart convent, St. Joseph, Mo."[8] And in July, it was reported in the South that the Montgomery, Alabama, club had made a concerted but unsuccessful effort to recruit Nick.[9]

By August, Kid Nichols had gone from simulating baseball games to playing in them again as the head of a local semi-pro team. In addition to games against rivals in Kansas City, the team spent a week playing in northern Kansas. Nick played first base, suggesting that either his pitching arm was still bothering him or that he thought it unfair to throw against far less experienced ballplayers. This development was even reported in *Sporting Life* toward the end of September.[10]

Sometime that autumn, Kid Nichols purchased the Crescent Bowling Alleys, at 1211 Walnut, which he rechristened the Nichols Bowling Academy.

For Kid Nichols, managing a bowling business didn't mean hour after hour of zero contact with his wife and daughter. In fact, *Kansas City Post* reporter J.P. Hughes chose to interview Mrs. Nichols about her husband's second-favorite sport. "I think that bowling is an ideal woman's game," Jennie Nichols said, as she supervised girls as they bowled. "It is a great muscle developer and gives the girls a form of exercise that they need. I have never felt better in my life since I took up the sport and there is scarcely a week when I do not roll from five to ten games. My daughter has a club of girls who come here every week, and a healthier crowd of young women you never saw." The article was accompanied by a photograph of Alice rolling a ball down the alley, with Jennie standing behind her.[11]

Jennie even took a team of Kansas City women to the American Bowling Congress tournament in Cincinnati in February. In addition to being a minor press sensation, Kid Nichols and the ladies were treated like royalty by Reds owner Garry Herrmann. They ended up staying two weeks, longer than they planned, because Herrmann insisted.[12]

Other bowling pursuits for Kid Nichols that winter included the "Novelty League," in which he and Jennie competed against other couples, and the "Kid Nichols Kids," for youngsters. The latter name would also be applied to baseball teams led by Nick. Speaking of his favorite game, during that winter Nick was one of the athletes recruited by Johnny Kling for a four-team indoor baseball league in Kansas City.[13]

During the first few months of 1908 Nick's name rarely showed up with regard to professional openings, though on June 10 it was announced that the Midgets of Springfield, Missouri, a Western Association club, had been negotiating with Nichols. Then on June 22 in Oshkosh, Wisconsin, the state where Kid Nichols was born, the board of directors of the city's minor league team held a meeting. One of the directors was I.S. MacNichol, the son-in-law of John Nichols, the half-brother of Charles. A few strings were pulled and soon an announcement appeared in the local paper that Kid Nichols would return to the pro ranks.

For the Oshkosh Indians of the Wisconsin-Illinois League he would replace manager George Bubser — who, as with Nick's demotion in St. Louis, would remain as a player.[14] The team had a win-loss record of 22–35 with Bubser at the helm and was in last place.

Kid Nichols reached Oshkosh in time for its home game on July 11 against the team from his birthplace, Madison, but he apparently only observed from the stands. On the 12th he made his debut on the diamond, and the team responded by shutting out Madison, 2–0. It was only the team's seventh game at its new Driving Park field, and the previous six had all resulted in defeats. On the 13th, Nick inserted himself in the lineup as a player, but in right field

Probably the team that traveled to Cincinnati in early 1908. Jennie Nichols is the bowler in the center.

rather than as the starting pitcher. The visiting team was the Pretzels of Freeport, Illinois.

The reporter for Oshkosh's daily was clearly thrilled to be covering a player of the Kid's caliber, as reflected in the descriptions of Nick's first game action. "The way he talked to the Indians and filled them with 'ginger' and fighting spirit was good to behold," the paper wrote. When Nick was due to bat in the third inning, he "was given a great demonstration when he stepped to the plate. Then everything was quiet when he batted. Two balls were called in order, then a strike — and presto — the new manager made a long, sweeping drive over left field that looked good for at least three bases and brought the grandstand to its feet, cheering madly. Ireland was after the ball like a flash, and when Nichols had almost touched second, the fielder was seen to make a last desperate leap, catching the sphere with one hand. Both Nichols and Ireland were given an ovation for the long drive and its brilliant catch."

After nine innings, the Indians found themselves in a scoreless tie. In the bottom of the tenth, Indians catcher Bill Warren popped one up beyond the gap between second and third. Freeport's player-manager, Thomas Schoonhoven, followed the ball as it drifted toward the foul line, only to muff it. Warren was credited with a double though the newspaper insisted that it should have been ruled an error. In any case, that brought up Manager Nichols. Nick didn't exactly hit behind the runner by grounding it toward short, but Warren sensed that he could make it to third, and he slid under the tag on Nick's fielder's choice. The next batter was pitcher Earl "Rube" Burwell, who won it for himself with a deep single to center. The large crowd cheered Nick and Rube as they walked in from second and first, and the newspaper was thrilled at the team's signs of life. "Hereafter Charles Nichols, the manager, will be referred to as 'King' Nichols as is the Indian custom for chiefs of unusually high esteem," the *Northwestern* declared.[15]

The Indians were shut out the next day but followed that up by winning a doubleheader, so Nick's tenure was indeed off to a good start. However, that didn't prevent a paper down in his birthplace of Madison from making a biting remark when he committed an error during one of his first games. "This proposition of playing old managers just because it looks like economy is poor judgment," said the *Wisconsin State Journal*.[16]

Still, within a week of his first game Nick's new job was news from coast to coast, and the *State Journal* soon changed its tone about the native son. When the paper wrote about a "Nichols Day" to be held at Madison's ballpark during the Oshkosh team's next visit, it bragged that Nick's "name is known to every youth in the land." The paper also reprinted the *Rockford Gazette*'s quip: "It's the Nichols that make the dollars and Madison needs the money."[17]

That game was scheduled for August 12, but in the interim, Nick had the pleasure of managing his Indians in a 23-inning game in nearby Fond du Lac, which Oshkosh won, 4–2. Both teams had scored twice by the second inning. Nick started in the outfield but removed himself in the tenth inning. Decades later, a paper in nearby Appleton reported that a resident still had the scorebook from that game. "Several of the oddities connected with this particular game included the fact that each pitcher went the distance, neither pitcher allowed a base on balls, neither hurler hit a batsman or delivered a wild pitch and neither catcher permitted a passed ball," reported the *Post-Crescent.*

After Kid Nichols was voted into the Hall of Fame, the *Post-Crescent* reported that the scorekeeper for that game "sent a letter of congratulations to Nichols and in the letter reminded the famous pitcher of the game. In a return letter two weeks later, Nichols said in part: 'I remember the game you spoke of very well — it was a most interesting game.... It was wonderful.'"[18] Nick's letter was kept with the scorebook.

A few days later, Nick had a sneak preview of how much his birthplace had changed when the Indians passed through Madison. "It is many years since I have visited Madison, and it seems good to be here again," Nick told the *State Journal.* "When I was last here Madison did not look so much like a real city. The town has improved wonderfully. Its well paved streets and its general cleanliness indicate a civic thrift. Madison is an excellent baseball town, and Howdy has a fine team."[19] Nick was presumably directing that final compliment at the Senators' manager, Howard Cassiboine.

In addition to the paving and cleaner surroundings, Madison would have looked very different to Kid Nichols because it had more than doubled its population since his family moved to Kansas City in the early 1880s. Another big difference could be found in the heart of downtown: the capitol building directly across from Robert Nichols' last butcher shop there, which young Charles would have seen so often, had been decimated by fire in 1904. When Nick returned in 1908, the current capitol building was about under construction in a process that would span a decade. One constant, at least, was that his oldest half-sibling, Mary Elizabeth Griffiths, still lived there with her large family.

In the first game of a doubleheader against La Crosse on the 9th, Nick pitched a complete game but his offense didn't give him quite enough help. He was the losing pitcher in a 3–2 contest, but at least he wasn't wild as he had been during his final month with Philadelphia two years earlier.

Though "Nichols Day" was scheduled for the 12th, Oshkosh played in Madison on the 11th, or at least made an attempt. The game was called after five innings played in a drizzle, before a small crowd. Nick hadn't inserted himself in the lineup. Because the game ended as a 1–1 tie, "Nichols Day" became a doubleheader.

That doubleheader, and "Nichols Day" itself, ended up being delayed again when it was decided that grounds were too wet on the 12th. One day later, the weather finally cooperated. "Nichols day at League park proved a good drawing card, and a large crowd of cordial fans turned out to welcome the hero of many battles," reported the *State Journal.* Kid Nichols pitched in the first game, and the paper reported that he possessed both speed and control. He shut out Madison for the first five innings and then yielded his only run in the sixth. He scattered seven hits while walking one and striking out eight. He even had two hits himself, one of which was a double. Thus, he emerged a 3–1 winner, his first professional win as a starting pitcher since September of 1906. He was about a month shy of his 39th birthday. Nick kept himself out of the lineup throughout the second game, which his team lost 1–0, but he had to have been very happy with "Nichols Day."

Back in Oshkosh on the 19th, Nick again pitched in a doubleheader. The starting pitcher for the La Crosse Pinks was another Wisconsin native who had made a name for himself in the majors, Emerson Pink Hawley. Pink, who was three years younger than Nick, had pitched in the majors for a decade, and peaked with a 31-win season for Pittsburgh in 1895, though he also won more than twenty games two of the three years after that. The two old pros hurled shutout ball for six innings and then Nick's squad broke through with a run in the seventh. Nick ended up struggling late, and after beaning a batter and walking three more in the ninth, he replaced himself with Bubser, who minimized the damage. Hawley also tired and a four-run eighth gave Oshkosh the victory, 5–3.

Nick defeated the Madison Senators a week later as part of a doubleheader in Oshkosh, improving his pitching record to three wins and one loss. Nick had also done a little relief pitching by that point, and during September he was starting pitcher twice but received a decision neither time, once because he lifted himself during an extra-inning game and the other time because of a tie. The last time that he wrote his name into the starting lineup was for the first game of a doubleheader on September 12 in Fond du Lac as a right fielder. He responded by homering to help the Indians win, 5–2. In the second game he made his final appearance as an unsuccessful pinch hitter in the fifth inning.

The season ended with Oshkosh Indians in seventh place in the eight-team league, with a win-loss record of 54–66. Given this overall record, and Bubser's at the time that Kid Nichols took over, Nick's 34–31 record as leader of the Indians was commendable. The *Northwestern* pointed out the improvement on the 19th, the day before Nick and Jennie were due to head back to Kansas City. His business obligations prevented him from a postseason trip out into the countryside to fish and shoot, but his great-grandchildren have a photograph of him golfing during his Oshkosh days, possibly his first exposure to that sport.

"Oshkosh baseball fans will always have a warm regard for Manager Charles Nichols," declared the *Northwestern*, which explained that he would always be "King" and not "Kid" Nichols to them.[20]

Wisconsin-Illinois League

1908

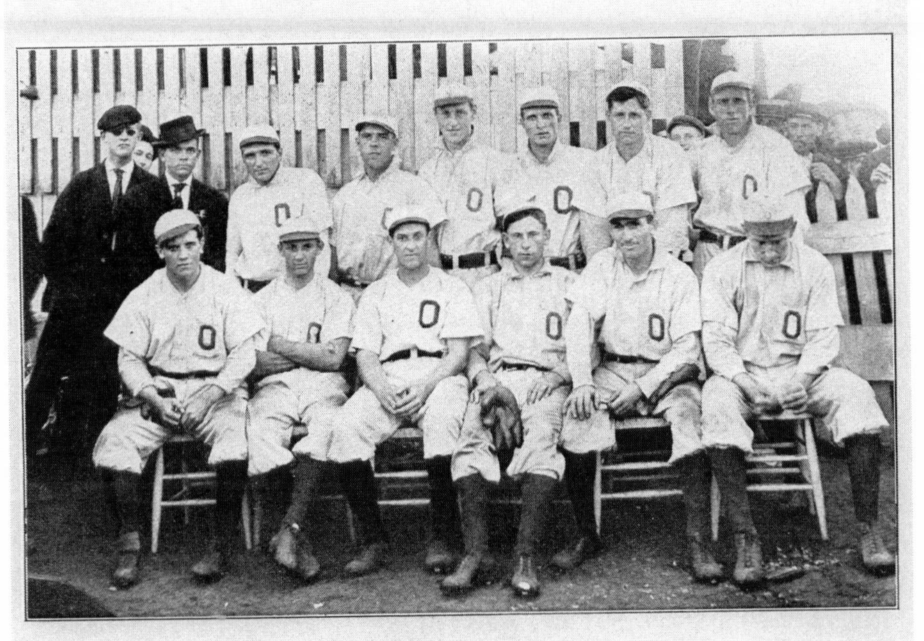

Oshkosh "Indians"

WARREN DOLAN BAUER PINKNEY CONVERSE BUBSER CURTIS
JOHNSON GROH NICHOLS BURWELL ANKLAM WHITE

THE CLUBS	Won	Lost	P. Ct.
1. Wausau	71	48	.597
2. Madison	66	54	.550
3. La Crosse	66	57	.537
4. Green Bay	65	58	.528
5. Freeport	58	63	.479
6. Fond du Lac	57	65	.467
7. Oshkosh	**54**	**66**	**.450**
8. Rockford	48	74	.394

(HOW THEY FINISHED)

26

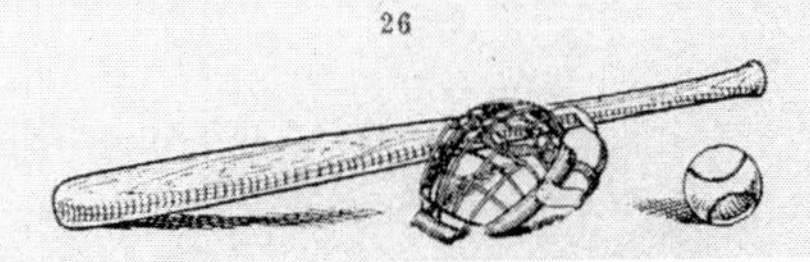

The 1908 Oshkosh Indians. Kid Nichols is seated third from the left.

Kid Nichols put himself in 35 games during that half-season, batted 128 times, made 23 hits, and scored 7 runs. As a fielder, he made 22 putouts, had seven assists, and committed three errors, for a fielding percentage of .906. His 3–1 record on the slab gave him career totals as a professional pitcher of 495 victories against 258 losses.

Two of Nick's 18-year-old charges in Oshkosh went on to have extended major league careers. One was Cozy Dolan, a starting outfielder for the Cardinals in 1914 and 1915. The other was Heinie Groh, who hit .292 over sixteen years in the NL, most notably with the Reds. In 1917 he led the NL in hits and in 1918 he led it in runs scored; in those two years he also led in both on-base percentage and doubles. In addition, in 1919 he led the NL in OPS (on-base percentage plus slugging percentage).

The remainder of 1908 was fairly quiet for Kid Nichols, but January of 1909 made up for that. A sublease began on the first day of the new year for him, in effect through March 31, 1912, with Bruns Bros. Amusement Co. for the old Royal bowling and pool hall, on the northeast corner of 8th and Grand Avenue in Kansas City. Toward the end of the month came the announcement that Jennie and Alice were among local women who might take part in a bowling meet. This was overshadowed within a few days by Nick's own bowling under very unusual circumstances that involved future Hall of Famer pitcher George Edward "Rube" Waddell. As the *Washington Post* reported, on the morning of the 26th Rube showed up in Kansas City "and proceeded to issue a number of challenges. He singled out John Kling first and defeated him six pool games. 'Kid' Nichols was the next to 'fall.' It was bowling this time, and George Edward won strictly on his merits." Rube's original purpose for traveling to the city was to arrange for a series of indoor baseball games. Instead, not only did the eccentric baseball personality succeed in these two challenges, but he also issued one to Jack Johnson, who had recently become the first African-American world heavyweight boxing champion.[21]

Whether or not Nick took Rube's challenge seriously, losing didn't really affect him, because at the end of the month his five-man bowling team set a record at a tournament in St. Louis, though it was broken the next year. The success of the Kid's team even made news out in California.[22] In Pittsburgh about six weeks later, Nick was named secretary of the American Bowling Congress.

In late March, Nick's name was again paired with Kling's in the press. Kling had helped the Cubs win consecutive World Series but prior to the 1909 season he had a dispute with team management over salary, not for the first time. While holding out, he announced plans to organize a semi-pro team in Kansas City's local weekend league, with Nick leading another team. This was front-page news in *Sporting Life*.[23]

Bowling tournament winners in early 1909. Kid Nichols is in the middle.

Kling and Nichols kept busy making arrangements in April and May, while Opening Day for the Cubs came and went without Kling reporting. The catcher instead announced his intention to take a semi-pro team from Kansas City on a tour. Kling was going to run the team and serve as its catcher, with Kid Nichols pitching.[24] Then in May, Kling and Nichols were reportedly attempting to buy the Lincoln franchise in the Western League, with the intent of relocating the club to Hutchinson, Kansas.[25]

Over the summer, Kling and Nichols were teammates in several semi-pro games in Kansas City. Then, to the chagrin of the ownership of the defending World Series champions, in early September the two men took their team to the Windy City. Around that time Chicago's semi-pro ranks attracted plenty of talent, as documented by Phil S. Dixon in his recent biography of Hall of Fame pitcher Andrew "Rube" Foster.[26]

In addition to Chicago papers reporting on these games, up in Oshkosh the *Northwestern* did as well, while reminding readers of the nice job Kid Nichols did with their Indians during the second half of 1908. "Charles Nichols, who managed the Oshkosh baseball team for two months last season, played with Kling's All Star semi-pro team of Kansas City against the Logan Squares and the West Ends at Chicago Monday," the paper reported. "Kling's team won both games and 'Kid' Nichols, as he was called when he was pitching in the major leagues, played an important part in the games. He made four hits in the two games, and fielded his position without an error." As was true for most of Nick's time in the Oshkosh lineup, he wasn't pitching.

Kling had also recruited a recent teammate to share the pitching load, in the form of Chick Fraser, a 14-year major leaguer who had gone 11–9 for the Cubs in 1908. But for this series in Chicago the biggest pitching splash was made by another hurler whom Kling had recruited, Sullivan Campbell, who no-hit a Chicago team on September 9. Kid Nichols again contributed hits to the victory. Campbell, who had played two years of minor league ball in Kansas prior to joining Kling's squad, would play two more as a pro in Nebraska.

"Johnny Kling's All-Stars" did very well in Chicago, but not in their last game in the city, played on September 11. They faced a famous African-American team known as the Leland Giants, formerly the Chicago Union Giants. Rube Foster wasn't able to play himself because he had suffered a broken leg in July. The most prominent player in the Leland lineup was future Hall of Famer John Preston "Pete" Hill, who batted third and played right field. Pitching in Foster's place was Walter Ball, who had spent a decade as the only black player on teams in Minnesota and North Dakota, starting in 1893. Ball limited Kling's team to six hits, two of which were earned by Kid Nichols, who batted eighth ahead of pitcher Chick Fraser. In addition to being covered in Chicago, the game was reported on back in Kansas City. "'Kid' Nichols' single and Fraser's double to right center averted a shutout for the visitors."[27] Nick scored the only run for his club in a 6–1 loss.

Kid Nichols kept a low profile for the rest of the year. In early 1910, he had a fateful conversation with a teenager who lived across the street. In February, Kid Nichols was living at 2417A Brooklyn Avenue and across the street, at 2416, lived Charles Dillon "Dutch" Stengel, who would later become famous under the nickname "Casey." Stengel had emerged as a multisport athlete in the area, including baseball. In 1908 he played with the Beatons, one of Nick's teams back in the 1880s, and in 1909 he was with the Kansas City Red Sox. It has been said that Kid Nichols even managed Stengel in the local athletic league in 1908 and 1909, but more likely they were merely on opposing teams.

In February of 1910, Stengel was signed by the Kansas City Blues, for the purpose of being given a tryout. In mid–April, he was released to a team in Kankakee, Illinois. Sometime around then, Nick decided to talk with "Dutch," who still recalled their meeting vividly more than 50 years later:

Kid Nichols, an old time pitcher who's in the Hall of Fame now, lived across the street from me then in Kansas City. He came over and gave me the best advice when I signed up to be a ballplayer. He said, "I understand you get in a lot of trouble at school and in a lot of arguments. Now when you start out in baseball, the best thing you can do is listen to your manager. And once in a while you'll have an old player teach you. Always listen to the man. Never say, 'I won't do that.' Always listen to him. If you're not going to do it, don't tell him so. Let it go in one ear, then let it roll around there for a month, and if it isn't any good, let it go out the other ear. If it is any good after a month, memorize it and keep it." And that's what his advice was in baseball. He said, "Now be sure you do that and you'll keep out of a lot of trouble."[28]

The rest, as the saying goes, is history as Stengel led the New York Yankees to seven World Series titles in twelve years.

During 1910, bowling and semi-pro ball kept Nick's name in the local papers with some regularity, but his only significant mention in national publications was during the second half of the year, after the publication of an interesting book, *Touching Second: The Science of Baseball,* by John J. Evers (the famous Cub) and Hugh S. Fullerton. An excerpt featuring Nick was published in at least five periodicals, which read in part:

Cy Young and "Kid" Nichols were the leading pitchers of fast balls, although both used curves while depending upon the "straight" one for their greatest success. They pitched the ball alike, throwing directly overhand, with the hand held as straight as possible and, at the instant of releasing the ball each gripped it tightly with the finger tips and loosely with the thumb. The finger pressure increased the speed of the natural revolution of the ball and caused it to jump more.[29]

During the first few months of 1911, three of Nick's relatives helped keep the family's name a fixture in local papers. His brother George had success in billiards, both at Nick's Grand billiard parlor and at Kling's, while Jennie received recognition for holding on to a record for bowling by women, which she had set a few years earlier, and Alice and a Mr. H. Everett issued a challenge to bowl against any other couple in the city.[30]

Nick himself would easily top them all in May by leading a baseball team in a game of some historical significance. A club from Keio University in Japan had spent three weeks playing collegiate teams in the United States, and on the 12th they faced Nick's Kansas City team, augmented with players from a few other local squads, including one from Johnny Kling's. The day before, the University of Kansas team beat Keio's 10 to 8 after the visitors' star pitcher, Kazuma Sugase, exited in the fourth inning with a sprained ankle. He didn't start in the game against Nick's team.

The Kansas City club, with Nick pitching, had the game in hand until the Keio players rallied for four runs in the eighth inning, after which Sugase came in to close a 7–6 victory. The *Star*'s postgame coverage included a large cartoon, in which Nick was depicted. Though the *Star* was a bit insensitive in its coverage, including the use of stereotypes, it also praised the Japanese team for astute play. One example it cited occurred when Nick was leading off second base and a teammate lined back to the Japanese pitcher, who without hesitation whirled and fired to second and doubled off Nichols, who was no more than six feet from the bag.[31]

The game was highlighted in the *Washington Post* where sportswriter Joe S. Jackson called Sugase "the Japanese Walter Johnson." In fact, Nick's team was mentioned in two separate pieces on that page.[32] The *Post* was publicizing Keio's upcoming game against Georgetown, which was attended by the entire staff of the Japanese embassy. Keio was edged in that one, 3–2.

In July, Kid Nichols took on a new role as a scout for the Detroit Tigers. On Independence Day he left Kansas City to watch teams play in the Texas League. Within that first week he watched the Austin team play in Dallas, and he was in Fort Worth from the 11th through at least the 15th, which included a visit from Austin. His primary scouting rival appeared to be the experienced Howard Earle, who worked for the Pirates. Another scout whom he encountered in Fort Worth was Hugo (sometimes "Hugh") Bezdek, the famous University of Chicago fullback who in 1911 was scouting for the Cubs. Hugo later became the first man to both manage a major league baseball team and serve as head coach of an NFL team.

Nick would also cross paths with coaches for the Cardinals and Athletics. A *Fort Worth Star-Telegram* article that mentioned several of these scouts featured a headline that referred to the "Famous Star" in their midst. "Though few people have known it, Kid Nichols, the greatest pitcher of his day, has been a daily attendant at Morris Park since last Tuesday," the paper noted. "Naturally quiet, he has been well concealed behind a score card in one of the upper boxes adjoining the telegraph booth. Smoking a big cigar, he has made notes on most of the Houston, Fort Worth and Austin young men."[33] Cigars had become Nick's one big vice perhaps as an outgrowth of his family's attempt to open a cigar store in the early 1890s, or the one that he helped Charlie Bennett launch a few years later.

On July 21, the *Dallas Morning News* reported that Earle had arranged for the Pirates to purchase pitcher John Henry Roberson, who went by Robinson, for $4,000. Robinson would make his major league debut on September 2, have some success with the Pirates in 1912 and 1913, and pitch parts of three other seasons. Kid Nichols named a few other pitchers whom he preferred over Robinson, including the pitcher with the next best record in the Texas League, Wiley Taylor of Austin's Senators — a team managed by Nick's old rival in Kansas City, Dale Gear. Taylor would make his major league debut four days after Robinson, for the Tigers. Kid Nichols was likely the scout who set that in motion. In contrast to Robinson, Taylor's career had no bright periods. He did get to pitch in 27 major league games between 1911 and 1914, but his win-loss record was 2–10 and his earned run average was 4.10.

Nick may have been trying to save face when he said that he preferred Taylor to Robinson, and if so, he shouldn't have felt embarrassed that Earle beat him to the punch. Kid Nichols was brand new as a scout, whereas Earle had been in that line of work for a few years. There just wasn't much untapped talent in the Texas League in 1911. Tex McDonald would hit .298 in the majors, but lasted only four years. Catcher Frank Gibson would play 23 games for Detroit in 1913 but he only made a meaningful contribution after returning to the majors in 1921 for the first of seven seasons with the Boston Braves. Gibson eventually compiled a .274 lifetime batting average in the major leagues, but he played in only 23 games in the Texas League during 1911, and with a batting average of just .159, not even Superman's vision powers could have detected potential major league value.

It's unclear how long Nick spent time observing Texas Leaguers, but he was back with his Kid Nichols' Kids team by August 19, when he pitched for them in Leavenworth, Kansas. While he was still scouting in July, one Kansas City paper printed stats for City League players, and before his trip south Nick had a win-loss record of 6–3.[34] He returned in time to lead his squad through an intense pennant race, which the Kids won on October 29 by defeating Johnny Kling's club. He pitched seventeen games for his Kids and won eleven.

The remainder of 1911 was quiet for Nick, but he received some very flattering press coverage in early 1912 when Cy Young named him to his list of the twenty greatest ballplayers. According to Young, "Kid Nichols forgot more baseball than 90 per cent of us ever knew."[35]

March brought Nick some additional national exposure, and a new line of work. In Chicago, his bowling teammate Louis Vielstitch set a new world's record in tournament competition. That trip to Chicago set in motion a new source of income for Kid Nichols. After the tournament Nick traveled up to Racine, Wisconsin, and arranged to sell cars manufactured by the J.I. Case Company, the firm that employed his half-brother John's son Howard. Nick also began selling Studebakers after returning to Kansas City. He had decided to pursue a new job when his lease on the Royal alleys expired that month.[36]

In 1912 Nichols and Kling continued as leaders of teams in the City League, and Nick's ex–Cardinal teammate Jake Beckley stepped in to manage in the league as well. By December, Kid Nichols had opened a billiards parlor at 1008-10 Walnut Street, two blocks from the Nichols Bowling Academy. Then on the 9th his half-brother John died back in Oshkosh. John received

The Diamond Theater, opened by Joe Tinker and Kid Nichols in 1913. Posters for three 1913 movies are discernible, "The Attack at Rocky Pass," "The Battle of Bloody Ford," and D. W. Griffith's "The Sheriff's Baby." Posters for a Patheplay movie and two Vitagraph releases were also displayed at that time.

robust military honors as his body was transported back to Madison for burial with his brother James and half-sister Fannie.

There was great joy for the Nichols family early in the new year when Alice married dentist Harlan "Doc" Everett in February. In addition to Alice and Harlan having been bowling buddies, he had managed the Kid Nichols' Kids while Nick was scouting for Detroit in 1911, and kept them in the City League pennant race. The ceremony was performed at St. Aloysius Catholic Church in Kansas City.

The next month was a grand opening for Kid Nichols and a new business partner, future Hall of Famer Joe Tinker, of Tinker-to-Evers-to-Chance fame. For two months or more the two men had been planning on opening a movie and vaudeville house at Fifteenth and Prospect, and on March 22 the Diamond Theater had its inaugural festivities. An ad that day in the *Kansas City Star* identified the theater's first selling points as its "absolutely fireproof" status and "splendid ventilation." The ad concluded by noting that the attraction for that evening would be that "Si Morgan will sing."[37] This presumably referred to Cy Morgan, a major league pitcher from 1903 to 1912 who was also known for being a movie singer—"talkies" weren't prevalent in movie theaters until after 1926. Morgan was with the Kansas City Blues for most of 1913 but late in the season he had a final stint back in the majors with the Reds.

By the end of that same month, news emerged that the semipro City League was going to expand beyond the Kansas City area and become an Intercity League of eight teams, with additions in Atchison, Leavenworth, and Lawrence, Kansas. Nichols and Kling would continue to lead teams, and soon enough it was announced that Nick's team would become the Nichols-Tinker club. Jake Beckley was one of the umpires.

During the summer of 1913 there would be two major occurrences in Kid Nichols' life. The first was on August 5, when the federal government awarded him U.S. Patent 1069629 for his "Amusement Apparatus," his unique version of an electronic scoreboard for displaying baseball games taking place across the country in close to real time. The next day was the sixth anniversary of the date on which he had applied for this patent. The second major event was Alice giving birth to Harlan Everett, Jr., Nick and Jennie's first grandchild.

Within two months of obtaining his patent, Kid Nichols put it to good use. Toward the end of September it was announced that the World Series games between the Giants and Athletics would be reproduced in Kansas City's Convention Hall. According to the *Kansas City Star*, the basic "scoreboard was designed by Harry Detrick, who has been granted a patent on many of the devices by which it is operated. It also contains one important feature, that of running lights between the bases, which was conceived originally by Charley Nichols, and which is used in this board by an arrangement with the former Boston pitcher." On October 7, more than 4,000 fans were in that hall for the first game, won by Philadelphia.[38]

In January of 1914, Kid and Jennie Nichols received exposure in publications far from Kansas City. Jennie was acknowledged as having held the women's record for highest "duckpin" bowling score from 1909 until it was broken that month by a woman in Washington, DC. Her husband was mentioned only briefly and was not identified as a former ballplayer of note. Nick was also mentioned in an item that appeared in *The Moving Picture World* about a donation that he and business partner Joe Tinker made to a charity called the Raggedy Stocking Fund.[39] At some point in 1914, the theater became Nick's only business holding.

In April of that year, a decision was made that Kid Nichols likely reacted to with sadness. Because major league baseball returned to Kansas City that year, in the form of the Federal League's Packers, and with the minor league Blues remaining popular, the Inter-City League was disbanded only a year after evolving from the City League. The *Star*'s coverage of this news included a long list of pros produced by the league, which originated in 1902. In addition to Casey Stengel, the league could claim Zack Wheat as a second future Hall-of-Famer. Another prominent alumnus was Claude Hendrix, three times a 20-game winner in ten major league seasons.[40]

Although Kid Nichols no longer had the City League as an outlet for his love of baseball, the National League pennant race that summer was an effective remedy. Nick's old Boston team, now called the Braves, pulled off one of the most incredible finishes in baseball history by jumping from last place on Independence Day to first. Then, when the Braves upset the heavily favored A's in the World Series, the games were conveyed to fans on an electronic scoreboard at Convention Hall that incorporated many more of Nick's design elements than a year earlier. It was explicitly "constructed under patents taken out by Charles A. Nichols," the *Star* noted, and differed "in many respects from any which has been used in Kansas City."[41]

Shortly after the World Series Kid Nichols received some publicity in scattered newspapers outside Missouri when Jack Doyle, first baseman for Baltimore during the legendary 1897 pennant battle and one of Amos Rusie's catchers, sang Nick's praises. Doyle regarded Walter Johnson and Rusie as the fastest pitchers he'd seen, but added that "there's one bygone pitcher who is overlooked. I mean Charley Nichols. Though not as fast as Rusie or Johnson he was good and fast, and his speed was all the more effective because [it was] sent up with an easy motion. Nichols was the best pitcher I ever saw to take another pitcher's game, and for that reason there never was another pitcher who was more valuable to his team than he was to the Bostons. By taking over another pitcher's game I mean going in when that other pitcher was in bad, and he could do that effectively even if he had pitched the day before. There haven't been any more useful pitchers than Nick."[42]

That winter was a quiet one for Kid Nichols on all fronts until he signed a contract in mid–February of 1915 that would return him to the collegiate coaching ranks. A month later he would begin to lead the Missouri Valley College team in Marshall, Missouri. His great-grandchildren still have the contract that he signed. His new job made the front page of *Sporting Life* and got him into a few other publications around the country, including in Boston.[43]

The college team's season was scheduled to open in mid–April with an away game against Central College in Fayette, Missouri, and the *Kansas City Star* noted that Nick would take the team there "in motor cars."[44] According to the *Spalding* yearbook covering that season, MVC lost both of its games to Central, on its way to a win-loss record of 3–6 against collegiate foes. MVC also lost a game against the Pittsburgh Rebels of the Federal League, 13–2.[45] At the end of the year the Federal League signed a peace agreement

The Missouri Valley College team that Kid Nichols led in 1915 and 1916. He is in the center of the men standing.

with the NL and AL, ending Kansas City's two-year stint as a major league city.

It's unclear when Kid Nichols and Joe Tinker backed out of the Diamond Theater, but with Tinker managing the Federal League's Chicago Whales for a second consecutive season in 1915 and Nick spending time as a college coach, they would have needed to find someone to manage the theater in Nick's absence. It seems more likely that they sold the Diamond, since by the summer of 1915 Nick was managing the Palace Theater in Kansas City for the Standard Amusement Company. By August, Nichols was serving as a road representative in southern Missouri and northern Arkansas for the newly formed Kleine-Edison Feature Film Service (George Kleine was given top billing at Thomas Edison's insistence at the time of the merger). By early 1916 Nick added Universal Pictures' "Blue Bird Photoplays" to his sales list.[46]

As the years pass following any prominent athlete's playing days, it's natural for his or her name to appear less and less often around the country, especially when the retired athlete doesn't live in a major league city. Nonetheless,

Kid Nichols was mentioned prominently twice during February of 1916. One instance was in an article by sportswriter William Phelon for *Baseball Magazine*. He wrote:

> One thing that certain pitchers, notably Kid Nichols, specialized in twenty years ago hasn't been tried in years, and seems to be utterly forgotten: Double-crossing the dangerous batsman; making him think he was to be presented with a free ticket, and then shooting them over while he reposed in haughty majesty. Nichols used to pull that on Anson, Connor and other mighty sluggers. It took a pitcher of iron nerve and elegant control to do it, but Kid Nichols had all of those articles in abundance. The modus operandi was simple, yet seems to have passed off the map. The catcher, just as he does to-day, would step off to one side, though not quite as far as is the present custom; then Nichols would send a couple of slow tosses out of reach. While the huge hitter posed like a monolith, and the crowd hooted, the catcher silently sidled in a little and whizz, whizz, the strikes began pelting in. A big, majestic slugger could be caught in that trap right along; a mechanical player would imagine that it was up to him to get a pass if he could, think that the first strike was a mistake, except [sic; accept] a third ball, and get another strike called on him before he got his senses — and a quick little hitter like Keeler would everlastingly kick the stuffing out of that ball. I saw Nichols pull that trick frequently on the 200-pound, slow-moving geezers, but Nick was too wise to try it on folks like Keeler and McGraw.[47]

Phelon may have had the mid–1892 incident with Cap Anson in mind, when Nick obtained a little revenge for Anson's intentional walk antics of the

Another shot of the Missouri Valley College team. Nick is in the dark sweater.

previous year, though the 1892 episode didn't quite match Phelon's description.

Also helping to keep Nick's name from fading was Honus Wagner, who was entering the second-to-last season of his Hall of Fame career. He named Kid Nichols among the six toughest pitchers he had ever faced. "I remember Nichols as a wonderful pitcher and a very fine man," Wagner added.[48]

By early March it was confirmed that Kid Nichols would coach Missouri Valley College a second year, despite the team's lack of success the previous season. An exhibition game against the Kansas City Blues was planned for April 13 and Nick said he might pitch half of the game if the weather warmed up enough for him to loosen his right arm sufficiently. Unfortunately, the game was rained out. The MVC club played much better ball in 1916, including two ninth-inning rallies on consecutive days in early May. The team ended its season in the Missouri Intercollegiate Conference with a record of 10–1–1, but a 12-inning tie against Westminster College meant that Kirksville, with a record of 10–1 but no ties, was awarded the conference pennant. Nick tried to overturn that ruling in early June, but without success.[49]

Kid Nichols' disappointment on behalf of his young players was followed the next month with sorrow when his remaining half-sibling back in Wisconsin, Mary Elizabeth Griffiths, passed away. She was 74. That left Nick with his brother George and sisters Sarah Colyer, Jessie Nickells, and Dora Northrop. He continued to maintain contact with some of Mary Elizabeth's children back in Madison.

In or around 1916 Nick and Jennie took up residence at 7433 Madison Avenue in Kansas City, in a home that still stands. This was after one year at 4031 Main. Before that, the couple had lived at 1528 Prospect Avenue from 1911 to 1914, a block from the Diamond Theater at 1433 Prospect. They would live at the house on Madison Avenue for about three years.

Thus with America's entry into World War I looming, Kid Nichols continued to experience instability regarding where he lived and worked. He was also developing a new passion. Articles in the *Kansas City Star* in August and November of 1916 revealed that baseball's role in his life was being replaced by golf. He had been known to dabble in it for more than two years, even winning prizes at the local Swope Park Golf Club, but his Class B victory on August 22 apparently inspired him to take the game more seriously. Of course, Nick didn't suddenly shun baseball; instead, he quickly credited it for helping his golf game.[50]

9

Calm in Kansas City

In 1917, Kid Nichols maintained a lower profile than in any other year during the previous three decades. With increasing regularity, on those occasions when Nick's name made it into newspapers, it was usually in some specific anecdote or in commentary on pitching. In 1918 there was somewhat surprising interest on the part of newspapers around the country in the possibility that the Missouri Intercollegiate Athletic Association would use Jake Beckley and Nick as umpires that season, but otherwise that year was as quiet as 1917.

In 1919, his name surfaced in Kansas City around the time of the World Series, due to the use of his patented scoreboard in the Convention Hall again for broadcasting purposes. This time, the *Star*'s coverage specified that Nick's lighting design for the basepaths was sophisticated enough to depict the separate actions of all runners when the bases were loaded, as well as rundown plays. The *Times* later noted when Jennie Nichols was observed in the crowd for one of the games.[1] It's too bad that this was the year of the infamous "Black Sox" scandal.

By late 1919 Kid Nichols was starting to turn golf into a year-round pursuit, and one that would take him very far from home. For example, in September, around the time of his 50th birthday, he played in Kalamazoo, Michigan, and in February of 1920 he was using his clubs in Pinehurst, North Carolina. In between those two excursions the second of his two grandchildren was born, a girl whom Alice and Harlan named Jane.

Kid Nichols' stature as a golfer received a boost that year in the pages of *American Golfer*, in an article by William Hanna on big leaguers who enjoyed that activity. The featured photograph was of Babe Ruth, shortly before his debut with the Yankees. Hanna noted that Nick took up golf after the age of forty, yet had "become sufficiently skilled at it to play in tournaments of the importance of the Trans-Mississippi." That migrating amateur tournament, which is still held today, originated in Kansas City in 1901 and Nick participated in it in 1918, when it was also held in Kansas City.[2]

Nick was still in the motion picture business in 1921, but starting in 1922 he also sold insurance for a few years, with the Southern Surety Company. Late in the summer of 1922 he was given a chance to return to his baseball home, Boston, for an old-timers' game. He worked out with the Kansas City Blues for a few days before his trip east. On September 11, he pitched the first two innings for one squad and Cy Young for the other. Regrettably, Nick's workouts with the Blues didn't help enough, and he was bashed for seven runs in the first frame. At least he escaped the second inning unscathed. Nick made the best of it, and played golf in New York about two weeks later, before returning to Kansas City. By the end of September it was confirmed that Nick's electronic scoreboard would again be used to show the World Series. The stated admission was to be 50 cents.

In November, Nick was prominently associated with bowling for the first time in about a decade. He became the local secretary of the Mid-West Tournament Company and helped them run a large competition in Kansas City. In this capacity he was linked for perhaps the first time to Barney Harvey, a local businessman who would become Nick's employer for a number of years.

Not quite a year after the 1922 old-timers' game Kid Nichols figured in an amusing story told by NL President John Heydler. "Last season, when I attended the 'Old Timers' Game' in Boston, I rode in a machine with Jimmy Collins, the old Boston third baseman; pitcher Kid Nichols, Larry Lajoie, as great a second baseman as ever lived, and old Cy Young," Heydler reported. "When we got out of the car at the field, a fan, looking over our party, said, 'I wish you boys were in your prime and I was your owner. I could sell you for $1,000,000 at the prevailing prices.'"[3]

The World Series in 1924 may have been the last hurrah for electronic scoreboards in Kansas City; radio broadcasts were becoming more commonplace. Nevertheless, 2,000 fans showed up at least once during that year's Series to follow a game on the board. The *Kansas City Star* had it set up in their parking lot, and the fans stood, brought their own stools, or sat in cars. Nick kept clippings about that year's board in the family's archives.

The following year brought two significant changes to Nick and Jennie's lives. Most importantly, they moved into a house with Alice, Harlan and their two kids, at 721 Valentine Road. Kid Nichols would live there until his death, which was still many years away. The house, which is just off of the Southwest Trafficway, looks largely unchanged today. After moving around so frequently during all of his previous decades in Kansas City, this decision would thus prove to be momentous. The other change was a new job for Nick as a manager for Harvey's Recreation, where he would work into the next decade. Nick also continued to sell insurance on the side until at least the historic stock market crash a few years later.

In 1926, Nick would receive some press exposure outside of Missouri when he anointed Walter Johnson as the greatest pitcher of all time. Nick had never seen Johnson pitch but he found "The Big Train's" statistics to be convincing. "Nichols also says talk of pitchers wearing out their arm is bunk," the report added.[4] In later decades, Nick would make such curmudgeonly comments with increasing frequency, though not at every opportunity. Kid Nichols may have been feeling a little older than usual around then, because this may have been the year when he began to wear eyeglasses regularly.

The year 1927 would start on a somber note for Kid Nichols, when his close friend Charlie Bennett died in February. In the next year or so Nick would sustain his multisport reputation by becoming bowling league champ of Kansas City's Co-Operative Club, and in early 1928 his grandson Harlan brought Nick into the national spotlight again when his latest "Kid Nichols' Kids" became the youngest team to be entered in a national bowling tournament.

In the spring of 1929 Nick would help the five-man Jenny Wren bowling team vie with a team from Atchison, Kansas, for top honors in the Inter-City

The Jenny Wren bowling team, around 1928. This may be among the earliest photographs of Kid Nichols wearing spectacles.

bowling league, and in November his management of the twenty-second annual tournament of the Middle West Bowling Association in Kansas would warrant a mention in the *New York Times*.[5]

In 1930, around the third anniversary of Charlie Bennett's death, Kid Nichols was afforded an opportunity to pay tribute to his friend in some eastern newspapers. "Charlie Bennett was more than a catcher to me," said Nichols. "He was my benefactor, idol and inspiration. What a man he was. No player ever showed more bravery. In all the time I pitched to him he never once met an emergency by signaling me for an intentional pass. I loved him for his courage as much as for his ability and all around manliness."[6]

In 1931 Kid Nichols apparently traveled to St. Louis for the last game of the World Series, against Philadelphia, based on a ticket stub pasted into one of his scrapbooks. Burleigh Grimes, a fellow Wisconsin native, won his second game of the Series for the Cardinals by a score of 4–2.

The next year Nick became involved in the national pastime in a more important manner. In March of 1932 he was acknowledged as one of the founders of an expanded Ban Johnson League in the area, for amateur ballplayers under the age of 21. Four years earlier, the Kansas City Junior League had been renamed to honor the late Bancroft Johnson, the longtime president of the American League. The plan launched in 1932 was designed to spread Ban Johnson Leagues across Missouri and Kansas, as well as neighboring states such as Oklahoma. By 1936 there were at least two leagues in each of those states and in Texas, with a total of more than four dozen teams. Kid Nichols was drafted to train and coach the Franklin Ice Cream club in 1932. This was prominent news not only in the central United States but also out east.[7]

The most famous alum of a Ban Johnson League would be Mickey Mantle, who played two years for Kansas' Baxter Springs Whiz Kids between World War II and the Korean War. There would be many others including pitcher Mort Cooper, the 1942 NL Most Valuable Player, and his brother Walker, NL All-Star catcher from 1942 to 1950; longtime White Sox catcher Sherm Lollar, a Whiz Kid with Mantle, and future Yankees manager Ralph Houk. More recent contributions included popular Royals second baseman Frank White; Rick Sutcliffe, the NL Rookie of the Year in 1979 and Cy Young Award winner in 1984, and pitcher David Cone, who played on five World Series champs in the late 20th century. The Ban Johnson League also served as an integration landmark while Kid Nichols was alive. "Even though Kansas City was ripe with its share of racial issues in 1947, I experienced little or no resistance when I entered the Ban Johnson League as its first black umpire that year," reported Bob Motley in his recent autobiography.[8]

In 1933, just as winter was turning to spring, Kid Nichols achieved a remarkable accomplishment in his other great sporting love: he won the Kansas

City bowling championship at the ripe old age of 63. This was news from New Hampshire to Utah. Nick could hardly have timed this triumph better, because to his tremendous sadness, it was a final opportunity for him to share with his beloved Jennie. She passed away on May 25 due to thrombosis (blood clotting within the circulatory system). She hadn't quite reached the age of 60. For the next few years, Charles Nichols was the most withdrawn of his entire adult life.

10

The Kid and Cooperstown

Directories for Kansas City in 1934 and 1935 didn't list a job for Kid Nichols, either due to the Great Depression or his own personal depression in the wake of his wife's death. It may have been a combination of both. By 1936, though, he had started working for the Pla-Mor bowling alleys, and he quickly became manager. He worked there for more than a decade.

Early in 1936, a first-of-its-kind event occurred that would eventually have a monumental effect on Nick's life. On January 29 the results of the initial election for the National Baseball Hall of Fame in Cooperstown, New York, were announced to an anxious public. In that inaugural class were five legends: Ty Cobb, Babe Ruth, Honus Wagner, the late Christy Mathewson, and Walter Johnson. Every year since, baseball fans have vigorously argued about which additional players merit selection, and which do not.

It took less than two months for a prominent sportswriter in the central United States to insist that Kid Nichols belonged. Cy Sherman, sports editor of the *Lincoln Journal* in Nebraska, didn't mince words when he wrote, "Deny the name Kid Nichols a place on the Cooperstown tablet? It would be nothing less than a baseball crime!" His declaration wasn't confined to his own newspaper, but it didn't exactly touch off a tidal wave.[1] Still, when Nick would travel to various big cities over the next decade or so, his candidacy may have made newspapers more inclined to interview him while he was in town.

One example occurred when he visited his birthplace, Madison, Wisconsin, in late June. A *Wisconsin State Journal* sportswriter printed a profile of Nick that was two columns wide and stretched the length of the page. He was traveling with his granddaughter Jane, who was sixteen at the time, and they stayed with Mr. and Mrs. Bert Sauthoff, one of his nieces and her husband. He also made contact with other children of his sister Mary Elizabeth, including Mrs. Bertha Cramton, whose son Charles would develop a particular rapport with Nick.[2]

Nick and Jane were passing through Madison on their way to a National Co-Operative Club convention in the Milwaukee area, where another newspaper demonstrated great interest. Nick and Jane were taken to the *Milwaukee Journal* by local resident Tom Nagle, a catcher for Nick during 1889 in Omaha and later for Chicago in the NL. Kid Nichols took that opportunity to praise Wee Willie Keeler as the best batter he ever faced.[3]

From Milwaukee Nick and Jane headed up to Oshkosh, and again the press greeted him warmly. This time, his brother John's grandsons, Neal and Tom MacNichol, took Nick and Jane to the local newspaper offices. Their father had been on the local ballclub's board of directors in 1908 when Nick was brought in as player-manager midseason. The *Northwestern* noted that Nick hadn't visited Wisconsin since 1919.[4] Nick's trip to Wisconsin had been in the planning stages since the fall of 1935, if not earlier, when Neal sent his "Uncle Charley" a copy of the twenty-year-old book *Oshkosh in Baseball*, which included a photograph of the 1908 squad. Nick's great-grandchildren still have this book. Neal's note said that his family was looking forward to seeing his uncle in mid–1936, and he thanked Nick for having sent him some unspecified item that allowed Neal to consider his first baseball scrapbook to be complete.

On and after December 19, Kid Nichols received atypical exposure in newspapers across the county as the result of an incident that had nothing to do with baseball, bowling, or golf. Instead, the impetus was his small, cheap, and outdated automobile:

> "Kid" Nichols, retired baseball pitcher, cherishes a 1924 model T "flivver." He drove it into a downtown parking lot.
>
> "You can't put that thing in here," said the attendant.
>
> "I'd like to know why," Nichols asked indignantly.
>
> "Because nobody around here can drive the contraption. We tried it the last time you parked in here," was the reply.

Before Christmas, this short tale appeared in newspapers across at least ten states, from California to New York.[5]

Cy Sherman's strong support and the warm reception that Nick received across Wisconsin did not lead to similar publicity in other parts of the country in 1937 and 1938. As in many recent years, Nick was again largely ignored by newspapers around the country. Exceptions were a very long and very flattering column in the *Philadelphia Inquirer*, probably by Perry Lewis, during the spring of 1937, and an article in the *Sporting News* during September of 1938 about Nick receiving Charlie Bennett's 1881 gold watch from Bennett's nephew, George Porter. That watch is on display in the Baseball Hall of Fame.[6]

In mid–1939 there was an eruption of interest in Kid Nichols, though it would last only a few weeks. On July 12 he played in his second old-timers' game, again in Boston, a day after attending the MLB All-Star Game in New York. As he prepared for his own all-star game, at the end of June he took time to praise Red Sox rookie Ted Williams to the Boston press. "I like that Williams boy," Nick said. "I saw him when he was with Minneapolis and can't say that I saw any weakness in his hitting."[7] Two weeks later he played for the NL team in the old-timers' game, with a roster that included pitcher Grover Alexander, shortstop Honus Wagner, his protégé Heinie Groh at third, and his longtime Beaneater teammate Fred Tenney at first. The AL squad included pitchers Walter Johnson and Cy Young, plus such luminaries as Tris Speaker, Eddie Collins, Frank Baker, and Stuffy McInnis. In contrast to his horrible first inning in the 1922 game, in a steady rain Nick pitched to five batters and completed the inning without allowing a run. The NL team won, 8–4.

Nick was interviewed by at least one East Coast radio station around then, and was the subject of a long and far-reaching profile in the *New York Daily Mirror* a week later. Author Dan Parker noted that Nick's trip, which he made with Jane, also included the World's Fair and other ballgames, including at the Polo Grounds. Nick opened up more than usual, including making the admission that when he quit the NL in 1906 he was broke, and had felt the need to hustle for a living ever since. Nick also bemoaned the fact that Jane's brother Harlan had a budding baseball career dashed by meningitis and typhoid fever.[8]

Another highlight of Nick's trip was the chance to see Jane, who had become a professional dancer, perform in the new show *Yokel Boy*, which rehearsed at Boston's Schubert Theatre before its Broadway opening at New York's Majestic Theatre on July 6. Notable cast members included Buddy Ebsen and Phil Silvers. During the first half of 1939 Jane had danced on Broadway in *Stars in Your Eyes*, which was headlined by Jimmy Durante and Ethel Merman. A few years later, just before Christmas of 1945, she would join the cast of *Follow the Girls*, which was about eighteen months into a two-year run. Jackie Gleason was one of that show's stars, and its cast also included Danny Aiello, who wasn't even a teenager yet. This was the same Danny Aiello who would be nominated for an Academy Award for his supporting role in Spike Lee's 1989 movie, *Do the Right Thing*.

Nick's 1939 trip out east was a thoroughly enjoyable one for him, but fate would only allow him to dwell on it for a few weeks. In mid–August Dora, his only younger sibling, passed away at the age of 66, and little more than a week later his only remaining brother, George, also died; he was 78. Nick's only surviving sibling was now Sarah Colyer, who was thirteen years older than him.

Nineteen-forty was another quiet year for Nick, and the only noteworthy highlight for him in 1941 was a trip back to Madison in July. At the age of 71 he decided it was time to apply for Social Security, but to do so needed a birth certificate. He had to return to Madison in order to have one created; fortunately, his sister Sarah was still alive to sign it as a witness to his birth. His return after five years resulted in another long profile in the *Wisconsin State Journal.* The paper noted that Nick was still with the Pla-Mor, as assistant manager for its 34 lanes, and that his bowling average had slipped in recent years to 185, down from 190. When the subject of baseball inevitably arose, Nick wasn't feeling too charitable.

"Aw, these youngsters today don't know what it is to pitch," he said. "I tell them they ought to be throwing five games every two weeks, and winning 35 a year, but they say they can't do it." He and the reporter then offered examples and statistics from Nick's own career to illustrate his point. In spite of Nick's disdain, he concluded the interview by proudly producing the lifetime pass to all major baseball games that he had received, undoubtedly two years earlier.[9] Today, his great-granddaughter Sharon Everett is in possession of it.

The year 1942 would begin on an upbeat note for Kid Nichols, and conclude with two more welcome events. At the end of January, his grandson Harlan married a woman named Henrietta Heiman, and on October 22, his granddaughter Jane became Mrs. Herbert W. Jones. Over the next decade Nick's six great-grandchildren were born, all while he was still alive. The first two, Sandra and Sharon, were born to Harlan and Henrietta. Next was Tom Jones, about a year before Harlan III. The two youngest are Cathy and Christy, Jane and Herbert's daughters. All six are alive and well. When his great-grandchildren grew old enough to say their first words, they would call Kid Nichols "Grandpa Nick." Sharon Everett looks back on him as a "kind, kind, gentle man." However, she said that the great-grandchildren didn't like Jerry, the Dalmatian Nick had throughout the 1940s.

On the last day of 1942 Nick was the subject of a lengthy, fawning profile in the *Sporting News,* accompanied by three photographs and a sidebar that provided detailed, year-by-year statistics from his playing days. Writer Dick Farrington had traveled from St. Louis to Kansas City to interview the 73-year-old Kid.

Farrington found him spending long days at the Pla-Mor, from 10:00 in the morning until an hour past midnight, and noted that Nick's duties included supervising the billiard room in addition to the bowling lanes. After Nick had talked about bowling at considerable length, Farrington gently reminded him that the purpose of his interview was to be baseball. "Here I am letting bowling put over a strike on baseball," Nichols replied. "That shouldn't be, eh?"

As the two discussed various facets of Nick's NL career, one of his longer comments was about his downfall in St. Louis during 1905. Nick didn't sugarcoat his feelings:

> Somehow, I always felt Stanley Robison had it in for me. But firing me as manager was only the beginning of our troubles. In Cincinnati one day — I think I had pitched the day before — Stanley ordered me to work on one of the gates. Players had to make themselves useful in more ways than one back in that period. Anyhow, I told Robison I wasn't going to watch any gate — that I was going over to the Latonia race track. To the track I went and Stanley Robison fired me off the club.
>
> I joined Philadelphia, and here's a good one. In my very first game with the Phillies in St. Louis, I beat the Cards, 2 to 1. That gave me a lot of personal satisfaction.

Nick did recall that game, a four-hitter for him on August 6, accurately. The interview also covered more recent topics, including Charlie Bennett's death in 1927 and the very recent death of Joe Gunson, who played a role in developing the catcher's mitt. Gunson was one of Nick's first catchers in the minor leagues, and Nick had visited him in Philadelphia in 1939.

Toward the end of the interview, Nick bragged about his two grandchildren. Jane had become a Rockette (Farrington called her a "Roxyette," using the famous dance troupe's original name) at Radio City Music Hall in New York, and Harlan was serving in the military. Not surprisingly, the interview ended with Farrington asking Nick if he longed to get into the Hall of Fame. When asked about that, Farrington reported that Kid Nichols "beamed."

"Sure thing," Nick replied. "I'd like to be in there. But they forget about us old codgers in a hurry. I've still got one real booster, however. He's Cy Sherman, who has written sports for nearly half a century in Lincoln, Neb. Maybe someday I'll make it." Farrington reported that Nick finished that thought "with a wistful grin," and concluded the article with this statement: "And you'll be reading about his nomination some day."[10]

Aside from Farrington's valuable contribution, the World War II years were largely invisible ones for Nick. Another isolated exception occurred during the summer of 1943, when *Boxoffice* printed an article about MGM honoring employees serving in the military. Among them were Sgt. Harlan Everett, Jr., and his good friend Lt. Walter Lambader. Harlan had become a booker for MGM, and in 1943 he was assigned to the Army–Air Force Technical School in Sioux Falls, South Dakota. The Nichols-Everett-Jones family archives has a photograph of Nick in that city a year later. At MGM's 1943 ceremony, Kid Nichols stood in for his grandson and appeared in the photograph accompanying the article.[11]

According to commentary in the *Kansas City Star*, around 1944 the campaign to get Kid Nichols into the Baseball Hall of Fame began to heat up.[12] If that's accurate, in contrast to recent decades, much of the work must have been done behind the scenes during its first four years.

The year 1946, at least, did bring Nick some attention, though mostly in the form of reminding people in Kansas City of the former superstar in their midst. In April he did receive a mention by Arthur Daley in the *New York Times*, who remarked, "The pitching arms of such relief artists as Ace Adams and Johnny Murphy would have atrophied if they had waited for Kid Nichols to weaken."[13]

Then in June, the *Kansas City Star* described a reunion of Kid Nichols and Cy Young, their first meeting since the old-timers' game in 1939. At the time, Young was sales promotion manager for Wilson Sporting Goods in Ohio, and he was visiting Nick at his Pla-Mor office. "We first met in 1890, when I was with Boston and Cy was with Cleveland," Nick recalled. "We both had about the same kind of a delivery — a high, fast ball right under the chin."

"And control," Young added. "These pitchers today," he started to continue, but just stopped and shook his head. Nick stepped in for him. "They pitch twenty games a season and think they've been worked hard," Nichols said, causing both of the pitching legends to laugh. "Why, we didn't figure we were earning our money unless we pitched thirty-five or forty games a season," Nick concluded.

"That's a fact," stated Young. "Why in 1903's world series Bill Dinneen and I pitched all eight games."

Nick declared that Babe Ruth had changed the game, and his friend elaborated. "It's not scientific anymore," Young noted. "Every batter steps up and tries to clout it out of the park."[14]

Though the two weren't quoted about the Hall of Fame, Nick's great-grandchildren consider Cy Young to have played a major role in the campaign on behalf of their great-grandfather. Not long after Young's visit, Nick's daughter Alice grew very frustrated by the lack of a campaign on her father's behalf. In late August she sent a letter to the Boston press in which she wrote, "Many of my Father's friends around here cannot understand just why you reporters in Boston have made no attempt to put him into the Hall of Fame." She did receive at least one very sympathetic reply, from Harold Kaese of the *Globe*, in which he said that "even if the game changes, the ball gets livelier and the schedule grows longer, let us put the great players of every generation into the Hall of Fame. Your dad, Kid Nichols, belongs there right now." Back in Kansas City, about four months after the interview with Cy Young appeared, the local *Swing* magazine was inspired to devote three full pages to a profile of Kid Nichols.[15]

To anyone who had been tracking Nick's results in Hall of Fame voting over that institution's first decade, 1946 may have seemed like the time to give up. In 1936, a special election for 19th century players had been conducted but nobody was selected. Nick's vote total was just shy of 4 percent, and that would be his high-water mark. In Base Ball Writers Association of America (BBWAA) voting for the Hall in 1938, 1939, 1942, and 1945, he never earned more than seven votes, and his highest percentage was barely above 2.5. The worst result came in 1946, when a special vote gave him half of one percent of the votes cast. The campaign supposedly launched around 1944 didn't yield any immediate fruit, though its leaders really couldn't be blamed; as baseball historian David Fleitz explained, the Hall's Permanent Committee made some strange choices in 1946. For starters, he noted that this committee enshrined Jack Chesbro, who won 198 games, while bypassing 300-game winners Tim Keefe, Mickey Welch, Pud Galvin, John Clarkson, and Nick, "all of whom were far better candidates for the Hall than Chesbro." Fleitz stressed that "the selection of Chesbro over Nichols is especially mystifying."

"It seems obvious, then, that in the mid–1940s the Permanent Committee was more impressed by single-season accomplishments than career records," Fleitz added. "They also bypassed Kid Nichols in favor of Rube Waddell and Ed Walsh."[16] Fleitz went on to note that the committee must have been impressed that Waddell, of the Athletics, who had even fewer career wins than Chesbro, set a record in 1904 by striking out 349 batters, and that Walsh had an astounding record of 40–15 in 1908 for the White Sox.

It would have been easy to understand if Kid Nichols had given up hope of getting into the Hall of Fame by 1947, but the only thing he did give up on then was bowling, and that was only under a doctor's orders. He had reportedly quit by the end of 1943, and maybe he did so, but later sources said this took effect after the war.

For whatever reason, in a stunning reversal Kid Nichols ended up all over the news during 1948. He may have lit the powder keg himself with an opinion piece under his own name in the January issue of *Baseball Digest*, "as told to Sam Molen." Whether it was Nick's idea or not, the title given to his two-page treatise was "Pitchers Are Sissies Now." In it, Nick expounded upon themes that he and Cy Young had raised together in 1946.

Nick noted that he was always asked the same question those days, why 30-win seasons for pitchers were uncommon. "One reason is that modern-day clubs carry too many pitchers, which prevents hurlers from working enough to bring out the best that is in them," Nick would answer. "The old-time clubs carried three pitchers; today, they have ten."

"Modern-day pitchers spend half their time trying to develop and master tricky deliveries," Nick added, then mentioned his own pitching success. "Yet, I had no fancy curves. Speed, change of pace and control are all any pitcher needs — if he masters them. And did you ever hear of Amos Rusie, Cy Young, Radbourne or Mathewson having an elbow operation for the removal of chipped bone? Such operations were unheard of until recent years. If the arm got sore, we went out and pitched until the soreness left — we had to, or we would have been dropped from the team."

He concluded with the kind of remarks that seem to surface from prominent baseball retirees of every generation:

> The game of baseball hasn't changed much in the past fifty years, but the players have a different philosophy toward the game. They want to make a lot of money and retire. I played the game at a time when the league had a salary ceiling of $2,400—the fabulous salaries later to be drawn by Ruth, Greenberg, Newsom and Feller were undreamed of. We played for the love of the game; there were few holdouts. We wanted to pitch every day; to win more games than the other guy—not for the money, but for the glory of winning.
> It's different today.[17]

Today's powers that be at the magazine thought enough of Nick's editorial to include it in a *Best of Baseball Digest* compilation in 2006. That same month, Nick's crotchetiness was offset a little by the well-known writer Grantland Rice, who reported that various managers, scouts and players had chosen Nick among the five pitchers on a list of "the most graceful ballplayers." As Rice summarized, "These men, in the main, made all plays look easy."[18]

In April, the campaign for Nick's Hall of Fame election received a shot in the arm when Ty Cobb firmly endorsed his candidacy. This clearly wasn't a hasty remark. In June, Rice reported that he had received a letter from Cobb. "I think everyone has overlooked one of the greatest pitchers of all time. His name is Kid Nichols. Here are just a few of his records from 1890 to 1906," Cobb wrote, and then he presented the statistical evidence. For Rice, that brought to mind a question he had posed to Christy Mathewson a few decades earlier, asking him to name the best pitcher he ever faced. "That's easy," Matty had replied "His name is Charles Kid Nichols of Boston. Nichols isn't a good pitcher. He is a great one."[19]

Kid Nichols certainly welcomed such advancement of his cause, but his life in Kansas City largely remained the same. One change was that by June of 1948 he had taken a job as an elevator operator at the Municipal Auditorium. More momentous was an event the next month.

On July 11, a baseball game was played at Blues Stadium for the Salvation Army's "Penny Ice" fund. Kid Nichols was honored prior to the game, which was between teams of Ban Johnson All-Stars representing Missouri and Kansas. The pregame activities also included the drum and bugle corps of the Wayne Miner post of the American Legion, an all-black unit.

When it came time to pay tribute to Nick, the local Co-Operative Club presented him with $636.50 that they had collected, for him to use however he saw fit. Four thousand fans had turned out, and joining Nick on the occasion were eight of his descendants spanning three generations, including his great-grandchildren Tom Jones and Sharon and Harlan Everett. Nick spent at least part of the evening with the boys on his lap. Though more than half of the fans left before the end of the long game, the Nichols family remained for its entirety, though all three kids had fallen asleep.

That same summer, Dan Parker, who had written a long and broad profile of Nick in mid–1939 for the *New York Daily Mirror*, decided to write another lengthy article on Kid Nichols, this time for nationwide distribution. He buttressed his new missive with references to Ty Cobb's stamp of approval. Parker concluded by declaring that thanks to "Cobb and others, the truth is finally 'outing' about this remarkable old-timer and he's bound to come into his rightful heritage by being admitted to baseball's Hall of Fame."[20]

By October, Kid Nichols decided to use his $636.50 windfall to see World Series games out east. For the first time since 1914, his old Boston team had won the NL pennant. He apparently thought that his lifetime pass included post-season games so his trip was almost ruined when he arrived at the Boston ballpark. Nick's predicament made news even out in California.[21]

"Only a kindly cop, who remembered the fabled pitching record compiled by the Kansas City flash, got him into the first game," Bill Duncliffe of the *Boston Evening American* subsequently reported for a news service. "After that, the Braves and the press took care of him. He was present at every game in Boston, and one in Cleveland. He didn't see much of any of them, though, and for a very good reason — some old time baseball fans hadn't quite forgotten the colossus of the '90s. So he wasn't able to analyze why the Braves lost the series. The fans saw him in the stands, and shook his hand, and built up a warmth of pleasure in his breast. 'Kid' Nichols discovered he wasn't completely forgotten."[22]

In some variations of Duncliffe's report he beat the drum for including Nick in the Hall of Fame, but for the next six months there would be little visible progress on that front. In February of 1949 Sec Taylor of the *Des Moines Sunday Register* wrote a very complimentary feature on Nick, but far more valuable from a strategic standpoint was commentary in the *Detroit News* toward the end of April that appeared under this headline that stretched across the entire page: "'Kid' Nichols Urged for BB Hall of Fame." The Detroit paper drew extensively from Taylor's work.[23]

In 1949, BBWAA members eligible to elect recent players into the Hall of Fame conducted initial balloting on February 11, with Charlie Gehringer of the Tigers missing election by a dozen votes. The results did trim the field to 20 for the final voting in early May. On the 5th it was announced that Gehringer had been chosen as that year's entry into the Hall, as was widely expected. What had to have been far more surprising was the announcement from the Hall three days later that its Permanent Committee had selected Charles "Kid" Nichols and the late Mordecai Brown. They became the fifteenth and sixteenth pitchers elected to the Hall. Nick was 79 years old.

At last! Probably taken in 1949.

"Happiness beamed from the sparkling eyes of one of baseball's great pitchers yesterday afternoon as he thumbed through the pages of numerous scrapbooks that hold the records of his brilliant diamond deeds of yesteryear," began the long front-page article in the next day's *Kansas City Times*. Nevertheless, the *Times* characterized Nick as not being very surprised, and the man's words confirmed that. It could be that advance word had leaked from the Permanent Committee. In any case, the paper also described him as "jubilant."

"That's fine, I'm glad to hear it," Nick said. "It's what I've been expecting. I've been hoping that I would be named before I passed on." He also shifted attention away from himself by commenting about the game as it was being played in the 1940s. He offered a new slant on his previous comments about pitchers. "I think there is too much managing today," he asserted. "A manager will yank a pitcher out too quick and ruin his confidence. There's too much shifting of lineups, too. We used the same men on the field day after day and they worked together like a team should instead of like strangers."

The *Times* added that Nick had given up golf, in addition to bowling, but exercised daily by walking his dog. He couldn't resist mentioning his family, including his son-in-law Harlan, whom Nick said usually attended or at least listened to Blues games with him. Nick was also looking forward to seeing his granddaughter Jane, whose family by then had relocated to Larchmont, New York.[24]

Over at the *Kansas City Star*, Ernest Mehl shed some light on his rapport with Nick. Mehl noted that he had gone with him to the first game of the 1948 World Series when Nick was almost turned away because he had no ticket. When Mehl crossed paths with Cy Young during that World Series, Cy remarked about what a pitcher Nick was. "In fact, he gave me some good beatings," Cy added.

Mehl believed that Bob Quinn, a Bostonian who had become President of the Hall of Fame in 1948, was among the key people who got Nick in. Thank goodness Kid Nichols didn't have to wait even longer, because Mehl said that Nick "had sought this honor so keenly it had become almost an obsession with him."[25] That night, Mehl had the privilege of interviewing Nick on the local station WDAF of NBC's radio network.

Naturally, the Kansas City papers wouldn't limit their coverage to a few days after this major development, and they pursued specific facets of Nick's life in detail. For instance, the *Star* printed an article by Louis W. Shouse on May 13 describing Kid Nichols as an inventor. The editor began by noting that Shouse had been a reporter for the *Times* more than 40 years earlier.

Shouse explained how, back in 1913, Nick had been able to add his own patented design elements to a scoreboard that was being built in Kansas City's Convention Hall to show the progress of actual baseball games. He explained that six men were needed to operate the board, and that during its first two years of usage, George J. Forster of the Kansas City Athletic Club's staff was instrumental in the team's smooth performance. Forster would eventually become a Brigadier General in the Army, a position he continued to hold in 1949. Due to scheduling conflicts the scoreboard wasn't used in 1915 or 1916, but it did serve its purpose for the World Series from 1917 through 1925.[26]

During the remainder of May, reactions to Nick's accolade were widespread and varied. Out in Boston, Harold Kaese of the *Globe*, with whom Alice Everett had corresponded three years earlier, wrote a long column in Nick's honor, and walked his readers through the highlights of his years with the Beaneaters. In *Grit* magazine, Roger Powers grumbled that Kid Nichols "should have been one of the first to be enshrined in the Hall of Fame." On the 23rd, papers from Pulaski, Virginia, to Ada, Oklahoma, noted that Ty Cobb had to be one of the most satisfied among Nick's many boosters. And in Kid Nichols' birthplace of Madison, Joe Hasel of WISC radio had an interview scheduled with Nick.[27]

With the induction ceremony scheduled for June 13, writing about Kid Nichols didn't subside much after May. *Co-Operator Magazine* bragged about their organization's member, including his seven-year perfect attendance record at their weekly luncheons, between his trip to Madison for a birth certificate in 1941 and his trip to Boston for the 1948 World Series, which the club itself enabled. Missouri Valley College similarly bragged that Nick had coached their baseball teams just before America entered World War I. The *Daily News* in Dayton, Ohio, proudly noted that Kid Nichols was traveling to Cooperstown with Russ Gentzler, a salesman for the Egry Register Co. headquartered in Dayton. Down in Florida, the *Miami Daily News Sunday Magazine* reported that Connie Mack had advocated Nick's selection shortly before the vote.[28] The *Buffalo Evening News* was happy to reveal that Gentzler's reason for heading east with Nick was to attend a convention at that city's Hotel Statler of the Society for the Preservation and Encouragement of Barber Shop Quartet Singing in America (SPEBSQSA), and that Nick, as an honorary member of a Kansas City barbershop quartet, would also be present.

The Buffalo paper may also have had something of a scoop when it said that in addition to Ty Cobb and Cy Young, such "great players of the old days" as Clark Griffith and Christy Mathewson had also clamored for Nick to be named to the Hall of Fame.[29] That would have required tremendous foresight for Matty, who died eleven years prior to his inclusion in the Hall's inaugural class of 1936. The writer must have been thinking of the very old quotation about Nick by Matty that Grantland Rice had circulated in 1948.

Kid Nichols' great-grandchildren have an interesting perspective on a photograph printed in papers during May and June. The photograph showed Nick seated, with a grin on his face as he looked at his great-grandson Harlan on his lap. Harlan was looking to the side with his arms extended, almost like an umpire gesturing that a batted ball was foul. The full photograph in the family's archives revealed that across from Harlan was his sister Sharon, sitting on the chair's wide arm. The two kids were holding their great-grandfather's old baseball bat from the 1880s, near the handle, with each other's hands alternating.[30] For some reason — today, with a laugh, Sharon blames sexism —

the journalists decided to edit her out of the photograph, cutting it almost in half as a result. When this slight was brought to Sharon's attention in 2011, she feigned great heartache about the photograph because as a young girl she was tomboyish and loved to play baseball with the neighborhood boys, even if they stuck her in right field all day and batted her last (if at all).

Kid Nichols with great-grandson Harlan Everett III and one of his sisters, Sharon. Taken in May of 1949 or earlier. Nick's great-grandchildren still have the bat.

Saturday, June 13, proved to be quite a day for Kid Nichols in Cooperstown. For the induction ceremony, Dodgers president Branch Rickey served as the master of ceremonies and the main speaker. He extolled the virtues of the "national pastime," calling it a road away from war and toward peace. He also singled out three other qualities: "First, the beauty of it. Second, the comparative freedom from danger of injury to participants. Third, the marvelous exactitudes and precision of measurements relating to human skills." When he introduced Kid Nichols as "one of the greatest pitchers of the olden days," Nick, undoubtedly moved by the entire experience, was apparently only able to reply, "I appreciate what they have done for me."[31]

The event, which drew a crowd of about 1,000 people, honored the 1948 inductees along with Nichols, Gehringer, and Brown. Gehringer caught flack for missing the ceremony but the disappointment subsided when he revealed that he had just gotten married, very quietly, and was on his honeymoon. In addition to Brown, 1948 inductee Herb Pennock was also deceased. Therefore, a photograph of the event showed the only 1948 inductee who was present, Pie Traynor, holding his plaque on one side and Nick holding his plaque on the other, with Rickey in between, arms outstretched toward each honoree.

Fred Clarke helped Rickey with the presentation, and he also caught Nick's ceremonial first pitch at the start of that day's exhibition game between Washington and Pittsburgh (which the Senators won, 8–7). Among the other dignitaries present were NL President Ford Frick and President Lou Perini and General Manager John Quinn of the Boston Braves. Photographs also surfaced of Nick at the groundbreaking of a new wing for the Hall, along with Frick and Hall president Bob Quinn, and of Nick taking a "practice pitch" on Cooperstown's mound, wearing what looks to be a Pirates cap.[32]

Others in attendance included those nearest and dearest to Nick's heart, namely his daughter Alice, granddaughter Jane, and her son Tom. At the time, Jane was pregnant with the older of Tom's two sisters, Cathy, so she has sometimes stressed that she was also present at the induction ceremony. Tom has a photograph from the event in which he appears with his great-grandfather and Pie Traynor, plus a third unidentified man. Months later, Traynor made a case that it was important to honor deserving players while they were still around to enjoy the experience, and that the Hall of Fame's voting system was too slow. Pie cited Kid Nichols as a case in point, and said being at Nick's induction was a touching sight. "Nichols was so proud of the honor that he took his daughter, grand-daughter and great-grandson to Cooperstown," Pie recalled. "There were four generations of one family present for the honor."[33]

In the end, Nick's trip out east lasted three months. On June 19 he saw Bob Feller and the Indians beat the Yankees, 4–2, in eleven innings. His great-grandchildren still have his scorecard from that game. In early July he took in a game in Greensboro, North Carolina, against Burlington. A photograph of him at the game, along with Jane and her father-in-law, appeared in the local paper. About a month later, he threw out the first pitch to his friend Frank Lay at a minor league game played in his honor in Kewanee, Illinois. Lay was an Amherst alumnus who may have helped get Nick into the Hall of Fame. Alas, Nick's pitch went into the dirt. In between numerous radio and some TV interviews, Nick worked in a chat with Casey Stengel and a trip to Washington, DC.[34]

Kid Nichols returned to Kansas City with just enough time to catch his breath prior to a special Kid Nichols Day event sponsored by his local Co-Operative Club. Lefty Gomez gave a short talk, and also among those present was Bruce Dudley, president of the American Association. Another organization in which Nick was also involved, by the way, was the Sertoma Club, which still exists today. Its focus is hearing loss.

That summer Kid Nichols again had contact with Fred Clarke, who was living in Winfield, Kansas. At the opening of the national semi-pro tournament in Wichita, the two Hall of Famers reminisced about a game in 1904 between Nick's Cardinals and Fred's Pirates. Nick's decision-making that day

At the Kansas City Co-Operative Club's event honoring Kid Nichols on August 16, 1949.

was strongly influenced by owner Frank Robison's dire warning about not being able to meet his payroll. Nick remembered the situation this way:

> Attendance hadn't been bad that year. There just wasn't any, but Fred Clarke, who was managing the Pittsburgh Pirates at the time, brought his team to town and for a change we had a lot of cash customers in the stands. Only it started raining in the first inning. It poured and then came down in bucket fulls. I was ready to throw in the towel when word came from the front office to play four and a half innings if we had to swim.

Kid Nichols before or after a broadcast in the spring of 1950. He's second from the right.

> Clarke was a good sport, though, and we kept playing. After four innings he came over and suggested that since we had been insane enough to go that long why not play the full nine. Water was ankle deep in the outfield but we played it out. St. Louis won 20–4. Beyond a doubt it was the wettest nine inning game in [the] history of baseball.

Clarke then chimed in. "I distinctly remember looking to my outfield in the third inning and all I could see was three baseball caps," he chuckled. "Well, the water was at least to the knees."[35]

After the summer ended, Kid Nichols was able to bask in the glow of his new status. It would be the only extended lull in his life. Sadly, during this respite his son-in-law Harlan passed away, on November 29, 1949. The cause of death was bronchopneumonia, following a heart attack. He was 63 years old.

In mid–1950 Kid Nichols looked well rested and was all smiles in a photograph that appeared in the local magazine *Swing*. The photograph was taken when Nick was taking part in a "Welcome Back, Baseball" broadcast on WHB. In the photograph with him were Parke Carroll, general manager of the Kansas

City Blues; Fred W. Pierson, president of the Blues Fans Club; Jay W. Wilson, chair of the Blues Fan Club; and Larry Roy, WHB sports director. Carroll would become well known late that same decade for his two-year stint as the GM of the Athletics, during which time he traded Roger Maris to the Yankees. Owen Bush, another on-air personality in Kansas City at the time, stood at the far left in the original photograph but was cropped from the version published. Bush would later enjoy a Hollywood career as a character actor, with many TV appearances during the 1960s.

That summer, Ernest Mehl decided to touch base with Nick on the occasion of the ballplayer's 81st birthday. Mehl devoted the first five paragraphs of his column to one of Nick's two great-grandsons, Tom Jones, who had been at his Hall of Fame induction. Tom, almost five years old then, was already in love with baseball and even sported a uniform with the number 42 on it. He named Tommy Henrich and Joe DiMaggio as his baseball heroes.[36]

Around 1950 or 1951, one of Nick's other great-grandchildren would keep him company for about three months. When Sharon Everett was in second grade, she was confined to bed for an extended period due to an illness that was feared to be rheumatic fever. She was told to stay in bed constantly but Sharon eventually got bored so she got up and did all kinds of things. She didn't limit herself to fun distractions, but even resorted to cleaning wastebaskets. When Nick finally caught her out of bed and drew a confession from her, he was angry not so much because she was disobeying the doctors' orders but because he feared that as the adult in charge, he'd be the one in big trouble.

As a result of spending so many hours with her Grandpa Nick, Sharon became very familiar with his habits. One she recalls distinctly is his fondness for saltines and hot milk. She and her sister Sandra, who is now a nun known as Sister Ann, believe that he once told them that his fondness for that combination dated back to his days with the Beaneaters.

The year 1951 would be a much busier year for Kid Nichols. Before January 9 Nick had accepted an invitation to attend a February gathering of living Hall of Famers to celebrate the National League's 75th anniversary. The ceremony was held at the Broadway Central Hotel in New York. On February 3, a large photograph from this event graced the top half of the front page of the *New York Daily News*. Seated in the photograph were Carl Hubbell, Kid Nichols (or "Charles Nicholas," as the caption read), Cy Young, Tris Speaker, and Fred Clarke. Standing behind them were Pie Traynor, Charlie Gehringer, Rogers Hornsby, Eddie Collins, Mickey Cochrane, Ed Walsh, Ty Cobb, Jimmie Foxx, and George Sisler. The one former player in the photograph who wasn't in the Hall of Fame was Arlie Latham, who sat on the end next to Fred Clarke. Latham would prove that hanging out with a bunch

At Toots Shor's New York restaurant in early February of 1951. From the left, the first two men standing are Fred Clarke and Mickey Cochrane, and seated are Kid Nichols, Ty Cobb, Charlie Gehringer and Mel Ott.

of legends didn't mean you would eventually be elected to membership yourself.

Famous New York restaurateur Toots Shor invited the players to his place and had a similar photograph taken there, with himself in the mix. That photograph didn't include Hubbell or Collins but it did include Latham, who for some reason chose to show the camera the bottom of his right shoe as he sat between Fred Clarke and Cy Young. Filling out the front row were George Sisler, Kid Nichols, Ty Cobb (with his arm around Nick's shoulder), and Charlie Gehringer. Toots Shor stood behind Sisler, and Rogers Hornsby was right behind Nick. Shor would use this photograph on the back of his menu for years.

The next month, Kid Nichols was on the program for a Knute Rockne Club event back in Kansas City, and then on May 1 he was given the honor of throwing out the first pitch on Opening Day for the Blues. A large photograph just after he released the ball appeared in the *Star* the next day, and among the dignitaries identified in it were Governor Forrest Smith, Yankees general

The photograph of Hall of Famers used on the back of Toots Shor's menu. Standing, from left, are Jimmie Foxx, Mel Ott, Mickey Cochrane, Ed Walsh, restaurateur Shor, Rogers Hornsby, Pie Traynor, and Tris Speaker. Seated are Fred Clarke, Arlie Latham (not in the Hall of Fame), Cy Young, George Sisler, Kid Nichols, Ty Cobb, and Charlie Gehringer.

manager George Weiss, and Del Webb, Blues president and part owner of the Yankees. Weiss would be elected to the Baseball Hall of Fame in 1971, and Webb would make a bigger name for himself as a nationally known real estate tycoon. Based on the trajectory of the ball and the elated expression on Nick's face, his heave from a seat behind the dugout may have sailed beyond the infield and out to the warning track.

Two weeks later, Charles Nichols' last living sibling, his much older sister Sarah Colyer, passed away at the age of 95. She had been a widow for thirty-five years, and at the time of her death was a resident of the Shea Nursing Home. Sarah must have been proud that her kid brother's adult life had been consistent with the anti-alcohol activism of her teen years.

Now that Kid Nichols was in the Hall of Fame, he didn't have to author his own submissions to *Baseball Digest.* In that magazine's June 1951 issue a seven-page feature on Nick was written by United Press sportswriter Sam

Smith, who delved into facets of Nick's career that hadn't received much attention.

"I was never much of a hitter," Nick told him, frankness that Smith found unexpected. Nick also reflected on the increase in the pitching distance to the current 60 feet, 6 inches after the 1892 season. "I never could see that the extra distance made much difference to me. There was a lot of discussion about it but it didn't seem to handicap me. My strikeout total dropped off but the number of hits off me, and bases on balls, did not change materially." However, Nick pointed out that one aspect of the game "which complicated a pitcher's life in those days was the way they'd change the mounds. We never knew whether a mound would be high or low when we were on the road. They used to change it around to cross us up."

Kid Nichols talked about salaries noting that Charlie Bennett had been paid $5,000 for 1890 in order to keep him from jumping to the Players' League, but that after it folded Bennett's pay was slashed to the official maximum of $2,400. Nick also gave examples of Bennett's toughness behind the plate. Smith ended his article with commentary from Casey Stengel about how Kid Nichols had influenced him.[37]

In July, Kid Nichols was informed that he had been elected to the inaugural class of the Wisconsin Athletic Hall of Fame, which was to be inducted in late November. Coverage was mainly restricted to that state, but this announcement actually reached Tokyo, Japan, where it was published in *Pacific Stars and Stripes*.[38] The other baseball players named along with Nick were Ginger Beaumont, Addie Joss, and Al Simmons. Rounding out that first class were bowler Chuck Daw, boxer Richie Mitchell, Marquette University track star Ralph Metcalfe (a gold medalist at the 1936 Olympics in Nazi Germany), pro wrestler Ed "Strangler" Lewis, and football figures Clark Hinkle, Don Hutson, Ernie Nevers, Pat O'Dea, Dave Schreiner, and Robert Zuppke.

Before his trip back to Wisconsin, in August Nick traveled to Wichita for the second year in a row, to be among a few Hall of Famers featured at the seventeenth annual nonprofessional baseball tournament there. Fred Clarke met him there again, and joining them were Connie Mack and George Sisler. Months earlier Honus Wagner and Mickey Cochrane had also agreed to attend but apparently didn't end up making it.[39]

The event in Milwaukee on November 28 proved to be quite an affair. Kid Nichols was able to share it with his grandson Harlan. In addition, his brother John's grandson, Tom MacNichol, traveled down from Oshkosh for the occasion.

The day after, the *Milwaukee Journal* devoted an entire page of photographs to this event. The first was of Beaumont, who was in a wheelchair. He had been the first batter in the 1903 World Series, and with him at the podium

Kid Nichols throwing out the first pitch for the Kansas City Blues on Opening Day, May 1, 1951. The ball is the white blur obscuring part of the girder on the left (*Kansas City Star*).

to honor him were the opposing aces in that series, Cy Young and Deacon Phillippe. The two pitchers also posed with Nick for two other photographs. Neither was used by that paper but Nick was one of the inductees pictured on that page, along with Hinkle, Hutson, Nevers, and Lewis. The legendary Jesse Owens was shown with his friend Metcalfe, and Connie Mack similarly posed with Simmons. The array of images also included pictures of the widows of Joss, Daw and Mitchell, each of whom accepted on behalf of her late husband. There was also a picture of the mother of Schreiner, who had been killed in fighting on Okinawa toward the end of World War II. The *Journal* included a shot from on high of the arena floor, which had enough seating for 800 people to enjoy the $10-a-plate dinners. There were also about a thousand youths in the bleachers to watch the plaques unveiled.[40]

After his big day in Milwaukee, Nick visited Madison, where he reunited with relatives, including Mr. and Mrs. Bert Sauthoff. On November 30 that city's *Capital Times* featured a photograph of him autographing a baseball for his "great-great nephew" Charles Cramton. After Madison, Nick also visited Oshkosh.

From left, Cy Young, Deacon Phillippe and Kid Nichols in Milwaukee on November 21, 1951, at the first Wisconsin Athletic Hall of Fame induction.

In April of 1952 Kid Nichols learned that he was a celebrity on at least two continents. That month he received fan letters from two teenagers in Japan named Yasuo Takeuchi and Hiroshi Ishido. The letters arrived separately, and after the first of them, Nick showed it to his longtime friend at the *Kansas City Star*, Ernest Mehl.

"There is something quite appealing in this letter and the veteran Nichols has been cherishing it ever since it was received," Mehl wrote. "The thought of a Japanese youngster looking up to him for what he once accomplished is as thrilling as anything which ever has happened to the onetime pitcher of the Braves."

"The letter illustrates as well as anything the great value of sports in blending relationships with foreign countries," Mehl continued. "There are many languages, but sports has only one and it is easily understood by all."[41]

Kid Nichols received three additional well-written letters that year from Yasuo Takeuchi, who informed Nick that he was 14 years old, stood five feet, five inches tall, weighed 88 pounds, and lived in Chiba Prefecture, 159 Kogane town, Tokatsu County, or Higashikatsushika-gun. From one of Yasuo's subsequent letters it was clear that Kid Nichols wrote back to him at least once. Nick's great-grandchildren have all five of these letters from abroad.

Around the same time as Mehl's heartfelt reaction to the first letter, Kid Nichols was given one a final opportunity to scold modern pitchers. In the March 17 issue of *Life* magazine, Ty Cobb tore into 1950s baseball in a screed called "They Don't Play Baseball Any More," though for the blurb on the front cover, the editors simplified his point to, "They Ruined Baseball." About a month later, Nick responded.

"A pitcher has got to keep his mind on his business," Nichols said. "He can't be effective if he just goes three innings or so and then starts thinking about relief." Today's fans should realize that this comment is far more fitting in the 21st century.

"A lot of things Cobb says are true," Nick continued, "especially about pitchers, but I can't go along with him all the way." Perhaps, after having been admitted to the Hall of Fame, Nick's views had softened. Regardless of his professed attitude, this article made it crystal clear that Kid Nichols was still madly in love with the game. "The Kid opened the 1952 baseball season with a scorecard in his hand and the radio tuned to the Boston Brave-Brooklyn Dodger game," the writer noted.[42] Nick's great-grandchildren have clear memories of him frequently listening to baseball games on the radio, and it wasn't unusual for them to see him keeping score.

Later that spring Kid Nichols served on a distinguished panel that was assigned the task of naming the best player ever to appear in a Kansas City uniform, based on their performance for the locals. The other judges were Mehl and C.E. McBride from the *Star*, Dutch Zwilling, the Federal League star, and J.G. Taylor Spink, publisher of the *Sporting News*. The top four vote-getters were Jimmy Zinn, Phil Rizzuto, Joe Hauser, and Jerry Priddy, with Tom Sheehan and Joey Kuhel tied for fifth. Each judge was allowed to vote for three in the final balloting, and Nick ranked his as Rizzuto, Kuhel, and Zinn.

On July 5, Kid Nichols wrote to the Baseball Hall of Fame to let them know that he had left that day for an event a few days later in Cincinnati. Nick had also been invited to a game between the Indians and Cubs at Cooperstown. On the 10th Nick was able to see his beloved Boston team play one last time, though they lost to the Reds, 5–3. The occasion was a special evening arranged by the "Ball Players of Yesterday," Cincinnati's association of former diamond pros. Nick was one of ten Hall of Famers on hand. The others were Connie Mack, Rogers Hornsby, Mickey Cochrane, Carl Hubbell, Cy Young, Jimmie Foxx, Charlie Gehringer, Tris Speaker, and Paul Waner.[43] Before the game this eminent group was introduced at home plate by former pitcher Waite

Hoyt, then the play-by-play voice of the Reds, who would be voted into the Hall in 1969.

Charles Nichols celebrated his 83rd birthday on September 14, 1952. On this occasion his gift from his daughter Alice, with whom he was still residing, was the *Official Encyclopedia of Baseball.* A photograph of the two with the volume was circulated widely via news service.[44]

In October, Ernest Mehl reported that he had visited his friend Nick at Kansas City's Menorah Hospital, where he was undergoing tests for a neck ailment. Again proving how obsessed he still was with major league baseball, Kid Nichols was more concerned about that year's World Series, and "he refused to submit to the tests until the seventh game had ended."[45] Nichols was ultimately diagnosed with carcinomatosis, meaning that considerable cancer was found in his body.

In 1953, toward the end of March, a young reporter named Bill Richardson interviewed Kid Nichols for the *Kansas City Star.* He had been on the staff for about two years, but when he retired in 1995, Richardson singled out this Q&A with Nick as the one he could recall among his earliest interviews with local figures. Richardson asked Nick about the top highlight of his career, and Nick said it occurred in August of 1892, when he won games in three cities on three consecutive days, beginning with a game between his Bostons and St. Louis in Kansas City.

"Three days, three different cities and three victories for one pitcher? Why was Nichols called on to hurl all three days?" Richardson asked. "As he recalls, the Boston club had only six pitchers and he was more available to work than the other five. Boston was engaged in a fight for the pennant at the time and Manager Frank Selee undoubtedly did not want to take any chances, so he called on his iron man. The Beaneaters eventually won the pennant as Nichols captured thirty-five victories."[46]

Less than two weeks later, on April 11, 1953, Charles "Kid" Nichols died at Menorah Hospital at the age of 83.

The very next day, Boston's National League team played the very last game of its existence, an exhibition victory against the Red Sox played in front of fewer than 8,000 fans in what was called "a bone-chilling drizzle."[47] On March 14 the franchise's owners had announced that they were moving the club to Milwaukee, which the NL approved in less than a week. On April 13, the Milwaukee Braves played their first major league game.

That night, back in Kansas City a rosary was recited for Charles Nichols at Our Lady of Good Counsel Catholic Church. His funeral was held there the next morning. Visiting that church today, it's easy to imagine that it hasn't changed since then.

The eight pallbearers were all from the Association of Professional Ball

Players of America: Joseph Kuhel, Patrick Collins, Joseph Bowman, Joseph Riggert, Lynn Nelson, Glen Wright, Al Wahlin (the local fire chief), and William Moore. In addition, there were seventeen honorary pallbearers, including Mehl, McBride, Sam Molen, and Dr. D.M. Nigro. More than 100 close friends attended the funeral mass, performed by Father Robert Martin, assistant pastor. Before the mass there was a brief service at the Freeman Funeral Home's chapel, and after mass took place the burial near the chapel, at Mt. Moriah Cemetery. Kid Nichols' grandson Harlan designed the simple grave marker.

Nick's daughter Alice recorded that the National League sent a wreath on an easel, containing red roses, snapdragons, Easter lilies, heather, and a pink bow. Warren Giles, who was only in his second year as NL President, also sent a telegram to her. It read:

> Just learned of your father's death and I extend to you my deep personal sympathy and the sympathy of our league. Kid Nichols wrote a great page in National League and baseball history. He will long be remembered for his great accomplishments on the diamond and for his personal charm, graciousness and understanding. I am sorry that an important commitment on Opening Day prevents my coming to Kansas City for the funeral. If there is anything our League office can do please call on us.

This telegram remains in one of the scrapbooks preserved by Kid Nichols' great-grandchildren. Giles would be elected to the Baseball Hall of Fame by the Veterans Committee in 1979, shortly after his death at age 82.

On the day after Kid Nichols' funeral, he was remembered by the Kansas City Blues and more than 17,000 fans. In a brief ritual before playing the Minneapolis Millers, Sergeants C.J. Bricker, H.R. Kurfiss and W.E. Long of the local Marine Corps recruiting service lowered the ballpark's American flag to half-staff in memory of Nick.

In addition to the wire service accounts that were widely printed right after his death, of course there were individualized efforts to honor Nick's passing, from Oshkosh's *Northwestern* to the *Sertoma News*, and the *Sporting News* published its own thorough and well-done "Necrology." One of the most revealing tributes was published two days after his death in the *Kansas City Star*. Mehl had been such a consistent source of insight about Kid Nichols over his final years, but this time it was C.E. McBride's turn.

McBride admitted that the Kid Nichols he knew, and knew well, "wasn't afraid to speak out when asked questions and he had well defined and emphatic opinions." Still, he characterized Nick as "a man with kindness in his heart and soft-spoken," as well as one who "never lived in the old-time glory of his baseball days." McBride then countered the image that Nick himself had painted by his frequent criticism of modern pitching.

"He kept pace with the game that enabled him to achieve a truly wonderful record. He loved baseball as it is played today," McBride insisted. "He considered the modern players on the whole greater than those of his day although he chaffed at times at their frailty." McBride then estimated that he had known Kid Nichols for 45 years.

"I'll always look with some personal satisfaction at the part I had in swinging Nick into Baseball's hall of Fame," McBride continued, and then shed new light on how that came about:

> It seemed like a hopeless task but Nick so craved the honor — and why not — that the job was well worth putting the shoulder to it, if one may say it that way. The Nichols records spoke for themselves but there were so very few around who had been witnesses of the marvelous hurling of the Kid from Kansas City.
>
> But there was one gentleman of baseball, not a writer, who knew all about Charley Nichols and was preparing to go to bat in his behalf. More about him later.
>
> By way of starting a campaign to install Nichols in the Hall of Fame, I enlisted the help of Grantland Rice, dean of the country's sports writers, and Harry G. Salsinger, sports editor of the *Detroit News*, a veteran baseball writer and a former president of the Baseball Writers Association of the major leagues. They wrote of the greatness of Nichols as told in the National league pitching records. Other baseball writers and sports columnists picked up the thread and wove stories that brought Nick much publicity.
>
> Still he didn't seem to be getting anywhere. Year after year the baseball writers voted players they knew or at least stars of more recent fame than Nichols into the Hall of Fame. Nichols had just about given up.
>
> Then this reporter thought of Bobby Quinn, who was the superintendent of the Cooperstown Hall. I had known Bob Quinn since he started in baseball with the Columbus club of the American Association. Known him well, too. Before taking the superintendency at the Hall of Fame, Quinn had been the general manager of both the Boston clubs so I figured he might know more than most baseball men about the remarkable career of Nichols with the Boston Nationals. I wrote to Bobby Quinn.
>
> And in Bob Quinn, who last year turned over the Hall of Fame job to Sid Keener, a St. Louis baseball writer and sports editor, I found the right man. A letter from Quinn brought not only cheery news but an item with which I was not familiar.
>
> Bob said that there was a committee of which he, as general manager of the Hall of Fame, was a member and that this committee had the right to select Hall of Fame members, when it deemed well to do so. Then Bob Quinn added that he was very familiar with Charley Nichols's amazing records, that the committee was considering the case and he added assurance that Nick would make the grade.
>
> That was it. Just a matter of time. With some elation I called Nick and told him I had received a letter from Bob Quinn that he would find very interesting. Nichols came in as soon as he could make it. I can see him now, sitting atop the long table back of *The Star*'s sports desk, reading the letter.
>
> "You're as good as IN right now," I commented to Nick.

His eyes were alight with the thrill of the message and then there came a pensive look as he said somewhat wistfully—"I hope they don't wait too long."

They didn't.

McBride then jumped ahead to the summer of 1951, when he and his wife took their two-year-old grandson C.E. McBride III to Cooperstown. "A joyous thrill was mine when I came to the picture of Charles A. (Kid) Nichols and the plaque dedicated to him."[48]

Kid Nichols would have been particularly pleased by the article written less than two weeks later by Frank Alexander of the *Star*. Though its topic was bowling rather than baseball, Alexander wrote about the accomplishments of the extended Nichols family. It singled out his wife Jennie, his granddaughter Jane's husband Herbert Jones, Nick and Jennie's daughter Alice, and Harlan Everett Sr., Jr., and III. This extended family profile appeared under the headline, "History Made by Champions in the Nichols-Everett Family."[49]

11

Commemorating the Kid

Even though Kid Nichols had made it into the Hall of Fame, it's only natural that with each subsequent decade, even the best players become less and less familiar. However, Nick did have one great champion for more than a decade after his death, his daughter Alice. She increased her advocacy after a transformative experience in 1956.

In the interim, major league baseball returned to Kansas City after an absence of four decades. Two years and one day after Kid Nichols died, the Kansas City Athletics played their first regular season game, hosting the Detroit Tigers on April 12, 1955.

Two years after Alice mourned the death of her father, whom she clearly revered, Alice suffered another terrible loss. Her dear daughter, Jane Jones, passed away on May 13, 1955. Jane was only 35 years old.

On July 23, 1956, the Hall of Fame inducted Hank Greenberg and Joe Cronin, who had been on the ballot for nine and ten years, respectively. Commissioner Ford Frick served as master of ceremonies in front of the Museum. Marguerita G. Scott, Society Editor for a paper in nearby Oneonta, New York, reported that good weather brought "a record crowd for the induction of new members to the Baseball Hall of Fame and the annual Hall of Fame game at Doubleday Field."

"A large representation of the fairer sex was to be found among whom were the ladies of many of the baseball great," she continued. "A few rows down we found a friendly lady, who proved to be the daughter of an old-timer in baseball, Charles 'Kid' Nichols of the Boston Nationals, now deceased. Mr. Nichols is also a member of the Hall of Fame having been inducted in 1949. With Mrs. Everett was her 12-year-old granddaughter, Sharon, of Kansas City, Kansas. Mrs. Everett said it was her first visit and they 'were enjoying it ever so much.' She lives in Kansas City, Missouri." A photograph of Alice and Sharon accompanied the article.[1] At some point thereafter, Alice received a Lifetime Pass to the Hall of Fame, which her grandchildren also have.

Emboldened by this experience, Alice exchanged letters with Hall of Fame officials over the next few years, several of which can be found in the file that the Hall maintains on her father. She was very interested in fleshing out information about her father, and would write down memories she had of him. For instance, in a note found among the many materials kept by her grandchildren, she recalled, "When my father played I remember he used to burn his bat, and treat it with something. They do not seem to do it now."

She would mix in such memories with information from old newspapers in her letters to the Hall. As a case in point, in her letter to Director Sid Keener dated September 15, 1957, she mentioned having provided information from Nick's scrapbooks so that the Hall could confirm certain statistics of his. She referred to scrapbooks for 1890-91 and the 1892 and 1893 seasons individually, but added that their "clippings of 1894 were destroyed by a chamber maid in a hotel." She surmised that her father got tired after 1895, because the next scrapbook was for 1899. Alice also alluded to her cousin Tom MacNichol's interest in her father's records. Alice sometimes copied long articles from the scrapbook in her own handwriting and provided them to the Hall.

As another example of her correspondence, she provided some genealogical information to the Hall's historian, Lee Allen. After presenting it, she concluded that the nationality of her "Papa" was "mainly American." On that same day she wrote a separate letter to Keener in which she reported on a recent visit to Detroit, where she met with Charlie Bennett's nephew, George Porter. George gave her the scorecard of the benefit game for his uncle that was played in Boston on August 27, 1894.

Keener replied in short order. "Once more may I compliment you for your continued enthusiasm for baseball," he wrote. "Well, why not. You are carrying on for your distinguished Father."

"It was thoughtful of you to take the time out to pen and forward all of that baseball data," he continued. "You have added another wonderful deed to your career by visiting George Porter, nephew of Charley Bennett."

In between her 1956 and 1960 trips, Alice made at least one other to the Hall, for the 1958 induction. As reported by one local paper, "Also introduced from the specially-erected platform in front of the Hall of Fame were Mrs. Honus Wagner, Mrs. Christy Mathewson and Mrs. John J. McGraw, widows of members of the Hall of Fame; Mrs. Betty Wagner Blair, Wagner's daughter; Mrs. A.P. McGinnis, daughter of the late Walter (Rabbit) Maranville; Mrs. Alice Nichols Everett, Sr., of Kansas City, Mo., daughter of Charles (Kid) Nichols; and Roy F. Mack, vice-president of the Kansas City Athletics and son of the immortal Connie Mack."[2]

Alice's grandchildren have a photograph from one of her visits that shows her seated with three other women, two of whom were Mrs. Mathewson and

Mrs. McGraw. Sitting between Alice and those two was a much younger woman, possibly Maranville's daughter.

Alice and her family weren't entirely alone in keeping the memory of Kid Nichols alive. Casey Stengel would do so from time to time as well, including in his own autobiography. Longtime Mets broadcaster Lindsey Nelson told of one instance that was unplanned:

> And there was the hot summer's night in 1964 when Warren Spahn was pitching for the Mets and was about to win. And if he did, that victory would put him ahead of Kid Nichols in the all-time listing of career victories. In the press box at Shea Stadium, the baseball writers were getting ready to make note of that historic achievement in their stories. But there was a problem. Nobody knew anything at all about Kid Nichols. Who the hell was Kid Nichols? Nobody had a clue. Then someone suggested that a runner be sent down to the dugout to query Casey Stengel. Surely Casey must have heard of Kid Nichols. He probably hadn't ever actually seen him, but he must have heard of him. He must have known whom he played for. When the messenger returned, he was still in a daze. When he had put his query to Casey, the grizzled old veteran had looked at him disbelievingly as though he had said, "Did you ever hear of a fellow named Franklin Roosevelt?" Casey said, "Hear of him? What the hell do you mean, hear of him? We lived on the same block in Kansas City and in fact he lived in the house directly across the street from where I lived."[3]

Two years later, after Stengel was inducted into the Hall of Fame, he made a point to single out two influences who happened to share the nickname "Kid," Nichols and Elberfeld. Norman "Kid" Elberfeld was an infielder who joined Brooklyn for a final year, in 1914, when Stengel was only in his second full season with that team. "They gave me some sound advice and helped me get started in professional baseball," Stengel said.[4] Because Casey proved to be such a popular figure, his advice from Nick would later be mentioned in multiple biographies.

In the spring of 1970, Kid Nichols was honored by his Wisconsin birthplace, when he was named to the Madison Pen and Mike Club Hall of Fame. Accepting on the family's behalf was his "grand nephew" Charles Cramton, who had appeared in a photograph with Nick in a local daily back in 1951.

In December, shortly after babysitting, Alice Nichols Everett suffered a coronary attack and passed away, at the age of 79. Her son Harlan notified the Hall of Fame, and they in turn reported her death in a Cooperstown newspaper. "A dynamic person of the type of her father who won 30 games a year seven times, Mrs. Everett was in steady touch with the museum, providing clippings from Kansas City newspapers," the Hall wrote. "She was a correspondent with the director's office and kept up on all the changes in the museum and library."[5] She was buried in the same cemetery as her father. Her son Harlan died in January of 2000 after an extended illness. He had retired in 1983 as an architectural draftsman for the Black & Veatch Corporation in 1983 and his wife Henrietta had passed away in 1991.

In the 1980s, the *Bill James Baseball Abstracts* revolutionized baseball fandom by introducing a wide variety of new statistics for analyzing players and teams — and more importantly, by fostering much more sophisticated and thoughtful analysis by other commentators. As a result, the career of Kid Nichols gained new exposure and greater appreciation.

For example, in *Total Baseball* by John Thorn and Pete Palmer in 1989, the Total Pitcher Index produced a top ten as follows:

1. Walter Johnson
2. Cy Young
3. **Kid Nichols**
4. Grover Cleveland Alexander
5. Lefty Grove
6. Christy Mathewson
7. John Clarkson
8. Tom Seaver
9. Bob Gibson
10. Warren Spahn[6]

Thus, it may not have raised too many eyebrows when baseball historians Lloyd Johnson and Bill Carle posited in 1996 that Nick "may have been the best pitcher of all time." In the first decade of this century, at least half a dozen baseball writers have declared him the best pitcher of the 1800s or a strong contender for that honor.[7] James himself had this to say when he ranked Kid Nichols ninth in *The New Bill James Historical Baseball Abstract*:

> Kid Nichols has been excluded from discussions about the greatest pitchers of all time, as much as anything, because of an accident of the calendar. Baseball exploded in popularity between 1905 and 1910, just as Nichols was leaving the game. Other things happened. Sports coverage by newspapers increased exponentially, and the wire services began to cover and report every game to a national audience. Nichols missed all that; his memory was pushed into baseball's medieval past almost before he got the clay out of his spikes. Although his record is essentially the same as Pete Alexander's or Christy Mathewson's, although he won 30 games seven times, few baseball fans know anything about him.
>
> Nichols was two years younger than Cy Young, but reached the majors in the same season as Cy, 1890. In their first nine seasons in the majors, Nichols out-pitched Young in almost every season. Altogether, he pitched 300 more innings than Young in those years (3642–3352) with a better ERA (2.97 to 3.10), despite pitching in a better hitter's park. He had a better strikeout/walk ratio than Cy Young, fewer baserunners allowed, and a markedly better won-lost record (276–132 for Nichols, 241–135 for Young). He was a better hitter than Cy Young.
>
> Young, of course, pitched equally well over the second half of his career, while Nichols faded at a normal rate.[8]

In 2003, the *Kansas City Star* summarized Bill James's comparison of the two great pitchers and added, "had he had he been able to keep going, today's pitchers might be trying for the Kid Nichols award."[9]

On August 12, 2004, Kid Nichols was honored by the Atlanta Braves, the continuing legacy of the Boston Beaneaters, when he was enshrined into their Hall of Fame along with Tommy Holmes and broadcasters Pete Van Wieren and Skip Caray. The Braves flew relatives in for the occasion. Before beginning her trip, Nick's second-oldest great-granddaughter, Sharon Everett, said, "It'll be like a family reunion. With all the cousins that will be there, I think it will be 17 altogether. It's special."[10] Sharon ended up drawing the short straw, and therefore was compelled to speak at the event.

"Fifty-five years ago, when he was inducted into the Hall of Fame, he said, 'this is truly the thrill of my life,'" she said. "So I know if he were here today, he would be saying the same thing. His heart was baseball, and this would be overwhelming for him." The Braves kept his memory alive later that decade with a large mural of Kid Nichols on their outfield wall.

Chapter Notes

Chapter 1

1. *Wisconsin State Journal* (Madison), September 14, 1869, page 2.

2. Bill Nowlin, *The Kid: Ted Williams in San Diego* (Cambridge, MA: Rounder Books, 2005).

3. Kid Nichols' birth certificate revealed what his father's middle initials stood for. Robert's death notice in the *Wisconsin State Journal*, November 20, 1899, page 1, and Mary Elizabeth's obituary in the *Wisconsin State Journal*, July 18, 1916, page 2, both state that the family moved to Madison in 1856, as does John's biography by C.W. Butterfield in *History of Dane County, Wisconsin* (Chicago: Western Historical, 1880), page 1017.

4. Sarah's maiden name was entered in a government registry when John obtained his marriage license.

5. The younger Sarah's date of birth and birthplace were entered on her death certificate issued by the State of Missouri.

6. A listing of city businesses was printed in a book by Lyman Copeland Draper, *Madison, The Capital of Wisconsin: Its Growth, Progress, Condition, Wants and Capabilities* (Madison: Calkins & Proudfit, 1857), pages 44–46. What was apparently the first Nichols meat market stood at the south point of the Capitol square. Additional sources for locations of his shop are *The Madison City Directory and Business Mirror* (Milwaukee: Smith, Du Moulin, 1858), page 50, *Madison City Directory* (Madison: B. W. Suckow, 1866), page 123, and *Madison Directory, 1868* (Madison: A. Bailey, 1868), page 78.

7. *The Madison City Directory and Business Mirror* (Milwaukee: Smith, Du Moulin, 1858), page 50, identified the Nichols family home as being located on the first block of East Johnson Street, two blocks northwest of the Capitol square. Other sources for locations of the Nichols residence include the city's property tax rolls and the *Madison City Directory* (Madison: B. W. Suckow, 1866), page 123.

8. *Madison Directory, 1868* (Madison: A. Bailey, 1868), page 78, listed the family's home on State Street, straight west of the Capitol, at the same address as another duo's grocery store, North & DePeyster.

9. C.W. Butterfield, *History of Dane County, Wisconsin* (Chicago: Western Historical, 1880), page 1017.

10. *Wisconsin State Journal*, September 25, 1863, page 1.

11. *Wisconsin Daily Patriot*, October 3, 1863, page 7.

12. "Madison Items," *Milwaukee Sentinel*, September 29, 1863, page 1; Forest Hill Cemetery Committee of Historic Madison, Inc., *Forest Hill Cemetery; A Biographical Guide to the Ordinary and the Famous Who Shaped Madison and the World* (Madison: Historic Madison, Inc., 2002).

13. *Wisconsin State Journal*, November 25, 1864, page 1.

14. *History of Dane County, Wisconsin*, pages 743–744.

15. Brian A. Podoll, *The Minor League Milwaukee Brewers, 1859–1952* (Jefferson, NC: McFarland, 2003), page 18.

16. Sam Smith, "Nichols: 'We Stayed In and Pitched,'" *Baseball Digest*, June 1951, page 76.

17. Record Book on the Games of the Capital Baseball Club, 1866–1869, in the archives of the Wisconsin Historical Society. The first time that the name Nichols appears — in a lineup without first names — was in a game between two Madison teams on July 6, 1866. James and John were first identified in that scorebook as catcher and first baseman, respectively, on the "Monona" team that lost 100 to 21 to the Capital team on July 25. (Monona is the name of one of the large lakes on which Madison is situated.) The brothers repeated at those positions for the Monona squad against the Capital City "second nine" on August 17, in a game for which a summary and box score were printed in the *Wisconsin State Journal*, August 19, 1866. Two games between Madison teams in September included an unspecified Nichols in one of the lineups. On September 19 and October 10 both brothers appeared in the Monona lineup versus the Capital team.

18. "The Match Game of Base Ball Between the Capitals and the Olympians," *Wisconsin State Journal*, June 17, 1867, page 4.
19. Record Book on the Games of the Capital Baseball Club, 1866–1869.
20. "Base Ball," *Wisconsin State Journal*, June 11, 1868, page 4.
21. "Base Ball," *Wisconsin State Journal*, June 24, 1868, page 4.
22. "Base Ball," *Wisconsin State Journal*, July 6, 1868, page 4.
23. "Base Ball," *Wisconsin State Journal*, July 10, 1868, page 4.
24. "Base Ball," *Wisconsin State Journal*, July 17, 1868, page 4.
25. "Base Ball — The Unions and the Capitals," *Wisconsin State Journal*, August 10, 1868, page 4.
26. See page 4 of the *Wisconsin State Journal* on August 13, 14, 15, and 17, 1868, which includes box scores.
27. "Base Ball Match This Afternoon," *Milwaukee Daily Sentinel*, August 27, 1868, and "The Match Game at Base Ball," *Milwaukee Daily Sentinel*, August 28, 1868, page 1.
28. *Wisconsin State Journal*, October 1, 1868.
29. Record Book on the Games of the Capital Baseball Club, 1866–1869.

Chapter 2

1. Henry McCormick, "No Foolin' Now," *Wisconsin State Journal*, June 25, 1936, page 21.
2. "Madison Honoring Kid Nichols at Last," *Wisconsin State Journal*, May 7, 1970, section 3, page 3.
3. "Meritorious Public School Pupils," *Wisconsin State Journal*, February 2, 1870, page 4, and "Merit Roll," *Wisconsin State Journal*, February 26, 1870, page 4.
4. "Merit Roll," *Wisconsin State Journal*, November 25, 1870, page 4.
5. Stuart D. Levitan, *Madison: The Illustrated Sesquicentennial History, Volume 1, 1856–1931* (Madison: University of Wisconsin Press, 2006), page 66.
6. See annual reports of the Trustees of the Soldiers' Orphans' Home of the State of Wisconsin, starting with the one for the fiscal year ending September 30, 1869.
7. H. W. Rood, "Grand Army Corner," *Madison Democrat*, April 26, 1908.
8. "Mrs. E. Garner 102 Years Old Dies Suddenly," *Capital Times* (Madison, Wisconsin), February 22, 1923, page 1.
9. *History of Dane County* (Chicago: Western Historical, 1906), page 971.
10. A. Brainerd, ed., *Madison City Directory and Business Advertiser for 1873* (Madison: Atwood & Culver, 1872).
11. *Wisconsin State Journal*, January 5, 1876, page 4.
12. "Degree Templars," *Wisconsin State Journal*, August 10, 1874, page 4.
13. "At the Opera House," *Wisconsin State Journal*, September 24, 1874, page 4, and "The Dramatic Entertainment," *Wisconsin State Journal*, September 25, 1874, page 4.
14. "The Oldest Lodge in the World," *Wisconsin State Journal*, March 19, 1878, page 4.
15. "Entertainments," *Wisconsin State Journal*, November 26, 1875, page 4.
16. See "The Good Templars," *Wisconsin State Journal*, February 2, 1876, and "Good Templars," *Wisconsin State Journal*, May 2, 1877, page 4.
17. David V. Mollenhoff, *Madison: A History of the Formative Years*, 2d Ed. (Madison: University of Wisconsin Press, 2003), page 158.
18. See "Base Ball," *Wisconsin State Journal*, August 9, 1875; "The Fated Men," *Wisconsin State Journal*, August 18, 1875, page 4; "Change," *Wisconsin State Journal*, August 20, 1875; "That Match Game," *Wisconsin State Journal*, August 23, 1875.
19. "Base Ball" and "Later," *Wisconsin State Journal*, September 2, 1875, both on page 4.
20. See "Base Ball Home Runs," *Wisconsin State Journal*, June 2, 1876, page 4, and "Base Ball — Bankers vs. Telegraphers," *Wisconsin State Journal*, June 5, 1876, page 4. The latter is a long account of the game, and includes a box score.
21. "The Base Ball Game," *Wisconsin State Journal*, June 10, 1876, page 4.
22. "Base Ball," *Wisconsin State Journal*, July 31, 1876, page 4.
23. "Stoughton Scooped," *Wisconsin State Journal*, June 30, 1877, page 4.
24. "Base Ball To-Morrow," *Wisconsin State Journal*, July 12, 1877, page 4.
25. "Base Ball in Madison," *Wisconsin State Journal*, August 7, 1877, page 4.
26. "Base Ball," *Wisconsin State Journal*, November 10, 1870, page 4.
27. "Giants Will Win Flag, Says Noted 'Kid' Nichols," *The Evening World* (New York), August 12, 1904, page 8.
28. "Kansas City Briefs," *Sporting Life*, April 7, 1894, page 6.
29. "Children to Distribute Flowers on Soldiers' Graves," *Wisconsin State Journal*, May 27, 1876, page 4.
30. *Wisconsin State Journal*, March 16, 1877, page 4.
31. *Wisconsin State Journal*, May 28, 1877, page 4.
32. *Wisconsin State Journal*, May 24, 1877.
33. "Stench Factories," *Wisconsin State Journal*, August 4, 1879, page 4.
34. *Wisconsin State Journal*, July 14, 1875.
35. "Fever in the Schools," *Wisconsin State Journal*, October 30, 1879, page 4.

36. "Died," *Wisconsin State Journal*, January 10, 1878, page 4.

37. See "A Hard Family," *Wisconsin State Journal*, July 25, 1879, page 4, and "Municipal Court," *Wisconsin State Journal*, August 4, 1879, page 4.

38. "Sudden Death," *Wisconsin State Journal*, December 8, 1880, page 4.

Chapter 3

1. An example of a column saying that he was 11 was written by Ernest Mehl, "Sporting Comment," *Kansas City Star*, September 14, 1950, and one saying that he was 12 was written by Dan Parker, "Winningest Pitcher," for several publications including *The American Weekly*, August 8, 1948.

2. For instance, specifying 1881 was an article by Sam Smith, "Nichols: 'We Stayed In and Pitched,'" *Baseball Digest*, June 1951, page 75, while 1882 was specified in an article by Dick Farrington, "Kid Nichols, Holder of Two 'Hidden' Major Hill Marks, Still Making His Way Via 15 Hours a Day at Age of 73," *Sporting News*, December 31, 1942, page 11.

3. "Charley Nichols' Mother Dead," *Kansas City Journal*, January 30, 1898, page 10.

4. *Hoye's Kansas City Directory for 1882* (Kansas City: Hoye City Directory Co., 1882).

5. Ernest Mehl, "Sporting Comment," *Kansas City Star*, September 14, 1950.

6. "Career of 'Kid' Nichols," *Kansas City Star*, March 8, 1903, page 11.

7. "Rev. Jenkins Acts," *Kansas City Journal*, August 3, 1897, page 1.

8. "Nichols Scores 'Perfect Game,'" *Walla Walla Union-Bulletin*, May 10, 1949, page 13.

9. "Independence," *Kansas City Times*, July 15, 1885, page 3; "Independence," *Kansas City Times*, August 5, 1885, page 3; "Sporting Matters," *Kansas City Evening Star*, August 10, 1885, page 2.

10. Mehl, September 14, 1950.

11. *Moberly Monitor-Index* (Missouri), May 10, 1949, page 11.

12. *Kansas City Times*, June 21, 1886, page 7; "Base Ball Briefs," *Kansas City Times*, July 6, 1886, page 2; "Brooklyn Park, Armourdale," *Kansas City Times*, July 18, 1886, page 10; "Local and Personal," *Kansas City Times*, August 9, 1886, page 8.

13. "Career of a Pitching Idol," *Kansas City Times*, March 3, 1895, page 5.

14. "Athletic Gallery — Harry Childs," *Kansas City Star*, September 4, 1909, page 5.

15. *Kansas City Times*, March 3, 1895.

16. Smith's article for *Baseball Digest* in mid–1951 said that Kid Nichols "tried for a job in 1885 with the city's professional team," but didn't elaborate.

17. *Kansas City Times*, March 3, 1895.

18. Mehl, September 14, 1950.

19. *Kansas City Times*, March 3, 1895.

20. "The Beatons," *Kansas City Times*, October 18, 1887, page 4. That paper gave Juvenal similar credit in its edition of June 24, 1887, on page 6.

21. "Juvenal Sues," *Hutchinson Daily News* (Kansas), July 14, 1888, page 5.

22. Among the few instances when his stint with the Beaton nine of Armourdale is mentioned are "Career of 'Kid' Nichols," *Kansas City Star*, March 8, 1903, page 11; Eddie Hurley, "Veteran Stars of Diamond in Gala Festival," *Boston Daily Advertiser*, September 11, 1922; and Ernest Mehl, "Sporting Comment," *Kansas City Star*, September 14, 1950.

23. For the full saga of Dick Juvenal, who was also sometimes called Richard, see "New Suits Filed Yesterday," *Kansas City Star*, August 27, 1890, page 3; "A South Side Sensation," *Kansas City Times*, September 25, 1890, page 6; "A Woman's Desperation," *Kansas City Star*, August 11, 1891, page 3; "Did Poison End Her Life?" *Kansas City Star*, September 12, 1891, page 1; "A Murder Attempted," *Kansas City Star*, September 14, 1891, page 1; "With His Divorced Wife Again," *Kansas City Times*, September 27, 1891, page 8; "Dick Juvenal Goes to Ohio," *Kansas City Star*, November 6, 1891, page 6.

24. *Kansas City Times*, March 3, 1895; *Kansas City Star*, March 8, 1903; Hurley, September 11, 1922; and Mehl, September 14, 1950.

25. "Armourdale," *Kansas City Times*, June 6, 1887, page 5.

26. *Kansas City Times*, March 3, 1895.

27. The memories reported in 1951 were conveyed by Sam Smith, "Nichols: 'We Stayed In and Pitched,'" *Baseball Digest*, June 1951, page 76.

28. "'Kid' Nichols an Old Timer," *St. Louis Republic*, May 17, 1903, Part IV, page 1.

29. "Kansas City Defeats Lincoln," *Omaha Daily Bee*, June 15, 1887, page 1.

30. *St. Louis Republic*, May 17, 1903.

31. "Nichols Won the Game," *Kansas City Star*, June 15, 1887, page 1.

32. "To-Day's Game," *Kansas City Times*, June 21, 1887, page 2; "Won Easily," *Kansas City Times*, June 22, 1887, page 2.

33. "Disgusted Cowboys," *Sporting Life*, July 13, 1887, page 3. The news item had a dateline of July 5.

34. *Kansas City Times*, June 22, 1887.

35. Bill Felber, "Two Hall of Famers Speak," *Base Ball: A Journal of the Early Game*, Fall 2010, page 24.

36. "Notes of the Game," *Kansas City Times*, July 5, 1887, page 2.

37. "Nichols' Game," *Kansas City Times*, July 27, 1887, page 2.

38. *Kansas City Times*, October 18, 1887.

39. "Only Practice," *Kansas City Times*, August 8, 1887, page 2.

40. W. C. Madden and Patrick J. Stewart, *Western League: A Baseball History, 1885 through 1999* (Jefferson, NC: McFarland, 2002), page 25.

41. "The Mannings Again Win," *Kansas City Times*, December 5, 1887, page 2; "Base Ball To-Day, *Kansas City Times*, December 11, 1887, page 2; "Foot Ball To-Day," *Kansas City Times*, November 20, 1887, page 3. In the football game, Nichols and a few other familiar Cowboy surnames were listed among the 11 players on the Menges team. Baseball on skates drew 800 spectators!

42. "Diamond Chips," *Kansas City Times*, December 21, 1887, page 2; "Nichols Not Yet Signed," *Kansas City Times*, February 2, 1888, page 2.

43. "Instructed to Report," *Kansas City Times*, March 10, 1888, page 3.

44. *St. Louis Republic*, May 17, 1903.

45. "Nicholls [sic] Wins," *Daily Picayune* (New Orleans), April 18, 1888, page 2.

46. "The Ball Tossers," *Springfield Republican* (Massachusetts), April 15, 1888, page 9.

47. *Daily Picayune* (New Orleans), June 5, 1888, page 2.

48. "Sports of the Day," *Kansas City Star*, July 23, 1888, page 2.

49. "Base Ball Briefs," *Kansas City Times*, August 5, 1888, page 3.

50. "The Local Clubs," *Kansas City Times*, October 7, 1888, page 3.

51. "Kansas City's Great Team," *Kansas City Times*, October 11, 1888, page 2.

52. "Trying to Sell a Team," *Kansas City Times*, November 2, 1888, page 3.

53. "Base Ball Notes," *Kansas City Times*, November 27, 1888, page 5; "Sold to St. Joseph," *Kansas City Times*, November 29, 1888, page 4.

54. "Roller Skating Race," *Kansas City Star*, January 4, 1889, page 1; "Kid Nichols Skates Well," *Kansas City Times*, February 10, 1889, page 5; "Nichols Again Out Skates Mack," *Kansas City Times*, February 22, 1889, page 4; "Bicycle Notes," *Kansas City Times*, March 25, 1889, page 8. On page 2 of its issue dated April 23, 1892, *Sporting Life* mentioned that Nichols and Boston teammate Harry Stovey were "expert bicycle riders."

55. For insight into the Beacon team of Omaha, see three articles in the *Omaha Daily Herald*: "Among the Sports," April 13, 1889, page 5; "Today's Ball Game," April 14, 1889, page 4; and "They Are All Ball Players," April 15, 1889, page 8.

56. "The Game at Exposition Park," *Kansas City Star*, April 27, 1889, page 1.

57. "St. Joseph's Claim on 'Kid' Nichols," *Kansas City Star*, May 1, 1889, page 1.

58. "Last Cincinnati Game," *Kansas City Star*, May 2, 1889, page 1.

59. *St. Louis Republic*, May 17, 1903.

60. "Players Reporting," *Omaha Daily Herald*, March 22, 1889, page 8.

61. "Sporting Notes," *Kansas City Star*, May 23, 1889, page 2.

62. "Notes of the Diamond Field," *Philadelphia Inquirer*, August 2, 1889, page 6.

63. "Chips from the Diamond," *Kansas City Times*, August 25, 1889, page 10.

64. "'Kid' Nichols," *Sioux County Herald* (Orange City, Iowa), September 5, 1889, page 3.

65. "'Kid' Nichols in the City," *Kansas City Times*, September 4, 1889, page 2.

66. "The Team for Next Season," *Kansas City Times*, September 22, 1889, page 10.

67. "Western Players Sought For," *Kansas City Times*, September 24, 1889, page 2.

68. "Boston's Latest Purchase," *St. Louis Republic*, September 25, 1889, page 6.

69. "The Omaha Club Bought," *Boston Daily Advertiser*, September 26, 1889, page 8.

70. "Another 'Kid' for Boston," *Boston Daily Globe*, September 27, 1889, page 5.

71. See these articles in the *Milwaukee Sentinel*: "The Dane County Fair," September 24, 1889, page 8; "Are Easy to Beat," September 28, 1889, page 7.

72. "Cincinnati Releases Elmer Smith," *St. Louis Republic*, October 12, 1889, page 6.

73. "Pitcher Nichols Signed," *Cincinnati Commercial Tribune*, October 13, 1889, page 3.

74. "'Kid' Nichols Sold for $3,000" and "Base Ball Bath," *Sioux County Herald* (Orange City, Iowa), October 17, 1889, page 2.

75. "Notes and Gossip," *Sporting Life*, October 23, 1889, page 5.

76. "Diamond Stories," *Philadelphia Inquirer*, December 3, 1899, page 13.

77. "The Way It Ended," *Wisconsin State Journal*, October 25, 1889, page 8.

78. "Nichols Does Not Know," *Kansas City Times*, October 26, 1889, page 2.

79. "Nichols Goes to the Hub," *Kansas City Times*, November 2, 1889, page 2.

80. "The Browns at Kansas City," *St. Louis Republic*, November 4, 1889, page 5.

81. "Positively the Last," *Kansas City Times*, November 4, 1889, page 2.

82. See these articles in the *Omaha Daily Bee*: "He Is a Very Smooth Man," October 30, 1889, page 2; "Flashes from the Diamond," November 3, 1889, page 9; "Items about Athletes," November 19, 1889, page 2.

83. "Triumvirate Owns 'Kid' Nichols," *Boston Daily Globe*, November 25, 1889.

84. *Philadelphia Inquirer*, December 3, 1899.

85. "Other Weddings," *Sporting Life*, February 12, 1890, page 1.

86. "Personal," *Omaha World Herald*, January 31, 1890, page 5.

87. "Bicycle vs Skates," *Omaha Daily Bee*, February 1, 1890, page 2.

88. "At the Coliseum," *Omaha Daily Bee*, February 5, 1890, page 2.
89. "The Kid and His Bride," *Omaha Daily Bee*, February 11, 1890, page 2.
90. "Personal," *Wisconsin State Journal*, March 11, 1890, page 4.
91. "Springfield," *Springfield Republican* (Massachusetts), March 18, 1890, page 6.
92. "Boston Base Ball Club," *Boston Daily Journal*, March 19, 1890, page 1.
93. "Base Ball," *Boston Daily Journal*, April 2, 1890, page 5.
94. "On the Base Ball Field," *New York Sun*, April 15, 1890, Page 4.
95. "Boston's Victory Over the New Havens," *New Haven Evening Register* (Connecticut), April 19, 1890, page 3.

Chapter 4

1. "National League: Boston 5 Brooklyn 2," *New York Evening World*, April 23, 1890, Baseball Extra, page 1.
2. "The League," *Boston Daily Journal*, April 24, 1890, page 3.
3. "Chips from the Diamond," *Kansas City Times*, April 24, 1890, page 5.
4. "One National League Game," *Philadelphia Inquirer*, April 27, 1890, page 6.
5. "Over the Fence in Centre Field," *New York Herald*, May 13, 1890, page 8.
6. "In Championship Form," *New York Daily Tribune*, May 13, 1890, page 5.
7. David L. Fleitz, *Ghosts in the Gallery at Cooperstown: Sixteen Little-Known Members of the Hall of Fame* (Jefferson, NC: McFarland, 2004), page 82.
8. *New York Daily Tribune*, May 13, 1890.
9. Frank Vaccaro, "Origins of the Pitching Rotation," *The Baseball Research Journal*, Fall 2011, page 30.
10. "Two at Once," *Boston Daily Globe*, June 17, 1890, page 5.
11. T. H. Murnane, "Murnane's Missive," *Sporting Life*, July 12, 1890, page 15.
12. "Hot from the Bat," *Omaha Daily Bee*, July 27, 1890, page 12.
13. "The League," *Boston Evening Journal*, August 13, 1890, page 7.
14. For example, see "Comiskey to Join the Quakers," *New York Herald*, September 13, 1890.
15. "Comiskey Nichols and Rhines," *Philadelphia Inquirer*, September 13, 1890, page 3.
16. "Comiskey to Play Here," *Philadelphia Record*, September 13, 1890, page 7.
17. "News Notes and Comments," *Sporting Life*, September 20, 1890, page 5.
18. "'Kid' Nichols Happy," *Boston Daily Globe*, December 12, 1890, page 20.
19. "Chips from the Diamond," *Kansas City Times*, January 18, 1891, page 6.
20. "Catcher Bennett's Visit," *Kansas City Times*, January 28, 1891, page 4.
21. "Pears and Hogriever Arrive," *Kansas City Times*, March 13, 1891, page 2.
22. "Chatter of the Crank," *Omaha Sunday Bee*, April 5, 1891, page 9.
23. "Not to Go South," *Boston Daily Journal*, March 27, 1891, page 4.
24. "The Ball Field," *Boston Daily Journal*, April 29, 1891, page 5.
25. "Boston in Third Place," *Boston Daily Journal*, June 13, 1890, page 6.
26. "The Ball Field," *Boston Daily Journal*, July 2, 1891, page 3.
27. George H. Dickinson, "New York News," *Sporting Life*, August 15, 1891, page 9.
28. Bill James, *The Baseball Book 1990* (New York: Villard, 1990), page 252.
29. David L. Fleitz, *Cap Anson: The Grand Old Man of Baseball* (Jefferson, NC: McFarland, 2005), page 209.
30. "The Ball Field," *Boston Daily Journal*, August 7, 1891, page 3.
31. "Questions Answered," *Sporting Life*, October 24, 1891, page 2.
32. "Won a Bitter Fight, *Chicago Herald*, August 7, 1891, page 7.
33. "'Anse' Knows the Game," *Boston Daily Globe*, August 7, 1891, page 12.
34. T. H. Murnane, "Echoes of the Game," *Boston Daily Globe*, August 8, 1891, page 11.
35. "Won It in the Tenth," *Chicago Herald*, August 8, 1891, page 7.
36. "Still in First Place," *Chicago Herald*, August 10, 1891, page 6.
37. "Sporting Notes and Queries," *Chicago Herald*, August 11, 1891, page 6.
38. Joe Murphy, "Chicago Gleanings," *Sporting Life*, August 15, 1891, page 3.
39. "Anson Downed by Fraud," *Daily Inter Ocean* (Chicago), October 1, 1891, page 2.
40. "Tim Murnane is Disgusted," *Chicago Herald*, October 1, 1891, page 2.
41. "On the Green Diamond," *Trenton Evening Times*, October 4, 1891, page 3.
42. David L. Fleitz, *The Irish in Baseball: An Early History* (Jefferson, NC: McFarland, 2009), page 63.
43. Peter Golenbock, *Wrigleyville: A Magical History Tour of the Chicago Cubs* (New York: St. Martin's Press, 1999), page 81.
44. "Baseball Directors Meet," *New York Herald*, October 6, 1891, page 11.
45. "Sporting Miscellany," *Boston Journal*, October 5, 1891, page 3.
46. "News, Gossip, Editorial Content," *Sporting Life*, October 31, 1891, page 3.
47. "Around the Office Stove," *Omaha Daily Bee*, November 8, 1891, page 15.

48. "General Sporting Notes," *Kansas City Star*, February 19, 1892, page 3.
49. "The Dickey Bird's Chirp," *Omaha Daily Bee*, March 6, 1892, page 15; "General Sporting Notes," *Kansas City Star*, March 21, 1892, page 3.
50. "Hard Hitting by Nash," *Boston Daily Globe*, March 30, 1892, page 5.
51. "Princeton's Excellent Game," *New York Times*, April 12, 1892.
52. "Brewers Beaten at Last," *Kansas City Times*, May 1, 1892, page 4.
53. "Harry Stovey Released," *Boston Daily Journal*, June 21, 1892, page 3.
54. "Boston's Revenge," *Boston Daily Advertiser*, June 23, 1892, page 5.
55. "Only the Ghosts of Giants," *New York Tribune*, June 28, 1892, page 3.
56. "Bean Eaters in Fancy Costume," *Kansas City Times*, July 12, 1892, page 3.
57. T. H. Murnane, "In New Uniforms," *Boston Daily Globe*, July 12, 1892, page 5. The first-half pennant race apparently excited scribes at the *Boston Journal* so much that in some editions that day they said Nichols hadn't won a game against Chicago in two-plus years in the majors, forgetting that he beat Anson's team in mid–September of 1891 to launch Boston's 18-game winning streak.
58. *Kansas City Times*, August 21, 1892, page 4.
59. "Case of Hoss and Toss," *Kansas City Times*, August 24, 1892, page 5.
60. "Along the Free Lunch Counter," *Omaha Daily Bee*, November 13, 1892, page 13. See also "The Bostons' Benefit," *Boston Daily Journal*, October 27, 1892, page 3; "The Boston Benefit," *Boston Daily Advertiser*, October 28, 1892, page 8.
61. "Base Ball Sprinters," *Boston Daily Journal*, October 28, 1892, page 2.
62. Jacob C. Morse, "Hub Happenings," *Sporting Life*, November 5, 1892, page 9.
63. "Settling Up Claims," *Boston Daily Globe*, November 17, 1892, page 13; "Cracks from the Flat Bat," *Omaha Daily Bee*, December 4, 1892, page 24.
64. "Chat of the Diamond," *Philadelphia Inquirer*, February 5, 1893, page 3.
65. "Sport on the Alleys," *Kansas City Star*, February 11, 1892, page 3; "Kid Nichols the Victor," *Kansas City Times*, March 4, 1893, page 2; "Among the Bowlers," *Kansas City Star*, March 25, 1893, page 3; "Base Ball Notes," *Boston Daily Globe*, March 22, 1893, page 5; and "Editorial Views, News, Comment," *Sporting Life*, February 25, 1893, page 2, among other mentions in that weekly during the first half of 1893.
66. "Scraps of Sports," *Daily Inter Ocean* (Chicago), March 12, 1893, page 6.
67. "Players Refuse Terms," *Boston Daily Globe*, March 13, 1893, page 18. Charles "Duke" Farrell had five years under his belt of what would be an 18-year major league career, but as the 1893 season began he had already changed clubs four times.
68. "Editorial Views, News, Comment," *Sporting Life*, April 1, 1893, page 2.
69. "'Kid' Nichols in Boston," *Kansas City Star*, April 6, 1893, page 3.
70. Bill James, *The Bill James Historical Baseball Abstract* (New York: Villard, 1988), page 38.
71. Ibid., page 39.
72. Elmer E. Bates, "Forest City Findings," *Sporting Life*, November 26, 1892, page 4.
73. "Yes, the Bostons," *Boston Daily Journal*, April 29, 1893, page 3.
74. Norman L. Macht, *Connie Mack and the Early Years of Baseball* (Lincoln: University of Nebraska Press, 2007), pages 100–101. A shorter version of this account, with slightly different phrasing, was related by Don C. Trenary of the *Milwaukee Journal* in "The Winningest 9," *Baseball Digest*, October-November 1962, page 39.
75. "Diamond Tips," *Lowell Sun* (Massachusetts), September 25, 1893, page 1.
76. "Notes of the Game," *Kansas City Times*, October 8, 1893, page 7.
77. "Fans Love Such a Game," *Kansas City Times*, October 8, 1893, page 7.
78. "Tickled Kansas City Fans," *Omaha Daily Bee*, October 9, 1893, page 2.
79. George V. Tuohey, *A History of the Boston Base Ball Club* (Boston: M. F. Quinn & Co., 1897), page 136.
80. "The City in Brief," *Cedar Rapids Evening Gazette* (Iowa), October 16, 1893, page 8. See also "Boston a Winner" on that same page.
81. "Lynn," *Boston Daily Globe*, October 21, 1893, page 2; see also "Lynn," *Boston Daily Globe*, October 14, 1893, page 8.
82. "Hotel Arrivals," *The Morning Call* (San Francisco), October 28, 1893, page 9.
83. "Boston's Crack Ball-Players," *Sacramento Daily Record-Union*, November 6, 1893, page 3.
84. "Baseball Notes," *Boston Daily Globe*, November 26, 1893, page 10; "Looking for Coachers," *Boston Daily Globe*, December 3, 1893, page 23.
85. "Indoor Baseball," *The Morning Call* (San Francisco), January 14, 1894, page 8.
86. "California Cullings," *Sporting Life*, January 27, 1894, page 4.
87. On page 4 of its January 27 issue *Sporting Life* reported that Nichols left on Monday the 15th but in "Personal and Pertinent," on page 3 of that same issue, it stated that Nichols left on the 16th.
88. *Sporting Life*, January 27, 1894, page 4.
89. As quoted in "Kansas Notes," *Kansas City Star*, February 6, 1894, page 4.
90. "Nichols at Home," *Sporting Life*, February 10, 1894, page 5.

91. "Kansas City Briefs," *Sporting Life*, April 7, 1894, page 6.
92. "From the Lunch Counter," *Sporting Life*, March 31, 1894, page 4.
93. "Smallest Men in the League," *Boston Daily Advertiser*, April 19, 1894, page 8.
94. "Kansas City Briefs," *Sporting Life*, April 7, 1894, page 6.

Chapter 5

1. T. H. Murnane, "Echoes of the Game," *Boston Daily Globe*, April 20, 1894, page 20.
2. "Baseball Is a 'Pink Tea' to What It Used to Be Once," *La Crosse Tribune and Leader-Press* (Wisconsin), August 31, 1917, page 7.
3. "Charley's Hope," *Boston Daily Globe*, June 2, 1894, page 15.
4. Henry Chadwick, "Henry Chadwick's Gossip," *St. Louis Republic*, June 10, 1894, page 11.
5. "Disgusted with Hoagland," *Plain Dealer* (Cleveland), August 15, 1894, page 3.
6. See these articles in the *Boston Daily Globe*: "Struggle of Giants," August 12, 1894, page 15; "Charley Bennett's Benefit," August 26, 1894, page 3; "Same Old Charley Bennett," August 27, 1894, page 11.
7. "Nearly 9000 Persons," *Boston Daily Advertiser*, August 28, 1894, page 8.
8. Donald J. Hubbard, *The Heavenly Twins of Boston Baseball: A Dual Biography of Hugh Duffy and Tommy McCarthy* (Jefferson, NC: McFarland, 2008), page 107.
9. "Before the Footlights," *Wilkes-Barre Times* (Pennsylvania), October 4, 1894, page 5.
10. "Both without an Error," *Boston Daily Journal*, October 6, 1894, page 3.
11. "Bowled a Gallant Game," *Kansas City Times*, November 23, 1894, page 2.
12. "Boston's Base Ball Team," *Philadelphia Inquirer*, January 6, 1895, page 6.
13. "Chat and Comment of Various Sports," *Philadelphia Inquirer*, January 25, 1895, page 4; "High Scores at Bowling," *The Sun* (Baltimore), January 25, 1895, page 6; "Broke the Bowling Record," *Salt Lake Tribune*, January 24, 1895, page 2.
14. "Live Base Ball Notes," *Kansas City Times*, January 27, 1895, page 2.
15. "Gossip of the Sports," *Kansas City Times*, March 11, 1895, page 2.
16. "A Fancy Sketch," *Sporting Life*, September 29, 1894, page 2.
17. J. C. Morse, "Hub Happenings," *Sporting Life*, October 6, 1894, page 6.
18. *Kansas City Times*, March 17, 1895, page 2.
19. *Kansas City Times*, March 18, 1895, page 2.
20. "Nichols Will Refuse to Sign," *Kansas City Daily Journal*, March 19, 1895, page 2.
21. "Nichols Still Kicking," *Kansas City Times*, March 19, 1895, page 3. See also "Gossip of the Sports" on the same page.
22. "'Kid' Nichols Won the Honors," *Kansas City Star*, March 23, 1895, page 3.
23. "May Lose Nichols," *Sporting Life*, March 23, 1895, page 2. Other coverage was printed on pages 8 and 13.
24. "Gossip of the Sports," *Kansas City Times*, March 23, 1895, page 3.
25. "Gossip of the Sports," *Kansas City Times*, April 2, 1895, page 4.
26. "Nichols Comes to Terms," *Boston Journal*, April 20, 1895, page 7.
27. "Sports," *Lima Daily News* (Ohio), April 25, 1898, page 3.
28. "Gossip of the Sports," *Kansas City Times*, July 22, 1895, page 2.
29. "League Averages," *St. Louis Republic*, July 21, 1895, section 2, page 11.
30. *Kansas City Times*, July 22, 1895.
31. J. C. Morse, "Hub Happenings," *Sporting Life*, August 31, 1895, page 7.
32. Morse, page 7.
33. "Base Ball Notes," *Boston Morning Journal*, October 1, 1895, page 3.
34. "For Temple Cup," *Boston Daily Globe*, October 3, 1895, page 3.
35. "Cleveland's First," *Boston Daily Journal*, October 3, 1895, page 3.
36. See these articles in the *Detroit Free Press*: "Benefit Game for Detroit Players," October 8, 1895, page 2; "Postponed the Game until To-Day," October 9, 1895, page 2; "The Giants Beat the Picked Players," October 10, 1895, page 2.
37. See "News and Comment," *Sporting Life*, December 28, 1895, page 4, and these articles in the issue of November 23: "Trip to Australia," page 1, and "A Big Undertaking," page 6.
38. As quoted in "General Sporting Notes," *The Plain Dealer* (Cleveland), February 25, 1896, page 8.
39. "Collins Signs," *Boston Daily Globe*, April 3, 1896, page 2.
40. "Notes of the Game," *Philadelphia Inquirer*, April 17, 1896, page 4.
41. "Base Ball's Triumph," *Boston Morning Journal*, April 21, 1896, page 1.
42. "One More," *Boston Daily Journal*, May 19, 1896, page 4.
43. "The Great Race," *Sporting Life*, July 11, 1896, page 2. Daily papers disagreed on how many hits each pitcher gave up. For example, on July 3 the *Boston Daily Advertiser* (page 2) said Nichols gave up two and McJames three, whereas the box score that day in the *Boston Morning Journal* (page 40) showed Nichols giving up three as well despite its narrative stating otherwise. "Not a sign of a hit did the Senators make until the eighth inning, and then one scratch and one legitimate was placed to their credit," the *Journal* wrote, adding later that Nichols retired Washing-

ton in order in the ninth. The one error that *Sporting Life* made in its brief summary was stating that the Senators' two hits were in the seventh, instead of the eighth. Longer narratives in the *Journal* and Washington's *Morning Times* (page 3) agree that Boston made two errors in the seventh and Nichols gave up two hits in the eighth.

44. "He's Still in It," *Boston Daily Globe*, August 15, 1896, page 8.

45. For example, see "Faultless Fielding Average," *Syracuse Daily Standard* (New York), October 18, 1896, page 8.

46. "News and Comment," *Sporting Life*, May 16, 1896, page 5.

47. *Cedar Rapids Evening Gazette* (Iowa), May 23, 1896, page 6; "In Short Metre," *Cedar Rapids Evening Gazette*, July 2, 1896, page 7.

48. "News and Comment," *Sporting Life*, July 11, 1896, page 6; William F. H. Koelsch, "New York News," *Sporting Life*, September 19, 1896, page 8.

49. "Not Nichols," *Boston Daily Advertiser*, September 21, 1895, page 7.

50. "Diamond Dust," *Milwaukee Journal*, September 28, 1896, page 8.

51. For example, see "May Get McCarthy," *St. Paul Globe*, October 1, 1896, page 5.

52. "Baseball Notes," *The Evening Times* (Washington, DC), October 9, 1896, page 3.

53. "News and Comment," *Sporting Life*, October 10, 1896, page 5, and October 17, 1896, page 3.

54. "Baseball Notes," *Boston Daily Globe*, October 7, 1896, page 2.

55. "Much Interest in Bowling," *Kansas City Daily Journal*, September 28, 1896, page 5.

56. "Bowling Averages," *Kansas City Daily Journal*, February 21, 1897, page 5.

57. M. J. Nixon, "Building up the Blues," *Sporting Life*, February 6, 1897, page 10.

58. "Wants to Practice Here," *Kansas City Journal*, March 11, 1897, page 5.

59. "Nichols Ordered to Report," *Kansas City Journal*, March 20, 1897, page 5; "Savannah Defeats Boston," *New York Times*, March 31, 1897.

60. "Diamond Dust," *Milwaukee Journal*, May 15, 1897, page 16.

61. "Base Ball Notes," *Boston Morning Journal*, June 3, 1897, page 3.

62. "Averages of the National League," *St. Louis Republic*, June 13, 1897, section 3, page 7.

63. "Baseball Notes," *Kansas City Journal*, June 26, 1897, page 5.

64. "Won with the Ash," *Boston Daily Advertiser*, June 25, 1897, page 1.

65. "Stenzel's 'Homer,'" *Boston Sunday Journal*, June 27, 1897, page 1. Though the paper agreed with the ruling about Stenzel's blast in the ninth inning, its account also included a very detailed analysis of how umpire Bob Emslie's interpretation of two rules, quoted by the paper, may have earlier cost Boston a crucial run.

66. "Heart in Mouth," *Boston Evening Journal*, July 2, 1897, page 3.

67. Bill Felber, *A Game of Brawl: The Orioles, the Beaneaters and the Battle for the 1897 Pennant* (Lincoln: University of Nebraska Press, 2007), page xxi.

68. "Inexplicable," *Boston Daily Journal*, September 22, 1897, page 3.

69. Charles Dryden, "Boston Played a Great Uphill Game and Won," *St. Louis Republic*, September 25, 1897, page 6.

70. "Closing Series of 1897," *The Evening Times* (Washington, DC), September 28, 1897, page 6; "Boston's Triumph," *The Plain Dealer* (Cleveland), September 28, 1897, page 6.

71. "Crowds at Times Bulletin," *The Times* (Washington, DC), September 28, 1897, page 6.

72. "On the Baseball Field," *New York Times*, September 28, 1897.

73. "Pennant Winners," *St. Louis Republic*, September 28, 1897, page 4.

74. "On the Run," *The Evening Telegraph* (Providence, RI), September 28, 1897, page 6.

75. James Tharp, "Beaneaters Too Much for Orioles" (ad), *The Times* (Washington, DC), September 28, 1897, page 6.

76. "Pitcher Nichols" (ad), *Boston Morning Journal*, September 28, 1897, page 1.

77. Bill James, *The Bill James Historical Baseball Abstract* (New York: Villard, 1988), page 47.

78. Kid Nichols' great-grandchildren possess the typed script for a radio interview with him in July of 1939, by a woman named Ann for a Boston radio station, at "Socony's 'Name-in-the-News' microphone." Socony was short for the Standard Oil Company of New York. Nichols was in New York City on July 11 and in Boston on July 12.

79. Jim Baker, writing in *The Bill James Historical Baseball Abstract*, page 55.

80. "An Off Day," *Boston Morning Journal*, October 5, 1897, page 1.

81. "Honor Paid," *Boston Daily Advertiser*, October 7, 1897, page 8.

82. "Bergen Is Missing," *Boston Daily Globe*, October 11, 1897, page 12.

83. "'Kid' Nichols at Home," *Kansas City Star*, October 21, 1897, page 2.

84. "A Banner Base Ball Town," *Kansas City Star*, October 25, 1897, page 3.

85. "News and Comment," *Sporting Life*, December 4, 1897, page 2.

86. "Nichols Sued for $10,000," *Kansas City Journal*, December 23, 1897, page 10.

87. "Frank Selee Here," *Kansas City Star*, December 29, 1897, page 3.

88. "Duffy Will Be Captain," *Boston Daily Globe*, February 20, 1898, page 16.

89. See these articles in the *Daily Picayune* (New Orleans), all on page 8: "Baseball. Kid

Nicholls [sic] Here," February 23, 1898; "Kid Nicholls [sic] Will Pitch Sunday," February 24, 1898, "A Game To-Day," March 6, 1898; "Setley Shows up Well in the Box," March 7, 1898.

90. "Baseball Notes," *Kansas City Journal*, March 24, 1898, page 5. See also "Praise for Pitcher Nichols," *Philadelphia Inquirer*, March 15, 1898, page 4.

91. T. H. Murnane, "Nichols Wants an Increase," *Boston Daily Globe*, March 22, 1898, page 12.

92. "Fiestas Hold the Ship," *Kansas City Star*, March 26, 1898, page 1; "Owls Win the First," *Kansas City Daily Journal*, March 23, 1898, page 5. On the latter page, see also "'Kid' Nichols Will Not Sign," which reported the dollar amounts in Nichols' salary demand differently than Murnane did.

93. "Minneapolis Men Arrive and Will Go into Training," *St. Louis Republic*, March 30, 1898, page 5.

94. See these *Boston Daily Globe* reports by T. H. Murnane: "Another Day of Rain," March 31, 1898, page 12, and "Four in the Ninth," April 10, 1898, page 3.

Chapter 6

1. "Superb Pitching," *Boston Evening Journal*, April 20, 1898, page 7.

2. "Glints from the Diamond," *Grand Rapids Herald* (Michigan), April 25, 1898, page 3.

3. W. S. Barnes, Jr., "Two Pitchers," *Boston Sunday Journal*, April 24, 1898, page 4.

4. "'Kid' Nichols in Town," *Kansas City Journal*, May 24, 1898, page 5.

5. "Kid Nichols' Brother Dead," *Kansas City Journal*, July 2, 1898, page 9.

6. "Baseball Notes," *Kansas City Journal*, August 19, 1898, page 5.

7. "Pennant Again," *Boston Daily Advertiser*, October 5, 1898, page 2.

8. Walter S. Barnes, Jr., "Bostons Leave for New York," *Boston Morning Journal*, October 16, 1898, page 3.

9. Bill James, *The New Bill James Historical Baseball Abstract* (New York: Free Press, 2001), page 978.

10. "Our Pennant," *Kansas City Journal*, September 21, 1898, page 5.

11. "Congratulations," *Boston Morning Journal*, October 13, 1898, page 3.

12. "Pennant for Champions," *Boston Evening Journal*, November 8, 1898, page 3.

13. Jacob C. Morse, "Hub Happenings," *Sporting Life*, November 12, 1898, page 6.

14. "Care of Arms," *Sporting Life*, November 12, 1898, page 6.

15. "The King Pitcher," *Sporting Life*, November 19, 1898, page 4.

16. "Baseball Notes," *Kansas City Journal*, August 26, 1898, page 5. Anson also chose Griffith and Breitenstein, while Chadwick named Young and Rusie. Chadwick also named Marty Bergen as one of his two catchers.

17. "News and Comment," *Sporting Life*, September 3, 1898, page 5; "Baseball Notes," *Kansas City Journal*, September 15, 1898, page 5; "Kid Nichols' Views," *Philadelphia Inquirer*, April 15, 1899, page 10.

18. "Live Sporting News," *Naugatuck Daily News* (Connecticut), November 26, 1898, page 3.

19. "Kid Nichols' Idea," *Boston Globe*, December 20, 1898, page 10.

20. Jacob C. Morse, "Hub Happenings," *Sporting Life*, February 4, 1899, page 7.

21. See two items in *Sporting Life*, January 28, 1899: "News and Comment," page 6; Jacob C. Morse, "Morse's Missive," page 8.

22. "Boston's Players," *Boston Globe*, February 13, 1899, page 3.

23. "Dreyfus to Soden," *The Sun* (Baltimore), April 4, 1899, page 6.

24. "In the Baseball World," *The Sun* (New York), April 16, 1899, page 9.

25. "Brooklyn Budget," *Sporting Life*, April 22, 1899, page 6.

26. "Talk with Mr. Hanlon," *The Sun* (Baltimore), April 17, 1899, page 6.

27. "Nichols Bros.' Laundry Burned," *Kansas City Journal*, June 7, 1899, page 6.

28. "Puffs from the Pipe," *Kansas City Journal*, July 16, 1899, page 5.

29. Ray Robinson, *Matty: An American Hero: Christy Mathewson of the New York Giants* (New York: Oxford University Press, 1993), p. 211; see also "Grant Sells Boston Braves," *Portsmouth Herald* (New Hampshire), February 21, 1923, page 2.

30. "In Sporting World," *The Daily Northwestern* (Oshkosh, Wisconsin), August 1, 1899, page 4.

31. "Sporting Gossip," *Boston Daily Advertiser*, September 26, 1899, page 5.

32. W. S. Barnes, Jr., "Two Good Finishes," *Boston Morning Journal*, September 30, 1899, page 3.

33. W. S. Barnes, Jr., "Errors Troubled," *Boston Morning Journal*, October 5, 1899, page 3.

34. W. S. Barnes, Jr., "Safely Second," *Boston Morning Journal*, October 14, 1899, page 10.

35. "Robert J. L. Nichols Dead," *Kansas City Journal*, November 21, 1899, page 5; "'Kid' Nichols' Father Dead," *Kansas City World*, November 20, 1899, page 1; "Obituary," *Wisconsin State Journal*, November 20, 1899, page 1; "Robert J. L. Nichols Is Dead," *Kansas City Star*, November 20, 1899, page 3.

36. "News of Nichols," *Sporting Life*, December 2, 1899, page 8.

37. "Bergen's Tragic End," *The Morning Herald* (Baltimore), January 20, 1900, page 8.

38. See "Hickman Joins Kid Nichols," *New Haven Register* (Connecticut), March 10, 1900; "Noted Baseball Men," *Meriden Daily Journal* (Connecticut), March 16, 1900, page 4; "Outdoor Work for Yale Teams," *The Sun* (New York), March 25, 1900, page 10; "College Athletes Busy," *New York Times*, April 1, 1900, page 19.

39. W. S. Barnes, Jr., "Bostons Start In," *Boston Journal*, April 3, 1900, page 3. On the 8th, the *Journal* published one of the first photos of Kid Nichols in any daily newspaper, a large and dramatic image of him in dark garb from neck to ankle, preparing to deliver a ball. It was credited to Robert G. White of Greenville, North Carolina.

40. W. S. Barnes, Jr., "Boston's Worst Defeat," *Boston Sunday Journal*, April 29, 1900, section 2, page 1.

41. *Boston Daily Globe*, May 21, 1900, page 5.

42. As reprinted in "Baseball Gossip," *Boston Daily Advertiser*, May 18, 1900, page 8.

43. "Will Stay at Home," *Boston Sunday Journal*, May 20, 1900, page 2.

44. "Baseball Notes," *Boston Daily Globe*, June 2, 1900, page 8.

45. "Coming Fast," *Boston Globe*, August 7, 1900, page 12.

46. "Nichols Has Signed," *Boston Globe*, March 11, 1901, page 17; "Brief Sporting Items," *New Castle News* (Pennsylvania), March 13, 1901, page 7; "Gossip of the Baseball Players," *St. Louis Republic*, March 14, 1901, page 4.

47. "Gossip of the Green Diamond," *St. Louis Republic*, March 12, 1901, page 4, attributed to the *Kansas City Journal*.

48. "Only Eight Games Played," *Daily True American* (Trenton, NJ), April 23, 1901, page 9.

49. Charles A. Nichols, "'Charlie' Nichols Shows Ambitious Pitchers How to Puzzle Heavy Batsmen," *Boston Post*, March 24, 1901.

50. Bill Felber, "Two Hall of Famers Speak," *Base Ball: A Journal of the Early Game*, Fall 2010, pages 24–25.

51. Felber, *A Game of Brawl*, page 35.

52. "Situation Is Mixed," *St. Paul Globe*, March 10, 1901, page 8.

53. See, for example, "Chicago Burglars Kill Two," *Janesville Daily Gazette* (Wisconsin), April 13, 1901, page 1.

54. W. S. Barnes, Jr., "Won in a Walk," *Boston Morning Journal*, April 20, 1901, page 3.

55. For example, see the *Boston Daily Globe*, May 17, 1901, page 28. The ad can be found in the next day's issue as well.

56. "Twelve Hard Innings," *Boston Morning Journal*, June 13, 1901, page 8.

57. "Four Men in the Box," *Boston Morning Journal*, June 28, 1901, page 8.

58. W. S. Barnes, Jr., "Great Record," *Boston Morning Journal*, July 8, 1901, page 3.

59. "Worried Pop Nichols," *Philadelphia Inquirer*, August 9, 1901, page 6.

60. "Win and Lose," and "Baseball Notes," *Boston Globe*, September 28, 1901, page 8.

61. "Suit over Frank Murphy" and "Nichols' Nose Broken," *Boston Globe*, October 11, 1901, page 8.

62. "'Kid' Nichols Here," *Kansas City Star*, October 30, 1901, page 3.

63. "Grievances to Be Submitted," *St. Louis Republic*, December 1, 1901, part 2, page 5.

64. "Expects No Trouble," *Boston Globe*, December 6, 1901, page 5.

65. "Absolute Deadlock," *Boston Morning Journal*, December 13, 1901, page 8.

66. "Nichols Got His Release," *Kansas City Star*, December 14, 1901, page 3.

Chapter 7

1. "Manager Nichols Is Back," *Kansas City Star*, December 17, 1901, page 3.

2. "Will Urge Players to Stand Together," *St. Louis Republic*, December 19, 1901, page 7.

3. "Kling Wants to Play Here," *Kansas City Star*, January 17, 1902, page 3.

4. See these articles in the *St. Paul Globe*: "Dale Gear Is Roasted," January 26, 1902, page 13; "Winter Notes from the Fan Mills," February 2, 1902, page 10.

5. "Nichols Back in Town," *Kansas City Star*, February 16, 1902, page 8.

6. "It's a Real League," *Minneapolis Journal*, March 15, 1902, page 5.

7. "Wing Shots of the United States," *St. Louis Republic*, March 31, 1902, page 4.

8. Dennis Pajot, *Baseball's Heartland War, 1902–1903: The Western League and American Association Vie for Turf, Players and Profits* (Jefferson, NC: McFarland, 2011), page 67.

9. "Western Rivals," *Sporting Life*, October 18, 1902, page 4.

10. "A Deserved Tribute to That Capable and Honorable Player, Charles Nichols," *Sporting Life*, July 12, 1902, page 5.

11. "Two for the Blue Stockings," *Kansas City Star*, September 1, 1902, page 4.

12. "The Blue Sox the Winners," *Kansas City Star*, September 23, 1902, page 3. Risley did linger long enough to practice with Nichols' squad during March of 1903, though by then he had been named player manager of the team in Iola, Kansas.

13. "Albuquerque Took the Last," *Kansas City Star*, October 19, 1902, page 7.

14. See these articles in the *Colorado Springs Gazette*: "'Kid' Nichols Says Weimer and Gibson May Not Go," October 23, 1902, page 6; "Ball Players and Their Wives Visited the Camp," October 24, 1902, page 6.

15. T. H. Murnane, *How to Play Base Ball* (New York: American Sports Publishing Com-

pany, 1903), pages 55, 57. In 1904 or '05, Nichols would contribute a lengthy lesson on pitching under his own byline as part of a "How to Play Baseball" feature in the *St. Louis Post-Dispatch*'s Sporting Inaugural.

16. For example, see "Wonderful Kid Nichols," *Meriden Daily Journal* (Connecticut), August 15, 1903, page 8.

17. "Nichols Lost His Temper" and "Gossip of the Diamond," *Kansas City Star*, August 17, 1903, page 3.

18. "Calls Off All Games in the Western League," *The Morning World-Herald* (Omaha), September 18, 1903, page 2.

19. "Circuit to Be the Same," *Kansas City Star*, September 20, 1903, page 10.

20. "Chat of the Western League," *Colorado Springs Gazette*, September 20, 1903, page 9.

21. See these articles in the *Santa Fe New Mexican*: "Santa Feans Down El Paso," October 14, 1903, page 1; "Santa Fe Downs Albuquerqueans," October 15, 1903, page 1; "All Are Tied for the Lead," October 17, 1903, page 1. Also see these articles, with box scores, in the *Albuquerque Journal*: "Each Team Now Has a Game," October 15, 1903, page 6; "Two Games Lost for Albuquerque," October 16, 1903, page 15; "Heated Baseball for Albuquerque," October 18, 1903.

22. "Wishes Team Good Luck," *Santa Fe New Mexican*, October 9, 1903, page 7.

23. Dan Ortiz, "Henry Alarid, Former Baseballer Tells of Victories in Olden Days," *Santa Fe New Mexican*, July 21, 1940, page 8. Henry identified "Bearwald" as a catcher with Colorado Springs, not with his 1903 club Denver, but Baerwald did play with Colorado Springs in 1901, 1902 and 1904. Henry associated Frantz with Brooklyn, but at that moment may have been confusing him with Schmidt and Jones.

24. L. M. Sutter, *New Mexico Baseball: Miners, Outlaws, Indians and Isotopes, 1880 to the Present* (Jefferson, NC: McFarland, 2010), page 37.

25. "Western League News," *Sporting Life*, October 24, 1903, page 5.

26. B. Wright, "St. Louis Sayings," *Sporting Life*, November 21, 1903, page 9.

27. "In Society," *Kansas City Star*, November 29, 1903, page 4.

28. "Bowling Now Popular," *Kansas City Star*, December 6, 1903, page 12.

29. "Nichols Now a Cardinal," *Kansas City Star*, January 10, 1904, page 8.

30. "Players Still Missing," *St. Louis Republic*, March 11, 1904, page 6.

31. "Grady and Nichols Clash," *Kansas City Star*, March 21, 1904, page 3.

32. "Cardinal 'Vets' and Colts to Play," *St. Louis Republic*, April 13, 1904, page 11.

33. "Kid Nichols in the Box," *Boston Daily Globe*, April 7, 1904, page 4.

34. "Frank Selee Hopeful," *Boston Daily Globe*, March 7, 1904, page 9.

35. "Old Baltimore-Boston Fight," *Boston Daily Globe*, March 24, 1904, page 17.

36. "New York Beats St. Louis, but Western Team Files a Protest," *New York Times*, May 8, 1904, page 11.

37. "Locals Protest Game to Pulliam," *St. Louis Republic*, May 8, 1904, part 3, page 7.

38. Harry C. Pulliam, "Official Verdict," *Sporting Life*, June 4, 1904, page 2.

39. "Manager Nichols Says Work Is Remedy for Sore Arm," *St. Louis Republic*, May 8, 1904, part 4, page 1.

40. "Old Friends Meet," *Boston Daily Globe*, June 2, 1904, page 11.

41. "St. Louis and Hub Teams Play One-Inning Game," *St. Louis Republic*, June 2, 1904, page 4.

42. "Nick Wins His Game in 12 Innings," *Boston Daily Globe*, June 5, 1904, page 4.

43. "Praise for Charlie Nichols," *Kansas City Star*, June 16, 1904, page 3.

44. "New York's Good Pitchers," *Kansas City Star*, July 13, 1904, page 3.

45. "Military Men at Ball Games," *St. Louis Republic*, July 22, 1904, page 7.

46. "Cardinals Defeat Superbas in Longest Game of the Season," *St. Louis Republic*, August 12, 1904, page 5.

47. "'Kid' Nichols Has Best of Old Age," *The Evening World* (New York), August 12, 1904, page 8. See also "Giants Will Win Flag, Says Noted 'Kid' Nichols" on that same page.

48. "Cardinals' Work Pleases the Fans," *St. Louis Republic*, July 31, 1904, part 2, page 4.

49. "Is Taylor a Bad Loner?" *Kansas City Star*, September 2, 1904, page 7. In this account, the Cardinal manager was referred to several times as "King Nick," and he was called that in the *St. Louis Republic* as well, e.g., on April 12, 1905 (page 9).

50. "Cardinals Lose Last to Brooklyn," *St. Louis Republic*, October 1, 1904, page 11.

51. "Bob Dunbar's Sporting Chat," *Boston Globe*, June 22, 1905, page 5.

52. *Spalding's Official Baseball Guide 1905* (New York: American Sports Publishing Company, 1904), page 12.

53. "May Join American," *Waterloo Daily Courier* (Iowa), November 2, 1904, page 5.

54. "Taylor Put on Trial by the Ball Magnates," *Philadelphia Inquirer*, February 15, 1905, page 13.

55. "Taylor Will Now Force James Hart to Prove Charges," *Philadelphia Inquirer*, February 16, 1905, page 13.

56. Arthur D. Hittner, *Honus Wagner: The Life of Baseball's "Flying Dutchman"* (Jefferson, NC: McFarland, 2003), page 133.

57. "Let the Batters Hit 'Em," *Kansas City Star*, February 27, 1905, page 3. Nick also de-

scribed the jump ball in *How to Pitch*, edited by John B. Foster for the Spalding Athletic Library series (No. 230), which was published in March of 1905.

58. "Burke Manager-Captain; Farrell Gets His Release," *St. Louis Republic*, May 4, 1905, page 9.

59. See these articles in the *St. Louis Republic*: "'Kid' Nichols May Join Phillies," July 9, 1905, part 3, page 7; "Notes of the Game," July 10, 1905, page 4.

60. "Baseball Notes," *Boston Daily Globe*, July 20, 1905, page 5.

61. "Phillies Split Even with Pirates," *Philadelphia Inquirer*, July 22, 1905, page 13.

62. "Phillies Land and Lose One to St. Louis Team," *Philadelphia Inquirer*, August 7, 1905, page 10.

63. "Phillies Jump M'Graw's Giants," *Philadelphia Inquirer*, September 1, 1905, page 13.

64. "Wonderful Charley Nichols," *Janesville Daily Gazette* (Wisconsin), September 11, 1905, page 8.

65. "Bowlers Getting Busy," *Kansas City Star*, September 12, 1905, page 3.

66. "Ball Clubs Soon Start on Trips," *Philadelphia Inquirer*, February 25, 1906, page 14.

67. "Spit Ball is a Dead One," *Logansport Pharos* (Indiana), February 15, 1906, page 3.

68. "The Situation at Kansas City," *Sporting Life*, March 10, 1906, page 7.

Chapter 8

1. "Echoes of the Diamond," *Washington Post*, December 2, 1906, sporting section, page 1; "Personal Comment on Men and Things in the Field of Sports," *Washington Times*, December 6, 1906.

2. "Ball Players Differ about Bowling," *Sporting Life*, March 9, 1907, page 3.

3. For example, see "A Roller Skating Game," *Kansas City Star*, January 6, 1907, page 10.

4. "'Kid' Nichols Pitched For 8 Pennant-Winners And Isn't Through Yet," *The Evening Telegram* (Salt Lake City), March 21, 1907, page 7.

5. "Nichols Out of Baseball," *Washington Post*, March 24, 1907, page 4.

6. "'Kid' Nichols' Latest Scheme," *Sporting Life*, June 1, 1907, page 24.

7. "The Enthusiasm of the Fans," *Kansas City Star*, May 20, 1907, page 5.

8. "Gossip of Society," *Kansas City Star*, June 19, 1907, page 2.

9. "Murphy Had Nothing for Montgomery Club," *Atlanta Constitution*, July 17, 1909, page 9.

10. "Chance Chief," *Sporting Life*, September 28, 1907, page 5.

11. J. P. Hughes, "Bowling as a Woman's Game," *Kansas City Post*, undated article in scrapbook kept by Kid Nichols' great-grandchildren. It is likely from December of 1907.

12. "Nichols Back from Cincinnati," *Kansas City Star*, February 27, 1908, page 9. Other insight into Jennie's bowling at this time appeared in the *Utica Herald Dispatch* (New York) on February 12, 1908, and decades later in the *Kansas City Star* on April 25, 1953, and January 12, 1957.

13. "Indoor Baseball League," *Kansas City Star*, February 9, 1908, page 12.

14. See these articles in the *Daily Northwestern* (Oshkosh, Wisconsin): "Everything Lovely," June 23, 1908, page 3; "Nichols to Manage," July 10, 1908, page 4.

15. "Winning Run in Tenth," *The Daily Northwestern* (Oshkosh, Wisconsin), July 14, 1908, page 8.

16. "Passed Balls," *Wisconsin State Journal* (Madison), July 16, 1908, page 7.

17. "Sporting Notes," *Wisconsin State Journal*, July 23 1908, page 7.

18. David F. Wagner, "Hall-of-Famer 'Kid' Nichols Played In '08 Oshkosh-Fond du Lac Game," *Appleton Post-Crescent* (Wisconsin), February 21, 1965, page 9. The man in possession of the scorebook then was William F. Wingren, who in 1908 was a senior at the Wisconsin State University-Oshkosh. As the paper explained, "Wingren came into possession of the scorebook and some correspondence about 10 years ago when a prominent Oshkosh attorney, Ed M. Hooper, died. Wingren's mother had been a secretary for Hooper and, upon his death, brought the scorebook to her son who was just beginning to take an interest in baseball. Hooper's connection with the game was that he had been scorekeeper." Wingren also had Hooper's letter.

19. "Nichols Likes It Here," *Wisconsin State Journal*, August 8, 1908, page 7.

20. "Back to Kansas City," *The Daily Northwestern* (Oshkosh, Wisconsin), September 19, 1908, page 14.

21. "Waddell Turns Fighter," *Washington Post*, January 27, 1909, page 29.

22. "Leaders in Bowling Tourney," *San Francisco Call*, February 1, 1909, page 8.

23. "Shine No More!" *Sporting Life*, April 3, 1909, page 1.

24. "Semi-Pros Follow Kling's Outlawry," *La Crosse Tribune* (Wisconsin), April 17, 1909, page 8.

25. "Sporting Editor's Notes," *Hutchinson News* (Kansas), May 13, 1909, page 3.

26. Phil S. Dixon, *Andrew "Rube" Foster: A Harvest on Freedom's Field* (Lexington, Kentucky: Xlibris Corporation, 2010), see especially pages 44–48, the latter two of which mention Kid Nichols.

27. "Klings Lost the Last One," *Kansas City Star*, September 12, 1909, page 12.

28. Casey Stengel, as told to Harry T. Paxton, *Casey at the Bat: The Story of My Life in Baseball* (New York: Random House, 1962), pages 58–59.

29. John J. Evers and Hugh S. Fullerton, *Touching Second: The Science of Baseball* (Chicago: Reilley & Britton, 1910), page 103.

30. See these articles in the *Kansas City Star*: "With the 3-Cushion Players," and "Nichols Has a Clean Record," January 22, 1911, page 11; "Nichols Is Undefeated," February 12, 1911, page 8; "Strikes and Spares," February 25, 1911, page 5; "Strikes and Spares," March 2, 1911, page 6.

31. See these articles in the *Kansas City Star*: "'Japs' Play Here Tomorrow," May 11, 1911, page 11; "Kansas Beat Keio 10 to 8," May 12, 1911, page 10; "Japs Use their 'Noodles,'" May 13, 1911, page 13.

32. Joe S. Jackson, "Sporting Facts and Fancies," *Washington Post*, May 19, 1911, page 8, and "Keio Team a Winner," same page.

33. "Kid Nichols, Famous Star of Boston, Spends Week in City," *Fort Worth Star-Telegram*, July 16, 1911, page 20

34. "City League Slab Records," *Kansas City Star*, July 22, 1911, page 9.

35. For example, "Cy Young Forgets His Own Record," *Washington Times*, January 5, 1912, page 14.

36. "Kid Nichols Lands a New Job," *Kansas City Star*, March 31, 1912, page 12; "Ball Player Is Good Auto Salesman," *San Francisco Call*, September 29, 1912, page 38.

37. Advertisement, *Kansas City Star*, March 22, 1913, page 4.

38. See these articles in the *Kansas City Star*: "Baseball in the Big Hall," September 28, 1913, page 13A; "A Crowd in the Big Hall," October 8, 1913, page 9.

39. Kirk C. Miller, "Woman Hangs up Duckpin Record," *Washington Times*, January 21, 1914, page 13; "Correspondence," *The Moving Picture World*, January 3, 1914, page 186.

40. "The Passing City League," *Kansas City Star*, April 25, 1914, page 7.

41. "World's Series in Big Hall," *Kansas City Star*, October 4, 1914, page 12.

42. For example, see "Sporting Comment," *The Anaconda Standard* (Montana), November 5, 1914, page 2.

43. "National League News," *Sporting Life*, February 27, 1915, page 1. See also, for example, "Nichols Is to Coach Missouri College Team," *Boston Evening Globe*, February 22, 1915, page 9, and "Kid Nicholls [sic] College Coach," *The Syracuse Herald* (New York), February 23, 1915, page 32.

44. "M. V. C. Opens against Central," *Kansas City Star*, April 15, 1915, page 2.

45. *Spalding's Official Base Ball Record: 1916* (New York: American Sports Publishing Company, 1916), page 377.

46. See these articles in *The Moving Picture World*, August 28, 1915: "On the Home Stretch," page 1459, and "Notes," page 1508. In the issue of January 15, 1916, see "A Good Batting Average to Him," page 460.

47. William A. Phelon, "Sidelights of the Season of 1915," *Baseball Magazine*, February 1916, page 53.

48. "Six Hardest Pitchers I Ever Faced," *Boston Daily Globe*, February 9, 1916, page 6.

49. See these articles in the *Kansas City Star*: "Tie Game Cost the Title," June 3, 1916, page 15, and "Claims a Tie for Baseball Title," June 4, 1916, page 15.

50. See these articles in the *Kansas City Star*: "Along the Fair Green," August 23, 1916, page 8, and "Baseball Helped Him," November 8, 1916, page 11.

Chapter 9

1. "A Good Board at Big Hall," *Weekly Kansas City Star*, September 30, 1919, page 13; "Reds Are the Favorite Here," *Kansas City Times*, October 19, 1919, page 10.

2. William B. Hanna, "Big Leaguers on the Links," *American Golfer*, April 10, 1920, page 14.

3. "Fan Observed They Were All Good Ball Players," *LeMars Semi-Weekly Sentinel* (Iowa), August 21, 1923, page 6.

4. "Nichols Picks Johnson," *Indiana Weekly Messenger* (Pennsylvania), April 29, 1926, page 7.

5. "Bowling Event Opens Thursday," *New York Times*, November 17, 1929.

6. For example, see "Bob Lowe and Kid Nichols Recall Memories of Charley Bennett, Famous Ball Player," *New Castle News* (Pennsylvania), February 20, 1930, page 15.

7. For example, see "Founders of Ban Johnson League See Idea Spreading over Nation," *Syracuse Herald* (New York), March 8, 1932, page 15.

8. Bob Motley with Byron Motley, *Ruling over Monarchs, Giants & Stars: Umpiring in the Negro Leagues & Beyond* (Champaign, IL: Sports Publishing, 2007), page 64.

Chapter 10

1. For example, see "All That's Sport," *Syracuse Herald* (New York), March 15, 1936, page 10.

2. Henry McCormick, "No Foolin' Now," *Wisconsin State Journal*, June 25, 1936, page 21.

3. Sam Levy, "Kid Nichols Praises Keeler as Best Batter," *Milwaukee Journal*, July 2, 1936, page 8.

4. "On the Sidelines," *Oshkosh Northwestern* (Wisconsin), July 7, 1936, page 13.

5. For example, see "Driving Flivver Is Lost Art Now," *San Antonio Light*, December 19, 1936, page 3.

6. "The Old Sport's Musings," *Philadelphia*

Inquirer, May 29, 1937; "Nichols Gets Keepsake," *Sporting News*, September 22, 1938, page 9.

7. "Bob Dunbar's Comment," *Boston Herald*, June 30, 1939; see also Boston's *Globe* and the *Evening Transcript* around then.

8. Dan Parker, "Kid Nichols Can Still Toss 'Em," *The Daily Mirror* (New York), July 20, 1939.

9. "Old Timer Snorts at Today's Ball Players," *Wisconsin State Journal*, July 10, 1941, section 2, page 13.

10. Dick Farrington, "Kid Nichols, Holder of Two 'Hidden' Major Hill Marks, Still Making His Way Via 15 Hours a Day at Age of 73," *Sporting News*, December 31, 1942, page 11.

11. "M-G-M Pays Tribute to Men in Services," *Boxoffice*, September 4, 1943, page 84.

12. Ernest Mehl, "Sporting Comment," *Kansas City Star*, May 12, 1949.

13. Arthur Daley, "Sports of the Times," *New York Times*, April 21, 1946, page 86.

14. "Cy Young and Kid Nichols Bring Back Old Memories," *Kansas City Star*, June 28, 1946, page 35.

15. "Friends of Kid Nichols Believe He's Overdue for Hall of Fame," *Kansas City Star*, December 19, 1948; Jack Staley, "The Kid from Kansas City," *Swing*, October 1946, pages 47–49.

16. David L. Fleitz, *Ghosts in the Gallery at Cooperstown: Sixteen Little-Known Members of the Hall of Fame* (Jefferson, NC: McFarland 2004), page 62.

17. Kid Nichols, as told to Sam Molen, "Pitchers Are Sissies Now," *Baseball Digest*, January 1948, pages 41–42.

18. For example, see Grantland Rice, "Sportlight," *Ellensburg Capital* (Washington), January 23, 1948, page 2.

19. Robert Moore, "Ty Cobb Plugs Pitcher Nichols For Baseball's Hall of Fame," *Florence Times* (Alabama), April 2, 1948, page 9; Grantland Rice, "Sportlight," *Big Piney Examiner* (Wyoming), June 17, 1948, page 7.

20. Dan Parker, "Winningest Pitcher," *The American Weekly*, August 8, 1948, page 18.

21. "Former Brave Hurler 'Shut Out,'" *The Independent* (Long Beach, California), October 7, 1948, page 19.

22. See "Boston Loss Saddens Top Brave Hero," *Bakersfield Californian*, October 12, 1948, page 21, which overlaps considerably with Bill Duncliffe's "Braves' Greatest Hero Almost Missed Series," *The Independent* (Long Beach, California), October 7, 1948, page 17.

23. Sec Taylor, "Sittin' in with the Athletes," *Des Moines Sunday Register*, February 27, 1949, sports section, page 1; "'Kid' Nichols Urged for BB Hall of Fame," *Detroit News*, April 26, 1949, page 23.

24. "Honor to Kid Nichols," *Kansas City Times*, May 9, 1949, page 1.

25. Ernest Mehl, "The Career of Kid Nichols Is Given a Fitting Climax," *Kansas City Star*, May 9, 1949, page 12.

26. Louis W. Shouse, "Nichols Famous as Hurler, but Few Know Him as Inventor," *Kansas City Star*, May 13, 1949, page 35. Shouse also described how he had been originally approached by Chicagoan Harry Dietrick (spelled "Detrick" in a *Star* article back in 1913) about constructing the scoreboard in Convention Hall. Shouse was in a position to approve it, and did. Kid Nichols happened to drop by a week or so after Dietrick began construction, and Shouse happened to mention the scoreboard to him. Shouse then arranged for a meeting between Dietrick and Nick, during which the latter said, reportedly quietly, "You may not know it, but this board is an infringement on a patent I hold." Because Dietrick's design included some unique features, the two agreed to work together in Convention Hall.

27. Harold Kaese, "Easier to Enter Hall of Fame Dead Than Alive," *Boston Globe*, May 10, 1949; "City News," *Atchison Daily Globe* (Kansas), May 15, 1949, page 11; Roger Powers, "Sports Chatter," *Grit*, May 22, 1949, page 9; radio listings in *Wisconsin State Journal* (Madison), May 25, 1925, page 24.

28. "Co-Operator 'Kid' Nichols Wins Baseball's Highest Honor," *Co-Operator Magazine*, June 1949, page 3; Jim Colegrove, "Sidelights on Sports," *Chillicothe Constitution-Tribune* (Missouri), June 2, 1949, page 2; Ed O'Neil, Jr., "Bone Chips? 'Bah!' Says Kid Nichols," *Dayton Daily News* (Ohio), June 6, 1949; Cullen Cain, "Quirk of Fate Bars Some Ballplayers from Hall of Fame," *Miami Daily News Sunday Magazine*, June 12, 1949, page 8.

29. Dick Johnston, "Former Mound Ace, Nichols, Content at 79 Just to Sing," *Buffalo Evening News*, June 10, 1949.

30. For example, this photo appeared in the *Morning Herald* (Hagerstown, Maryland), May 16, 1949, page 16. It would appear in other papers over the next month, at a minimum.

31. "Branch Rickey Praises Sport," *Lewiston Daily Sun* (Maine), June 14, 1949, page 8.

32. For the photo of Traynor, Rickey, and Nichols, see the *Pittsburgh Press*, June 14, 1914, page 29, which is accompanied by an article that lists additional "brass" present. For the photo of Nick with Frick and Quinn, see the *Oneonta Star* (New York), June 15, 1949, page 11. For the photo of Nick warming up, see the *Titusville Herald* (Pennsylvania), June 21, 1949, page 8.

33. "Players Should Be Named to Hall of Fame Now — Traynor," *The Evening Standard* (Uniontown, Pennsylvania), February 22, 1950, page 13.

34. See the photo accompanying the article by Irwin Smallwood, "Nichols Says Pitchers Need Harder Work," *Greensboro Daily News* (North Carolina), July 5, 1949; "Well Played, Says

Nichols," *The Star-Courier* (Kewanee, Illinois), August 5, 1949; John Lundgren, "Liniment Lament," *Burlington Hawk-Eye Gazette* (Iowa), June 20, 1949, page 4; and "Kid Nichols Is Back Home After the Trip of His Life," *Kansas City Star*, August 7, 1949, page 3B.

35. Skipper Patrick, "Sports Roundup," *Jefferson City Post-Tribune* (Missouri), August 22, 1949, page 5.

36. Ernest Mehl, "Sporting Comment," *Kansas City Star*, September 14, 1950.

37. Sam Smith, "Nichols: 'We Stayed In and Pitched,'" *Baseball Digest*, June 1951, pages 75–81.

38. "Badger State Starts Sports Hall of Fame," *Pacific Stars and Stripes*, August 5, 1951, page 12.

39. "Six Baseball Greats to Attend Tournament," *Cedar Rapids Gazette* (Iowa), April 15, 1951, page 39; "Mack Claims Players Smarter but Weaker," *San Antonio Express*, August 18, 1951, page 18.

40. "Wisconsin's Athletic Hall of Fame Dedication Draws Famous Sports Figures of Past," *Milwaukee Journal*, November 29, 1951, page 24.

41. Ernest Mehl, "Sporting Comment," *Kansas City Star*, April 16, 1952.

42. "Today's Pitchers Soft, Is Kid Nichols' Claim," *Milwaukee Journal*, April 18, 1952, page 2.

43. "Cincy Hands Braves Third Straight Loss," *Galveston Daily News*, July 11, 1952, page 26.

44. For example, see *Long Beach Press-Telegram*, September 15, 1952, page 10.

45. Ernest Mehl, "Sporting Comment," *Kansas City Star*, October 26, 1952, page 23.

46. See these *Kansas City Star* articles by Bill Richardson: "Kid Nichols Won Three Games in Three Cities in Three Days," March 30, 1953, page 12; "That's -30-," July 16, 1995, page C2.

47. "Braves Close Glorious Era with Win over Red Sox," *Evening Citizen* (Ottawa, Canada), April 13, 1953, page 25.

48. C. E. McBride, "Selection for the Hall of Fame Gave Kid Nichols Pride and Joy," *Kansas City Star*, April 13, 1949.

49. Frank Alexander, "History Made by Champions in the Nichols-Everett Family," *Kansas City Star*, April 25, 1953.

Chapter 11

1. Marguerita G. Scott, "Ladies of Baseball Greats Adorn Hall of Fame Ceremonies, Game," *Oneonta Star* (New York), July 25, 1956, page 10.

2. "Hall of Fame Wing Is Dedicated; Nats 5, Phils 4," *The Otsego Farmer* (Cooperstown, New York), August 7, 1958, page 1.

3. Lindsey Nelson, *Hello, Everybody, I'm Lindsey Nelson* (New York: William Morrow, 1985), page 283.

4. Bob Root, "Rooting Here & Where with Bob Root," *Sarasota Journal*, August 9, 1966, page 15.

5. "Kid Nichols' Daughter Dies," *The Freeman's Journal* (Cooperstown, NY), December 16, 1970.

6. John Thorn and Pete Palmer, *Total Baseball* (New York: Warner Books, 1989).

7. Lloyd Johnson and Bill Carle, "The Road to Cooperstown Goes through Kansas City," in *Unions to Royals : The Story of Professional Baseball in Kansas City* (Cleveland Society for American Baseball Research, 1996), pages 46–47. For Nick's stature as a 19th century pitcher, see Rob Neyer and Eddie Epstein, *Baseball Dynasties: The Greatest Teams of All Time* (New York: W. W. Norton, 2000), page 89; Mark L. Armour and Daniel R. Levitt, *Paths to Glory: How Great Baseball Teams Got That Way* (Dulles, VA: Brassey's, 2003), page 95; Ed Koszarek, *The Players League: History, Clubs, Ballplayers and Statistics* (Jefferson, NC: McFarland, 2006), page 325; Donald Hubbard, *The Heavenly Twins of Boston Baseball: A Dual Biography of Hugh Duffy and Tommy McCarthy* (Jefferson, NC: McFarland, 2008), page 90; Derek Gentile, *Baseball's Best 1,000: Rankings of the Skills, the Achievements, and the Performance of the Greatest Players of All Time* (New York: Black Dog & Leventhal, 2008), page 66. The latter ranked Kid Nichols the 46th best *player* overall.

8. Bill James, *The New Bill James Historical Baseball Abstract* (New York: Free Press, 2001), page 852.

9. "All-Stars, Our Stars," *Kansas City Star*, July 13, 2003, page C8.

10. Jeffrey Flanagan, "Cover Jinx Could Explain Royals' Seasonlong Struggles," *Kansas City Star*, August 15, 2004, sports section, page 2

Bibliography

Periodicals

Albuquerque Journal, New Mexico, 1903
Boston Daily Advertiser, 1889–1922
Boston Globe, 1889–1949
Boston Journal, 1890–1901
The Call, San Francisco, 1893–1912
Cedar Rapids Evening Gazette, Iowa, 1893–1951
Chicago Herald, 1891
Colorado Springs Gazette, 1902–1903
Daily Northwestern, Oshkosh, Wisconsin, 1899–1936
Daily Picayune, New Orleans, 1888–1898
Detroit Free Press, 1895
Kansas City Journal, 1895–1899
Kansas City Star, 1887–2004
Kansas City Times, 1885–1949
Milwaukee Journal, 1896–1952
Milwaukee Sentinel, 1863–1889
The Moving Picture World, 1914–1916
New York Herald, 1890–1891
New York Times, 1892–1946
Omaha Daily Bee, 1887–1893
Omaha Daily Herald, 1889–1903
Philadelphia Inquirer, 1889–1937
The Plain Dealer, Cleveland, 1894–1897
St. Louis Republic, 1889–1905
St. Paul Globe, 1896–1902
Santa Fe New Mexican, 1903–1940
Sporting Life, 1887–1915
The Sun, Baltimore, 1895–1899
Syracuse Herald, New York, 1915–1936
Washington Post, 1906–1911
Washington Times, 1906–1914
Wisconsin State Journal, Madison, 1863–1970

Selected Articles

Carleton, Jetta, and Jack Staley. "The Kid from Kansas City." *Swing* 2, no. 10 (October 1946): 47–49.
Farrington, Dick. "Kid Nichols, Holder of Two 'Hidden' Major Hill Marks, Still Making His Way Via 15 Hours a Day at Age of 73." *Sporting News,* 31 December 1942, 11.
Felber, Bill. "Two Hall of Famers Speak." *Base Ball: A Journal of the Early Game* 4, no. 2 (Fall 2010): 12–30.
Hanna, William B. "Big Leaguers on the Links." *American Golfer,* 10 April 1920, 14.
Nichols, Kid, as told to Sam Molen. "Pitchers are Sissies Now." *Baseball Digest* 7, no. 1 (January 1948): 41–42.
Parker, Dan. "Kid Nichols Can Still Toss 'Em." *The* (New York) *Daily Mirror,* 20 July 1939.
_____. "Winningest Pitcher." *The American Weekly,* 8 August 1948.
Phelon, William A. "Sidelights of the Season of 1915." *Baseball Magazine* 16, no. 4 (February 1916): 49–54.
Smith, Sam. "Nichols: 'We Stayed In and Pitched.'" *Baseball Digest* 10, no. 6 (June 1951): 75–81.
Vaccaro, Frank. "Origins of the Pitching Rotation." *The Baseball Research Journal* 40, no. 2 (Fall 2011): 27–35.

Books

Armour, Mark L., and Daniel R. Levitt. *Paths to Glory: How Great Baseball Teams*

Got That Way. Dulles, VA: Brassey's, 2003.
Butterfield, C.W. *History of Dane County, Wisconsin*. Chicago: Western Historical, 1880.
Chadwick, Henry, ed. *Spalding's Official Baseball Guide*. New York: A.G. Spalding & Brothers, 1904.
Dixon, Phil S. *Andrew "Rube" Foster: A Harvest on Freedom's Field*. Lexington, KY: Xlibris, 2010.
Draper, Lyman Copeland. *Madison, The Capital of Wisconsin: Its Growth, Progress, Condition, Wants and Capabilities*. Madison, WI: Calkins & Proudfit, 1857.
Evers, John J., and Hugh S. Fullerton. *Touching Second: The Science of Baseball*. Chicago: Reilley & Britton, 1910.
Felber, Bill. *A Game of Brawl: The Orioles, the Beaneaters and the Battle for the 1897 Pennant*. Lincoln: University of Nebraska Press, 2007.
Fleitz, David L. *Cap Anson: The Grand Old Man of Baseball*. Jefferson, NC: McFarland, 2005.
_____. *Ghosts in the Gallery at Cooperstown: Sixteen Little-Known Members of the Hall of Fame*. Jefferson, NC: McFarland, 2004.
_____. *The Irish in Baseball: An Early History*. Jefferson, NC: McFarland, 2009.
Forest Hill Cemetery Committee of Historic Madison. *Forest Hill Cemetery; A Biographical Guide to the Ordinary and the Famous Who Shaped Madison and the World*. Madison, WI: Historic Madison, 2002.
Foster, John B., ed. *How to Pitch*. Spalding Athletic Library Series, no. 230. New York: American Sports Publishing, 1905.
_____. *Spalding's Official Base Ball Record*. New York: A.G. Spalding & Brothers, 1916.
Gentile, Derek. *Baseball's Best 1,000: Rankings of the Skills, the Achievements, and the Performance of the Greatest Players of All Time*. New York: Black Dog & Leventhal, 2008.
Golenbock, Peter. *Wrigleyville: A Magical History Tour of the Chicago Cubs*. New York: St. Martin's Press, 1999.
Hittner, Arthur D. *Honus Wagner: The Life of Baseball's "Flying Dutchman."* Jefferson, NC: McFarland, 2003.
Hubbard, Donald J. *The Heavenly Twins of Boston Baseball: A Dual Biography of Hugh Duffy and Tommy McCarthy*. Jefferson, NC: McFarland, 2008.
James, Bill. *The Baseball Book 1990*. New York: Villard, 1990.
_____. *The Bill James Historical Baseball Abstract*. New York: Villard, 1988.
_____. *The New Bill James Historical Baseball Abstract*. New York: Free Press, 2001.
Johnson, Lloyd, and Bill Carle. "The Road to Cooperstown Goes through Kansas City." In *Unions to Royals: The Story of Professional Baseball in Kansas City*, edited by Lloyd Johnson, Steve Garlick and Jeff Magalif. Cleveland: Society for American Baseball Research, 1996.
Koszarek, Ed. *The Players League: History, Clubs, Ballplayers and Statistics*. Jefferson, NC: McFarland, 2006.
Levitan, Stuart D. *Madison: The Illustrated Sesquicentennial History, Volume 1, 1856–1931*. Madison: University of Wisconsin Press, 2006.
Macht, Norman L. *Connie Mack and the Early Years of Baseball*. Lincoln: University of Nebraska Press, 2007.
Madden, W. C., and Patrick J. Stewart. *Western League: A Baseball History, 1885 through 1999*. Jefferson, NC: McFarland, 2002.
Mollenhoff, David V. *Madison: A History of the Formative Years*, 2d ed. Madison: University of Wisconsin Press, 2003.
Motley, Bob, with Byron Motley. *Ruling over Monarchs, Giants & Stars: Umpiring in the Negro Leagues & Beyond*. Champaign, IL: Sports Publishing, 2007.
Murnane, T. H. *How to Play Base Ball*. New York: American Sports Publishing, 1903.
Nelson, Lindsey. *Hello, Everybody, I'm Lindsey Nelson*. New York: William Morrow, 1985.

Neyer, Rob, and Eddie Epstein. *Baseball Dynasties: The Greatest Teams of All Time.* New York: W. W. Norton, 2000.

Oshkosh Base Ball Club. *Oshkosh in Base Ball.* Oshkosh: Castle-Pierce, 1913.

Pajot, Dennis. *Baseball's Heartland War, 1902–1903: The Western League and American Association Vie for Turf, Players and Profits.* Jefferson, NC: McFarland, 2011.

Podoll, Brian A. *The Minor League Milwaukee Brewers, 1859–1952.* Jefferson, NC: McFarland, 2003.

Robinson, Ray. *Matty: An American Hero: Christy Mathewson of the New York Giants.* New York: Oxford University Press, 1993.

Stengel, Casey, as told to Harry T. Paxton. *Casey at the Bat: The Story of My Life in Baseball.* New York: Random House, 1962.

Sutter, L. M. *New Mexico Baseball: Miners, Outlaws, Indians and Isotopes, 1880 to the Present.* Jefferson, NC: McFarland, 2010.

Thorn, John, and Pete Palmer, with David Reuthers, eds. *Total Baseball.* New York: Warner Books, 1989.

Tuohey, George V. *A History of the Boston Base Ball Club.* Boston: M. F. Quinn, 1897.

Index

Numbers in ***bold italics*** indicate pages with photographs